SMP AS/A2

# Core 3
## for AQA

CAMBRIDGE
UNIVERSITY PRESS

**The School Mathematics Project**

**SMP AS/A2 Mathematics writing team** Spencer Instone, John Ling, Paul Scruton, Susan Shilton, Heather West

**SMP design and administration** Melanie Bull, Pam Keetch, Nicky Lake, Cathy Syred, Ann White

The authors thank Sue Glover for the technical advice she gave when this AS/A2 project began and for her detailed editorial contribution to this book. The authors are also very grateful to those teachers who advised on the book at the planning stage and commented in detail on draft chapters.

CAMBRIDGE UNIVERSITY PRESS
Cambridge, New York, Melbourne, Madrid, Cape Town, Singapore, São Paulo

Cambridge University Press
The Edinburgh Building, Cambridge CB2 2RU, UK

www.cambridge.org
Information on this title: www.cambridge.org/9780521605298

First published 2005

Printed in the United Kingdom at the University Press, Cambridge

A catalogue record for this publication is available from the British Library

ISBN-13   978-0-521-60529-8 paperback
ISBN-10   0-521-60529-6 paperback

Typesetting and technical illustrations by The School Mathematics Project

The authors and publisher are grateful to the Assessment and Qualifications Alliance for permission to reproduce questions from past examination papers. Individual questions are marked AQA.

# Using this book

Each chapter begins with a **summary** of what the student is expected to learn.

The chapter then has sections lettered A, B, C, … (see the contents overleaf). In most cases a section consists of development material, worked examples and an exercise.

The **development material** interweaves explanation with questions that involve the student in making sense of ideas and techniques. Development questions are labelled according to their section letter (A1, A2, …, B1, B2, …) and answers to them are provided.

**D** Some development questions are particularly suitable for discussion – either by the whole class or by smaller groups – because they have the potential to bring out a key issue or clarify a technique. Such **discussion questions** are marked with a bar, as here.

**K** **Key points** established in the development material are marked with a bar as here, so the student may readily refer to them during later work or revision. Each chapter's key points are also gathered together in a panel after the last lettered section.

The **worked examples** have been chosen to clarify ideas and techniques, and as models for students to follow in setting out their own work. Guidance for the student is in italic.

The **exercise** at the end of each lettered section is designed to consolidate the skills and understanding acquired earlier in the section. Unlike those in the development material, questions in the exercise are denoted by a number only.

**Starred questions** are more demanding.

After the lettered sections and the key points panel there may be a set of **mixed questions**, combining ideas from several sections in the chapter; these may also involve topics from earlier chapters.

Every chapter ends with a selection of **questions for self-assessment** ('Test yourself').

Included in the mixed questions and 'Test yourself' are **past AQA exam questions**, to give the student an idea of the style and standard that may be expected, and to build confidence.

Chapter 10 on **proof** gives students an opportunity to understand a variety of proofs and to prove some statements for themselves. Because it uses mathematical content that appears at various points in the Core 3 course, the chapter is placed at the end of the book; however it may be drawn on at appropriate points earlier in the course.

# Contents

# 1 Functions

In this chapter you will learn
- what is meant by a function, including one–one and many–one functions
- about the domain and range of a function
- how to find a composite function
- how to find an inverse function and draw its graph

## A What is a function? (answers p 156)

The concept of a **function** began its development in the 18th century and is now fundamental to almost every branch of mathematics. A function is essentially a rule or process that generates exactly one output for every given input.

An example of a function is one where the inputs are people and the outputs are their favourite colours. So an input could be Jane Jones and the output would be her favourite colour, say, red.

In mathematics, we often deal with functions where both the inputs and outputs are numbers.

For a rule such as $y = x + 2$, we can think of the values of $x$ as the inputs and the values of $y$ as the outputs. For example, an input of $x = 5$ gives an output of $y = 5 + 2 = 7$.

Not all rules generate exactly one output for each given input: not all rules give functions.

**A1** Below are four rules that connect $x$ and $y$.

$$y = x^2 \qquad y^2 = x \qquad x^2 + y^2 = 25 \qquad y = \sqrt{x}$$

$\sqrt{x}$ means the **positive** square root of $x$.

(a) Match each rule with one of the graphs below.

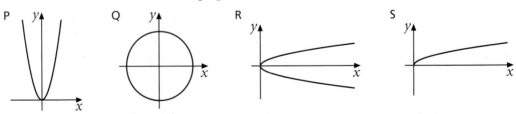

(b) For each rule, find the corresponding value or values of $y$ when $x = 4$.

$y = x^2 + 1$ is an example of a rule for a function as each input value of $x$ generates **exactly one** corresponding output value of $y$.

For example, when $x = 3$ then $y = 10$.

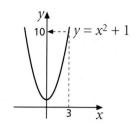

However, $x^2 + y^2 = 25$ is not a rule for a function as each input value of $x$ between $-5$ and $5$ generates **two** corresponding values of $y$.

For example, when $x = 3$ then $y = 4$ and $y = -4$.

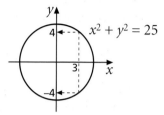

**A2** Which of these are not rules for functions?

| $y = x^2 - 3$ | $y^2 - x^2 = 0$ | $y = \sqrt{x+3}$ | $y^3 = x$ | $y^4 = x$ |

**A3** For the rule $y = \sqrt{x}$, can you find the value of $y$ when $x = -5$?

When defining a function you need to specify the set of input values to be used. This set of input values is called the **domain** of the function.

For example, the rule $y = \sqrt{x}$ generates one value of $y$ for each input value of $x$ that is positive or 0. We cannot find the square root of a negative number so we can use the rule to define a function if we use non-negative input values. So a suitable domain is the set of values $x \geq 0$.

A definition of a function consists of two parts.

The **rule**    This tells you how values of the function are calculated.

The **domain**    This tells you the set of values to which the rule is applied.

We can use letters to stand for functions, the most usual ones being f, g and h. For example, if we call the square root function f, we can write it as

$$f(x) = \sqrt{x}, \ x \geq 0$$

where the rule is $f(x) = \sqrt{x}$ and the domain is the set of values $x \geq 0$.

(We could write the same function as $f(y) = \sqrt{y}, \ y \geq 0$: using $y$ to stand for the input values does not change the rule or the domain.)

Sometimes, the context in which a rule is applied can restrict the domain.

For example, the rule $g(x) = x^3$ can be applied to any real number $x$ and so the domain of g could be the complete set of real numbers (the complete set of rational and irrational numbers).

However, if we use the rule $g(x) = x^3$ to determine the volume of a cube of side $x$, it would be inappropriate to include negative values in the domain.

**A4** A circle is cut out of a square of metal as shown. The centre of the circle is at the centre of the square.

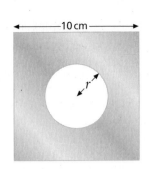

The radius of the circle is $r$.
The area of metal remaining is $A(r)$.

(a) Which of the following is the rule for the function A?

| | |
|---|---|
| $A(r) = 10 - \pi r^2$ | $A(r) = \pi r^2 - 100$ |
| $A(r) = 100 - \pi r^2$ | $A(r) = \pi r^2 - 10$ |

(b) Find the value of $A(3)$, correct to two decimal places.

(c) Which of the following do you think is an appropriate domain for the function A?

| | | | | | |
|---|---|---|---|---|---|
| $r \leq 100$ | $r \leq 5$ | $0 \leq r \leq 10$ | $0 \leq r \leq 100$ | $0 \leq r \leq 5$ | $r \leq 10$ |

To sketch a graph of a function, you need to exclude input values that are not in its domain.

---

### Example 1

Sketch the graph of $y = f(x)$ where $f(x) = x^2 + 1$, $x \geq -2$.

### Solution

The graph of the rule $y = x^2 + 1$ for all real values of $x$ is as shown.

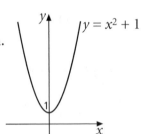

The domain of f is $x \geq -2$.
$f(-2) = (-2)^2 + 1 = 5$ so
the graph of $y = f(x)$ is as shown.

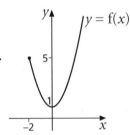

*The point $(-2, 5)$ is included in the graph, so is shown by a solid circle.*

*An open circle can be used to show that an end-point is not included in a graph.*

---

A useful shorthand for the set of real numbers is $\mathbb{R}$.

The statement '$x \in \mathbb{R}$' means '$x$ belongs to the set of real numbers'.

Sometimes we want the domain of a function to be all real numbers except a particular value.

For example, $f(t) = \dfrac{1}{t - 2}$ is not defined for $t = 2$ (as division by 0 is not possible)

so a suitable domain for f is $t \in \mathbb{R}, t \neq 2$ (the set of all real numbers except 2).

**A5** Sketch the graph of $y = f(x)$ for each function below.

(a) $f(x) = x^2 - 1, \ x \leq 3$

(b) $f(x) = 2^x, \ x \in \mathbb{R}$

(c) $f(x) = 3x + 1, \ x > -1$

(d) $f(x) = \dfrac{2}{x}, \ x \in \mathbb{R}, \ x \neq 0$

There is an alternative notation for the rule of a function.
For example, rather than writing $f(x) = x^2$ we can write

$f: x \mapsto x^2$ (Read '$f: x \mapsto x^2$' as '$f$, such that $x$ maps to $x^2$')

This notation suggests the idea of the input $x$ being 'converted' to the output $x^2$.
You can also use an ordinary arrow ($\rightarrow$) for this purpose.

For example, the input 3 is converted to the input $3^2$ or 9.
We could write either $f(3) = 9$ or $f: 3 \mapsto 9$.

**A6** Sketch the graph of $y = f(x)$ where $f: x \mapsto \sqrt{x+2}, \ x \geq -2$.

## Exercise A (answers p 156)

**1** Match each function to its sketch graph.

(a) $f(x) = x^2, \ x \geq 1$

(b) $f(x) = x^2, \ x \geq -2$

(c) $f(x) = x + 2, \ x \in \mathbb{R}$

(d) $f(x) = x + 2, \ x \leq 0$

(e) $f(x) = \sqrt{x}, \ x \geq 1$

(f) $f(x) = \sqrt{x-1}, \ x \geq 1$

(g) $f(x) = \dfrac{1}{x}, \ x \in \mathbb{R}, \ x \neq 0$

(h) $f(x) = \dfrac{1}{x}, \ x > 1$

P

Q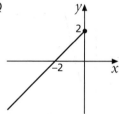

R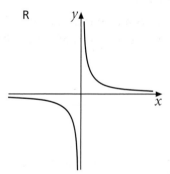

S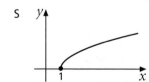

T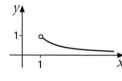

U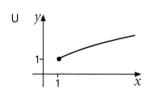

V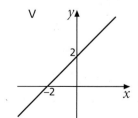

W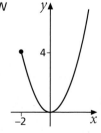

**2** Sketch the graph of $y = f(x)$ for each of these functions.

(a) $f(x) = x - 2, \ x \le 1$  (b) $f(x) = x^2 - 3, \ x > -2$

(c) $f: x \mapsto 9 - x^2, \ x \in \mathbb{R}$  (d) $f: x \mapsto \sqrt{x} + 2, \ x \ge 0$

(e) $f(x) = x - 3, \ -1 \le x \le 10$  (f) $f(x) = x^2, \ -2 < x < 4$

**3** A rule for a function is $f(c) = \dfrac{1}{c + 3}$.

(a) Evaluate    (i) $f(2)$    (ii) $f(-2)$    (iii) $f(0)$    (iv) $f(-5)$

(b) Which value of $c$ cannot be included in the domain of f?

## B Many–one and one–one functions (answers p 156)

**B1** (a) For the function $f(x) = 2x + 7, \ x \in \mathbb{R}$, solve the equation $f(x) = 25$.

(b) For the function $g(x) = x^2, \ x \in \mathbb{R}$, solve the equation $g(x) = 4$.

(c) For the function $h(x) = x^3, \ x \in \mathbb{R}$, solve the equation $h(x) = 27$.

**K** A **many–one function** is a function where there are two or more different inputs that generate the same output.

For example, for the function $f(x) = x^2$

we have    $f(2) = 2^2 = 4$
and    $f(-2) = (-2)^2 = 4$

Two different inputs ($-2$ and $2$) generate the
same output ($4$) so the function $f(x) = x^2$ is many–one.

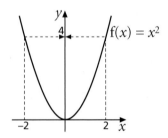

**K** Any function which is not many–one is a **one–one function**.
Each output can be generated by only one input.

**B2** A function g is defined for all real values of $x$ by
$g(x) = x^3 - 3x + 1$. A sketch of $y = g(x)$ is shown.
Explain how the sketch shows that g is many–one.

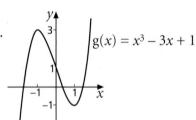

**B3** A function is defined by $f(x) = x^3 - x, \ x \in \mathbb{R}$.

(a) Evaluate $f(1), f(0)$ and $f(-1)$.

(b) Is f a one–one function?

**B4** Classify each function as one–one or many–one.

(a) $f(x) = x^2 - 2, \ x \in \mathbb{R}$  (b) $f(n) = n^3, \ n \in \mathbb{R}$

(c) $f: t \mapsto 3t + 5, \ t \in \mathbb{R}$  (d) $f: x \mapsto x^4, \ x \in \mathbb{R}$

**Exercise B** (answers p 157)

**1** Two functions are defined as

$$f(x) = x^2 + 1, \ x < 1$$
$$g(x) = x^2 + 1, \ x > 1$$

(a) Draw a sketch graph for each function.

(b) Which one of these functions is one–one?

**2** A function is defined by $f(t) = t^2 + 2t, \ t \geq -2$.

(a) Solve the equation $f(t) = 0$.

(b) Show that the equation $f(t) = 3$ has only one solution.

**3** (a) Evaluate $\sin 0$ and $\sin \pi$.

(b) Show that the function $g(\theta) = \sin \theta$ with domain $0 \leq \theta \leq 2\pi$ is many–one.

(c) Solve the inequality $g(\theta) > \frac{1}{2}$.

**4** A function is defined by $h: x \mapsto \cos x, \ 0 \leq x \leq \pi$.
Is the function h one–one or many–one? Explain how you decided.

**5** A square is cut out of a square piece of metal as shown. The point $O$ is the centre of both squares.

The length of one edge of the smaller square is $x$ cm. The area of metal remaining is $A(x)$ cm$^2$.

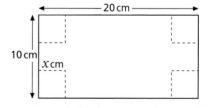

(a) Show that the rule for the function A is

$$A(x) = 144 - x^2$$

(b) What is a suitable domain for the function A?

(c) (i) Sketch the graph of $y = A(x)$.

(ii) Classify the function A as one–one or many–one.

(d) Solve the equation $A(x) = 100$.

**\*6** A manufacturer has some sheets of card. Each sheet measures 20 cm by 10 cm.

A cuboid-shaped box is to be made from each sheet by cutting a square ($x$ cm by $x$ cm) from each corner and folding up.

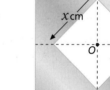

The sheet of card is assumed to be of negligible thickness and rigid.

(a) Show that the volume of the box, $V(x)$ cm$^3$, is given by

$$V(x) = 4x^3 - 60x^2 + 200x$$

(b) What is a suitable domain for the function V?

(c) Show that the function V is many–one.

(d) The manufacturer wants to make boxes with a volume of 144 cm$^3$. What value of $x$ should the manufacturer use?

## C The range of a function

**K** The **range** of a function is the complete set of possible output values.

For example, consider the function f defined by $f(x) = x^2 - 4x + 5, \ x > 0$.

In completed-square form $x^2 - 4x + 5 = (x-2)^2 - 4 + 5$
$$= (x-2)^2 + 1$$
which is a minimum when $x = 2$.

The value $x = 2$ is in the domain of f so the minimum value of $f(x)$ is $f(2)$ which is 1.
Hence the range is the set of all the real numbers greater than or equal to 1.
We can write the range as $f(x) \geq 1$.

A sketch graph illustrates this.

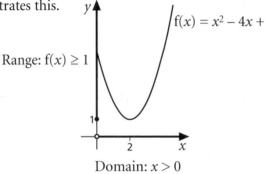

Range: $f(x) \geq 1$

$f(x) = x^2 - 4x + 5$

Domain: $x > 0$

---

### Example 2

Draw a sketch graph of the function defined by $f(x) = 2x + 1, \ -3 < x < 4$.
State its range.

### Solution

*The graph is a straight line so find the end-points.*

When $x = -3$, $2x + 1 = 2\times-3 + 1 = -5$

When $x = 4$, $2x + 1 = 2\times4 + 1 = 9$

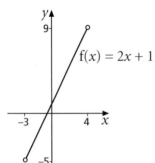

$f(x) = 2x + 1$

*The end-points $(-3, -5)$ and $(4, 9)$ are not included in the graph and so are shown by open circles.*

The range is $-5 < f(x) < 9$.

---

**Example 3**

Draw a sketch graph of the function defined by $g(t) = 3^t$, $t \in \mathbb{R}$.
State its range.

**Solution**

$g(0) = 3^0 = 1$

As $t$ becomes large and positive, $g(t)$ gets larger very quickly.
As $t$ becomes large and negative, $g(t)$ gets smaller and smaller, getting closer and closer to 0.

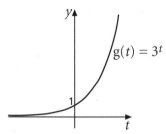

The graph gets closer and closer to the horizontal axis but does not reach it,
so the range is $g(t) > 0$.

**Exercise C** (answers p 157)

**1** For each function below, draw a sketch graph and state the range of the function.

(a) $f(x) = x + 3$, $x \geq 1$

(b) $g(x) = x^2 + 3$, $x \in \mathbb{R}$

(c) $h(x) = 1 - x^2$, $x \in \mathbb{R}$

(d) $f(x) = \sin x$, $0 \leq x \leq 2\pi$

(e) $g(x) = 3^x$, $x > -1$

(f) $h(x) = 2^x$, $x \leq 2$

(g) $f(x) = (x - 2)^2 + 3$, $x \in \mathbb{R}$

(h) $g(x) = (x + 1)^2 - 2$, $x \geq 0$

**2 (a)** Write the expression $x^2 - 6x + 10$ in completed-square form.

**(b) (i)** Sketch the graph of $y = f(x)$ where f is defined by

$$f: x \mapsto x^2 - 6x + 10, \ x \leq 2$$

**(ii)** Find the range of f.

**3 (a)** Sketch the graph of the function $g(\theta) = \cos(2\theta)$ where the domain of g is $0 \leq \theta \leq \frac{1}{2}\pi$.

**(b)** State the range of g.

**4** The function f is defined by $f(x) = x^2 + 2x + 6$, $x \in \mathbb{R}$.

**(a)** Find the range of f.

**(b)** Hence show that the equation $f(x) = 3$ has no real solution.

**5** The function h is defined as $h(t) = t^2 - 4t - 5$, $-1 \leq t \leq 6$.

**(a)** Show that this function is many–one.

**(b)** Find the range of h.

**6** The function h is defined by
$$h(x) = \frac{1}{x} + 2, \ x \in \mathbb{R}, \ x \neq 0$$

A sketch of its graph is shown.

(a) Solve these equations.

    (i) $h(x) = 2\frac{1}{3}$         (ii) $h(x) = 3$

    (iii) $h(x) = 4$        (iv) $h(x) = 1$

(b) Explain why the equation $h(x) = 2$ has no solution.

(c) Which set of values below is the range of h?

| $h(x) \in \mathbb{R}$ | $h(x) \in \mathbb{R}, \ h(x) \neq 2$ | $h(x) \in \mathbb{R}, \ h(x) \neq 0$ |
|---|---|---|

**7** What is the range of each function?

(a) $f(x) = \frac{1}{x} - 5, \ x \in \mathbb{R}, \ x \neq 0$     (b) $f(x) = \frac{4}{x} + 3, \ x \in \mathbb{R}, \ x \neq 0$

**8** The function g is defined by
$$g(x) = \frac{1}{x}, \ x \in \mathbb{R}, \ x \geq 2$$

Sketch the graph of the function and find its range.

**9** The function f is defined by
$$f: t \mapsto 2^{-t}, \ t > -2$$

Find the range of f.

**10** The function g is defined by
$$g(x) = \frac{1}{\sqrt{x}}, \ x \geq \frac{1}{9}$$

(a) Solve the equation $g(x) = 2$.

(b) Find the range of g.

## D Composite functions (answers p 158)

**D1** A gas meter indicates the amount of gas in cubic feet used by a consumer.
The number of therms of heat from $x$ cubic feet of gas is given by the function f where
$$f(x) = 1.034x, \ x \geq 0$$

A particular gas company's charge in £ for $t$ therms is given by the function g where
$$g(t) = 15 + 0.4t, \ t \geq 0$$

(a) How many therms of heat are produced from 500 cubic feet of gas?

(b) What is the cost of using 100 therms?

(c) Find the cost of using these amounts of gas from this gas company.

    (i) 100 cubic feet     (ii) 400 cubic feet     (iii) 1000 cubic feet

To find the cost of using, say, 50 cubic feet of gas you must use both functions: first f and then g. This can be illustrated by the following diagram.

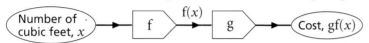

We can write this in stages as $gf(50) = g(f(50)) = g(51.7) = 28.18$.

**D2** Evaluate $gf(200)$.

For an input of $x$ cubic feet of gas we have the following diagram.

Number of cubic feet, $x$ → f → $f(x)$ → g → Cost, $gf(x)$

The function gf is called a **composite** function as it is a composition of two functions, f and g. gf means first f and then g.

**D3 (a)** Find the rule, in its simplest form, for the function gf where $gf(x)$ is the cost of using $x$ cubic feet of gas.

**(b)** Use your rule to find the cost of 550 cubic feet of gas.

---

**Example 4**

Functions f and g are defined for all real values of $x$ by $f(x) = x^2 + 1$
and $g(x) = 5x - 7$

Calculate $fg(2)$, $gf(2)$ and $ff(2)$.

**Solution**

$fg(2) = f(g(2)) = f(5 \times 2 - 7) = f(3) = 3^2 + 1 = 10$
$gf(2) = g(f(2)) = g(2^2 + 1) = g(5) = 5 \times 5 - 7 = 18$
$ff(2) = f(f(2)) = f(2^2 + 1) = f(5) = 5^2 + 1 = 26$

---

**Example 5**

Functions f and g are defined for all real values of $x$ by $f(x) = (x + 4)^2$
and $g(x) = 2x - 1$

Find an expression for $fg(x)$.

**Solution**

$fg(x) = f(g(x)) = f(2x - 1)$
$\qquad = ((2x - 1) + 4)^2$
$\qquad = (2x + 3)^2$

$x$ → g → $2x - 1$ → f → $((2x - 1) + 4)^2$

---

**D4** Functions f and g are defined for all real values of $x$ by

$$f(x) = 10 - x^2$$
and $$g(x) = 3x + 2$$

(a) Evaluate these.

    (i) fg(0)                (ii) gf(4)                (iii) ff(−2)

(b) Find an expression for each of these.

    (i) gf($x$)               (ii) fg($x$)              (iii) gg($x$)

## Exercise D (answers p 158)

**1** Functions f and g are defined for all real values of $x$ by

$$f(x) = x^2$$
and $$g(x) = 3x + 1$$

(a) Evaluate these.

    (i) fg(2)                (ii) gf(2)                (iii) gg(2)

(b) Find an expression for gf($x$).

(c) Show that $fg(x) = 9x^2 + 6x + 1$.

(d) (i) Find an expression, in its simplest form, for gg($x$).

    (ii) Use your result to evaluate gg(−1).

    (iii) Solve the equation $gg(x) = 49$.

**2** For each pair of rules below, find expressions for fg($x$) and gf($x$).

(a) $f(x) = 2x + 3$     (b) $f(x) = x^2$         (c) $f(x) = 3x + 2$     (d) $f(x) = 1 - x^2$

    $g(x) = x^3$           $g(x) = \dfrac{1}{x+1}$       $g(x) = 5 - x$         $g(x) = 1 - 2x$

**3** Functions f and g are defined for all real values of $x$ by

$$f\colon x \mapsto x^2 - 4x + 1$$
$$g\colon x \mapsto kx + 5, \text{ where } k \text{ is a constant}$$

Given that $gf(1) = 2$, find the value of $k$.

**4** Functions f and g are defined by

$$f(x) = \frac{1}{x}, \ x > 0$$

$$g(x) = \frac{1}{3x - 1}, \ x > 1$$

Solve $fg(x) = 14$.

**5** Functions f and g are defined by

$$f\colon x \mapsto x - 10, \ x \in \mathbb{R}$$
$$g\colon x \mapsto \sqrt{x}, \ x \geq 0$$

(a) Find f(1).

(b) Explain why the composite function gf cannot be formed.

**6** Functions f and g are defined by

$$f(x) = \frac{1}{(x-1)(x+3)}, \quad x > 1$$

$$g(x) = \frac{5}{x}, \quad x > 0$$

Solve $gf(x) = 25$.

**7** A theatre manager notices that if he raises the temperature on the central heating thermostat he can increase the sales of ice cream in the interval.

He observes that the proportion of the audience buying ices is given by the function P where

$$P(c) = 1 - \frac{10}{c}, \quad 15 \le c \le 25$$

and where $c$ is the temperature in degrees Celsius.

(a) What proportion of the audience buys ice cream when the temperature is $15\,°C$?

(b) At what temperature will half of the audience buy ices?

(c) What is the range of the function P?

The function $f(t) = \frac{5}{9}(t - 32)$ gives the temperature in degrees Celsius where $t$ is the temperature in degrees Fahrenheit.

(d) What proportion of the audience buys ice cream when the temperature is $65\,°F$?

(e) Find the rule for the composite function that determines the proportion of the audience that will buy ices when the temperature is $t\,°F$.

(f) One evening, 55% of the audience buy ices.
What is the temperature in degrees Fahrenheit?

*(g) Work out an appropriate domain for the function Pf.

## E Inverse functions (answers p 159)

**E1** Functions f and g are defined for all real values of $x$ by

$$f(x) = 2x + 5$$

$$g(x) = \frac{x-5}{2}$$

(a) Evaluate $gf(5)$ and $fg(5)$.

(b) Evaluate $gf(-3)$ and $fg(-3)$.

(c) Find an expression for $gf(x)$.

> **K** A function that reverses, or 'undoes', the effect of f is its **inverse** and is denoted by $f^{-1}$.
> So $f^{-1}f(x) = x$.
>
> (In this context, $f^{-1}$ does not mean $\frac{1}{f}$.)

So we can write $f(x) = 2x + 5$ and $f^{-1}(x) = \frac{x-5}{2}$.

**E2** The rule for the function f is $f(x) = 3x - 1$.

(a) (i) Show that $f(7) = 20$.

(ii) Hence write down the value of $f^{-1}(20)$.

(b) Which of the rules below is the rule for the inverse of f?

A $\quad f^{-1}(x) = 3x + 1$

B $\quad f^{-1}(x) = \frac{1}{3}x + 1$

C $\quad f^{-1}(x) = \dfrac{x + 1}{3}$

D $\quad f^{-1}(x) = \dfrac{x - 1}{3}$

**K** One way to find a rule for the inverse of a function is to write the function in terms of $x$ and $y$ and then rearrange to obtain a rule for $x$ in terms of $y$.

For example, to find the rule for the inverse of $\qquad g(x) = 2x - 1$
first write the rule as $\qquad\qquad\qquad\qquad\qquad\quad y = 2x - 1$
then rearrange to obtain $\qquad\qquad\qquad\qquad\quad y + 1 = 2x$

$$\Rightarrow \tfrac{1}{2}(y + 1) = x$$

So we can write the inverse as $g^{-1}(y) = \frac{1}{2}(y + 1)$

We could write the inverse rule as, say, $g^{-1}(k) = \frac{1}{2}(k + 1)$ or $g^{-1}(p) = \frac{1}{2}(p + 1)$ or use any other letter we choose.

We usually use $x$ which gives $g^{-1}(x) = \frac{1}{2}(x + 1)$ for the inverse rule.

**E3** For each rule, find an expression for $f^{-1}(x)$, where $f^{-1}$ is the inverse of f.

(a) $f(x) = 4x + 3$  (b) $f(x) = \frac{1}{5}x + 3$  (c) $f: x \mapsto 2(x - 7)$

**E4** For each rule, find an expression for $g^{-1}(x)$, where $g^{-1}$ is the inverse of g.

(a) $g(x) = 10 - x$  (b) $g: x \mapsto -x$  (c) $g(x) = \dfrac{1}{x}$

**K** An inverse exists for any one–one function.
If a function is many–one, then an inverse function does not exist.

For example, for the many–one function $f(x) = x^2$ we have two different inputs (−2 and 2) that generate the same output (4) so reversing the effect of f gives two possible outputs for an input of 4.

A function must give exactly one output for each input so an inverse function for $f(x) = x^2$ does not exist.

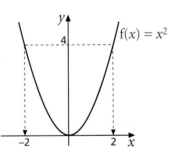

**E5** Which of these functions does not have an inverse?

A $f(x) = x^2 - 5, \ -3 \le x \le 3$  B $f(x) = x^2 - 5, \ 1 \le x \le 6$

**E6** The domain of a function g is $-2 \le x \le 6$. The graph of $y = g(x)$ is shown.

(a) Write down the value of

    (i) $g(3)$  (ii) $g^{-1}(3)$  (iii) $g^{-1}(4)$  (iv) $g^{-1}(-1)$

(b) Why is it not possible to evaluate $g^{-1}(10)$?

(c) What is the domain of the function $g^{-1}$?

(d) Write down the range of the function $g^{-1}$.

(e) Sketch the graph of the function $y = g^{-1}(x)$.

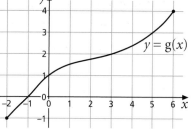

**K**   The domain of an inverse function $f^{-1}$ is the range of the function f.

**E7** For each function below,

    (i)  using the same scale on the $x$- and $y$-axes, sketch the graph of $y = f(x)$

    (ii) find an expression for $f^{-1}(x)$

    (iii) find the domain of $f^{-1}$

    (iv) add the graph of $y = f^{-1}(x)$ to your sketch of $y = f(x)$

(a) $f(x) = 2x + 1, \; x \ge -2$         (b) $f(x) = \frac{1}{4}(x - 2), \; x < 10$

(c) $f(x) = x^2, \; x > 1$              (d) $f: x \mapsto x^3 + 1, \; 0 \le x \le 2$

**K**   Using the same scale on the $x$- and $y$-axes, the graphs of a function and its inverse have reflection symmetry in the line $y = x$.

---

### Example 6

A function f is defined for $x \ge 0$ by $f(x) = (x + 1)^2 + 2$.
Find an expression for the inverse $f^{-1}(x)$.
Sketch the graph of the inverse function $f^{-1}$ and state its domain.

### Solution

*First write the function in terms of x and y.*

$$y = (x + 1)^2 + 2$$
$$\Rightarrow \quad y - 2 = (x + 1)^2$$

*Take the positive square root as $x \ge 0$.*

$$\sqrt{y - 2} = x + 1$$
$$\Rightarrow \quad \sqrt{y - 2} - 1 = x$$

*We need an expression for $f^{-1}(x)$.*

So $f^{-1}(x) = \sqrt{x - 2} - 1$

*You can first sketch the graph of*
*$y = (x + 1)^2 + 2$ for $x \in \mathbb{R}$,*
*remembering to use the same*
*scale on the $x$- and $y$-axes.*

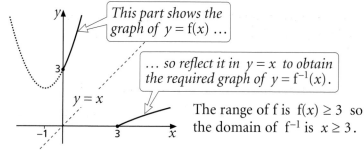

This part shows the graph of $y = f(x)$ ...

... so reflect it in $y = x$ to obtain the required graph of $y = f^{-1}(x)$.

The range of f is $f(x) \ge 3$ so the domain of $f^{-1}$ is $x \ge 3$.

## Example 7

A function g has the rule defined by $g: x \mapsto \dfrac{3}{2x-1}$.

Find an expression for the inverse $g^{-1}(x)$.

### Solution

*First write the rule in terms of x and y.*  $\qquad\qquad y = \dfrac{3}{2x-1}$

*Multiply both sides by $(2x-1)$.*  $\qquad\qquad y(2x-1) = 3$

*Expand the brackets.*  $\qquad\qquad\qquad\qquad 2xy - y = 3$

$\qquad\qquad\qquad\qquad\qquad\qquad \Rightarrow \qquad 2xy = 3 + y$

$\qquad\qquad\qquad\qquad\qquad\qquad \Rightarrow \qquad x = \dfrac{3+y}{2y}$

*We need an expression for $g^{-1}(x)$.*  $\qquad$ So $g^{-1}(x) = \dfrac{3+x}{2x}$

---

### Exercise E (answers p 160)

**1** Function f is defined by $f(x) = 5x + 1$, $x \in \mathbb{R}$.
Find an expression for $f^{-1}(x)$.

**2** Function g is defined by $g(x) = \frac{1}{4}x - 3$, $0 \leq x \leq 16$.
  (a) Find an expression for $g^{-1}(x)$.   (b) Find the domain and range of $g^{-1}$.

**3** The function $f(t) = \frac{5}{9}(t - 32)$ gives the temperature in degrees Celsius where $t$ is the temperature in degrees Fahrenheit. The domain of the function is $t \geq -459.4$.
  (a) Find an expression for $f^{-1}(t)$.
  (b) What is the domain of $f^{-1}$?
  (c) Convert $-70\,°C$ into a temperature in degrees Fahrenheit.

**4** Explain why no inverse exists for function f where f is defined by $f(x) = x^2$, $x \geq -4$.

**5** Function h is defined by $h: x \mapsto 2 - 3x$, $x > 0$.
  (a) Find an expression for $h^{-1}(x)$.
  (b) What is the domain of $h^{-1}$?
  (c) Solve the equation $h^{-1}(x) = h(x)$.

**6** Function f is defined by $f(x) = (x - 2)^2 - 5$, $x > 2$.
  (a) Find an expression for $f^{-1}(x)$.
  (b) What is the domain of $f^{-1}$?

**7** Function g is defined by $g: x \mapsto x^2 + 6x + 10$, $x > -2$.
  (a) Write $x^2 + 6x + 10$ in completed-square form.
  (b) Find an expression for $g^{-1}(x)$.

**8** Find an expression for each inverse function $f^{-1}(x)$ and write down its domain.

(a) $f(x) = \sqrt{x} + 2,\ x \geq 0$

(b) $f(x) = x^3 - 5,\ x \in \mathbb{R}$

(c) $f(x) = \dfrac{2}{3+x},\ x > 0$

(d) $f(x) = \dfrac{5}{x} - 4,\ x < 0$

**9** The graph sketched is of the function defined by

$$f: x \mapsto 3^{-x} - \tfrac{1}{3},\ x \geq 0$$

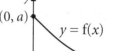

(a) Work out the values of $a$ and $b$.

(b) Sketch the curve with equation $y = f^{-1}(x)$.

(c) What is the domain of $f^{-1}$?

**10** Function f is defined by $f(x) = \dfrac{2x+3}{x-2}$.

Show that $f^{-1}(x) = f(x)$ for $x \in \mathbb{R},\ x \neq 2$.

---

## Key points

- A **function** is a rule or process that generates exactly one output for every input. A definition of a function consists of

    a **rule** that tells you how values of the function are calculated

    a **domain** that is the set of values to which the rule is applied                          (p 7)

- An alternative notation for the rule of a function is to use an arrow. For example, rather than writing $f(x) = x^2$ we can write $f: x \mapsto x^2$.                          (p 9)

- A **many–one function** is a function where two or more different inputs generate the same output. Any function where each output can be generated by only one input is a **one–one function**.                          (p 10)

- The **range** of a function is the complete set of possible output values.                          (p 12)

- The function gf is called a **composite** function and tells you to 'do f first and then g': $gf(x) = g(f(x))$.                          (p 15)

- A function that reverses, or 'undoes', the effect of f is its **inverse** and is denoted by $f^{-1}$. So $f^{-1}f(x) = x$.
  Only one–one functions have inverses.
  The domain of an inverse function $f^{-1}$ is the range of the function f.                          (pp 17–19)

- One way to find a rule for the inverse of a function is to write the function in terms of $x$ and $y$ and then rearrange to obtain a rule for $x$ in terms of $y$.                          (p 18)

- Using the same scale on the $x$- and $y$-axes, the graphs of a function and its inverse have reflection symmetry in the line $y = x$.                          (p 19)

## Test yourself (answers p 160)

**1** Functions f and g are defined for all real values of $x$ by

$$f: x \mapsto 5 - 3x$$
$$g: x \mapsto x^3 - 4$$

(a) Solve the inequality $f(x) < 1$.

(b) The composite function fg is defined for all real values of $x$.
Find $fg(x)$, expressing your answer in the form $p + qx^3$, where the values of $p$ and $q$ are to be found.

(c) The graph of $y = g(x)$ is sketched below with equal scales on the $x$- and $y$-axes.

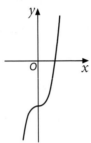

Copy the graph of $y = g(x)$ and on the same axes sketch the graph of $y = g^{-1}(x)$.

(d) Find an expression for $g^{-1}(x)$.                                    AQA 2001

**2** Functions f and g are defined with their respective domains by

$$f(x) = \frac{1}{x^3 + 1}, \quad x \in \mathbb{R}, \ x \neq -1$$

$$g(x) = 2x^2, \quad x \geq 0$$

(a) Find $fg(x)$, giving your answer in its simplest form.

(b) (i) Sketch the graph of $y = g(x)$.

(ii) What is the range of g?

(iii) Solve the equation $g(x) = 18$.

(c) What is the domain of $g^{-1}$?

(d) The graph of $y = g(x)$ and the graph of $y = g^{-1}(x)$ intersect at two points.
Find the $x$-coordinates of these two points.

**3** State which of the following graphs $G_1$, $G_2$ or $G_3$ does not represent a function.
Give a reason for your answer.

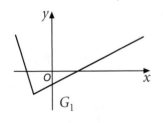
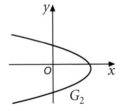
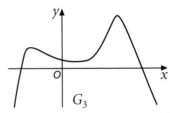

AQA 2002

**4** The function f has domain $x \geq 4$ and is defined by $f(x) = (x - 3)^2 + 1$.

   **(a) (i)** Find the value of f(4) and sketch the graph of $y = f(x)$.

      **(ii)** Hence find the range of f.

   **(b)** Explain why the equation $f(x) = 1$ has no solution.

   **(c)** The inverse function of f is $f^{-1}$. Find $f^{-1}(x)$.             AQA 2003

**5** The function f is defined for all real values of $x$ by $f(x) = (x + 2)(x - 2)$.

   **(a)** Sketch the graph of $y = f(x)$, showing where the graph crosses both axes.

   **(b)** Find the range of f.

   **(c)** Explain why the function f does not have an inverse.

**6** Functions f and g are defined with their respective domains by

$$f: x \mapsto \frac{4}{3 + x}, \quad x > 0$$

$$g: x \mapsto 9 - 2x^2, \quad x \in \mathbb{R}$$

   **(a)** Find fg$(x)$, giving your answer in its simplest form.

   **(b) (i)** Sketch the graph of $y = g(x)$.

      **(ii)** Find the range of g.

   **(c) (i)** Solve the equation $g(x) = 1$.

      **(ii)** Explain why the function g does not have an inverse.

   **(d)** The inverse of f is $f^{-1}$.

      **(i)** Find $f^{-1}(x)$.

      **(ii)** Solve the equation $f^{-1}(x) = f(x)$.             AQA 2003

**7** Functions f and g are defined for all real values of $x$ by

$$f(x) = x^2 - 4x + 7$$

$$g(x) = x + k, \text{ where } k \text{ is a positive constant}$$

   **(a)** Find the range of f.

   **(b)** Given that fg$(3) = 12$, find the value of $k$.

   **(c)** Solve the equation gf$(x) = 14$.

# 2 The modulus function

In this chapter you will learn
- what is meant by 'the modulus function'
- how to draw the graph of a modulus function
- how to solve an equation or inequality that involves a modulus function and relate the solution to the graphs

## A Introducing the modulus function (answers p 161)

$|x|$ is the symbol for 'the modulus of $x$' or 'the absolute value of $x$'.
The modulus or absolute value of a real number can be thought of as its 'distance' from 0 and is always positive.

For example, $|4| = 4$ and $|-2| = 2$.

Many graphic calculators use 'Abs $(x)$' for $|x|$.

---

**Example 1**

Given that $f(x) = |2x - 5|$, find the value of f(1).

**Solution**

$f(1) = |2 \times 1 - 5| = |-3| = 3$

---

**Exercise A** (answers p 161)

**1** Evaluate these.

(a) $|-3| + 1$      (b) $|-3 + 1|$      (c) $|7 - 1|$      (d) $|1 - 7|$

**2** A function is defined by $f(x) = |2x - 3|$.
Evaluate these.

(a) f(1)          (b) f(2)          (c) f(0)          (d) f(6)          (e) f(−3)

**3** A function is defined by $g(x) = |4 - x| + 1$.
Evaluate these.

(a) g(3)          (b) g(6)          (c) g(−1)          (d) g(10)          (e) $g\left(5\frac{1}{2}\right)$

**4** A function is defined by $h(x) = |x^2 - 5|$.
Evaluate these.

(a) h(1)          (b) h(3)          (c) h(0)          (d) h(−2)          (e) h(−4)

**5** Functions f and g are defined by $f(x) = |x - 3|$ and $g(x) = x + 1$.
Evaluate these.

(a) fg(0)          (b) gf(0)          (c) ff(1)          (d) gf(−2)          (e) fg(2)

## B Graphs (answers p 161)

You can check each graph on a graph plotter.

**B1** (a) Copy and complete this table of values.

| $x$ | -3 | -2 | -1 | 0 | 1 | 2 | 3 |
|-----|----|----|----|---|---|---|---|
| $|x|$ | | | | | | | |

(b) Evaluate these.

(i) $\left|\frac{1}{2}\right|$            (ii) $\left|-\frac{3}{4}\right|$            (iii) $|-2.25|$

(c) Draw the graph of $y = |x|$.

**B2** (a) Copy and complete this table of values.

| $x$ | -3 | -2 | -1 | 0 | 1 | 2 | 3 |
|-----|----|----|----|---|---|---|---|
| $|x + 1|$ | | | | | | | |

(b) Draw the graph of $y = |x + 1|$.

**B3** (a) Draw up a table of values for the equation $y = |x^2 - 4|$.

(b) Draw the graph of $y = |x^2 - 4|$.

**B4** Match each equation with its sketch graph.

(a) $y = |x - 2|$          (b) $y = |x + 5|$          (c) $y = |2x|$

(d) $y = \left|\dfrac{1}{x}\right|$          (e) $y = |x^2 - 3|$          (f) $y = |x^3 - x|$

**A**
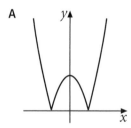

**B**
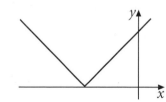

**C**
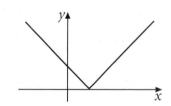

**D**
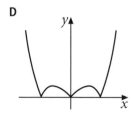

**E**
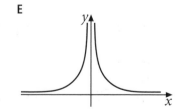

**F**
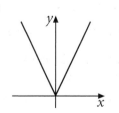

**B5** Show that the graph of $y = |x - 2|$ is the same as the graph of $y = |2 - x|$.

One method to sketch the graph of $y = |2x - 1|$ is shown below.

First sketch the graph of $y = 2x - 1$.

Identify which parts of the graph lie beneath the $x$-axis (showing where the values of $2x - 1$ are negative).

Change the negative values to positive ones by reflecting in the $x$-axis.

Sketch the final graph of $y = |2x - 1|$.

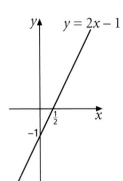 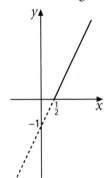 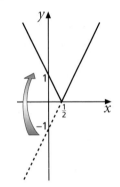 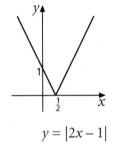

This method can be used to sketch the graph of any modulus function.

---

### Example 2

A function is defined by $f(x) = x^2 - 4x + 3$.
Draw the graph of $y = |f(x)|$ showing clearly where the graph meets each axis.

### Solution

$f(0) = 3$ so the graph of $y = f(x)$ cuts the $y$-axis at $(0, 3)$.

$x^2 - 4x + 3 = (x - 3)(x - 1)$
So the graph of $y = f(x)$ cuts the $x$-axis at $(1, 0)$ and $(3, 0)$.

As there is a vertical line of symmetry, the vertex is halfway between 1 and 3 at $x = 2$.
$f(2) = -1$ so the vertex of the graph $y = f(x)$ is $(2, -1)$.

The graph of $y = f(x)$ is

So the graph of $y = |f(x)|$ is

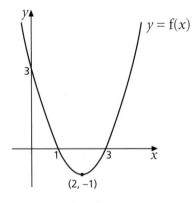 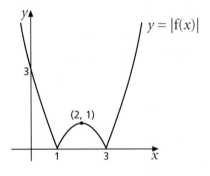

---

**Exercise B** (answers p 162)

In these questions, show clearly the points where each graph meets the axes.
Where possible, check your graph on a graph plotter.

**1** Sketch the graph of each equation, using a separate diagram for each one.

(a) $y = |x + 5|$    (b) $y = |3x - 5|$    (c) $y = |2x + 8|$

**2** Sketch the graph of each equation, using a separate diagram for each one.

(a) $y = |x^2 - 1|$    (b) $y = |x^2 - x|$    (c) $y = |x^2 - x - 6|$

**3** Show that the graph of $y = |x^2 - 9|$ is the same as the graph of $y = |9 - x^2|$.

**4** The diagram below shows a sketch of the curve with equation $y = f(x)$, $-2 \leq x \leq 4$.

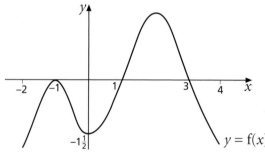

Draw a sketch of the curve with equation $y = |f(x)|$.

**5** Sketch the graph of $y = |\sin x|$, $-2\pi \leq x \leq 2\pi$.

**6** A function is defined as $g(x) = (x + 1)(x - 2)(x - 3)$, $-1 \leq x \leq 3$.
Sketch the graph of $y = |g(x)|$.

**7** A function is defined as $h(x) = 2^x - 1$, $-2 \leq x \leq 3$.
Sketch the graph of $y = |h(x)|$.

**8** The function f is defined as $f: x \mapsto |x + k|$, $x \in \mathbb{R}$, where $k$ is a positive constant.
Sketch the graph of $y = f(x)$.

**9** Each of the graphs below has a vertical line of symmetry.
Determine the equation of each graph.

(a)

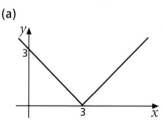

(b)

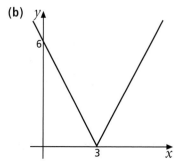

(c)

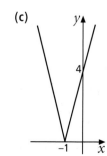

## C Equations and inequalities (answers p 162)

**C1** Show that $x = -4$ is a solution of the equation $|x + 1| = 3$.
Find another solution of this equation.

**C2** Solve these equations.

    (a) $|x + 4| = 5$      (b) $|x - 1| = 5$      (c) $|x + 3| = 1$      (d) $|x + 6| = 0$

**C3** Explain how you know that the equation $|x + 2| = -1$ has no solution.

An equation such as $|2x + 1| = 3$ is straightforward to solve.
There are two possibilities: either $2x + 1 = 3$ or $2x + 1 = -3$.

$$2x + 1 = 3 \quad \Rightarrow \quad x = 1$$
$$\text{and } 2x + 1 = -3 \quad \Rightarrow \quad x = -2$$

So there are two solutions, $x = 1$ and $x = -2$.

A graph illustrates this.

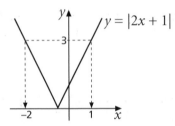

**C4** Solve these equations.

    (a) $|2x + 3| = 5$         (b) $|3x + 1| = 2$         (c) $|2x - 5| = 4$

**D** **C5** Can the equation $|3x + 2| = x$ be solved?

We can see that the equation $|2x + 1| = x$ does not have a solution when we
sketch the graphs of $y = |2x + 1|$ and $y = x$ on the same axes.

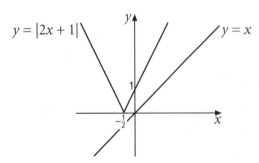

The graphs do not intersect so the equation $|2x + 1| = x$ cannot have a solution.

**C6** (a) By sketching graphs, show that the equation $|2x + 1| = -x$ has two solutions.

    (b) Find these solutions.

When solving equations that involve a modulus function, it often helps to start with a sketch.

For example, we can see from a sketch that the equation $|2x - 1| = x$ has two solutions (as the graphs of $y = |2x - 1|$ and $y = x$ intersect at two points).

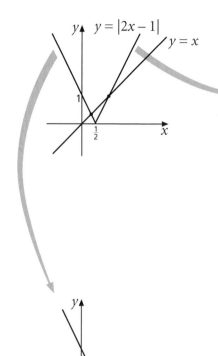

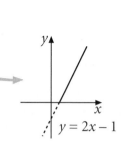

The right-hand 'arm' of the graph of $y = |2x - 1|$ is part of the graph of $y = 2x - 1$.

So for the point of intersection on this arm we have $2x - 1 = x$, which has a solution $x = 1$.

The left-hand arm of the graph of $y = |2x - 1|$ is part of the graph of $y = -(2x - 1)$, which is $y = 1 - 2x$.

So for the point of intersection on this arm we have $1 - 2x = x$, which has a solution $x = \frac{1}{3}$.

So the solutions of the equation $|2x - 1| = x$ are $x = 1$ and $x = \frac{1}{3}$.

**C7** Solve the equation $|2x - 5| = x + 1$.

**C8** (a) Draw a sketch of $y = |x^2 - 9|$.

(b) Use your sketch to write down the number of solutions of each equation below.
  (i) $|x^2 - 9| = 7$      (ii) $|x^2 - 9| = -3$      (iii) $|x^2 - 9| = 16$

(c) Find all the solutions of the equation $|x^2 - 9| = 7$.

**C9** (a) On the same diagram, draw sketches of $y = |3x - 6|$ and $y = |x|$.

(b) Find all the solutions of the equation $|3x - 6| = |x|$.

(c) Solve the inequality $|3x - 6| < |x|$.

**C10** Show that the equation $|x^2 - 1| = x - 2$ has no solutions.

**C11** Solve the inequality $|4x + 1| \geq 3$.

**C12** Solve the equation $|x| = 12 - x^2$.

## Example 3

A function is defined by $f(x) = (x + 1)(x - 5)$.
Solve $|f(x)| = 8$.

### Solution

*A sketch shows the equation will have four solutions.*

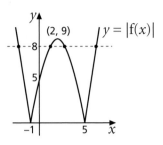

For $|f(x)| = 8$, either $f(x) = 8$ or $f(x) = -8$, so solve
$(x + 1)(x - 5) = 8$ and $(x + 1)(x - 5) = -8$.

$$(x + 1)(x - 5) = 8$$
$$x^2 - 4x - 5 = 8$$
$$\Rightarrow \quad x^2 - 4x - 13 = 0$$
$$\Rightarrow \quad (x - 2)^2 - 17 = 0$$
$$\Rightarrow \quad (x - 2)^2 = 17$$
$$\Rightarrow \quad x - 2 = \pm\sqrt{17}$$
$$\Rightarrow \quad x = 2 \pm \sqrt{17}$$

$$(x + 1)(x - 5) = -8$$
$$\Rightarrow \quad x^2 - 4x - 5 = -8$$
$$\Rightarrow \quad x^2 - 4x + 3 = 0$$
$$\Rightarrow \quad (x - 1)(x - 3) = 0$$
$$\Rightarrow \quad x = 1, 3$$

So the four solutions are $x = 2 + \sqrt{17}, 2 - \sqrt{17}, 1, 3$.

---

## Example 4

Solve the equation $|3x - 5| = |x + 1|$.

### Solution

*A sketch shows that the equation has two solutions.*

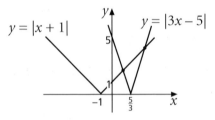

*The right-hand solution is the intersection of* $y = 3x - 5$ *and* $y = x + 1$, *so solve* $3x - 5 = x + 1$.

$$3x - 5 = x + 1 \quad \Rightarrow \quad 2x = 6$$
$$\Rightarrow \quad x = 3$$

*The left-hand solution is the intersection of* $y = -(3x - 5)$ *and* $y = x + 1$, *so solve* $-(3x - 5) = x + 1$.

$$-(3x - 5) = x + 1 \quad \Rightarrow \quad -3x + 5 = x + 1$$
$$\Rightarrow \quad 4x = 4$$
$$\Rightarrow \quad x = 1$$

So the two solutions are $x = 1, 3$.

---

**Example 5**

Solve the inequality $|3x - 4| > x + 2$.

**Solution**

A sketch of $y = |3x - 4|$ and $y = x + 2$ shows that the equation $|3x - 4| = x + 2$ has two solutions.

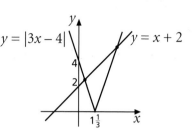

Solve $3x - 4 = x + 2$ and $-(3x - 4) = x + 2$.

$$3x - 4 = x + 2$$
$$\Rightarrow \quad 2x = 6$$
$$\Rightarrow \quad x = 3$$

$$-(3x - 4) = x + 2$$
$$\Rightarrow \quad -3x + 4 = x + 2$$
$$\Rightarrow \quad 4x = 2$$
$$\Rightarrow \quad x = \tfrac{1}{2}$$

$|3x - 4| > x + 2$ when the graph of $y = |3x - 4|$ is above the graph of $y = x + 2$.

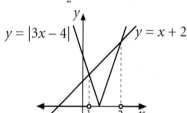

The solution is $x < \tfrac{1}{2}$ and $x > 3$.

---

**Exercise C** (answers p 163)

**1** Solve each equation.

(a) $|x + 6| = 9$      (b) $|2x - 1| = 10$      (c) $\left|\dfrac{8}{x}\right| = 2$

(d) $|x^2 - 2| = 1$      (e) $|3 - 2x^2| = 6$      (f) $|x^3 - 13| = 14$

**2** Solve each inequality.      (a) $|x - 5| < 2$      (b) $|3x + 4| \geq 1$

**3** (a) On the same diagram, draw sketches of $y = |x - 2|$ and $y = x + 1$.

(b) Solve the equation $|x - 2| = x + 1$.

(c) Hence find the solution of $|x - 2| < x + 1$.

**4** Solve each equation.

(a) $|3x - 2| = 2x + 1$      (b) $|2x - 1| = 5 - x$      (c) $|x + 2| = x^2$

(d) $|x| = x^2$      (e) $|x + 5| = x^2 - 1$      (f) $x^2 - 9 = |2x - 1|$

**5** (a) Show that the equation $|x + 4| = |x - 1|$ has only one solution.

(b) Solve the inequality $|x + 4| \geq |x - 1|$.

**6** Solve each equation.

(a) $|x + 3| = |2x - 1|$      (b) $|2x + 3| = |2x - 9|$      (c) $|3x + 5| = |x + 3|$

**7** Solve each inequality.

(a) $|2x - 3| \leq |2x + 5|$    (b) $|3x + 2| < x + 6$    (c) $|x + 9| < 2x$

(d) $|x - 5| \geq |\frac{1}{2}x + 1|$    (e) $|x + 12| > x^2$    (f) $x^2 - 3 \geq |3 - x|$

**8 (a)** On the same diagram, draw sketches of $y = |x|$ and $y = 20 - x^2$.

(b) Find the solution of $|x| = 20 - x^2$.

**9 (a)** On the same diagram, draw sketches of $y = |2x + 1|$ and $y = 7 - x^2$.

(b) Find the solution of $|2x + 1| < 7 - x^2$.

**10** Solve $|x^2 + x - 6| < |3x + 4|$.

## D Further graphs and equations (answers p 163)

**D1** The function f is defined for all real values of $x$ by $f(x) = |x| + 3$.

(a) Evaluate f(4) and f(−1).

(b) Which of the sketches below shows the graph of $y = f(x)$?

A
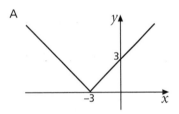

B
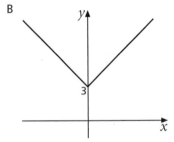

C
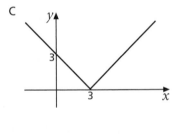

(c) What is the range of f?

(d) Explain why the equation $f(x) = 1$ has no solution.

(e) Solve the equation $f(x) = 5$.

**D2** The function g is defined by $g(x) = 2|x - 1|$.

(a) Which of the sketches below shows the graph of $y = g(x)$?

A
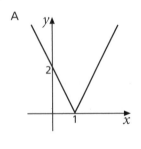

B
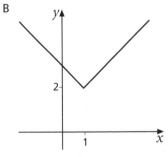

C
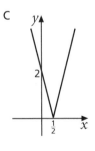

(b) Solve the equation $g(x) = 8$.

**D3** Sketch the graph of $y = f(x)$ where f is defined by $f(x) = 2|x| - 1$.

**D4** The function g is defined by $g(x) = |2x - 3| + 1$.

(a) Sketch the graph of $y = g(x)$.

(b) Explain why the equation $g(x) = 0$ has no solution.

(c) Solve the equation $g(x) = 8$.

**D5** The function f is defined by $f(x) = -|x + 2|$.

(a) Evaluate f(1) and f(−2).

(b) Which of the sketches below shows the graph of $y = f(x)$?

A 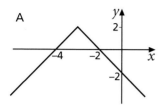 B 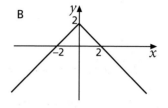 C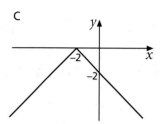

(c) What is the range of f?

**D6** Sketch the graph of $y = g(x)$ where g is defined by $g(x) = -|x| + 3$.

---

### Example 6

Sketch the graph of $y = f(x)$ where f is the function defined by $f(x) = 3 - 2|x + 1|$.
State its range.

### Solution

*One method is to sketch the graph in stages.*

$$y = |x + 1| \quad\longrightarrow\quad y = 2|x + 1| \quad\longrightarrow\quad y = -2|x + 1| \quad\longrightarrow\quad y = 3 - 2|x + 1|$$

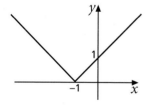 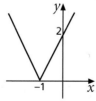 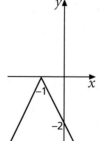 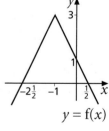

The range is $f(x) \le 3$.

---

**D7** (a) Sketch the graph of $y = f(x)$ where f is defined by $f(x) = 4 - |2x + 5|$.

(b) What is the range of f?

**D8** Functions f and g are defined by $f(x) = 6 - x$ and $g(x) = |x - 2|$.

(a) Write down, and simplify if necessary, expressions for fg(x) and gf(x).

(b) Sketch the graph of $y = fg(x)$.

## Example 7

A function is defined by $g(x) = 7 - |3x - 1|$.
Solve the equation $g(x) = 3$.

### Solution

$$7 - |3x - 1| = 3$$
$$\Rightarrow \qquad |3x - 1| = 4$$

Solve $3x - 1 = 4$ *and* $3x - 1 = -4$.

| | |
|---|---|
| $3x - 1 = 4$ | $3x - 1 = -4$ |
| $\Rightarrow \quad 3x = 5$ | $\Rightarrow \quad 3x = -3$ |
| $\Rightarrow \quad x = \frac{5}{3}$ | $\Rightarrow \quad x = -1$ |

So the solutions are $x = \frac{5}{3}, -1$.

---

## Example 8

A function is defined by $f(x) = |2x + 1| - 3$.
Solve the inequality $f(x) < x$.

### Solution

Solve $|2x + 1| - 3 < x$.

A sketch of $y = |2x + 1| - 3$ *and* $y = x$ *shows that*
*the equation* $|2x + 1| - 3 = x$ *has two solutions.*

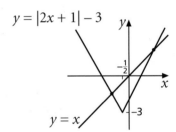

Solve $(2x + 1) - 3 = x$ *and* $-(2x + 1) - 3 = x$.

| | |
|---|---|
| $(2x + 1) - 3 = x$ | $-(2x + 1) - 3 = x$ |
| $\Rightarrow \qquad 2x - 2 = x$ | $\Rightarrow \qquad -2x - 4 = x$ |
| $\Rightarrow \qquad x - 2 = 0$ | $\Rightarrow \qquad 3x = -4$ |
| $\Rightarrow \qquad x = 2$ | $\Rightarrow \qquad x = -\frac{4}{3}$ |

$|2x + 1| - 3 < x$ *when the graph of* $y = |2x + 1| - 3$
*is below the graph of* $y = x$.

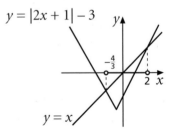

The solution is $-\frac{4}{3} < x < 2$.

*An alternative method is to rearrange* $|2x + 1| - 3 < x$ *to obtain* $|2x + 1| < x + 3$ *and*
*consider the graphs of* $y = |2x + 1|$ *and* $y = x + 3$.

---

## Example 9

Solve the equation $x|x-1| = 1$.

### Solution

$$x|x-1| = 1$$
$$\Rightarrow \quad |x-1| = \frac{1}{x}$$

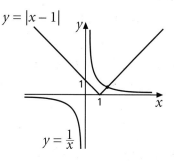

A sketch of $y = |x-1|$ and $y = \frac{1}{x}$ shows that the equation $|x-1| = \frac{1}{x}$ has one solution, which is when $x-1 = \frac{1}{x}$.

$$x - 1 = \frac{1}{x}$$
$$\Rightarrow \quad x(x-1) = 1$$
$$\Rightarrow \quad x^2 - x - 1 = 0$$
$$\Rightarrow \quad x = \frac{-(-1) \pm \sqrt{(-1)^2 - 4 \times 1 \times (-1)}}{2}$$
$$\Rightarrow \quad x = \frac{1 \pm \sqrt{5}}{2}$$

From the graph we can see that $x$ is positive so the solution is $x = \frac{1}{2}(1 + \sqrt{5})$.

---

## Exercise D (answers p 164)

**1** Sketch the graph of $y = f(x)$ for each function.
State the range of f each time.

(a) $f(x) = |x| + 2$      (b) $f(x) = 3|x+1|$      (c) $f(x) = 2|x| + 3$

(d) $f(x) = |2x-1| - 3$      (e) $f(x) = 5 - |x|$      (f) $f(x) = 6 - |3x+1|$

**2** Solve each equation.

(a) $2|x| = \frac{1}{2}x + 15$      (b) $|3x-1| - 5 = x$      (c) $4 - |x| = x$

**3** The function f is defined for all real values of $x$ by $f(x) = 8 - |2x+5|$.

(a) Solve the equation $f(x) = 1$.

(b) Show that there are no solutions to $f(x) = 9$.

(c) Solve the inequality $f(x) \leq 2$.

**4** The function g is defined for all real values of $x$ by $g(x) = 1 + |3x-7|$.

(a) Solve the equation $g(x) = x$.

(b) Show that the equation $g(x) = x - 2$ has no solutions.

**5** Solve the inequality $|x+2| < 3|x|$.

**6** The function h is defined by $h(x) = |x-1| + 4$.
Solve $h(x) > 2x$.

**7 (a)** On the same set of axes, sketch the graphs of $y = |2x - 1|$ and $y = \dfrac{1}{x}$.

**(b)** Explain how your graphs show that there is only one solution of the equation $x|2x - 1| = 1$. Solve the equation.

**8** The function f is defined by $f(x) = |x|$, $x \in \mathbb{R}$.
Show that $f^{-1}$ does not exist.

**9** Functions f and g are defined for all real values of $x$ by
$$f(x) = |x^2 - 3| \text{ and } g(x) = x + 2$$

**(a)** Write down, and simplify if necessary, expressions for $fg(x)$ and $gf(x)$.

**(b)** Sketch the graph of $y = gf(x)$.

**10** Functions f and g are defined for all real values of $x$ by
$$f(x) = |x + 1| \text{ and } g(x) = x - 3$$

**(a)** Solve the equation $gf(x) = 5$.

**(b)** Solve the inequality $fg(x) < x$.

**11** The function g is defined by $g(x) = |x| + x$.

**(a)** Sketch the graph of $y = g(x)$.

**(b)** Solve the equation $g(x) = 10$.

**12** Solve the equation $|x| - 1 = |x^2 - 3|$.

**13** The function f is defined by $f(x) = x(x - 4)$.

**(a)** Sketch the graph of $y = |f(x)|$.

**(b)** Sketch the graph of $y = f(|x|)$.

---

## Key points

- $|x|$ is the symbol for 'the modulus of $x$' or 'the absolute value of $x$'.
  The modulus of a real number can be thought of as its 'distance' from 0 or
  its 'size' and is always positive. For example, $|4| = 4$ and $|-2| = 2$. (p 24)

- The graph of $y = |x|$ is

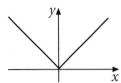

(p 25)

- One method of sketching $y = |f(x)|$ is first to sketch the graph of $y = f(x)$.
  Take any part of the graph that is below the $x$-axis and reflect it in the $x$-axis to
  obtain the graph of $y = |f(x)|$. (p 26)

- When solving equations that involve a modulus function, it is usually
  a good idea to sketch graphs first to determine the number of solutions. (p 29)

## Test yourself (answers p 166)

**1** The function f is defined for all real values of $x$ by

$$f(x) = |x + 1| + 6$$

**(a)** Sketch the graph of $y = f(x)$ and state the range of f.

**(b)** Evaluate ff(−5).

**(c)** Solve the equation $f(x) = 10$.

**2** The function f is defined for all real values of $x$ by

$$f(x) = |2x − 3| − 1$$

**(a)** Sketch the graph of $y = f(x)$. Indicate the coordinates of the points where the graph crosses the $x$-axis and the coordinates of the point where the graph crosses the $y$-axis.

**(b)** State the range of f.

**(c)** Find the values of $x$ for which $f(x) = x$.                    AQA 2002

**3** The function f is defined for all real values of $x$ by

$$f(x) = 3 − |2x − 1|$$

**(a) (i)** Sketch the graph of $y = f(x)$. Indicate the coordinates of the points where the graph crosses the coordinate axes.

**(ii)** Hence show that the equation $f(x) = 4$ has no real roots.

**(b)** State the range of f.

**(c)** By finding the values of $x$ for which $f(x) = x$, solve the inequality $f(x) < x$.  AQA 2003

**4** Solve the equation $|3x + 1| = |3x − 5|$.

**5 (a)** Sketch, on the same diagram, the graphs of

$$y = |2x + 3| \text{ and } y = 2x^2 − 9$$

stating the coordinates of any points where the graphs meet the axes.

**(b)** Deduce the number of roots of the equation $|2x + 3| = 2x^2 − 9$. Determine the value of each of these roots.                    AQA 2001

**6** Solve the inequality $|x − 2| > 2|x + 1|$.

**7** The function g is defined by

$$g: x \mapsto |x + a| + b, \ x \in \mathbb{R}$$

where $a$ and $b$ are positive constants.

**(a)** Sketch the graph of $y = g(x)$, showing the coordinates of any points where the graph cuts the axes.

**(b)** State the range of g.

**(c)** Given that the graph cuts the $y$-axis at $(0, 8)$ and that the graph has $x = −2$ as a vertical line of symmetry, find the values of $a$ and $b$.

# 3 Transforming graphs

In this chapter you will
- revise how to transform the graph of $y = f(x)$ to obtain graphs of the form $y = af(x)$, $y = f(ax)$, $y = f(x) + a$ and $f(x + a)$
- learn how to combine transformations to obtain a new graph and a new equation

## A Single transformations: revision (answers p 167)

If one graph is a transformation of another, then the equations of the two graphs are related.

For example, transforming the graph of $y = x^2$ by translating it by $\begin{bmatrix} 0 \\ 3 \end{bmatrix}$ gives a new graph with equation $y = x^2 + 3$.

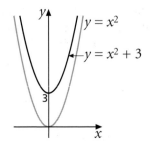

Function notation helps us think about how the equations of transformed graphs are related. For example, suppose the graph of $y = f(x)$ is transformed by a stretch of scale factor 2 in the $x$-direction. Thus the $x$-coordinate of each point is doubled.

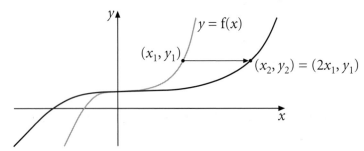

Let $(x_1, y_1)$ be a point on $y = f(x)$ and let $(x_2, y_2)$ be its image on the stretched curve.

Then $(x_2, y_2) = (2x_1, y_1)$, giving

$$x_2 = 2x_1 \text{ which rearranges to } x_1 = \tfrac{1}{2}x_2$$
$$\text{and } y_2 = y_1 \text{ which rearranges to } y_1 = y_2$$

We know that $y_1 = f(x_1)$, so it must be true that
$$y_2 = f\left(\tfrac{1}{2}x_2\right)$$
and so $y = f\left(\tfrac{1}{2}x\right)$ is the equation of the image.

So to find the equation of $y = f(x)$ after a stretch of scale factor 2 in the $x$-direction we replace $x$ by $\tfrac{1}{2}x$ to obtain $y = f\left(\tfrac{1}{2}x\right)$.

**K** In general, in a stretch of scale factor $k$ in the $x$-direction, $x$ is replaced in the equation by $\frac{1}{k}x$. So the graph of $y = f(x)$ is mapped on to the graph of $y = f\left(\frac{1}{k}x\right)$.

It follows that, in a stretch of scale factor $\frac{1}{k}$ in the $x$-direction, $x$ is replaced in the equation by $\left(\frac{1}{\left(\frac{1}{k}\right)}\right)x$, which is equivalent to $kx$.

**K** So the graph of $y = f(x)$ is mapped on to the graph of $y = f(kx)$ by a stretch of scale factor $\frac{1}{k}$ in the $x$-direction.

For example, $y = 2^x$ is changed to $y = 2^{4x}$ by replacing $x$ by $4x$. So the graph of $y = 2^x$ is transformed on to the graph of $y = 2^{4x}$ by a stretch of scale factor $\frac{1}{4}$ in the $x$-direction.

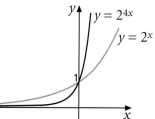

Now suppose that $y = f(x)$ is transformed by a stretch of scale factor 2 in the $y$-direction. Thus the $y$-coordinate of each point is doubled.

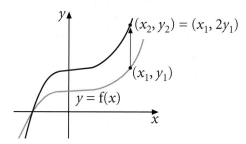

Let $(x_1, y_1)$ be a point on $y = f(x)$ and let $(x_2, y_2)$ be its image on the stretched curve. Then $(x_2, y_2) = (x_1, 2y_1)$, giving

$$x_2 = x_1 \quad \text{which rearranges to} \quad x_1 = x_2$$

and $y_2 = 2y_1$ which rearranges to $y_1 = \frac{1}{2}y_2$

We know that $y_1 = f(x_1)$, so it must be true that

$$\tfrac{1}{2}y_2 = f(x_2)$$

and so $\frac{1}{2}y = f(x)$ is the equation of the image.

This can be rearranged to give $y = 2f(x)$.

So to find the equation of $y = f(x)$ after a stretch of scale factor 2 in the $y$-direction we replace $y$ by $\frac{1}{2}y$ to obtain $\frac{1}{2}y = f(x)$ or $y = 2f(x)$.

**K** In general, a stretch of scale factor $k$ in the $y$-direction transforms an equation by replacing $y$ with $\frac{1}{k}y$. So the graph of $y = f(x)$ is mapped on to the graph of $\frac{1}{k}y = f(x)$, which rearranges to $y = kf(x)$.

For example, a stretch of scale factor 3 in the y-direction replaces $y$ with $\frac{1}{3}y$.
So stretching the graph of $y = \cos x$ by a factor of 3 in the y-direction transforms it on to the graph of $\frac{1}{3}y = \cos x$ or $y = 3\cos x$.

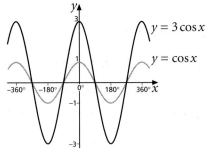

**A1** Show that the image of $y = x^2 + 1$ after a stretch of factor $\frac{1}{2}$ in the x-direction is $y = 4x^2 + 1$.

**A2** Show that a translation of $\begin{bmatrix} a \\ 0 \end{bmatrix}$ maps the graph of $y = f(x)$ on to the graph of $y = f(x - a)$.

**A3** What is the image of $y = |x|$ after a translation of $\begin{bmatrix} 3 \\ 0 \end{bmatrix}$?

**A4** What is the image of $y = f(x)$ after a translation of $\begin{bmatrix} 0 \\ a \end{bmatrix}$?

**A5** Find the image of $y = 3^x$ after a translation of $\begin{bmatrix} 0 \\ 5 \end{bmatrix}$.

**A6** What is the image of $y = f(x)$ after

(a) reflection in the x-axis          (b) reflection in the y-axis

**A7** What is the image of $y = x^2 + x$ after reflection in the y-axis?

---

**Example 1**

Find the equation of the image of $y = x^2 + 3x$ after a translation of $\begin{bmatrix} -2 \\ 0 \end{bmatrix}$.

**Solution**

For a translation of $\begin{bmatrix} -2 \\ 0 \end{bmatrix}$ we replace $x$ by $x + 2$.

So $y = x^2 + 3x$ becomes $y = (x + 2)^2 + 3(x + 2) = x^2 + 4x + 4 + 3x + 6 = x^2 + 7x + 10$.
So the equation of the image is $y = x^2 + 7x + 10$.

---

**Example 2**

The function f is defined by $f(x) = x^3 - x$.
Show that $f(2x) = 8x^3 - 2x$.

The diagram shows the graph of $y = x^3 - x$.
Copy it and add the sketch of $y = 8x^3 - 2x$.

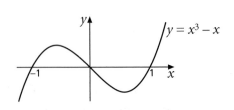

**Solution**

$f(2x) = (2x)^3 - (2x) = 8x^3 - 2x$ as required.

$x$ is replaced by $2x$, so the transformation is a stretch of factor $\frac{1}{2}$ in the x-direction as shown.

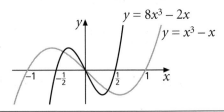

**Exercise A** (answers p 167)

**1** Describe the transformation that transforms $y = f(x)$ on to each of these.

(a) $y = 3f(x)$      (b) $y = f(3x)$      (c) $y = \frac{1}{3}f(x)$      (d) $y = f\left(\frac{1}{3}x\right)$

**2** Find the image of $y = x^3$ after a stretch of factor 2 in the $y$-direction.

**3** The function f is defined by $f(x) = x^2 - x$.
The diagram shows the graph of $y = x^2 - x$.

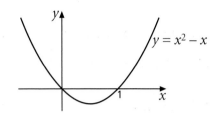

(a) Show that $f(5x) = 25x^2 - 5x$.

(b) Hence describe the transformation that maps $y = x^2 - x$ on to $y = 25x^2 - 5x$.

(c) Sketch the graph of $y = 25x^2 - 5x$.

**4** Describe the transformation that transforms $y = f(x)$ on to each of these.

(a) $y = f(x) + 3$      (b) $y = f(x + 3)$      (c) $y = f(x) - 3$      (d) $y = f(x - 3)$

**5** What transformation maps the graph of $y = \sin x$ on to the graph of $y = \sin(x + 90)$?

**6** The function f is defined by $f(x) = x^2 + x$.

(a) Show that $f(x - 4) = x^2 - 7x + 12$.

(b) Hence describe the transformation that maps $y = x^2 + x$ on to $y = x^2 - 7x + 12$.

**7** The function f is defined by $f(x) = x^3 - 4x$.
The diagram shows the graph of $y = x^3 - 4x$ and
its image after a translation in the $x$-direction.

Find the equation of the translated graph
in the form $y = ax^3 + bx^2 + cx + d$.

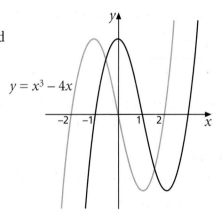

**8** (a) Find the image of $y = x^4 + x^2$ after reflection in the $y$-axis.

(b) Hence show that the graph of $y = x^4 + x^2$ has the $y$-axis as a line of symmetry.

**9** (a) Find the image of $y = 5^x$ after    (i) a translation of $\begin{bmatrix} -1 \\ 0 \end{bmatrix}$

                                 (ii) a stretch of scale factor 5 in the $y$-direction

(b) Show that these images are the same.

| $y = f(x)$ is transformed on to ... | by a ... | that ... |
|---|---|---|
| $y = f(x) + a$ | translation of $\begin{bmatrix} 0 \\ a \end{bmatrix}$ | replaces $y$ by $(y - a)$ |
| $y = f(x - a)$ | translation of $\begin{bmatrix} a \\ 0 \end{bmatrix}$ | replaces $x$ by $(x - a)$ |
| $y = f(x + a)$ | translation of $\begin{bmatrix} -a \\ 0 \end{bmatrix}$ | replaces $x$ by $(x + a)$ |
| $y = kf(x)$ | stretch of factor $k$ in the $y$-direction | replaces $y$ by $\frac{1}{k}y$ |
| $y = f\left(\frac{1}{k}x\right)$ | stretch of factor $k$ in the $x$-direction | replaces $x$ by $\frac{1}{k}x$ |
| $y = f(kx)$ | stretch of factor $\frac{1}{k}$ in the $x$-direction | replaces $x$ by $kx$ |
| $y = -f(x)$ | reflection in the $x$-axis | replaces $y$ by $-y$ |
| $y = f(-x)$ | reflection in the $y$-axis | replaces $x$ by $-x$ |

## B Combining transformations (answers p 167)

**B1** The graph of $y = x$ is first translated by $\begin{bmatrix} 0 \\ 2 \end{bmatrix}$ and then stretched by factor 3 in the $y$-direction. Sketch a graph of the final image and determine its equation.

**B2** (a) The graph of $y = x$ is first translated by $\begin{bmatrix} 1 \\ 0 \end{bmatrix}$ and then reflected in the $y$-axis. Find the equation of the final image.

(b) The graph of $y = x$ is first reflected in the $y$-axis and then translated by $\begin{bmatrix} 1 \\ 0 \end{bmatrix}$. What is the equation of the final image?

**B3** The graph of $y = x^2$ is first stretched by factor 3 in the $y$-direction and then translated by $\begin{bmatrix} 0 \\ -5 \end{bmatrix}$.
Show that the equation of the final image is $y = 3x^2 - 5$.

**B4** Find the image of $y = x^2$ after each sequence of transformations.

(a) A translation of $\begin{bmatrix} 0 \\ 1 \end{bmatrix}$ followed by a reflection in the $x$-axis

(b) A translation of $\begin{bmatrix} 5 \\ 0 \end{bmatrix}$ followed by a stretch of factor 2 in the $y$-direction

(c) A translation of $\begin{bmatrix} -3 \\ 0 \end{bmatrix}$ followed by a translation of $\begin{bmatrix} 0 \\ -2 \end{bmatrix}$

(d) A stretch of factor 6 in the $y$-direction followed by reflection in the $x$-axis

**B5** Describe a sequence of transformations that will map $y = x^2$ on to each of these.
(a) $y = \frac{1}{2}(x + 1)^2$       (b) $y = 7 - x^2$

**D** **B6** Which of these is the image of $y = f(x)$ after a translation of $\begin{bmatrix} 1 \\ 0 \end{bmatrix}$ followed by a stretch of factor 3 in the $y$-direction?

**A** $y = 3f(x + 1)$ **B** $y = 3f(x - 1)$ **C** $y = \frac{1}{3}f(x + 1)$ **D** $y = \frac{1}{3}f(x - 1)$

**B7** Which of these is the image of $y = f(x)$ after a reflection in the $y$-axis followed by a stretch of factor 2 in the $x$-direction?

**A** $y = -2f(x)$ **B** $y = f\left(-\frac{1}{2}x\right)$ **C** $y = \frac{1}{2}f(-x)$ **D** $y = f(-2x)$

We can use algebra to determine equations of graphs after a sequence of transformations.

---

### Example 3

The graph of $y = x^2$ is first stretched by factor 3 in the $y$-direction and then translated by $\begin{bmatrix} 2 \\ 0 \end{bmatrix}$.
Find the equation of the final image and sketch its graph.

### Solution

For the image of $y = x^2$ after a stretch of factor 3 in the $y$-direction, replace $y$ by $\frac{1}{3}y$.
So the image is $\frac{1}{3}y = x^2$, which is equivalent to $y = 3x^2$.

For the image of $y = 3x^2$ after a translation of $\begin{bmatrix} 2 \\ 0 \end{bmatrix}$, replace $x$ by $(x - 2)$.
So the final image is $y = 3(x - 2)^2$.

The sequence of graphs is

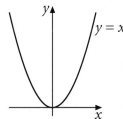 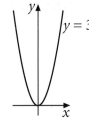 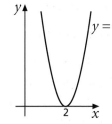

*The final graph is the required result.*

---

### Example 4

The graph of $y = f(x)$ is first stretched by factor $\frac{1}{2}$ in the $x$-direction and then stretched by factor 5 in the $y$-direction.

Write down the coordinates of the image of the point $(4, 1)$ and find the equation of the final image.

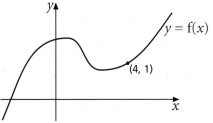

### Solution

*The first stretch multiplies the x-coordinate by $\frac{1}{2}$ and the second multiplies the y-coordinate by 5.*

The coordinates of the image of the point are $\left(\frac{1}{2} \times 4, 5 \times 1\right) = (2, 5)$.

For the image of $y = f(x)$ after a stretch of factor $\frac{1}{2}$ in the $x$-direction, replace $x$ by $2x$.
So the image is $y = f(2x)$.

For the image of $y = f(2x)$ after a stretch of factor 5 in the $y$-direction, replace $y$ by $\frac{1}{5}y$.
So the final image is $\frac{1}{5}y = f(2x)$, which is equivalent to $y = 5f(2x)$.

---

**Example 5**

The diagram shows the graph of $y = 3 \times 2^{-x}$.

Describe a sequence of transformations by which this graph can be obtained from the graph of $y = 2^x$.

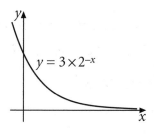

**Solution**

$y = 3 \times 2^{-x}$ is equivalent to $\frac{1}{3}y = 2^{-x}$.

From $y = 2^x$ we can obtain $\frac{1}{3}y = 2^{-x}$ by replacing $y$ by $\frac{1}{3}y$ and $x$ by $-x$.

So a sequence of transformations is a stretch of factor 3 in the $y$-direction followed by a reflection in the $y$-axis (or vice versa).

---

**Example 6**

The diagram shows the graph of $y = f(x)$, where f is defined for $0 \leq x \leq 3$.

Sketch the graph of $y = 2f(x + 1)$.

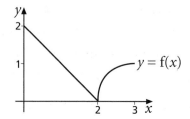

**Solution**

$y = 2f(x + 1)$ is equivalent to $\frac{1}{2}y = f(x + 1)$.

From $y = f(x)$ we can obtain $\frac{1}{2}y = f(x + 1)$ by replacing $y$ by $\frac{1}{2}y$ and $x$ by $(x + 1)$.

So a sequence of transformations is a stretch of factor 2 in the $y$-direction followed by

a translation of $\begin{bmatrix} -1 \\ 0 \end{bmatrix}$ (or vice versa).

Hence a sequence of graphs is

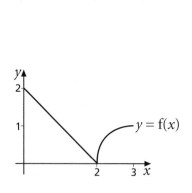

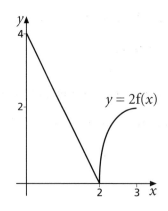

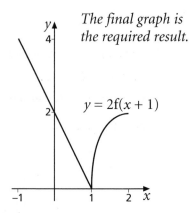

*The final graph is the required result.*

**Exercise B** (answers p 168)

**1** The graph of $y = x^2$ is first translated by $\begin{bmatrix} 1 \\ 0 \end{bmatrix}$ and then translated by $\begin{bmatrix} 0 \\ 5 \end{bmatrix}$.
What is the equation of the final image?

**2** The graph of $y = x^3$ is first stretched by a factor of 2 in the $x$-direction and then translated by $\begin{bmatrix} 0 \\ -2 \end{bmatrix}$. Find the equation of the final image in the form $y = px^3 + q$, where $p$ and $q$ are constants.

**3** The graph of $y = |x|$ is first translated by $\begin{bmatrix} 3 \\ 0 \end{bmatrix}$ and then stretched by a factor of 2 in the $y$-direction.

(a) What is the equation of the final image?

(b) Sketch the graph of the final image, showing clearly where the graph meets each axis.

**4** Describe a sequence of geometrical transformations that will map

(a) the graph of $y = x^2$ on to $y = \frac{1}{2}(x - 1)^2$

(b) the graph of $y = |x|$ on to $y = |3x| - 5$

(c) the graph of $y = 4^x$ on to $y = 4^{x+1} + 3$

**5** State a sequence of geometrical transformations that will map $y = f(x)$ on to

(a) $y = 2f(4x)$          (b) $y = 3f(x + 1)$          (c) $y = \frac{1}{4}f(x - 2)$

**6** The diagram shows the graph of $y = f(x)$ where the domain of f is $-2 \le x \le 2$. The point $P\left(1, \sqrt{3}\right)$ lies on the curve.

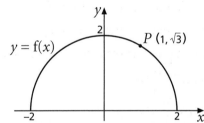

Sketch the graph of $y = \frac{1}{2}f(x - 2)$, showing clearly the coordinates of the image of $P$.

**7** The function f is defined by $f(x) = x^2$.

(a) Show that $\frac{1}{2}f(x - 4) = \frac{1}{2}x^2 - 4x + 8$.

(b) Hence find a sequence of transformations that maps $y = x^2$ on to $y = \frac{1}{2}x^2 - 4x + 8$.

**8** The diagram shows the graph of $y = f(x)$, $x \ge 0$.

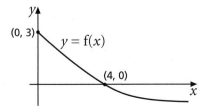

Sketch the graph of $y = 3f(4x)$, showing clearly where the graph meets each axis.

**9** The diagram shows the graph of $y = f(x)$.

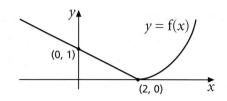

Sketch the graph of $y = 2f(x + 1)$, showing clearly the images of $(0, 1)$ and $(2, 0)$.

**10** The diagram shows the graph of $y = f(x)$.

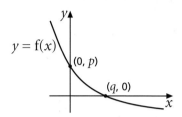

If the graph is transformed to give the graph of $y = f\left(\frac{1}{4}x\right) + 3$, what are the images of $(0, p)$ and $(q, 0)$?

**11** The diagram shows the graph of $y = f(x)$.

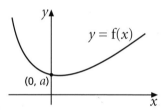

Sketch the graph of $y = 2f(-x)$, showing the coordinates of the image of $(0, a)$.

## C Order of transformations (answers p 168)

Sometimes the order that transformations are applied in matters and sometimes it does not.

**C1** (a) The graph of $y = x$ is first translated by $\begin{bmatrix} 0 \\ 3 \end{bmatrix}$ and then stretched by factor 2 in the $y$-direction.

Sketch a graph of the final image and find its equation.

(b) Now $y = x$ is transformed using the same transformations but in the opposite order, first stretching by factor 2 in the $y$-direction and then translating by $\begin{bmatrix} 0 \\ 3 \end{bmatrix}$.

Find the equation of the final image.

(c) Are the final images the same?

**C2** (a) The graph of $y = x^2$ is first translated by $\begin{bmatrix} 2 \\ 0 \end{bmatrix}$ and then reflected in the $y$-axis.

Sketch a graph of the final image and find its equation.

(b) Now $y = x^2$ is transformed using the same transformations but in the opposite order, first reflecting in the $y$-axis and then translating by $\begin{bmatrix} 2 \\ 0 \end{bmatrix}$.

Find the equation of the final image.
What do you notice?

**C3** (a) The graph of $y = x^2$ is first translated by $\begin{bmatrix} 1 \\ 0 \end{bmatrix}$ and then reflected in the $x$-axis. Find the equation of the final image.

(b) Now $y = x^2$ is transformed using the same transformations but in the opposite order, first reflecting in the $x$-axis and then translating by $\begin{bmatrix} 1 \\ 0 \end{bmatrix}$. Find the equation of the final image.

(c) Can you explain why both these final images are the same?

We can use algebra to decide when order matters in applying a sequence of transformations.

Consider the graph of $y = x$ and the transformations • a translation by $\begin{bmatrix} 0 \\ 2 \end{bmatrix}$

• a stretch of factor 3 in the $y$-direction

When $y = x$ is translated by $\begin{bmatrix} 0 \\ 2 \end{bmatrix}$ we replace $y$ by $y - 2$ to obtain $y - 2 = x$, which is equivalent to $y = x + 2$.

If we now stretch by a factor of 3 in the $y$-direction we replace $y$ by $\frac{1}{3}y$ to obtain $\frac{1}{3}y = x + 2$, which is equivalent to $y = 3(x + 2)$ or $y = 3x + 6$.

The sequence of graphs is

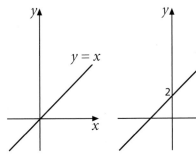

Now apply the transformations in the opposite order.

When $y = x$ is stretched by a factor of 3 in the $y$-direction we replace $y$ by $\frac{1}{3}y$ to obtain $\frac{1}{3}y = x$, which is equivalent to $y = 3x$.

If we now translate by $\begin{bmatrix} 0 \\ 2 \end{bmatrix}$ we replace $y$ by $y - 2$ to obtain $y - 2 = 3x$, which is equivalent to $y = 3x + 2$.

The sequence of graphs is

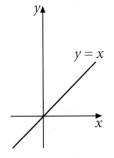
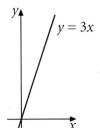
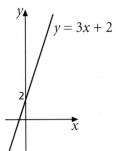

We can see clearly that the equations and the final images are different: the order matters here.

**C4 (a)** The graph of $y = x^2$ is first translated by $\begin{bmatrix} -1 \\ 0 \end{bmatrix}$ and then reflected in the $y$-axis.
Use algebra to find the equation of the final image.

**(b)** Now $y = x^2$ is transformed using the same transformations but in the opposite order. Find the equation of the final image.

**(c)** Are the final images the same?

**C5 (a) (i)** Show that the image of $y = |x|$ after a translation of $\begin{bmatrix} 4 \\ 0 \end{bmatrix}$ followed by a stretch of factor 2 in the $x$-direction is $y = |\frac{1}{2}x - 4|$.

**(ii)** Hence sketch the graph of $y = |\frac{1}{2}x - 4|$.

**(b)** Now find the image of $y = |x|$ after applying the same transformations in the opposite order.

We can use algebra to decide when order matters for $y = f(x)$.

Consider the transformations • a translation by $\begin{bmatrix} 3 \\ 0 \end{bmatrix}$

• a stretch of factor $\frac{1}{2}$ in the $x$-direction.

When $y = f(x)$ is translated by $\begin{bmatrix} 3 \\ 0 \end{bmatrix}$ we replace $x$ by $x - 3$ to obtain $y = f(x - 3)$.

If we now stretch by a factor of $\frac{1}{2}$ in the $x$-direction we replace $x$ by $2x$ to obtain $y = f(2x - 3)$.

Now apply the transformations in the opposite order.

When $y = f(x)$ is stretched by a factor of $\frac{1}{2}$ in the $x$-direction we replace $x$ by $2x$ to obtain $y = f(2x)$.

If we now translate by $\begin{bmatrix} 3 \\ 0 \end{bmatrix}$ we replace $x$ by $x - 3$ to obtain $y = f(2(x - 3))$, which is $y = f(2x - 6)$.

The equations of the final images are different: the order matters here.

> **K** When applying two transformations, the order does not matter if one transformation involves replacing $x$ and the other involves replacing $y$.
> If both transformations involve replacing $x$ (or $y$), then the order could matter.

---

### Example 7

Determine a sequence of transformations that will transform the graph of $y = f(x)$ on to the graph of $y = f(3x - 1)$.

### Solution

First $y = f(x)$ can be transformed to $y = f(x - 1)$ by replacing $x$ by $x - 1$.

Then $y = f(x - 1)$ can be transformed to $y = f(3x - 1)$ by replacing $x$ by $3x$.

So a sequence of transformations is a translation of $\begin{bmatrix} 1 \\ 0 \end{bmatrix}$ followed by a stretch of factor $\frac{1}{3}$ in the $x$-direction.

---

## Example 8

Determine a sequence of transformations that will map $y = x^3$ on to $y = (3 - x)^3$ and hence sketch the graph of $y = (3 - x)^3$.

### Solution

First $y = x^3$ can be transformed to $y = (x + 3)^3$ by replacing $x$ by $x + 3$.

Then $y = (x + 3)^3$ can be transformed to $y = (3 - x)^3$ by replacing $x$ by $-x$.

So a sequence of transformations is a translation of $\begin{bmatrix} -3 \\ 0 \end{bmatrix}$ followed by reflection in the $y$-axis.

The sequence of graphs is

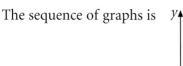 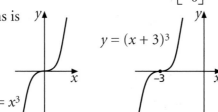 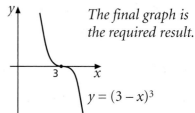

*The final graph is the required result.*

---

## Exercise C (answers p 169)

**1 (a)** The graph of $y = x^2$ is first translated by $\begin{bmatrix} 0 \\ -2 \end{bmatrix}$ and then stretched by factor 5 in the $y$-direction.

Find the equation of the final graph.

**(b)** Now $y = x^2$ is transformed using the same transformations but in the opposite order, first stretching by factor 5 in the $y$-direction and then translating by $\begin{bmatrix} 0 \\ -2 \end{bmatrix}$.

Find the equation of the final graph. What do you notice?

**2** The graph of $y = 3^x$ is first reflected in the $y$-axis and then translated by $\begin{bmatrix} 5 \\ 0 \end{bmatrix}$.

Show that the equation of the image is $y = 3^{5 - x}$.

**3** Find the image of $y = f(x)$ after each sequence of transformations.

**(a)** A stretch of factor $\frac{1}{2}$ in the $y$-direction followed by a translation of $\begin{bmatrix} 0 \\ -3 \end{bmatrix}$

**(b)** A translation of $\begin{bmatrix} 0 \\ 4 \end{bmatrix}$ followed by a reflection in the $x$-axis

**(c)** A translation of $\begin{bmatrix} -1 \\ 0 \end{bmatrix}$ followed by a stretch of factor $\frac{1}{4}$ in the $x$-direction

**(d)** Reflection in the $y$-axis followed by a translation of $\begin{bmatrix} 4 \\ 0 \end{bmatrix}$

**4 (a)** Find the image of $y = f(x)$ after a translation of $\begin{bmatrix} a \\ 0 \end{bmatrix}$ followed by a stretch of factor $\frac{1}{k}$ in the $x$-direction.

**(b)** Use your result to describe a sequence of transformations that will map $y = f(x)$ on to $y = f(3x - 5)$.

**5** Determine a sequence of transformations that will map $y = |x|$ on to $y = |2x - 9|$.

**6** The graph of $y = f(x)$ is translated by $\begin{bmatrix} 3 \\ 0 \end{bmatrix}$ and stretched by factor 2 in the $y$-direction. Show that using these transformations in any order will result in the same final image.

**7 (a)** Find the image of $y = f(x)$ after a stretch of factor $k$ in the $y$-direction followed by a translation of $\begin{bmatrix} 0 \\ a \end{bmatrix}$.

**(b)** Use your result to describe a sequence of transformations that will map $y = f(x)$ on to $y = 3f(x) - 5$.

**8** Find a sequence of transformations that will map $y = f(x)$ on to

**(a)** $y = \frac{1}{3}f(x) + 1$        **(b)** $y = -f(x) + 5$        **(c)** $y = f(2x - 8)$

**(d)** $y = 3f(x) - 6$        **(e)** $y = f\left(\frac{1}{2}x + 4\right)$        **(f)** $y = f(3 - x)$

**9 (a)** What is the image of $y = f(x)$ after

    **(i)** a stretch of scale factor 2 in the $y$-direction followed by a translation of $\begin{bmatrix} 0 \\ 10 \end{bmatrix}$

    **(ii)** a translation of $\begin{bmatrix} 0 \\ 5 \end{bmatrix}$ followed by a stretch of scale factor 2 in the $y$-direction

**(b)** What can you deduce from your answers to part (a)?

**10 (a)** What is the image of $y = f(x)$ after

    **(i)** a reflection in the $x$-axis followed by a translation of $\begin{bmatrix} 0 \\ -2 \end{bmatrix}$

    **(ii)** a translation of $\begin{bmatrix} 0 \\ 2 \end{bmatrix}$ followed by a reflection in the $x$-axis

**(b)** What can you deduce from your answers to part (a)?

**\*11 (a)** The graph of $x^2 + y^2 = 1$ is transformed by a stretch of factor 3 in the $x$-direction, followed by a stretch of factor $1\frac{1}{2}$ in the $y$-direction, followed by a translation of $\begin{bmatrix} -1 \\ 2 \end{bmatrix}$. Show that the equation of the transformed graph is $x^2 + 4y^2 + 2x - 16y + 8 = 0$.

**(b)** Sketch the graph of $x^2 + 4y^2 + 2x - 16y + 8 = 0$.

**(c)** What are the equations of its axes of symmetry?

---

### Key points

- The rules for the basic transformations are on page 42.

- A graph can be transformed using a combination of basic transformations. You can determine the equation of the final image by applying the rules for the basic transformations in order.

  For example, to find the result of transforming $y = f(x)$ by a translation of $\begin{bmatrix} 0 \\ 5 \end{bmatrix}$ followed by a stretch of factor $\frac{1}{2}$ in the $x$-direction, first replace $y$ by $y - 5$ and then replace $x$ by $2x$ to obtain $y - 5 = f(2x)$ or $y = f(2x) + 5$.     (pp 43–44)

- When applying two transformations, the order does not matter if one transformation involves replacing $x$ and the other involves replacing $y$. If both transformations involve replacing $x$ (or $y$), then the order could matter. (pp 47–48)

## Test yourself (answers p 170)

**1** The diagram shows a sketch of $y = \frac{1}{2}(x + 1)^3$.

Describe fully a sequence of geometrical transformations that would map the graph of $y = x^3$ on to the graph of $y = \frac{1}{2}(x + 1)^3$.

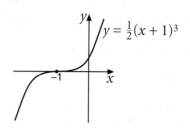

**2** A sketch of the graph of $y = f(x)$ is shown.
The point $P\,(3, 2)$ lies on the graph.

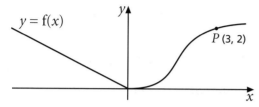

(a) Describe fully a sequence of transformations that maps the graph of $y = f(x)$ on to the graph of $y = 4f(x - 3)$.

(b) Sketch the graph of $y = 4f(x - 3)$.
Label the image of the point $P$, giving its coordinates.

**3** Describe a sequence of transformations by which the graph of $y = 4 \times 5^{-x}$ can be obtained from the graph of $y = 5^x$.

**4** The diagram shows the sketch of a curve with equation $y = f(x)$.
The curve meets the axes at the points $(a, 0)$ and $(0, b)$.

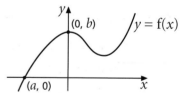

(a) Describe a sequence of transformations by which the graph of $y = f(x)$ can mapped on to the graph of $y = 2f(3x)$.

(b) Sketch the curve with equation $y = 2f(3x)$, showing clearly where the curve meets the coordinate axes.

**5** The graph of $y = x^2$ is first translated by $\begin{bmatrix} 0 \\ -3 \end{bmatrix}$ and then stretched by factor 2 in the $y$-direction.
Find the equation of the final image.

**6** Determine a sequence of transformations that will map $y = f(x)$ on to

(a) $y = 3f(x) + 4$    (b) $y = f(-x) - 7$    (c) $y = f(5x - 3)$

**7** Find the image of $y = f(x)$ after reflection in the $x$-axis followed by a translation of $\begin{bmatrix} 0 \\ 6 \end{bmatrix}$.

# 4 Trigonometry

In this chapter you will learn about
- the inverse functions of cosine, sine and tangent
- the reciprocal functions secant, cosecant and cotangent
- transformations of the above functions
- identities and equations involving the above functions

## A Inverse circular functions (answers p 171)

This is part of the graph of $y = \sin x$, where $x$ is measured in radians.

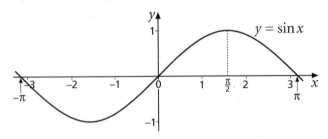

**A1** Using the same scale on each axis, make a sketch copy of the graph above.

Draw the line $y = x$ on your sketch.

Draw the reflection of $y = \sin x$ in the line $y = x$ on your sketch.

Mark carefully the position of the reflection of the point $\left(\frac{\pi}{2}, 1\right)$.

**A2** You saw in chapter 1 that reflecting the graph of a function in the line $y = x$ may give the graph of an inverse function.

Does it give an inverse function in this case? If not, why not?

In order that the reflection of $y = \sin x$ in the line $y = x$ may represent a function, we need to restrict the domain of $y = \sin x$, so that $y = \sin x$ is a one–one function.

**A3** Which of these are one–one functions?

$$f(x) = \sin x, \ -\frac{\pi}{2} \le x \le \frac{\pi}{2} \qquad g(x) = \sin x, \ 0 \le x \le \pi \qquad h(x) = \sin x, \ \frac{\pi}{2} \le x \le \frac{3\pi}{2}$$

How we restrict the domain of $y = \sin x$ so it has an inverse is to some extent arbitrary, but the convention is that we restrict $x$ to the interval $-\frac{\pi}{2} \le x \le \frac{\pi}{2}$.

The inverse function of $\sin x$ is denoted by $y = \sin^{-1} x$.

$\left(\text{Note that } \sin^{-1} x \text{ never means } \dfrac{1}{\sin x}.\right)$

The range of $\sin^{-1} x$ is the restricted domain of $\sin x$, that is $-\frac{\pi}{2} \le \sin^{-1} x \le \frac{\pi}{2}$.

We call the range of $\sin^{-1} x$ the **principal values** of $\sin^{-1} x$.

So, for example, $\sin^{-1} 1 = \frac{\pi}{2}$ $\left(\frac{\pi}{2} \text{ is the principal value for the angle whose sine is 1}\right)$.

**A4** What is the domain of $\sin^{-1} x$?

The graph of $y = \sin^{-1} x$ is shown on the right.

We also write $\arcsin x$ or $\mathrm{asin}\, x$ for $\sin^{-1} x$.

K    The domain of $y = \sin^{-1} x$ is $-1 \le x \le 1$.

     The range of $y = \sin^{-1} x$ is $-\dfrac{\pi}{2} \le y \le \dfrac{\pi}{2}$.

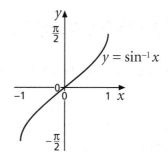

**A5** Using degrees, $\sin^{-1} 1 = 90°$. In degrees, write down the value of

    **(a)** $\sin^{-1} \frac{1}{2}$       **(b)** $\sin^{-1}\left(\dfrac{1}{\sqrt{2}}\right)$       **(c)** $\sin^{-1} 0$       **(d)** $\sin^{-1}(-1)$

**A6** In order for $\tan x$ to have an inverse, we restrict its domain to $-\dfrac{\pi}{2} \le x \le \dfrac{\pi}{2}$.

    **(a)** With this domain, what is the range of $\tan x$?

    **(b)** Using equal scales on the $x$- and $y$-axes, sketch the graph of $y = \tan x$ with domain as stated above.

    **(c)** On the same graph, sketch and label the inverse function of $\tan x$, which is $y = \tan^{-1} x$.

    **(d)** Write down the domain and range of $y = \tan^{-1} x$.

---

**Example 1**

Write down, in degrees, the value of

**(a)** $\sin^{-1}\left(-\dfrac{1}{\sqrt{2}}\right)$       **(b)** $\tan^{-1}\left(-\dfrac{1}{\sqrt{3}}\right)$

**Solution**

*You need to know, or to be able quickly to work out, the sine, cosine and tangent of $0°$, $30°$, $45°$, $60°$ and $90°$.*

**(a)**                           $\sin 45° = \dfrac{1}{\sqrt{2}}$, so $\sin(-45°) = -\dfrac{1}{\sqrt{2}}$.

*$\sin^{-1} x$ is between $-90°$ and $90°$.*    Hence $\sin^{-1}\left(-\dfrac{1}{\sqrt{2}}\right) = -45°$.

**(b)**                           $\tan 30° = \dfrac{1}{\sqrt{3}}$, so $\tan(-30°) = -\dfrac{1}{\sqrt{3}}$.

*$\tan^{-1} x$ is between $-90°$ and $90°$.*    Hence $\tan^{-1}\left(-\dfrac{1}{\sqrt{3}}\right) = -30°$.

**Exercise A** (answers p 171)

**1** In order for $\cos x$ to have an inverse, we restrict its domain to $0 \le x \le \pi$.

(a) Using equal scales on the $x$- and $y$-axes, sketch the graph of $y = \cos x$ with the above domain.

(b) On the same graph, sketch the inverse function of $\cos x$, $y = \cos^{-1} x$.

(c) Write down the domain and range of $y = \cos^{-1} x$.

**2** (a) Write down the solution in degrees, between $0°$ and $90°$, of $\cos \theta° = \frac{1}{2}$.

(b) Hence write down the two solutions to $\cos \theta° = -\frac{1}{2}$ between $0°$ and $360°$.

(c) What is the principal value of $\cos^{-1}\left(-\frac{1}{2}\right)$ in degrees?

**3** Write down the value, in degrees, of each of the following

(a) $\cos^{-1}(-1)$      (b) $\cos^{-1}\left(\frac{\sqrt{3}}{2}\right)$      (c) $\cos^{-1} 0$      (d) $\tan^{-1}(-\sqrt{3})$

**4** Write down, in radians, the value of each of these.

(a) $\cos^{-1} 1$      (b) $\cos^{-1}\left(-\frac{1}{2}\right)$      (c) $\tan^{-1}(-1)$      (d) $\sin^{-1}\left(-\frac{\sqrt{3}}{2}\right)$

(e) $\cos^{-1} 0$      (f) $\tan^{-1} 0$      (g) $\cos^{-1}\left(-\frac{1}{\sqrt{2}}\right)$      (h) $\sin^{-1}\left(-\frac{1}{2}\right)$

**5** Solve these where possible.

(a) $\sin^{-1} x = \frac{\pi}{4}$      (b) $\sin^{-1} x = \frac{\pi}{6}$      (c) $\sin^{-1} x = -\frac{\pi}{4}$      (d) $\sin^{-1} x = \pi$

**6** (a) Work these out.

(i) $\sin\left(\sin^{-1}\frac{1}{2}\right)$      (ii) $\tan\left(\tan^{-1} 1\right)$      (iii) $\cos\left(\cos^{-1}\frac{\sqrt{3}}{2}\right)$      (iv) $\sin\left(\sin^{-1}-\frac{1}{2}\right)$

(b) Is it always true that $\sin\left(\sin^{-1} x\right) = x$?

**7** (a) Work these out.

(i) $\sin^{-1}\left(\sin\frac{\pi}{6}\right)$      (ii) $\sin^{-1}\left(\sin\frac{5\pi}{6}\right)$      (iii) $\sin^{-1}\left(\sin\frac{7\pi}{6}\right)$      (iv) $\sin^{-1}\left(\sin\frac{13\pi}{6}\right)$

(b) Is it always true that $\sin^{-1}\left(\sin x\right) = x$?

**8** (a) Which of the following domains ensures that the function $f(x) = \sin 2x$ is one–one?

A $-\pi \le x \le \pi$      B $-\frac{\pi}{2} \le x \le \frac{\pi}{2}$      C $-\frac{\pi}{4} \le x \le \frac{\pi}{4}$

(b) With the chosen domain, what is the range of $f(x)$?

(c) Write down the domain and range of the inverse function, $f^{-1}(x)$.

**\*9** (a) Using your answers to question 8, suggest a possible inverse function for $y = \sin 2x$.

(b) Check your suggestion, using a graph plotter, by

(i) reflecting the graph of $y = \sin 2x$ in the line $y = x$

(ii) plotting the graph of your suggestion and checking that it coincides with (i).

## B Sec, cosec and cot (answers p 171)

The most useful trigonometrical functions are cosine, sine and tangent.
However there are three other closely related functions – secant, cosecant
and cotangent (usually abbreviated to sec, cosec and cot).

These are defined as

$$\sec x = \frac{1}{\cos x} \qquad\qquad \operatorname{cosec} x = \frac{1}{\sin x} \qquad\qquad \cot x = \frac{1}{\tan x}$$

**B1** (a) When $x = \frac{\pi}{4}$, what is the value of $\cos x$?

  (b) What is the value of $\sec x$ when $x = \frac{\pi}{4}$?

**B2** What is the value of $\sec x$ when

  (a) $x = \frac{\pi}{6}$      (b) $x = \frac{\pi}{3}$      (c) $x = 0$      (d) $x = -\frac{\pi}{4}$

**B3** Write down the value of $\operatorname{cosec} x$ when

  (a) $x = \frac{\pi}{2}$      (b) $x = -\frac{\pi}{2}$      (c) $x = \frac{\pi}{4}$      (d) $x = -\frac{\pi}{6}$

**B4** Evaluate these.

  (a) $\cot \frac{\pi}{4}$      (b) $\cot \frac{\pi}{6}$      (c) $\cot \left(-\frac{\pi}{3}\right)$      (d) $\cot \frac{5\pi}{4}$

**D**

**B5** (a) What happens when you try to evaluate $\operatorname{cosec} 0$?

  (b) Write down two other values of $x$ for which $\operatorname{cosec} x$ is not defined.

  (c) Describe accurately the complete set of values of $x$
  for which $\operatorname{cosec} x$ is not defined.

**B6** (a) Write down three values of $x$ for which $\sec x$ is not defined.

  (b) Describe clearly the complete set of values of $x$
  for which $\sec x$ is not defined.

The diagram shows part of the graph of $\cos x$.
Part of the graph of $\sec x$ is also shown.

**B7** (a) Copy the diagram and complete
  the graph of $y = \sec x$ for $-\pi \le x \le 2\pi$.

  (b) Describe clearly the domain of $\sec x$
  (you will need to use your answer to B6).

  (c) Write down an expression for
  the range of $y = \sec x$.

  (d) What is the period of $\sec x$?

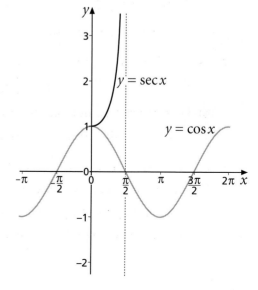

**B8 (a)** Sketch the graph of $\sin x$.

**(b)** On your diagram, sketch the graph of $\operatorname{cosec} x$.

**(c)** Write down expressions for the domain and range of $\operatorname{cosec} x$.

**(d)** What is the period of $\operatorname{cosec} x$?

The cotangent of $x$, $\cot x$, is defined as $\dfrac{1}{\tan x}$.

Using the relationship between $\sin x$ and $\cos x$, we can establish a relationship between $\sec x$ and $\tan x$.

$$\sin^2 x + \cos^2 x = 1$$

Dividing by $\cos^2 x$ we obtain $\qquad \dfrac{\sin^2 x}{\cos^2 x} + 1 = \dfrac{1}{\cos^2 x}$

$$\Rightarrow \qquad \tan^2 x + 1 = \sec^2 x$$

**B9** Divide the relationship $\sin^2 x + \cos^2 x = 1$ by $\sin^2 x$ to obtain a relationship between $\operatorname{cosec} x$ and $\cot x$.

---

**Example 2**

Show that $\dfrac{\tan \theta}{1 + \tan^2 \theta} = \sin \theta \cos \theta$.

**Solution**

$$\frac{\tan \theta}{1 + \tan^2 \theta} = \frac{\tan \theta}{\sec^2 \theta} = \frac{\tan \theta}{\dfrac{1}{\cos^2 x}} = \tan \theta \times \cos^2 \theta = \frac{\sin \theta}{\cos \theta} \times \cos^2 \theta = \sin \theta \cos \theta$$

---

**Example 3**

Given that $\tan \theta = 2$, find exact values for    **(a)** $\cot \theta$    **(b)** $\sec \theta$    **(c)** $\operatorname{cosec} \theta$

**Solution**

**(a)** $\cot \theta = \dfrac{1}{\tan \theta} = \frac{1}{2}$

One possible pair of values for $\sin \theta$ and $\cos \theta$ is $\sin \theta = \dfrac{2}{\sqrt{5}}$ and $\cos \theta = \dfrac{1}{\sqrt{5}}$.

However, both sine and cosine could be negative $\left(\text{for an angle between } \pi \text{ and } \dfrac{3\pi}{2}\right)$.

In this case, $\sin \theta = -\dfrac{2}{\sqrt{5}}$ and $\cos \theta = -\dfrac{1}{\sqrt{5}}$. Hence

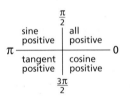

**(b)** $\sec \theta = \dfrac{1}{\cos \theta} = \dfrac{1}{\dfrac{1}{\sqrt{5}}}$ or $\dfrac{1}{-\dfrac{1}{\sqrt{5}}} = \sqrt{5}$ or $-\sqrt{5}$

**(c)** $\operatorname{cosec} \theta = \dfrac{1}{\sin \theta} = \dfrac{1}{\dfrac{2}{\sqrt{5}}}$ or $\dfrac{1}{-\dfrac{2}{\sqrt{5}}} = \dfrac{\sqrt{5}}{2}$ or $-\dfrac{\sqrt{5}}{2}$

**Example 4**

Simplify $\operatorname{cosec}\left(\dfrac{\pi}{2}-x\right)$.

**Solution**

$$\operatorname{cosec}\left(\frac{\pi}{2}-x\right)=\frac{1}{\sin\left(\dfrac{\pi}{2}-x\right)}=\frac{1}{\cos x}=\sec x$$

$$\sec x=\frac{1}{\cos x}\qquad\qquad\operatorname{cosec} x=\frac{1}{\sin x}\qquad\qquad\cot x=\frac{1}{\tan x}$$

$$\sec^2 x=1+\tan^2 x\qquad\qquad\operatorname{cosec}^2 x=1+\cot^2 x$$

**Exercise B** (answers p 172)

1 (a) Sketch the graph of $\tan x$ for $-2\pi<x<2\pi$.
  (b) On your diagram, sketch also the graph of $\cot x$.
  (c) Give the domain and range of $\cot x$, clearly stating any values that are excluded.
  (d) What is the period of $\cot x$?

2 Find the exact values of
  (a) $\operatorname{cosec}\dfrac{\pi}{3}$   (b) $\cot\dfrac{\pi}{3}$   (c) $\sec\left(-\dfrac{\pi}{3}\right)$   (d) $\operatorname{cosec}\left(-\dfrac{\pi}{3}\right)$

3 Simplify these.
  (a) $\operatorname{cosec} x\tan x$   (b) $\tan x\cot x$   (c) $\sin x\operatorname{cosec} x$   (d) $\sec x\sin x$

4 Simplify these.
  (a) $\dfrac{\cos\theta}{\sin\theta}$   (b) $\dfrac{\operatorname{cosec}\theta}{\sec\theta}$   (c) $\sec\left(\dfrac{\pi}{2}-x\right)$   (d) $\cot(\pi+x)$

5 Simplify the following.
  (a) $\dfrac{\sin x}{1+\cot^2 x}$   (b) $\cos x\sqrt{1+\tan^2 x}$

6 Prove the following identities.
  (a) $\tan\theta+\cot\theta=\sec\theta\operatorname{cosec}\theta$   (b) $\cot\theta\sec\theta=\operatorname{cosec}\theta$

7 Simplify these.
  (a) $\operatorname{cosec}^2 x-1$   (b) $(\sec x+1)(\sec x-1)$   (c) $\dfrac{\tan x}{1-\sec^2 x}$

8 Show that $\operatorname{cosec} x+\cot x=\dfrac{1}{\operatorname{cosec} x-\cot x}$   $(\operatorname{cosec} x\neq\cot x)$.

9 Given that $\sin\theta=\frac{4}{5}$, and that $\theta$ is in the first quadrant, find exact values of
  (a) $\cos\theta$   (b) $\tan\theta$   (c) $\sec\theta$   (d) $\operatorname{cosec}\theta$

10 Given that $\dfrac{\pi}{2}\leq\theta\leq\pi$ and $\cot\theta=-2\frac{2}{5}$, find exact values of
  (a) $\tan\theta$   (b) $\cos\theta$   (c) $\sin\theta$   (d) $\operatorname{cosec}\theta$

11 Given that $\tan\theta=1$, what are the possible values of
  (a) $\cot\theta$   (b) $\sin\theta$   (c) $\cos\theta$   (d) $\operatorname{cosec}\theta$

## C Solving equations (answers p 173)

When solving equations involving $\sec x$, $\text{cosec}\, x$ or $\cot x$, it is often best to substitute so that the equation involves $\sin x$, $\cos x$ or $\tan x$ instead.

You may also be able to make use of the relations $\sec^2 x = 1 + \tan^2 x$ and $\text{cosec}^2 x = 1 + \cot^2 x$.

### Example 5

Solve the equation $\sec x = 2$ for $0 \leq x \leq 2\pi$.

**Solution**

$$\sec x = 2$$

*Substitute for $\sec x$.*
$$\frac{1}{\cos x} = 2$$

$$\Rightarrow \quad \cos x = \tfrac{1}{2}$$

$$\Rightarrow \quad x = \frac{\pi}{3} \text{ or } 2\pi - \frac{\pi}{3} = \frac{5\pi}{3}$$

### Example 6

Solve $\cot^2 \theta° = 3$, where $-180° \leq \theta° \leq 180°$.

**Solution**

$$\cot^2 \theta° = 3$$

*Substitute $\dfrac{1}{\tan \theta°}$ for $\cot \theta°$.*
$$\frac{1}{\tan^2 \theta°} = 3$$

$$\Rightarrow \quad \tan^2 \theta° = \tfrac{1}{3}$$

$$\Rightarrow \quad \tan \theta° = \pm \frac{1}{\sqrt{3}}$$

If $\tan \theta° = \dfrac{1}{\sqrt{3}}$, then $\theta° = 30°$ or $-150°$; if $\tan \theta° = -\dfrac{1}{\sqrt{3}}$, then $\theta° = -30°$ or $150°$.
Hence $\theta° = -150°, -30°, 30°$ or $150°$.

### Example 7

Solve the equation $\tan^2 x + \sec x = 1$ for $0 \leq x \leq 2\pi$.

**Solution**

$$\tan^2 x + \sec x = 1$$

*You need to get a quadratic in a single variable, so substitute $\tan^2 x = \sec^2 x - 1$.*

$$\sec^2 x - 1 + \sec x = 1$$

$$\Rightarrow \quad \sec^2 x + \sec x - 2 = 0$$

*Factorise.*
$$(\sec x + 2)(\sec x - 1) = 0$$

$$\Rightarrow \quad \sec x = -2 \text{ or } \sec x = 1$$

$$\Rightarrow \quad \cos x = -\tfrac{1}{2} \text{ or } \cos x = 1$$

$$\Rightarrow \quad x = \frac{2\pi}{3} \text{ or } \frac{4\pi}{3} \text{ or } x = 0 \text{ or } 2\pi$$

**C1** Solve $\tan^2 x + \sec x = 1$ by substituting $\tan x = \dfrac{\sin x}{\cos x}$ and $\sec x = \dfrac{1}{\cos x}$ as the first step, and then solving a quadratic in $\cos x$.

Check your answer is identical to that in example 7.

**Exercise C** (answers p 173)

**1 (a)** Solve $\sec\theta° = \sqrt{2}$, giving exact answers within the range 0° to 360°.

 **(b)** Hence solve $\sec^2\theta° = 2$ $(0° \le \theta° \le 360°)$.

**2** Solve $\cot\theta° = 3$, giving answers in the range −180° to 180° to the nearest degree.

**3** Solve for $0 \le x \le 2\pi$

 **(a)** $\cot x = 1$ **(b)** $\operatorname{cosec} x = 1$ **(c)** $\operatorname{cosec}^2 x = 1$ **(d)** $3\operatorname{cosec}^2 x = 4$

**4** Solve, giving answers in the range −π to π to two decimal places,

 **(a)** $\sec x = 3$ **(b)** $\sec^2 x = 9$ **(c)** $\operatorname{cosec} x = 3$ **(d)** $\cot x = \frac{1}{2}$

**5 (a)** By replacing $\sec^2 x$ by $1 + \tan^2 x$, show that the equation

 $$\sec^2 x + \tan x = 3$$

 is equivalent to the equation

 $$\tan^2 x + \tan x - 2 = 0$$

 **(b)** Factorise the left-hand side of this equation.

 **(c)** Solve the equation to find all the values of $x$ between −π and π.

**6** By substituting for $\cot^2\theta$ in terms of $\operatorname{cosec}^2\theta$, solve $2\cot^2\theta + \operatorname{cosec}\theta + 1 = 0$ for $-\pi \le \theta \le \pi$.

**7** Solve $2\tan^2 x - 7\sec x + 5 = 0$, giving answers between 0 and 2π to one decimal place.

**8** Solve $3\cot x + 2\tan x = 5$. Give answers between 0° and 90° to one decimal place.

**9** Solve the following equations for $0° \le \theta° \le 360°$.
 Give your answers to two decimal places.

 **(a)** $2\sec^2\theta° = 9\tan\theta° + 7$ **(b)** $\operatorname{cosec}^2\theta° = 3\cot\theta° + 5$

**10** Solve $\sec x = \tan x$ for $0 \le x \le 2\pi$.
 Explain your result with the aid of a graph.

**11** The diagram shows the graphs of $y = \sin x$ and $y = \cot x$ $(0 \le x \le 2\pi)$.

 Find the coordinates of the points $A$ and $B$, to two decimal places.

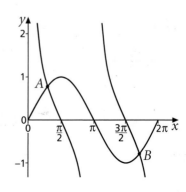

## D Transforming graphs (answers p 173)

In chapter 3 you saw how transforming the graph of a function affects its equation.

The diagrams below show how $y = \sin x$ (shown in grey) is changed after the transformations shown.

$y = a \sin x$:
stretch in the $y$-direction, scale factor $a$

$y = \sin bx$:
stretch in the $x$-direction, scale factor $\dfrac{1}{b}$

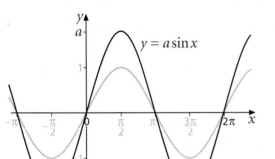

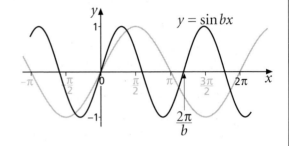

$y = \sin (x + c)$: a translation by $\begin{bmatrix} -c \\ 0 \end{bmatrix}$

$y = (\sin x) + d$: a translation by $\begin{bmatrix} 0 \\ d \end{bmatrix}$

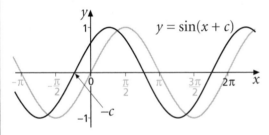

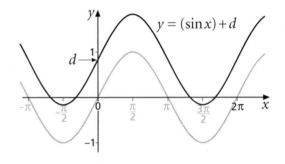

$y = -\sin x$:
reflection in the $x$-axis

$y = \sin (-x)$:
reflection in the $y$-axis

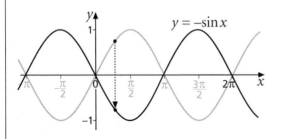

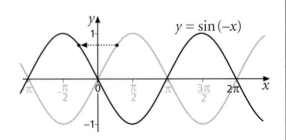

**D1** Without doing any plotting, state the two transformations that will transform $y = \sin x$ on to each of these.

(a) $y = \frac{1}{3} \sin(-x)$

(b) $y = \sin(2x) + 3$

(c) $y = 3 - \sin x$ (note: $3 - \sin x = -(\sin x) + 3$)

**D2** (a) What is the equation of the image of $y = \cos x$ after each of the following?

(i) A translation by $\begin{bmatrix} 0 \\ 2 \end{bmatrix}$, followed by a stretch in the $x$-direction, scale factor 4

(ii) A stretch in the $y$-direction, scale factor 2, followed by a translation by $\begin{bmatrix} 1 \\ 0 \end{bmatrix}$

(iii) A stretch in the $x$-direction, scale factor 3, followed by a stretch in the $y$-direction, scale factor 2

(b) For each part of (a), sketch $y = \cos x$ and the result of the transformations.

**D3** For each of the graphs below,

(i) state two transformations that will transform $y = \sin x$ (shown in grey on each diagram) on to the given graph

(ii) hence write down the equation of the graph

(a)

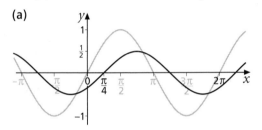

(b)

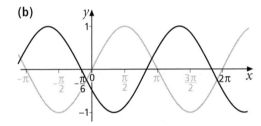

(c)

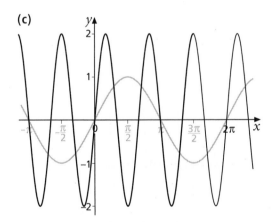

(d)

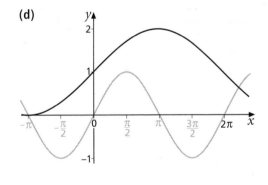

## Example 8

Sketch the graph of $y = \cos\theta°$ $(-360° \leq \theta° \leq 360°)$, and its image after a stretch in the $\theta$-direction, scale factor 2, followed by a stretch in the $y$-direction, scale factor 1.5.

What is the equation of the image?

### Solution

The graph of $y = \cos\theta°$ is shown in grey; shown dotted after the stretch in the $\theta$-direction, and solid after the stretch in the $y$-direction.

The graph of $y = \cos\theta°$ becomes

$y = \cos\frac{1}{2}\theta°$ after a stretch in the $\theta$-direction, scale factor 2.

The graph of $y = \cos\frac{1}{2}\theta°$ becomes $y = 1.5\cos\frac{1}{2}\theta°$ after a stretch in the $y$-direction, scale factor 1.5.

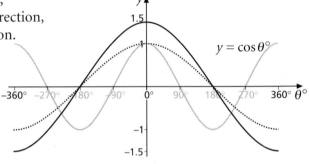

The final graph has the equation $y = 1.5\cos\frac{1}{2}\theta°$.

*It is sensible to now check this by drawing the graph of $y = 1.5\cos\frac{1}{2}\theta°$ on a graph plotter and seeing whether it agrees with the graph you have sketched.*

---

## Example 9

State two transformations which, when applied to the graph of $y = \tan x$, will give the graph of $y = \tan 2x - 1$. Hence sketch the graph of $y = \tan 2x - 1$, where $-2\pi \leq x \leq 2\pi$.

### Solution

The graph of $y = \tan 2x - 1$ can be obtained from that of $y = \tan x$ by first applying a stretch in the $x$-direction, scale factor $\frac{1}{2}$ (giving $y = \tan 2x$)

and then by applying the translation $\begin{bmatrix} 0 \\ -1 \end{bmatrix}$ to $y = \tan 2x$ (giving $y = \tan 2x - 1$).

Hence the graph is

*It is sensible to check this on a graph plotter.*

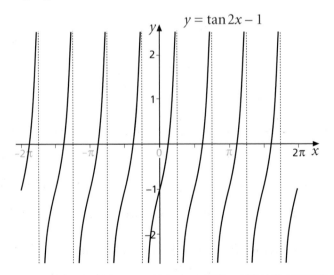

## Example 10

Sketch the graph of $y = \cos^{-1} 2x$. State its domain and range.

**Solution**

*Start by sketching the graph of $y = \cos^{-1} x$.*

The graph of $y = \cos^{-1} x$ is shown dotted on the right.

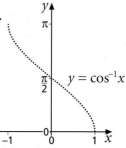

We obtain the graph of $y = \cos^{-1} 2x$ from that of $y = \cos^{-1} x$ by replacing $x$ by $2x$, that is by applying a stretch in the $x$-direction with scale factor $\frac{1}{2}$.

Transforming $y = \cos^{-1} x$ in this way we obtain the graph of $y = \cos^{-1} 2x$ (shown solid).

The domain is $-\frac{1}{2} \leq x \leq \frac{1}{2}$, and the range is $0 \leq y \leq \pi$.

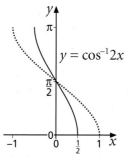

## Exercise D (answers p 174)

**1** Each of these graphs shows $y = \cos x$ after a single transformation. Identify the transformation and thus the equation of each graph.

**(a)**

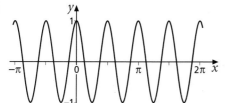

**(b)**

**(c)**

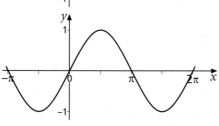

**(d)**

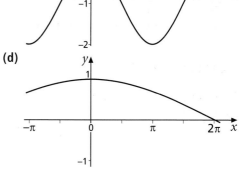

**2 (a)** Find the equation of the resulting graph when $y = \tan x$ is transformed by

   **(i)** a stretch, scale factor 2, in the $x$-direction, followed by a translation by $\begin{bmatrix} 0 \\ -1 \end{bmatrix}$

   **(ii)** a reflection in the $y$-axis, followed by a stretch, factor $\frac{1}{2}$, in the $x$-direction

   **(iii)** a translation by $\begin{bmatrix} 1 \\ 0 \end{bmatrix}$ followed by reflection in the $x$-axis

   **(iv)** a translation by $\begin{bmatrix} 0 \\ 1 \end{bmatrix}$ followed by reflection in the $y$-axis

**(b)** For each part of (a), sketch $y = \tan x$ and the result of the transformations.

**3 (a)** The point $A\left(\frac{\pi}{6}, \frac{1}{2}\right)$ lies on the graph of $y = \sin x$.

What are the coordinates of the image of $A$ after a stretch, factor 2, in the $y$-direction, followed by a translation by $\begin{bmatrix} \frac{\pi}{4} \\ 0 \end{bmatrix}$?

**(b)** The graph of $y = \sin x$ is transformed by the pair of transformations in (a). What is the equation of the transformed graph?

**(c)** Check that the coordinates of the image of $A$ satisfy the equation of the transformed graph.

**4** For each of the graphs below,

    **(i)** state two transformations that will transform $y = \cos x$ (shown in grey on each diagram) on to the given graph

    **(ii)** hence write down the equation of the graph

**(a)**

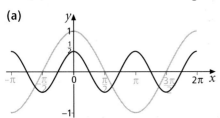

**(b)**

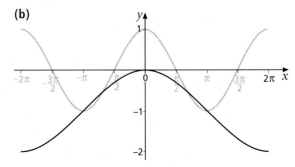

**(c)**

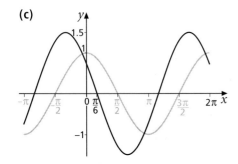

**(d)**

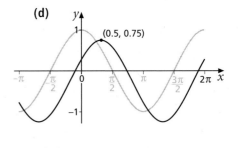

**5** For $-2\pi \le x \le 2\pi$ sketch the graphs of

    **(a)** $y = \sin x$         **(b)** $y = |\sin x|$         **(c)** $y = \sin |x|$

    Check using a graph plotter.

**6 (a)** Sketch the graph of $y = \sec x$ for $-\pi \le x \le \pi$.

**(b)** On the same diagram, sketch the graph of $y = \sec x$ after a stretch in the $y$-direction, scale factor $\frac{1}{2}$, followed by a stretch in the $x$-direction, scale factor $\frac{1}{3}$.

**(c)** What is the equation of the resulting graph? Check with a graph plotter.

**7** The graph of $y = \cos 3x$ is shown $(-\pi \le x \le \pi)$.

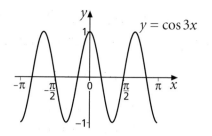

(a) Identify the coordinates of each maximum and minimum of $y = \cos 3x$ in the interval $-\pi \le x \le \pi$.

(b) Copy the graph and on your copy draw the graph of $y = |\cos 3x|$.

(c) Use your answers to (a) to solve the equation $|\cos 3x| = 1 \; (-\pi \le x \le \pi)$.

**8** (a) Find the equation of the resulting graph when $y = \sin^{-1} x$ is first stretched, scale factor 2, in the $y$-direction and then translated by $\begin{bmatrix} 1 \\ 0 \end{bmatrix}$.

(b) Sketch the resulting graph.
Check using a graph plotter.

**9** $f(x)$ is defined by $f(x) = \sin \frac{1}{2}x$ for $x \in \mathbb{R}, -\pi \le x \le \pi$;
$g(x)$ is defined by $g(x) = |x|$ for $x \in \mathbb{R}$.

(a) State the range of $f(x)$.

(b) State the domain and range of $f^{-1}(x)$.

(c) Which of the following functions is $f^{-1}(x)$?

$\boxed{f^{-1}(x) = \sin^{-1} 2x}$ $\boxed{f^{-1}(x) = \sin^{-1} \frac{1}{2}x}$ $\boxed{f^{-1}(x) = 2\sin^{-1} x}$ $\boxed{f^{-1}(x) = \frac{1}{2}\sin^{-1} x}$

(d) Write down an expression for $fg(x)$.

(e) Sketch $y = fg(x)$.

**\*10** Use a graph plotter for this question.

(a) Draw the graph of $y = \tan x$ and $y = \cot x$ on the same axes.

(b) The two graphs appear to be the same shape.
Perform two transformations on the graph of $y = \cot x$ to superimpose the graph on to that of $y = \tan x$ to confirm this observation.

(c) Write down the equation of the graph of $y = \cot x$ after the two transformations in part (b).

(d) Prove algebraically that your equation in (c) is identical to $y = \tan x$.

## E Order of transformations (answers p 176)

In section D, the order in which two transformations were applied to (for example) $y = \sin x$ did not in general matter.

This will always be the case if one transformation affects only $x$, and the other transformation affects only $y$, as you saw in chapter 3.

However, consider transforming $y = \sin x$ by applying first a stretch of factor 2 in the $x$-direction, then a translation by $\begin{bmatrix} \frac{\pi}{3} \\ 0 \end{bmatrix}$.

After a stretch of factor 2 in the $x$-direction, $x$ is replaced by $\frac{1}{2}x$, so $y = \sin x$ becomes $y = \sin \frac{1}{2}x$.

After a translation by $\begin{bmatrix} \frac{\pi}{3} \\ 0 \end{bmatrix}$, $x$ is replaced by $x - \frac{\pi}{3}$,

so $y = \sin \frac{1}{2}x$ becomes $y = \sin \frac{1}{2}\left(x - \frac{\pi}{3}\right)$, which is $y = \sin\left(\frac{1}{2}x - \frac{\pi}{6}\right)$.

The sequence of graphs is

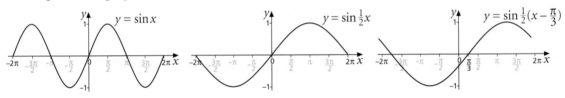

**E1** (a) Sketch a sequence of graphs for when the transformations above are applied to $y = \sin x$ in the opposite order.

(b) What is the equation of the image of $y = \sin x$ after the transformations?

---

### Example 11

Find a sequence of transformations that will transform the graph of $y = \sin x$ on to the graph of $y = \sin(2x + 1)$. Thus sketch $y = \sin(2x + 1)$.

**Solution**

First $y = \sin x$ is transformed on to $y = \sin(x + 1)$ by replacing $x$ by $x + 1$, that is by a translation by $\begin{bmatrix} -1 \\ 0 \end{bmatrix}$.

Then $y = \sin(x + 1)$ is transformed on to $y = \sin(2x + 1)$ by replacing $x$ by $2x$, that is by a stretch, scale factor $\frac{1}{2}$, in the $x$-direction.

The sequence of graphs is

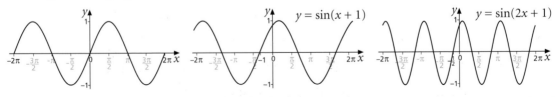

**E2** The transformed curve in example 11 passes through $(-\frac{1}{2}, 0)$.

How could you transform $y = \sin x$ on to $y = \sin(2x + 1)$,

where one of the transformations is a translation by $\begin{bmatrix} -\frac{1}{2} \\ 0 \end{bmatrix}$?

---

**Example 12**

The graph of $y = \sin x$ is first translated by $\begin{bmatrix} 0 \\ 1 \end{bmatrix}$ and then stretched
by a factor of $\frac{1}{3}$ in the $y$-direction.

What is the equation of the resulting graph?

**Solution**

A translation by $\begin{bmatrix} 0 \\ 1 \end{bmatrix}$ has the effect of replacing $y$ by $(y - 1)$,

so $y = \sin x$ becomes $y - 1 = \sin x$, which is $y = \sin x + 1$.

A stretch in the $y$-direction, scale factor $\frac{1}{3}$, has the effect of replacing $y$ by $3y$.
So $y = \sin x + 1$ becomes $3y = \sin x + 1$, which is $y = \frac{1}{3}\sin x + \frac{1}{3}$.

The sequence of graphs is

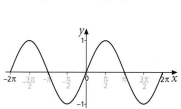 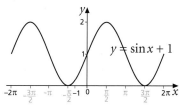 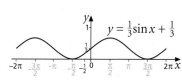

---

**E3 (a)** What is the resulting equation if the transformations in example 12
are applied in the opposite order?

**(b)** Sketch the sequence of graphs arising from applying the transformations
in this order.

## Exercise E (answers p 177)

**1 (a)** What is the equation of the resulting graph if the graph of $y = \cos x$
is first stretched in the $x$-direction, factor $\frac{1}{2}$, and then translated by $\begin{bmatrix} 3 \\ 0 \end{bmatrix}$?

**(b)** What is the equation of the graph if the two transformations are
applied in the reverse order?

**2** Find the equation of the image of the graph of $y = \tan x$ after

**(a)** a translation by $\begin{bmatrix} 3 \\ 0 \end{bmatrix}$ followed by reflection in the $y$-axis

**(b)** a reflection in the $y$-axis followed by a stretch in the $x$-direction, factor 2

**(c)** a stretch in the $x$-direction, factor $\frac{1}{2}$, followed by a translation by $\begin{bmatrix} 3 \\ 0 \end{bmatrix}$

**(d)** a translation by $\begin{bmatrix} -1 \\ 0 \end{bmatrix}$ followed by a stretch in the $x$-direction, factor 3

**(e)** a reflection in the $y$-axis followed by a translation by $\begin{bmatrix} 2 \\ 0 \end{bmatrix}$

**3** Find the equation of the image of the graph of $y = \cos x$ after

(a) a stretch in the $y$-direction, factor 2, followed by a translation of $\begin{bmatrix} 0 \\ -1 \end{bmatrix}$

(b) a translation of $\begin{bmatrix} 0 \\ 2 \end{bmatrix}$ followed by reflection in the $x$-axis

(c) a reflection in the $x$-axis followed by a translation of $\begin{bmatrix} 0 \\ 3 \end{bmatrix}$

(d) a translation of $\begin{bmatrix} 0 \\ -3 \end{bmatrix}$ followed by a stretch in the $y$-direction, factor $\frac{1}{3}$

(e) a reflection in the $x$-axis followed by a stretch in the $y$-direction, factor 5

**4 (a)** State a pair of transformations, making the order clear, which will map

(i) $y = \sin\theta$ on to $y = \sin(3\theta - 1)$      (ii) $y = \sin\theta$ on to $y = \sin 2(\theta - 3)$

(iii) $y = \cos\theta$ on to $y = 2\cos\theta + 1$      (iv) $y = \cos\theta$ on to $y = \frac{1}{2}(\cos\theta - 1)$

(b) For each part of (a), sketch the original graph and the result of the transformations. Check with a graph plotter.

**5** On each diagram below, the graph of $y = \cos x$ is shown in grey.
The image of $y = \cos x$ after two transformations is shown in black.
The image of the point $A$ (0, 1) is $A'$, and is shown on each diagram.

Identify a pair of transformations for each diagram, and hence the equation of the transformed curve.

(a)

(b)

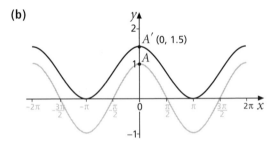

(c)

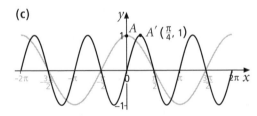

(d)

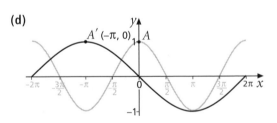

**6** Two functions are defined as $f(x) = \mathrm{cosec}\, x$ and $g(x) = |x|$.

(a) On separate graphs, sketch $\mathrm{fg}(x)$ and $\mathrm{gf}(x)$ for $-3\pi \le x \le 3\pi$.

(b) Does $\mathrm{fg}(x) = \mathrm{gf}(x)$?

(c) Suggest a domain that will make $\mathrm{fg}(x) = \mathrm{gf}(x)$.

## Key points

- The inverse function of $\sin x$ is denoted by $y = \sin^{-1} x$, $\arcsin x$ or $\operatorname{asin} x$, and has domain $-1 \le x \le 1$ and range $-\dfrac{\pi}{2} \le y \le \dfrac{\pi}{2}$.

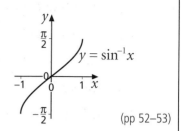

(pp 52–53)

- The inverse function of $\cos x$ is denoted by $y = \cos^{-1} x$, $\arccos x$ or $\operatorname{acos} x$, and has domain $-1 \le x \le 1$ and range $0 \le y \le \pi$.

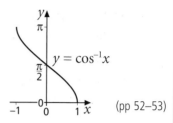

(pp 52–53)

- The inverse function of $\tan x$ is denoted by $y = \tan^{-1} x$, $\arctan x$ or $\operatorname{atan} x$, and has domain $x \in \mathbb{R}$ and range $-\dfrac{\pi}{2} < y < \dfrac{\pi}{2}$.

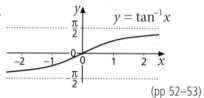

(pp 52–53)

- $\sec x$ is defined as $\dfrac{1}{\cos x}$.

  $y = \sec x$ has domain $x \in \mathbb{R}$, $x \ne \pm\dfrac{\pi}{2}, \pm\dfrac{3\pi}{2}, \pm\dfrac{5\pi}{2}, \ldots$

  and range $y \le -1$ and $y \ge 1$;

  its period is $2\pi$.

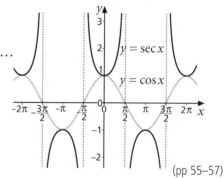

(pp 55–57)

- $\operatorname{cosec} x$ is defined as $\dfrac{1}{\sin x}$.

  $y = \operatorname{cosec} x$ has domain $x \in \mathbb{R}$, $x \ne 0, \pm\pi, \pm 2\pi, \pm 3\pi, \ldots$

  and range $y \le -1$ and $y \ge 1$;

  its period is $2\pi$.

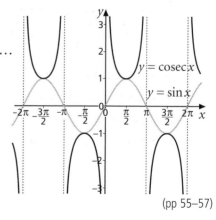

(pp 55–57)

- $\cot x$ is defined as $\dfrac{1}{\tan x}$.

  $y = \cot x$ has domain $x \in \mathbb{R},\, x \neq 0, \pm\pi, \pm2\pi, \pm3\pi, \dots$
  and range $y \in \mathbb{R}$; its period is $\pi$.
  ($\tan x$ is shown in grey on the graph.)

  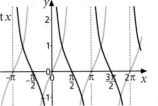

  (pp 55–57)

- $\sec^2 x = 1 + \tan^2 x$                 (p 57)

- $\operatorname{cosec}^2 x = 1 + \cot^2 x$         (p 57)

## Test yourself (answers p 178)

**1** Write down, in radians, the exact value of

(a) $\sin^{-1}\frac{1}{2}$      (b) $\tan^{-1}\left(\dfrac{1}{\sqrt{3}}\right)$      (c) $\cos^{-1}\left(-\dfrac{\sqrt{3}}{2}\right)$      (d) $\cos^{-1}\left(-\frac{1}{2}\right)$

**2** Give exact values of

(a) $\operatorname{cosec} 30°$      (b) $\sec 45°$      (c) $\cot 60°$      (d) $\sec(-60°)$

**3** Simplify these.

(a) $\cot x \sec x$      (b) $\dfrac{1}{(1 - \operatorname{cosec} x)(1 + \operatorname{cosec} x)}$      (c) $\dfrac{\sec^2 x}{(\sec x - 1)(1 + \sec x)}$

**4** Solve $\operatorname{cosec}^2 x + \cot x - 1 = 0$ giving answers as multiples of $\pi$ in the range 0 to $2\pi$.

**5** Solve the equation $3\cot^2 x + 8\operatorname{cosec} x + 1 = 0$,
giving all values of $x$ to the nearest degree in the interval $0° \leq x \leq 360°$.

**6** State the two transformations that will map $y = \tan x$ on to

(a) $y = 2\tan(-x)$      (b) $y = \tan(2x) + 1$    (c) $y = -\tan\left(\frac{1}{2}x\right)$      (d) $y = 2 - \tan x$

**7** What is the equation of the image of $y = \sin x$ after each of these?

(a) A stretch in the $x$-direction, factor 4, followed by a translation by $\begin{bmatrix} 0 \\ 2 \end{bmatrix}$

(b) A reflection in the $y$-axis, followed by a stretch in the $y$-direction, factor 2

(c) A translation by $\begin{bmatrix} -1 \\ 0 \end{bmatrix}$ followed by a reflection in the $x$-axis

**8** The diagram shows a sketch of the curve with
equation $y = \sin 2x$ for $-\dfrac{\pi}{2} \leq x \leq \dfrac{\pi}{2}$.

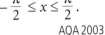

(a) Find, in radians, the values of $x$ in the interval
$-\dfrac{\pi}{2} \leq x \leq \dfrac{\pi}{2}$ for which $\sin 2x = -\frac{1}{5}$.

(b) (i) Draw on a single diagram sketches of the
graphs with equations $y = |x|$ and $y = |\sin 2x|$ for $-\dfrac{\pi}{2} \leq x \leq \dfrac{\pi}{2}$.

    (ii) Hence state the number of times the graph of the curve with
equation $y = |\sin 2x| - |x|$ intersects the $x$-axis in the interval $-\dfrac{\pi}{2} \leq x \leq \dfrac{\pi}{2}$.

AQA 2003

**9** For each of the graphs below,

    **(i)** state the two transformations that will transform $y = \sin x$ on to the given graph ($y = \sin x$ is shown in grey on each diagram)

    **(ii)** hence write down the equation of the graph

**(a)**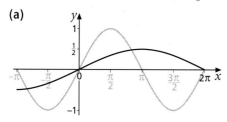

**(b)**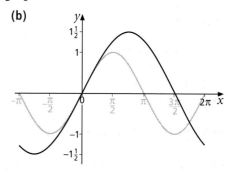

**10** Find the equation of the resulting curve if $y = \sin x$ is

    **(a)** reflected in the $x$-axis and then translated by $\begin{bmatrix} 0 \\ 1 \end{bmatrix}$

    **(b)** translated by $\begin{bmatrix} 0 \\ 1 \end{bmatrix}$ and then reflected in the $x$-axis

    **(c)** stretched in the $x$-direction, factor $\frac{1}{3}$, and then translated by $\begin{bmatrix} 2 \\ 0 \end{bmatrix}$

    **(d)** translated by $\begin{bmatrix} 2 \\ 0 \end{bmatrix}$ and then stretched in the $x$-direction, factor $\frac{1}{3}$

**11** Find a pair of transformations, making the order in which they are performed clear, which will map $y = \operatorname{cosec} x$ on to

    **(a)** $y = \operatorname{cosec}\left(\frac{1}{2}x + 1\right)$    **(b)** $y = \operatorname{cosec} 3(x - 2)$    **(c)** $y = 2(\operatorname{cosec} x) - 3$

**12** The diagram shows a sketch of the graph of $y = \cos 2x$ with a line of symmetry $L$.

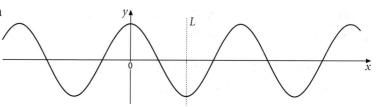

    **(a) (i)** Describe the geometrical transformation by which the graph of $y = \cos 2x$ can be obtained from that of $y = \cos x$.

    **(ii)** Write down the equation of the line $L$.

The function f is defined for the restricted domain $0 \le x \le \dfrac{\pi}{2}$ by $f(x) = \cos 2x$.

    **(b) (i)** State the range of the function f.

    **(ii)** Write down the domain and range of the inverse function $f^{-1}$, making it clear which is the domain of $f^{-1}$ and which is its range.

    **(iii)** Sketch the graph of $y = f^{-1}(x)$.

The function g is defined for all real numbers by $g(x) = |x|$.

    **(c) (i)** Write down an expression for $gf(x)$.

    **(ii)** Sketch the graph of $y = gf(x)$.

AQA 2002

# 5 Natural logarithms and e$^x$

In this chapter you will learn
- what is meant by the number e
- how to find the natural logarithm of a number
- how to solve equations that involve e$^x$ and ln$x$
- about the graphs of $y = e^x$ and $y = \ln x$

## A Introducing e (answers p 179)

**A1** You invest £1 in a savings scheme that gives 100% interest per annum!
How much money would you have at the end of one year?

**A2** Now suppose that the interest is given as 50% compound interest twice a year.
Show that an investment of £1 will have grown to £2.25 at the end of the year.

**A3** Now suppose that the interest is given as $33\frac{1}{3}$% compound interest three times a year.
Show that an investment of £1 will have grown to $£\left(1 + \frac{1}{3}\right)^3$ at the end of the year.
Work out this amount to the nearest penny.

Imagine this process continuing indefinitely.

**A4** (a) Show that, if interest is calculated $n$ times in one year year at a rate of $\dfrac{100}{n}$% each
time, then an investment of £1 will have grown to $£\left(1 + \dfrac{1}{n}\right)^n$ at the end of the year.

(b) Calculate the final amount if interest is added on 100 times a year.

(c) What happens to this final amount as $n$ gets larger and larger?

**A5** (a) Use a graph plotter to plot the graph of $y = \left(1 + \dfrac{1}{x}\right)^x$ for $x > 0$.

(b) Given that there is a limit for $\left(1 + \dfrac{1}{x}\right)^x$ as $x \to \infty$, find this limit correct to three
decimal places.

In 1683, as part of some work on compound interest, the Swiss mathematician Jacob Bernouilli
tried to find the limit of $\left(1 + \dfrac{1}{n}\right)^n$ as $n$ tends to infinity. He showed that the limit had to lie
between 2 and 3. Some years later, Leonhard Euler, another Swiss mathematician, used the
letter e to stand for this limit and gave an approximation for it to 18 decimal places as

$$e \approx 2.718\,281\,828\,459\,045\,235$$

This is the first time that a number was defined by a limiting process.

Euler probably chose e to stand for this number as the first four letters of the alphabet, a, b, c
and d, already had common mathematical uses. It is very unlikely that it has anything to do
with Euler's name: despite his great achievements in mathematics, he was a modest man.

The constant e is needed in various areas of mathematics, particularly in problems involving
growth and decay.

**A6** Let f be a function defined for all non-negative integers by

$$f(n) = \frac{1}{0!} + \frac{1}{1!} + \frac{1}{2!} + \frac{1}{3!} + \ldots + \frac{1}{n!}.$$

(0! is conventionally defined as 1.)

(a) Show that $f(3) = 2\frac{2}{3}$.

(b) Evaluate these, correct to six decimal places.

(i) $f(5)$         (ii) $f(8)$         (iii) $f(10)$         (iv) $f(15)$

(c) What do you notice about your results in part (b)?

In 1748, in *Introductio in analysin infinitorum*, Euler showed that

$$e = \frac{1}{0!} + \frac{1}{1!} + \frac{1}{2!} + \frac{1}{3!} + \ldots$$

and this is a much more efficient way of calculating the value of e.

Euler proved that e is irrational, so its decimal expansion never terminates or repeats. No matter how many digits in the expansion of e you know, the only way to find the next one is to calculate it using a definition such as the one above.

In general, the decimal expansion of e did not give rise to the same enthusiasm as that of π. However, by 1884 e had been calculated correct to 346 decimal places and in 1999 Sebastian Wedeniwski calculated e to 869 894 101 places!

**Exercise A** (answers p 179)

**1** Without using a calculator, decide whether each statement is true or false.

(a) $e + 1 > 4$      (b) $\frac{e}{3} < 1$      (c) $2e > 5$      (d) $e^2 < 9$

(e) $\sqrt{e} < 2$      (f) $e^3 > 8$      (g) $\frac{1}{e} < 0$      (h) $e^{\frac{1}{3}} > 1$

(i) $e^{\pi} > 8$      (j) $e^{-2} > 0$      (k) $e^{-\frac{1}{2}} < 0$      (l) $e^0 = 1$

**2** Use the $e^x$ key on your calculator to evaluate these, correct to four decimal places.

(a) $e^2$      (b) $e^{-3}$      (c) $\sqrt{e}$      (d) $e^{-\frac{1}{4}}$      (e) $\frac{1}{4}e$

**3** Each of these is an approximation for e.
Put them in order, from the least accurate to the most accurate.

A $\quad 3 - \sqrt{\dfrac{5}{63}}$      B $\quad \dfrac{271801}{99990}$      C $\quad 2 + \dfrac{54^2 + 41^2}{80^2}$      D $\quad \left(\pi^4 + \pi^5\right)^{\frac{1}{6}}$

## B Natural logarithms (answers p 179)

**B1** Use trial and improvement to solve these equations, correct to two decimal places.

(a) $e^x = 7$          (b) $e^x = 2$

You know from earlier work on logarithms that, if a number $y$ is expressed as $y = a^x$, then we say that $x$ is the log-to-base-$a$ of $y$ and write it as $x = \log_a y$.

So, for example, if $2 = e^x$ then $x$ is the log-to-base-e of 2 and can be written as $x = \log_e 2$.

> **K** Logarithms to the base e have a special name and their own notation: they are called **natural logarithms** and we write $\log_e x$ as $\ln x$.
>
> In general, $e^x = y \Leftrightarrow x = \ln y$.
>
> It can be useful to express this as $e^{\ln y} = y$ or $\ln e^x = x$.

The letters 'ln' are an abbreviation of the French 'logarithme naturel'. The expression '$\ln x$' is usually pronounced as 'el-en-of-$x$' or 'lon-$x$'.

**B2 (a)** Find the ln key on your calculator and use it to calculate $\ln 2$ to six decimal places.

**(b)** Use your result to verify that $e^{\ln 2} = 2$.

**B3** Without using a calculator, write down the value of $e^{\ln 4}$.

**B4 (a)** Use your calculator to evaluate $e^{1.3863}$ correct to three decimal places.

**(b)** Hence, without using a calculator, write down the value of $\ln 4$, correct to one decimal place.

**B5** Solve these equations, correct to four decimal places.

(a) $e^x = 10$      (b) $e^x = 2.5$      (c) $e^x = 0.5$      (d) $e^x = 0.1$

**B6** Explain why the equation $e^x = -5$ has no real solution.

**B7 (a)** Write $\dfrac{1}{e^3}$ in the form $e^k$ for some integer $k$.

**(b)** Hence, without using a calculator, write down the value of $\ln \dfrac{1}{e^3}$.

**B8** Without using a calculator, write down the value of these.

(a) $\ln e^5$      (b) $\ln e$      (c) $\ln \dfrac{1}{e^2}$      (d) $\ln \sqrt{e}$      (e) $\ln 1$

**B9** Explain why a value for $\ln(-2)$ does not exist.

Of course, the laws of logarithms apply to natural logarithms.

> **K** Where $a, b > 0$,
> - $\ln a + \ln b = \ln ab$
> - $\ln a - \ln b = \ln\left(\dfrac{a}{b}\right)$
> - $\ln a^k = k \ln a$ (for all values of $k$)

**B10** Show that $2\ln 3 + 5\ln 2$ is equivalent to the single logarithm $\ln 288$.

**B11** Write each of these as a single logarithm.

(a) $\ln 3 + \ln 2$      (b) $\ln 8 - \ln 4$      (c) $2\ln 6$      (d) $2\ln 4 + 3\ln 2$

**B12** (a) Use your calculator to find $\ln 5$ to six decimal places.

(b) Hence write down the value of each of these, correct to one decimal place.

(i) $\ln 25$        (ii) $\ln 5e$        (iii) $\ln \dfrac{e}{5}$

**B13** Show that $\ln(8e^2) = 2 + 3\ln 2$.

You will see in the next chapter that there are many calculus problems where $e^x$ and natural logarithms arise. This is one reason that $e^x$ and $\ln x$ are such important functions.

In this chapter you will simplify expressions, solve equations and draw graphs where $e$ and natural logarithms are involved. This is important preparation for working with $e$ and natural logarithms in calculus.

---

### Example 1

Solve the equation $e^{x+1} = 5$, giving your answer as an exact value.

**Solution**

$$e^{x+1} = 5$$
$$\Rightarrow \quad x + 1 = \ln 5$$
$$\Rightarrow \quad x = \ln 5 - 1$$

---

### Example 2

Solve the equation $\ln x^3 = 7$, giving your answer correct to four decimal places.

**Solution**

$$\ln x^3 = 7$$
$$\Rightarrow \quad 3\ln x = 7$$
$$\Rightarrow \quad \ln x = \tfrac{7}{3}$$
$$\Rightarrow \quad x = e^{\frac{7}{3}}$$
$$\quad\quad = 10.3123 \text{ (to 4 d.p.)}$$

---

### Example 3

Solve the equation $e^{-5x} - 3 = 0$, giving your answer correct to four decimal places.

**Solution**

$$e^{-5x} - 3 = 0$$
$$\Rightarrow \quad e^{-5x} = 3$$
$$\Rightarrow \quad -5x = \ln 3$$
$$\Rightarrow \quad x = -\tfrac{1}{5}\ln 3$$
$$\quad\quad = -0.2197 \text{ (to 4 d.p.)}$$

---

## Example 4

Write the expression $4\ln(x+1) - \ln x$ as a single logarithm.

**Solution**

$$4\ln(x+1) - \ln x = \ln(x+1)^4 - \ln x$$
$$= \ln \frac{(x+1)^4}{x}$$

## Example 5

Solve the equation $\ln(2x-1) + \ln 3 = 2$, giving your answer as an exact value.

**Solution**

$$\ln(2x-1) + \ln 3 = 2$$
$$\Rightarrow \quad \ln(3(2x-1)) = 2$$
$$\Rightarrow \quad \ln(6x-3) = 2$$
$$\Rightarrow \quad 6x - 3 = e^2$$
$$\Rightarrow \quad 6x = e^2 + 3$$
$$\Rightarrow \quad x = \tfrac{1}{6}(e^2 + 3)$$

## Exercise B (answers p 179)

**1** Solve each equation, giving each solution correct to three decimal places.

(a) $e^x = 3$      (b) $4e^{-x} = 1$      (c) $e^x + 1 = 4.5$

(d) $e^{x+1} = 20$      (e) $e^{3x} = 0.2$      (f) $e^{\frac{1}{2}x} - 2 = 6$

(g) $2e^{4x} - 3 = 0$      (h) $e^{1-3x} = \tfrac{1}{2}$      (i) $e^{\frac{1}{4}x+1} - 1 = 0$

**2** The growth of a colony of bacteria is modelled by the equation $y = 4e^t$, where $t$ is measured in hours and $y$ is the number of bacteria.

(a) Estimate the number of bacteria after

   (i) 1 hour      (ii) $3\tfrac{1}{2}$ hours      (iii) 10 hours

(b) How long does it take for the colony to grow to 500 bacteria?

**3** When a particular drug is injected into the body, the amount in the bloodstream is modelled by the equation $A = 5e^{-0.2t}$, where $t$ is the time in hours after the dose is administered, and $A$ is the amount remaining, in milligrams.

(a) What is the initial amount of drug in the bloodstream?

(b) How much of the drug (to the nearest 0.01 mg) remains in the blood after

   (i) 1 hour      (ii) 5 hours      (iii) 24 hours

(c) How long does it take for the amount of drug to decrease to below 0.01 mg?

**4** Show that $x = \tfrac{1}{3}(\ln 5 + 2)$ is the solution of the equation $e^{3x-2} = 5$.

**5** Find the exact solution of each equation.

(a) $e^{2x+1} = 5$        (b) $e^{3x-4} = 1$        (c) $e^{1-\frac{1}{2}x} - 3 = 1$

**6** Without using a calculator, show that     (a) $\ln\frac{1}{2} = -\ln 2$     (b) $e^{-\ln 4} = \frac{1}{4}$

**7** Solve $e^{-2x} = \frac{1}{3}$ and write the solution in the form $x = a\ln b$, where $b$ is a positive integer.

**8** Find the exact solution of the equation $3e^{-5x} = \frac{1}{2}$.

**9** Solve each equation, giving each solution correct to three decimal places.

(a) $\ln x = 4$        (b) $\ln 2x = -3$        (c) $3\ln x = 5$

(d) $\ln(x+1) = 0.6$      (e) $\ln(2x-3) = 1.5$     (f) $\ln\left(1 - \frac{1}{3}x\right) = -1.2$

**10** Show that $x = \frac{1}{4}(e^2 + 1)$ is the solution of the equation $\ln(4x - 1) = 2$.

**11** Find the exact solution of each equation.

(a) $\ln 4x = 5$        (b) $\ln(x-1) = -2$      (c) $\ln(2x+3) = 1$

**12** Write each of these as a single logarithm.

(a) $3\ln x$        (b) $\ln 4x + \ln 5$        (c) $\ln\frac{1}{2}x + \ln 2x$

(d) $2\ln 5 + \ln x$     (e) $\ln x - \ln 2$        (f) $\frac{1}{2}\ln 9 - \ln x$

**13** Find the exact solution of each equation.

(a) $\ln x + \ln 5 = 2$     (b) $\ln x - \ln 3 = 1$      (c) $\ln x + \ln 2x = 3$

(d) $3\ln 2 + \ln 5x = 0$   (e) $\ln(x+1) + \ln 2 = 5$    (f) $\ln(5-x) - \ln 4 = 1$

**14** (a) Show that any solution to the equation $\ln(x+2) + \ln x = \ln 8$ must satisfy the equation $x^2 + 2x - 8 = 0$.

(b) Which of the solutions of $x^2 + 2x - 8 = 0$ is a solution of $\ln(x+2) + \ln x = \ln 8$? Explain your answer fully.

**15** Solve each of these equations.

(a) $\ln(x+3) - \ln x = \ln 5$       (b) $\ln(x+1) + \ln x = \ln 6$

(c) $\ln(6x-5) = 2\ln x$         (d) $\ln(2x-1) + \ln 3x = 2\ln x$

**16** (a) Show that the equation $e^{2x} - 4e^x + 3 = 0$ is equivalent to $y^2 - 4y + 3 = 0$ where $y = e^x$.

(b) Solve $e^{2x} - 4e^x + 3 = 0$, giving your solutions as exact values.

**17** Solve each equation, giving all solutions as exact values.

(a) $e^{2x} - 6e^x + 5 = 0$     (b) $e^{2x} = 2e^x$        (c) $e^{2x} - 3e^x = 4$

**18** Solve $2\ln(x+1) - \ln x = \ln 6$, giving your solutions as exact values.

**19** Solve each equation, giving all solutions as exact values.

(a) $9e^x = 4e^{-x}$        (b) $e^{2x+1} = 3e^x$        (c) $5 - e^x = 4e^{-x}$

## C Graphs (answers p 180)

The graph of $y = e^x$ is an exponential curve.

When $x = 0$ then $y = e^0 = 1$, so the $y$-intercept is 1.
As $x$ gets very large and negative then $e^x$ gets closer
and closer to 0 so the $x$-axis is an asymptote.

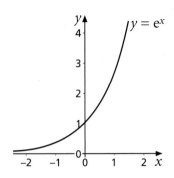

**C1** Write down the range of the function $y = e^x$ where $x \in \mathbb{R}$.

We know that $y = e^x \Leftrightarrow x = \ln y$ so $e^x$ and $\ln x$ are inverse functions and
the graph of $y = \ln x$ is the reflection of $y = e^x$ in the line $y = x$.

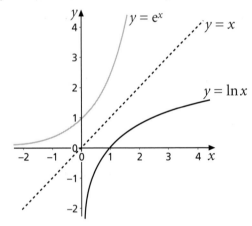

**C2** Write down the largest suitable domain for the function $y = \ln x$.

**C3** Sketch the graph of $y = f(x)$ for each function.

    **(a)** $f(x) = e^{-x}, \ x \in \mathbb{R}$             **(b)** $f(x) = 2e^x, \ x \in \mathbb{R}$

    **(c)** $f(x) = \ln(x + 1), \ x > -1$       **(d)** $f(x) = \ln(3x), \ x > 0$

**C4** Write down the range of each function in C3.

---

### Example 6

Sketch the graph of $y = e^{x-1} - 3$, showing clearly the exact coordinates of
any points where the graph meets the axes.

### Solution

The graph of $y = e^{x-1} - 3$ is obtained from $y = e^x$ by a translation of 1 unit to the right and
3 units down. So $y = -3$ is an asymptote of the graph of $y = e^{x-1} - 3$.

When $x = 0$, $y = e^{-1} - 3 = \dfrac{1}{e} - 3$ so the graph cuts the $y$-axis at $\left(0, \dfrac{1}{e} - 3\right)$.

When $y = 0$, $e^{x-1} - 3 = 0$

$\Rightarrow \quad e^{x-1} = 3$

$\Rightarrow \quad x - 1 = \ln 3$

$\Rightarrow \quad x = \ln 3 + 1$

so the graph cuts the $x$-axis at $(\ln 3 + 1, 0)$.

Hence a sketch is:

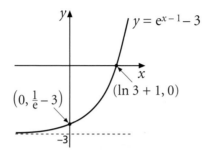

*The asymptote is shown by a dotted line.*

*Finding approximate decimal values for any important coordinates helps you draw a realistic sketch:*

$\left(0, \dfrac{1}{e} - 3\right) \approx (0, -2.6)$ *and*

$(\ln 3 + 1, 0) \approx (2.1, 0)$

---

### Example 7

A function is defined by the rule $f(x) = \ln(2x + 5)$.

Sketch the graph of $y = f(x)$, showing clearly the coordinates of any points where the graph meets the axes.

Write down the largest suitable domain for the function f.

### Solution

*$y = \ln(2x + 5)$ is a transformation of $y = \ln x$ so we know the general shape.*

When $x = 0$, $y = \ln 5$ so the graph cuts the $y$-axis at $(0, \ln 5)$.

When $y = 0$, $\ln(2x + 5) = 0$

$\Rightarrow \quad 2x + 5 = 1$

$\Rightarrow \quad x = -2$

so the graph cuts the $x$-axis at $(-2, 0)$.

*$x = 0$ is an asymptote to $y = \ln x$ so $2x + 5 = 0$ is an asymptote to $y = \ln(2x + 5)$.*

*$2x + 5 = 0$ when $x = -2\frac{1}{2}$ so the line $x = -2\frac{1}{2}$ is a vertical asymptote.*

Hence a sketch is:

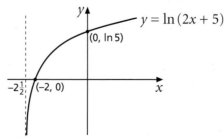

*The asymptote $x = -2\frac{1}{2}$ is shown by a dotted line.*

The largest suitable domain is $x > -2\frac{1}{2}$.

## Example 8

On the same axes, sketch the graphs of $y = e^{3x}$ and $y = 3e^{-x}$.
Find the $x$-coordinate of the point of intersection, correct to four significant figures.

### Solution

The graph of $y = e^{3x}$ is obtained from $y = e^x$ by a stretch of factor $\frac{1}{3}$ in the $x$-direction.

The graph of $y = 3e^{-x}$ is obtained from $y = e^x$ by a stretch of factor 3 in the $y$-direction followed by reflection in the $y$-axis (or vice versa).

Hence a sketch is:

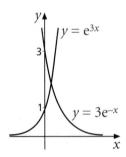

The $x$-coordinate of the point of intersection is the solution of the equation $e^{3x} = 3e^{-x}$.

$$e^{3x} = 3e^{-x} \quad \Rightarrow \quad e^{3x} = \frac{3}{e^x}$$

$$\Rightarrow \quad e^{3x} \times e^x = \frac{3}{e^x} \times e^x$$

$$\Rightarrow \quad e^{4x} = 3$$

$$\Rightarrow \quad 4x = \ln 3$$

$$\Rightarrow \quad x = \tfrac{1}{4}\ln 3 = 0.2747 \text{ (to 4 s.f.)}$$

---

### Exercise C (answers p 181)

**1** A function is defined by $f(x) = e^x + 5, \; x \in \mathbb{R}$.

  (a) Evaluate $f(0)$.

  (b) Sketch the graph of $y = f(x)$, indicating the position of the horizontal asymptote.

  (c) What is the range of f?

**2** Sketch the graph of $y = f(x)$ where $f(x) = e^{x+5}, \; x \in \mathbb{R}$.
Indicate clearly the exact coordinates of the point where the graph cuts the $y$-axis.

**3** What transformation will map the graph of $y = e^x$ on to the graph of $y = e^{\frac{1}{3}x}$?

**4** (a) What transformation will map the graph of $y = \ln x$ on to the graph of $y = \ln x - 1$?

  (b) Show that the graph of $y = \ln x - 1$ meets the $x$-axis at the point $(e, 0)$.

**5** For each function, sketch the graph of $y = f(x)$, indicating clearly the exact coordinates of any points where the graph meets the $x$-axis.

  (a) $f(x) = \ln x - 3, \; x > 0$           (b) $f(x) = 3\ln x, \; x > 0$

  (c) $f(x) = -\ln x, \; x > 0$          (d) $f(x) = 1 - \ln x, \; x > 0$

**6** Describe a sequence of geometrical transformations by which the graph of $y = 5e^{-x}$ can be obtained from that of $y = e^x$.

**7** Sketch the graph of $y = e^{-x} - 4$, indicating clearly the exact coordinates of any points where the graph meets the axes.

**8** A function is defined by $f(x) = e^{x+2} - 5$, $x \in \mathbb{R}$.

(a) Evaluate f(−2).

(b) Sketch the graph of $y = f(x)$, indicating clearly the exact coordinates of any points where the graph meets the axes.

(c) What is the equation of the asymptote?

(d) What is the range of f?

(e) Solve the equation $f(x) = 1$.

**9** (a) What transformation will map the graph of $y = \ln x$ on to the graph of $y = \ln(x + 2)$?

(b) Sketch the graph of $y = \ln(x + 2)$, showing clearly the exact coordinates of any points where the graph meets the axes and the position of the vertical asymptote.

**10** A function is defined by f: $x \mapsto 2e^{-x} - 1$, $x \in \mathbb{R}$.
A sketch of $y = f(x)$ is shown.

(a) What is the value of $a$?

(b) Show that $b = \ln 2$.

(c) What is the range of f?

(d) Solve the equation $f(x) = 3$.

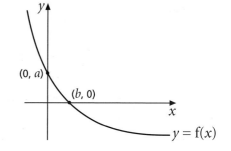

**11** The rule for a function is g: $x \mapsto 3 + \ln(2x + 1)$.
A sketch of $y = g(x)$ is shown.

(a) What are the values of $p$ and $q$?

(b) What is the equation of the vertical asymptote?

(c) Solve the equation $g(x) = -2$.

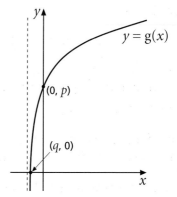

**12** A function is defined by $f(x) = 5 - 2\ln(x + 3)$, $x > -3$.
Sketch the graph of $y = f(x)$.

**13** (a) On the same axes, sketch the graphs of $y = e^{-x}$ and $y = 3e^x$.

(b) The two curves $y = e^{-x}$ and $y = 3e^x$ intersect at the point P.

(i) Show that the x-coordinate of the point P is a root of the equation $e^{2x} = \frac{1}{3}$.

(ii) Find the x-coordinate of the point P, correct to four significant figures.

**14** A cup of coffee, initially at boiling point, cools according to Newton's law of cooling, so that after $t$ minutes its temperature, $T°C$, is given by

$$T = 15 + 85e^{-\frac{t}{8}}$$

(a) Sketch the graph of $T$ against $t$.

(b) How long does the coffee take to cool to $40\,°C$?

**15** A function is defined by $f(x) = |e^x - 3|, \ x \in \mathbb{R}$.

(a) Evaluate $f(0)$.

(b) Evaluate these, correct to two decimal places.

    (i) $f(2)$                (ii) $f(1)$                            (iii) $f(-3)$

(c) Solve the equation $f(x) = 0$.

(d) Sketch the graph of $y = f(x)$, showing clearly the exact coordinates of any points where the graph meets the axes.

(e) What is the range of f?

(f) Show that the equation $f(x) = 1$ has two solutions.
    Solve $f(x) = 1$, giving the solutions in exact form.

(g) Solve $f(x) = 5$.

**16** A function is defined by $g(x) = \ln|x - 2|, \ x \neq 2$.

(a) Evaluate $g(3)$ and $g(1)$.

(b) Sketch the graph of $y = g(x)$, showing clearly the exact coordinates of any points where the graph meets the axes.

(c) Solve $g(x) = 3$, giving the solutions in exact form.

## D Inverses

You have seen that one way to find a rule for the inverse of a function is to write the function in terms of $x$ and $y$ and then rearrange to obtain a rule for $x$ in terms of $y$.

For example, let f be the function defined by       $f(x) = e^x + 1, \ x \in \mathbb{R}$.

To find the inverse first write the rule as            $y = e^x + 1$

Then rearrange to obtain                     $y - 1 = e^x$

$$\Rightarrow \quad \ln(y - 1) = x$$

So the inverse rule is $f^{-1}(x) = \ln(x - 1)$.

The range of f is the set of real numbers given by $f(x) > 1$ so the domain of $f^{-1}$ is $x > 1$.

Hence we can define the inverse fully by

$$f^{-1}(x) = \ln(x - 1), \ x > 1$$

The range of $f^{-1}$ is $f^{-1}(x) \in \mathbb{R}$ (the domain of f).

You have also seen that reflecting the graph of a function in the line $y = x$ gives the graph of its inverse.

The graphs of $y = f(x)$ and $y = f^{-1}(x)$ are:

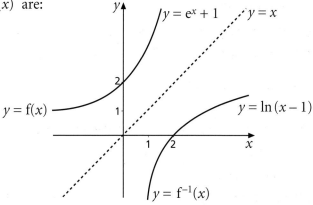

---

### Example 9

The function f is defined for $x > 0$ by $f(x) = \ln(3x) - 6$.
Find an expression for $f^{-1}(x)$.

#### Solution

*First write the rule as*
$$y = \ln(3x) - 6$$

*Rearrange.*
$$y + 6 = \ln(3x)$$

$$\Rightarrow \quad e^{y+6} = 3x$$

$$\Rightarrow \quad \tfrac{1}{3}e^{y+6} = x$$

So $f^{-1}(x) = \tfrac{1}{3}e^{x+6}$.

---

### Example 10

The function g is defined for $x \in \mathbb{R}$ by $g(x) = 2e^{x-5} + 3$.
Find an expression for $g^{-1}(x)$.
State the domain and range of $g^{-1}$.

#### Solution

*First write the rule as*
$$y = 2e^{x-5} + 3$$

*Rearrange.*
$$y - 3 = 2e^{x-5}$$

$$\Rightarrow \quad \tfrac{1}{2}(y - 3) = e^{x-5}$$

$$\Rightarrow \quad \ln\left(\tfrac{1}{2}(y-3)\right) = x - 5$$

$$\Rightarrow \quad \ln\left(\tfrac{1}{2}(y-3)\right) + 5 = x$$

So $g^{-1}(x) = \ln\left(\tfrac{1}{2}(x-3)\right) + 5$.

The range of g is $g(x) > 3$ so the domain of $g^{-1}$ is $x > 3$.
The domain of g is $x \in \mathbb{R}$ so the range of $g^{-1}$ is $g^{-1}(x) \in \mathbb{R}$.

**Exercise D** (answers p 182)

**1** For each rule, find an expression for $f^{-1}(x)$, where $f^{-1}$ is the inverse of f.

(a) $f(x) = e^{2x}$          (b) $f(x) = e^{x+2}$          (c) $f(x) = e^x + 2$

(d) $f(x) = 2e^x$          (e) $f(x) = e^{2-x}$          (f) $f(x) = e^{-x} - 2$

**2** For each rule, find an expression for $g^{-1}(x)$, where $g^{-1}$ is the inverse of g.

(a) $g(x) = \ln(5x)$          (b) $g(x) = \ln(x+5)$          (c) $g(x) = 5 + \ln x$

(d) $g(x) = 5\ln x$          (e) $g(x) = \ln(\frac{1}{5}x)$          (f) $g(x) = 5\ln x - 1$

**3** A function is defined by $f(x) = e^{x-1} + 2$, $x \in \mathbb{R}$.

(a) What is the range of f?

(b) Find an expression for $f^{-1}(x)$.

(c) State the domain and range of $f^{-1}$.

(d) On the same axes, sketch the graphs of $y = f(x)$ and $y = f^{-1}(x)$. Show clearly any asymptotes and state their equations.

**4** A function is defined by $g(x) = \ln(x+1) - 2$, $x > -1$.

(a) (i) Find an expression for $g^{-1}(x)$.

    (ii) Hence find the exact solution to the equation $g(x) = 7$.

(b) State the domain and range of $g^{-1}$.

**5** A function is defined by $f(x) = 2e^x + 3$, $x \in \mathbb{R}$.

(a) Find an expression for $f^{-1}(x)$.

(b) (i) State the domain of $f^{-1}$.

    (ii) Hence show that the equation $f(x) = 1$ has no solution.

**6** A function is defined by $h(x) = \ln(2x-4)$, $x > 2$.

(a) Find an expression for $h^{-1}(x)$.

(b) On the same axes, sketch the graphs of $y = h(x)$ and $y = h^{-1}(x)$. Show clearly any asymptotes and state their equations.

**7** A function is defined by $f(x) = 3e^{-x}$, $x \geq -2$.

(a) What is the maximum value of $f(x)$?

(b) Find an expression for $f^{-1}(x)$.

(c) What is the domain and range of $f^{-1}$?

**8** A particular type of car depreciates in value according to the mathematical model
$$V = 14\,000\,e^{-0.3t}$$
where £$V$ is the value $t$ years after it is sold as new.

(a) Find a formula for $t$ in terms of $V$.

(b) Sarah buys one of these cars as new at the beginning of the year 2005. During which year does the value of the car fall to below £5000?

## Key points

- e is an irrational number; its value is 2.718 281 828 correct to nine decimal places. (pp 72–73)

- Natural logarithms use e as a base and we write $\log_e x$ as $\ln x$:
  $$e^x = y \Leftrightarrow x = \ln y$$
  (p 74)

- $y = \ln x$ and $y = e^x$ are inverse functions so the graph of $y = \ln x$ is the reflection of $y = e^x$ in the line $y = x$.

  $e^x$ is positive for all $x$ so $\ln x$ is defined only for positive values of $x$.

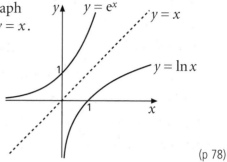

(p 78)

## Mixed questions (answers p 183)

**1 (a)** The diagram shows the graph of $y = f(x)$, where the function f is defined for all values of $x$ by
$$f(x) = 5e^{-x}$$

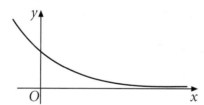

  **(i)** Write down the coordinates of the point where the graph intersects the $y$-axis.

  **(ii)** State the range of the function f.

  **(iii)** Find the value of $f(\ln 6)$, giving your answer as a fraction.

**(b)** The function g is defined for all values of $x$ by
$$g(x) = x + 10$$

  **(i)** Show that $gf(x) = 5(e^{-x} + 2)$.

  **(ii)** State the range of the function gf.

  **(iii)** Sketch the graph of $y = gf(x)$.

  **(iv)** Show that $gf(x) = 11 \Rightarrow x = \ln 5$.

**(c)** A dish of water is left to cool in a room where the temperature is $10\,^{\circ}\text{C}$.
At time $t$ minutes, where $t \geq 0$, the temperature of the water in degrees Celsius is
$$5(e^{-t} + 2)$$

  **(i)** State the temperature of the water at time $t = 0$.

  **(ii)** Calculate the time at which the temperature of the water reaches $11\,^{\circ}\text{C}$.
  Give your answer to the nearest tenth of a minute.

AQA 2003

**2** A function is defined by $f(x) = 1 + 3e^{-x}, \ x \in \mathbb{R}$.

   **(a)** Sketch the graph of $y = f(x)$.    **(b)** Solve the inequality $f(x) < 2$.

**3** The functions f and g are defined by     $f: x \mapsto \ln\left(\tfrac{1}{2}x - 3\right), \ x > 6$

                                                   $g: x \mapsto 4e^{2x}, \ x \in \mathbb{R}$

   **(a)** Find an expression for $f^{-1}(x)$.

   **(b)** Evaluate $gf(8)$.

   **(c)** Show that $gf(x) = (x - 6)^2$.

**4** The functions f and g are defined by     $f(x) = 1 + \ln x, \ x > 0$

                                                   $g(x) = (ex)^2, \ x \in \mathbb{R}$

   **(a)** Evaluate $g(5)$ correct to two decimal places.

   **(b)** Describe the geometrical transformation by which the graph of $y = f(x)$ can be obtained from the graph of $y = \ln x$.

   **(c)** Find an expression for $f^{-1}(x)$.

   **(d)** Show that $fg(x) = 3 + 2\ln x$.

   **(e)** Sketch the graph of $y = |fg(x)|$.

**5** The function f is given by $f: x \mapsto \ln(3x - 9), \ x > 3$.

   **(a)** Find, to three significant figures, the value of $x$ for which $f(x) = 5$.

   The function g is given by $g: x \mapsto \ln|3x - 9|, \ x \neq 3$.

   **(b)** Sketch the graph of $y = g(x)$.

## Test yourself (answers p 184)

**1** Write each of these expressions in the form $a \ln p + b \ln q$.

   **(a)** $\ln(pq)$         **(b)** $\ln(p^3 q^2)$         **(c)** $\ln\left(\dfrac{p^2}{q}\right)$         **(d)** $\ln\sqrt{\dfrac{p^2}{q}}$

**2** The functions f and g are defined for all real numbers by

        $f: x \mapsto e^{4x}$

        $g: x \mapsto \tfrac{1}{4}x - 3$

   **(a)** Evaluate $fg(12)$.

   **(b)** Find an expression for $f^{-1}(x)$.

   **(c)** Sketch on the same diagram the graphs of $y = f(x)$ and $y = f^{-1}(x)$, indicating the relationship between the graphs.

   **(d)** Sketch the graph of $y = |gf(x)|$, indicating clearly the exact coordinates of any points at which the graph meets the axes.

**3** Describe, in each of the following cases, a single transformation which maps the graph of $y = e^x$ on to the graph of the function given.

   **(a)** $y = e^{3x}$           **(b)** $y = e^{x-3}$           **(c)** $y = \ln x$           AQA 2001

**4** Find the exact solution of the equation $\ln(3y + 2) - \ln 5 = 2$.

**5** The function f is defined by $f(x) = e^{x-3} + 2, \; x \in \mathbb{R}$.

    **(a)** Sketch the graph of $y = f(x)$, showing clearly the coordinates of any points where the graph meets the axes.

    **(b)** What is the range of f?

    **(c)** Solve the equation $f(x) = 7$.

    **(d)** Find an expression for $f^{-1}(x)$ and state the domain of $f^{-1}$.

**6** The diagram shows the graphs of $y = x$ and $y = f(x)$.

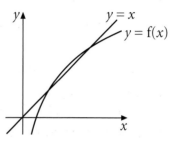

    **(a) (i)** Describe the geometrical transformation by which the graph of $y = f^{-1}(x)$ can be obtained from the graph of $y = f(x)$.

      **(ii)** Copy the above diagram and sketch on the same axes the graph of $y = f^{-1}(x)$.

    **(b)** The function f is defined for $x > 0$ by $f(x) = 3\ln x$.

      **(i)** Describe the geometrical transformation by which the graph of $y = f(x)$ can be obtained from the graph of $y = \ln x$.

      **(ii)** Find an expression for $f^{-1}(x)$.                    *AQA 2002*

**7** The diagram shows the graph of $y = f(x)$, where f is defined for all real numbers by
$$f(x) = 2e^{-x}$$

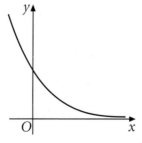

    **(a)** Describe a sequence of geometrical transformations by which the above graph can be obtained from the graph of $y = e^x$.

    **(b)** Copy the above diagram and sketch on the same axes the graph of $y = f^{-1}(x)$.

    **(c)** Find an expression for $f^{-1}(x)$.

    **(d)** State the domain and range of $f^{-1}$.

    **(e)** A time $t$ hours after an injection, a hospital patient has $f(t)$ milligrams per litre of a certain drug in his blood. Find the time after the injection at which the patient has 0.5 milligrams per litre of the drug in his blood.      *AQA 2001*

**8** A function is defined by $g(x) = \ln(5 - 2x), \; x < 2\frac{1}{2}$.

    **(a)** Find an expression for $g^{-1}(x)$.     **(b)** What is the domain of $g^{-1}$?

# 6 Differentiation

In this chapter you will learn how to
- differentiate $e^x$, $\ln x$, $\sin x$, $\cos x$ and $\tan x$
- differentiate a product of two functions, a quotient of two functions and a function of a function

---

**Key points from Core 1 and Core 2**

- The derivative of $x^n$ is $nx^{n-1}$.

- The derivative of $f(x) + g(x)$ is $f'(x) + g'(x)$.
  The derivative of $kf(x)$ is $kf'(x)$.

- If $f'(a) > 0$, f is increasing at $x = a$. If $f'(a) < 0$, f is decreasing at $x = a$.

- Points where $f'(x) = 0$ are called stationary points of the function f.
  If $f'(a) = 0$ and $f''(a) > 0$, then $x = a$ is a local minimum.
  If $f'(a) = 0$ and $f''(a) < 0$, then $x = a$ is a local maximum.

---

## A Exponential functions (answers p 185)

The functions $y = 2^x$ and $y = 3^x$ are exponential functions. Their graphs are shown here.

Because $2^0$ and $3^0$ are both 1, both graphs go through $(0, 1)$.

In fact, for any value of $a$, the graph of $y = a^x$ goes through $(0, 1)$.

At $(0, 1)$, the graph of $y = 3^x$ is steeper than the graph of $y = 2^x$.

We shall first find the gradient of each graph at $(0, 1)$.

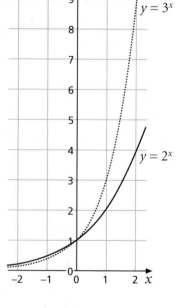

This diagram shows a close-up of the graph of $y = 2^x$ as it passes through $(0, 1)$, labelled $A$.

The coordinates of the point $B$ on the graph are $(h, 2^h)$, where $h$ is small.

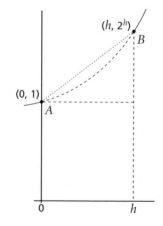

**A1 (a)** Show that the gradient of the line $AB$ is $\dfrac{2^h - 1}{h}$.

**(b)** Find the value of this expression when $h = 0.1$.

**(c)** Do the same for $h = 0.05, 0.01, 0.001$ and $0.0001$.

**(d)** What conclusion do you draw about the gradient of $y = 2^x$ at the point $(0, 1)$?

**A2** If the graph of $y = 2^x$ is replaced by the graph of $y = 3^x$, the coordinates of $B$ become $(h, 3^h)$ and the gradient of $AB$ is $\dfrac{3^h - 1}{h}$.

Find the value of this expression when $h = 0.1$, $0.01$, $0.001$ and $0.0001$ and hence find an approximate value for the gradient of $y = 3^x$ at the point $(0, 1)$.

You should find that at the point $(0, 1)$ the gradient of $y = 2^x$ is approximately $0.69$ and the gradient of $y = 3^x$ is approximately $1.1$.

This suggests that somewhere between 2 and 3 is a value of $a$ for which the gradient of $y = a^x$ at the point $(0, 1)$ is equal to 1.

We would expect this value to be nearer to 3 than to 2, because $1.1$ is nearer to 1 than is $0.69$. You could use a spreadsheet to find this value by trial and improvement.

It can be shown, by methods that are beyond the scope of this book, that the required number has the value $2.718\,281\,8\ldots$, which is the number denoted by e.

**A3** Verify by using a calculator that when you substitute $h = 0.1, 0.01, 0.001, \ldots$ into the expression $\dfrac{e^h - 1}{h}$, the results get closer and closer to 1.

The graph of $y = e^x$ is shown on the right. Its gradient at the point $(0, 1)$ is 1.

We now need to investigate the gradient at any other point of the graph, say the point $P$ where $x = p$.

This diagram is a close-up of the graph as it passes through $P$, whose coordinates are $(p, e^p)$.

$Q$ is a nearby point on the graph, where $x = p + h$ and $h$ is small. The coordinates of $Q$ are $(p + h, e^{p + h})$.

The gradient of the line $PQ$ is
$$\frac{e^{p + h} - e^p}{h}$$

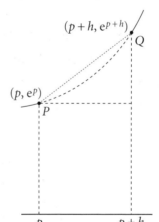

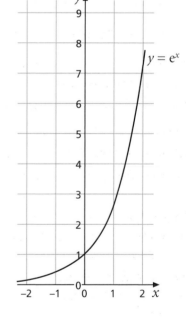

**A4 (a)** Show that this expression can be written as
$$\frac{e^p(e^h - 1)}{h}$$

**(b)** Explain why, as $h$ gets smaller and smaller, the value of this expression gets closer and closer to $e^p$. What conclusion do you draw about the gradient of $y = e^x$ at the point where $x = p$?

The result of A4 (b) is this: the gradient of the curve $y = e^x$ when $x = p$ is $e^p$.
This can be stated simply as:

**K** The derivative of $e^x$ is $e^x$.

This is the main reason the number e is important in mathematics.

**A5** Write down the derivative of each of these.

(a) $3e^x + 4$          (b) $5e^x + 4x$          (c) $2e^x - x^2$          (d) $e^x + \dfrac{2}{x}$

**A6** Use the fact that $e^{x+2} = e^2 e^x$ to find the derivative of $e^{x+2}$.
(Remember that $e^2$ is just a number.)

---

### Example 1

Given that $f(x) = 3e^x - \dfrac{1}{x}$, show that f(x) is increasing for $x > 0$.

### Solution

$f(x) = 3e^x - x^{-1}$

$f'(x) = 3e^x - (-1)x^{-2} = 3e^x + \dfrac{1}{x^2}$. When $x > 0$, $e^x > 0$ and $\dfrac{1}{x^2} > 0$, so $3e^x + \dfrac{1}{x^2} > 0$.

So f(x) is increasing for $x > 0$.

---

### Exercise A (answers p 185)

**1** Find the derivative of each of these.

(a) $e^x - 5x$          (b) $x^2 + 4e^x$          (c) $e^x - 3\sqrt{x}$          (d) $3e^x + x^3 - 1$

**2** Find $f'(x)$ given that

(a) $f(x) = 2e^x - x^{-2}$    (b) $f(x) = 6e^x + \dfrac{1}{x}$    (c) $f(x) = x^{\frac{3}{2}} + 2e^x$    (d) $f(x) = \dfrac{1}{\sqrt{x}} + 2e^x$

**3** (a) Find $\dfrac{dy}{dx}$ given that $y = e^x - 3x$.

(b) Show that $\dfrac{dy}{dx} = 0$ when $x = \ln 3 = 1.099$ to 3 d.p.

(c) From (b) it follows that the graph of $y = e^x - 3x$ has a stationary point where $x = 1.099$. Find the y-coordinate of this stationary point, to 3 d.p.

(d) By differentiating $\dfrac{dy}{dx}$ find $\dfrac{d^2y}{dx^2}$ for the function $y = e^x - 3x$.

(e) Find the value of $\dfrac{d^2y}{dx^2}$ at the stationary point.

(f) What type of stationary point is it? Give the reason for your answer.

**4** Show that the function f given by $f(x) = e^x - \dfrac{1}{x^3}$ is increasing for $x > 0$.

## B The derivative of ln x (answers p 185)

Because $\ln x$ is the inverse of $e^x$, the graph of $y = \ln x$ is the reflection of $y = e^x$ in the line $y = x$.

$P$ is the point on the graph of $y = \ln x$ where $x = 3$. So $P$ is $(3, \ln 3)$.

The corresponding point $Q$ on $y = e^x$ is $(\ln 3, 3)$.

On the graph of $y = e^x$ the gradient is equal to the value of $y$, which is 3 at $Q$.

From the diagram, the gradient of $y = \ln x$ at $P$ is the reciprocal of 3, which is $\frac{1}{3}$.

There is nothing special about the number 3 here.

For all positive values of $x$, the derivative of $\ln x$ is $\frac{1}{x}$.

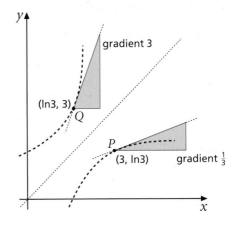

This can be shown more formally. But first we need a more general result.

The definition of $\frac{dy}{dx}$ involves making small changes $\delta x$ and $\delta y$ to $x$ and $y$ and seeing what happens to the ratio $\frac{\delta y}{\delta x}$ as $\delta x$ and $\delta y$ get smaller and smaller.

We can also look at the ratio $\frac{\delta x}{\delta y}$, which is equal to $\frac{1}{\frac{\delta y}{\delta x}}$.

The limiting value of $\frac{\delta x}{\delta y}$ as $\delta x$ and $\delta y$ get smaller and smaller

is the derivative of $x$ with respect to $y$. It is denoted by $\frac{dx}{dy}$, which is equal to $\frac{1}{\frac{dy}{dx}}$.

It follows that

$$\frac{dy}{dx} = \frac{1}{\frac{dx}{dy}}$$

This relationship helps us to differentiate the function $\ln x$, which is the inverse of $e^x$.

Let $y = \ln x$

This can be rewritten as $\qquad x = e^y$

Differentiate with respect to $y$: $\quad \dfrac{dx}{dy} = e^y$

Use the relationship above: $\quad \dfrac{dy}{dx} = \dfrac{1}{\frac{dx}{dy}} = \dfrac{1}{e^y} = \dfrac{1}{x}$

The derivative of $\ln x$ is $\frac{1}{x}$.

**B1** Differentiate each of these with respect to $x$.

(a) $\ln x + x^2$      (b) $\ln x - \sqrt{x}$      (c) $\ln x + 5e^x$      (d) $\frac{1}{x} - \ln x$

**B2** Explain why $\ln 3x = \ln 3 + \ln x$ and hence explain why the derivative of $\ln 3x$ is $\frac{1}{x}$.

**B3 (a)** Explain why $\ln(5x^2) = \ln 5 + 2\ln x$ and hence differentiate $\ln(5x^2)$.

**(b)** Differentiate **(i)** $\ln(2x^3)$ **(ii)** $\ln(\sqrt{x})$ **(iii)** $\ln(x^{-3})$ **(iv)** $\ln\left(\dfrac{1}{x}\right)$

---

## Example 2

Find $f'(x)$ given that $f(x) = 5x^4 - \ln(5x^4)$.

### Solution

$f(x) = 5x^4 - (\ln 5 + 4\ln x) = 5x^4 - \ln 5 - 4\ln x$

$$f'(x) = 20x^3 - 4\left(\frac{1}{x}\right) = 20x^3 - \frac{4}{x} \quad (\ln 5 \text{ is a constant, so its derivative is } 0.)$$

---

## Example 3

Find the stationary point on the graph of $y = 8x^2 - \ln x$ and determine its type.

### Solution

$\dfrac{dy}{dx} = 16x - \dfrac{1}{x}$. At a stationary point, $16x - \dfrac{1}{x} = 0 \implies 16x^2 - 1 = 0 \implies x = \pm\frac{1}{4}$.

When $x = \frac{1}{4}$, $y = \frac{8}{16} - \ln\frac{1}{4} = 1.886$ (to 3 d.p.)

When $x = -\frac{1}{4}$, there is no value of $y$ because $\ln\left(-\frac{1}{4}\right)$ does not exist.

So the stationary point is $(0.25, 1.886)$.

$\dfrac{d^2y}{dx^2} = 16 + \dfrac{1}{x^2}$. When $x = \frac{1}{4}$, $\dfrac{d^2y}{dx^2} = 16 + 16 = 32$. As $32 > 0$, the point is a minimum.

---

## Exercise B (answers p 185)

**1** Differentiate these with respect to $x$.

**(a)** $x^2 + \ln x$      **(b)** $3\ln x - x^3$      **(c)** $\sqrt{x} - 2\ln x$      **(d)** $\ln x + e^x$

**2** Express $\ln(7x^3)$ in the form $\ln a + b\ln x$ and hence differentiate $\ln(7x^3)$.

**3** Find $f'(x)$ given that

**(a)** $f(x) = \ln(6x^2)$    **(b)** $f(x) = \ln(4x^5)$    **(c)** $f(x) = \ln(2\sqrt{x})$    **(d)** $f(x) = \ln\left(3x^{\frac{3}{2}}\right)$

**4** Express $\ln\left(\dfrac{3}{x^2}\right)$ in the form $\ln a - b\ln x$ and hence differentiate $\ln\left(\dfrac{3}{x^2}\right)$.

**5** Find $\dfrac{dy}{dx}$ given that

**(a)** $y = e^x + \ln(2x^3)$   **(b)** $y = \ln\left(\dfrac{3}{x}\right)$    **(c)** $y = \ln\left(x^{\frac{2}{3}}\right)$    **(d)** $y = x^{-\frac{1}{2}} + \ln\left(x^{-\frac{1}{2}}\right)$

**6 (a)** Show that the graph of $y = \ln x - x$ has a stationary point at $x = 1$.

**(b)** Show that the stationary point is a maximum.

**7** Find the stationary point on the graph of $y = x^4 - \frac{1}{4}\ln x$ and determine its type.

## C Differentiating a product of functions (answers p 185)

Suppose that the variables $u$ and $v$ are defined in terms of $x$ by

$$u = x^2 \qquad v = 2x + 1$$

Let $y = uv$.

It is a simple matter to find $\dfrac{dy}{dx}$ in this case, because $y = x^2(2x + 1) = 2x^3 + x^2$.

**C1** (a) Find $\dfrac{dy}{dx}$.

(b) $y$ is the product of $u$ and $v$. Show that $\dfrac{dy}{dx}$ is **not** the product of $\dfrac{du}{dx}$ and $\dfrac{dv}{dx}$.

You can't differentiate the product of two functions by differentiating each one separately and multiplying the results. However, there is a rule for differentiating a product, and this is what we shall now investigate.

Let $u$ and $v$ be two variables that are functions of $x$.
The product $uv$ represents the area $y$ of a rectangle.

Suppose that $x$ increases by a small amount $\delta x$.

As a result, $u$ increases by a small amount $\delta u$, and $v$ by a small amount $\delta v$, and the area $y$ by a small amount $\delta y$.

These diagrams show the rectangle before and after the increases.

The second rectangle can be split up like this:

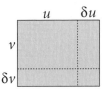

**C2** Show that $\delta y = u\,\delta v + v\,\delta u + \delta u\,\delta v$.

When the equation above is divided throughout by $\delta x$ it becomes

$$\frac{\delta y}{\delta x} = u\frac{\delta v}{\delta x} + v\frac{\delta u}{\delta x} + \frac{\delta u}{\delta x}\delta v$$

Now let $\delta x$ get smaller and smaller.

$\dfrac{\delta y}{\delta x}$ gets closer and closer to $\dfrac{dy}{dx}$. $\dfrac{\delta u}{\delta x}$ gets closer and closer to $\dfrac{du}{dx}$.

$\dfrac{\delta v}{\delta x}$ gets closer and closer to $\dfrac{dv}{dx}$. $\delta v$ gets closer and closer to 0.

So if $y = uv$, then $\dfrac{dy}{dx} = u\dfrac{dv}{dx} + v\dfrac{du}{dx}$. This rule is called the **product rule**.

The rule can also be stated using function notation:

The derivative of $f(x)g(x)$ is $f'(x)g(x) + f(x)g'(x)$.

**C3** Let $u = x^2$ and $v = 2x + 1$, as in question C1.
Use the product rule to find the derivative of $uv$.
Check that the result agrees with the previous one.

**C4** Let $f(x) = x^3$ and $g(x) = x^2 - 3$.

(a) Use the product rule to find the derivative of $f(x)g(x)$.

(b) Find the derivative of $f(x)g(x)$ in a different way by first multiplying $f(x)$ and $g(x)$ and then differentiating. Check that the two results agree.

**C5** Use the product rule to find the derivative of $x^3 e^x$.

**C6** Use the product rule to find $\dfrac{dy}{dx}$ given that $y = x^4 \ln x$.

**C7** Differentiate these with respect to $x$.

(a) $(x^2 - 3x)e^x$        (b) $(x^2 - 3x)\ln x$        (c) $x^{\frac{1}{2}}\ln x$

---

### Example 4

(a) Find the exact values of the coordinates of the stationary points on the graph of $y = x^2 e^x$.

(b) Determine the type of each stationary point.

### Solution

(a) Use the product rule with $u = x^2$ and $v = e^x$.

$$\frac{du}{dx} = 2x, \ \frac{dv}{dx} = e^x, \ \text{so} \ \frac{dy}{dx} = u\frac{dv}{dx} + v\frac{du}{dx} = x^2 e^x + e^x(2x) = (x^2 + 2x)e^x$$

At stationary points, $\dfrac{dy}{dx} = 0$

$\Rightarrow \qquad (x^2 + 2x)e^x = 0$

$\Rightarrow \qquad x(x + 2)e^x = 0 \qquad$ *(factorising $x^2 + 2x$)*

$\Rightarrow \qquad x = 0 \ \text{or} \ x = -2 \qquad$ (because $e^x$ is never 0)

When $x = 0$, $y = 0^2 e^0 = 0$. When $x = -2$, $y = (-2)^2 e^{-2} = 4e^{-2}$.

So the stationary points are $(0, 0)$ and $(-2, 4e^{-2})$.

(b) *To find* $\dfrac{d^2y}{dx^2}$, *you have to differentiate* $\dfrac{dy}{dx}$, *which is* $(x^2 + 2x)e^x$.

Use the product rule with $u = x^2 + 2x$ and $v = e^x$.

$$\frac{d^2y}{dx^2} = u\frac{dv}{dx} + v\frac{du}{dx} = (x^2 + 2x)e^x + e^x(2x + 2) = (x^2 + 4x + 2)e^x$$

When $x = 0$, $\dfrac{d^2y}{dx^2} = 2$. This is greater than 0, so $(0, 0)$ is a minimum.

When $x = -2$, $\dfrac{d^2y}{dx^2} = (4 - 8 + 2)e^{-2}$. This is less than 0, so $(-2, 4e^{-2})$ is a maximum.

---

**Exercise C** (answers p 186)

**1** Differentiate these with respect to $x$.

(a) $x^5 e^x$  (b) $x^{\frac{1}{2}} e^x$  (c) $x^2 \ln x$  (d) $3x e^x$

(e) $e^x \ln x$  (f) $e^x \sqrt[3]{x}$  (g) $x^{-2} \ln x$  (h) $x^{-2} e^x$

**2** Find $f'(x)$ given that

(a) $f(x) = e^x(2x + 3)$  (b) $f(x) = (4x - 1) \ln x$  (c) $f(x) = e^x(x^2 + 1)$

(d) $f(x) = (\sqrt{x} - 1) \ln x$  (e) $f(x) = e^x\left(1 - \dfrac{1}{x}\right)$  (f) $f(x) = e^x(x + \ln x)$

**3** The expression $x^2(x + 1)e^x$ can be rewritten as either $(x^3 + x^2)e^x$ or $x^3 e^x + x^2 e^x$.

(a) Use the product rule to differentiate $(x^3 + x^2)e^x$ with respect to $x$.

(b) Use the product rule to differentiate each of $x^3 e^x$ and $x^2 e^x$ and hence write down the derivative of $x^3 e^x + x^2 e^x$.
Check that the result agrees with (a).

(c) Find the derivative of $x^2(x + 1) \ln x$.

**4 (a)** Find $\dfrac{dy}{dx}$ given that $y = xe^x$.

(b) Show that the graph of $y = xe^x$ has a stationary point at $x = -1$.

(c) Find the $y$-coordinate of this stationary point.

(d) By finding $\dfrac{d^2 y}{dx^2}$, determine the type of this stationary point.

**5 (a)** Given that $f(x) = e^x(x^2 - 7x + 13)$, find $f'(x)$.

(b) Express $f'(x)$ in the form $e^x(x - a)(x - b)$.

(c) Find the values of $x$ for which $f(x)$ has a stationary value.

(d) Determine the type of each stationary value.

**6** You are given that $y = x \ln x \ (x > 0)$.

(a) Find the gradient of the graph of $y = x \ln x$ at the point where $x = e$.

(b) Show that the point on the graph of $y = x \ln x$ where $x = \dfrac{1}{e}$ is a stationary point.

(c) Show that this stationary point is a minimum.

**7 (a)** Given that $y = x^2 \ln x \ (x > 0)$, show that $\dfrac{dy}{dx} = x(1 + 2 \ln x)$.

(b) Hence show that the graph of $y = x^2 \ln x$ has a stationary point at $x = e^{-0.5}$.

(c) Determine the type of this stationary point.

## D Differentiating a quotient (answers p 186)

In the previous section we looked at $\dfrac{dy}{dx}$ where $y$ is the product $uv$ of two functions.

In this section we consider the case where $y$ is the quotient $\dfrac{u}{v}$ of two functions.

The relationship $y = \dfrac{u}{v}$ can be rewritten in product form as $u = yv$.

We can use the product rule to differentiate with respect to $x$:
$$\frac{du}{dx} = y\frac{dv}{dx} + v\frac{dy}{dx}$$

Rearrange this equation to make $\dfrac{dy}{dx}$ the subject:
$$\frac{dy}{dx} = \frac{\dfrac{du}{dx} - y\dfrac{dv}{dx}}{v}$$

Now use the fact that $y = \dfrac{u}{v}$ to replace $y$:
$$= \frac{\dfrac{du}{dx} - \dfrac{u}{v}\left(\dfrac{dv}{dx}\right)}{v}$$

Finally multiply top and bottom by $v$:
$$= \frac{v\dfrac{du}{dx} - u\dfrac{dv}{dx}}{v^2}$$

> **K**
>
> If $y = \dfrac{u}{v}$, then $\dfrac{dy}{dx} = \dfrac{v\dfrac{du}{dx} - u\dfrac{dv}{dx}}{v^2}$. This is called the **quotient rule**.
>
> It can also be written using function notation:
>
> The derivative of $\dfrac{f(x)}{g(x)}$ is $\dfrac{f'(x)g(x) - f(x)g'(x)}{[g(x)]^2}$.

**D1** Use the quotient rule to differentiate each of these.

(a) $y = \dfrac{x^2}{x+1}$  (b) $y = \dfrac{x}{x^3-1}$  (c) $y = \dfrac{\ln x}{x}$  (d) $y = \dfrac{e^x}{x-1}$

---

### Example 5

Given that $y = \dfrac{1+x^2}{1+e^x}$, find $\dfrac{dy}{dx}$.

### Solution

Use the quotient rule with $u = 1 + x^2$ and $v = 1 + e^x$.

$$\frac{du}{dx} = 2x, \quad \frac{dv}{dx} = e^x, \quad \text{so} \quad \frac{dy}{dx} = \frac{v\dfrac{du}{dx} - u\dfrac{dv}{dx}}{v^2} = \frac{(1+e^x)2x - (1+x^2)e^x}{(1+e^x)^2}$$

This can be tidied up by collecting, in the numerator, the terms in $e^x$:

$$\frac{dy}{dx} = \frac{2x + e^x(-x^2 + 2x - 1)}{(1+e^x)^2}$$

---

**Exercise D** (answers p 186)

**1** Differentiate these with respect to $x$.

(a) $\dfrac{x^2}{2x+3}$
(b) $\dfrac{x^3}{x-1}$
(c) $\dfrac{x}{x^2+1}$
(d) $\dfrac{2x}{x^2+x+1}$

(e) $\dfrac{x-1}{x^2-x+1}$
(f) $\dfrac{x}{2x^3-1}$
(g) $\dfrac{x^2}{x^3+1}$
(h) $\dfrac{x^2-1}{x^3+5x+1}$

**2** (a) Use the quotient rule to differentiate $\dfrac{e^x}{x^2}$ with respect to $x$.

(b) The expression $\dfrac{e^x}{x^2}$ can also be written as a product $x^{-2}e^x$.

Use the product rule to differentiate $x^{-2}e^x$ and check that the result agrees with that of (a).

**3** Find $f'(x)$ given that

(a) $f(x) = \dfrac{e^x}{x+1}$
(b) $f(x) = \dfrac{e^x}{x^2+1}$
(c) $f(x) = \dfrac{x^2}{e^x+1}$

(d) $f(x) = \dfrac{\ln x}{x-1}$
(e) $f(x) = \dfrac{\ln x}{x^2+1}$
(f) $f(x) = \dfrac{e^x}{\ln x}$

**4** (a) Given that $y = \dfrac{x}{x+1}$, show that $\dfrac{dy}{dx} = \dfrac{1}{(x+1)^2}$.

(b) Hence show that there are no stationary points on the graph of $y = \dfrac{x}{x+1}$.

**5** (a) Given that $f(x) = \dfrac{x+1}{(x^2+3)}$, show that $f'(x) = \dfrac{-(x-1)(x+3)}{(x^2+3)^2}$.

(b) Hence find the values of $x$ for which $f(x)$ is stationary.

**6** Given that $f(x) = \dfrac{x}{(x^2+4)}$, find the values of $x$ for which $f'(x) = 0$.

**7** Find the coordinates of the stationary point on the graph of $y = \dfrac{e^x}{x-2}$.

**8** (a) Given that $y = \dfrac{\ln x}{x}$ $(x>0)$, find  (i) $\dfrac{dy}{dx}$  (ii) $\dfrac{d^2y}{dx^2}$

(b) Find the coordinates of the stationary point on the graph of $y = \dfrac{\ln x}{x}$.

(c) Determine the type of this stationary point.

**9** Show that the graph of $y = \dfrac{x^2}{\ln x}$ $(x>0)$ has just one stationary point whose coordinates are $(e^{0.5}, 2e)$.

## E Differentiating sin x, cos x and tan x (answers p 187)

Here is the graph of $y = \sin x$, where $x$ is in radians.

The diagram below shows a close-up of the graph as it passes through the origin $O$.

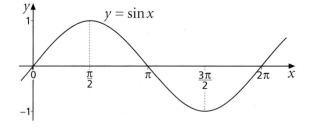

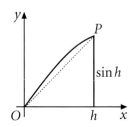

The coordinates of the point $P$ on the graph are $(h, \sin h)$, where $h$ is small.

The gradient of $OP$ is $\dfrac{\sin h}{h}$.

**E1** Find the value of $\dfrac{\sin h}{h}$ when $h = 0.1, 0.01$ and $0.001$.

(Make sure your calculator is set to work in radians.)

What conclusion do you draw about the gradient of $y = \sin x$ at $x = 0$?

**D**

**E2** (a) What is the gradient of $y = \sin x$ at each of these points?

$$x = \frac{\pi}{2} \qquad x = \pi \qquad x = \frac{3\pi}{2} \qquad x = 2\pi$$

(b) From the graph above, you can see that between $x = 0$ and $x = \dfrac{\pi}{2}$ the gradient of $y = \sin x$ decreases from 1 to 0, slowly at first but then more rapidly.

Sketch the graph of the gradient $\dfrac{dy}{dx}$ between $x = 0$ and $x = \dfrac{\pi}{2}$ and extend the sketch graph up to $x = 2\pi$.

What do you think its equation is?

**E3** Here is the graph of $y = \cos x$.

Sketch the graph of $\dfrac{dy}{dx}$.

What do you think its equation is?

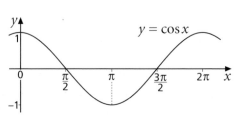

It can be proved, by methods beyond the scope of this book, that

The derivative of $\sin x$ is $\cos x$.

The derivative of $\cos x$ is $-\sin x$.

An important reason for using radians is that they give simple results like these.

**E4** Write down the derivative of each of these.

(a) $\sin x + 3x + x^2$  (b) $\sqrt{x} - \cos x$  (c) $3e^x + 4\sin x$  (d) $5\ln x - 2\cos x$

To differentiate $\tan x$, we use the fact that $\tan x = \dfrac{\sin x}{\cos x}$.

**E5** (a) Given that $y = \tan x = \dfrac{\sin x}{\cos x}$, use the quotient rule to show that $\dfrac{dy}{dx} = \dfrac{\cos^2 x + \sin^2 x}{\cos^2 x}$.

(b) Explain why this expression for $\dfrac{dy}{dx}$ is equivalent to $\sec^2 x$.

**Ⓚ** The derivative of $\tan x$ is $\sec^2 x$.

**E6** What happens to $\sec^2 x$ as $x$ gets closer and closer to $\dfrac{\pi}{2}$?
How is this related to the behaviour of the graph of $y = \tan x$?

---

**Example 6**

Find $f'(x)$ given that  (a) $f(x) = e^x \sin x$  (b) $f(x) = \dfrac{\tan x}{x^2 + 1}$

**Solution**

(a) Use the product rule.  $f'(x) = e^x \cos x + (\sin x)e^x = e^x(\cos x + \sin x)$

(b) Use the quotient rule.  $f'(x) = \dfrac{(x^2 + 1)\sec^2 x - (\tan x)2x}{(x^2 + 1)^2} = \dfrac{(x^2 + 1)\sec^2 x - 2x\tan x}{(x^2 + 1)^2}$

---

**Exercise E** (answers p 188)

**1** Differentiate these with respect to $x$.

(a) $\sin x + \cos x$  (b) $\sin x - x^2$  (c) $3\sin x - 2\cos x$  (d) $x + 2\tan x$

**2** Differentiate these with respect to $x$.

(a) $3x\cos x$  (b) $\dfrac{\cos x}{x}$  (c) $\dfrac{\sin x}{x^2}$  (d) $e^x \tan x$

**3** Given that $f(x) = \dfrac{\sin x}{x}$, show that $f'(x) = \dfrac{\cos x}{x} - \dfrac{\sin x}{x^2}$.

**4** (a) Find $f'(x)$ given that $f(x) = 3\sin x + 4\cos x$.

(b) Show that if $f'(x) = 0$, then $\tan x = 0.75$ and find the values of $x$ in the interval $0 \le x \le 2\pi$ for which $f'(x) = 0$.

**5** Given that $f(x) = \dfrac{\cos x}{x^2}$, show that $f'\left(\dfrac{\pi}{2}\right) = -\dfrac{4}{\pi^2}$.

**6** Given that $f(x) = \sin x - \tan x$, find the values of $x$ in the interval $0 \le x \le 2\pi$ for which $f'(x) = 0$.

**7** Given that $y = \cot x = \dfrac{\cos x}{\sin x}$, use the quotient rule to show that $\dfrac{dy}{dx} = -\text{cosec}^2 x$.

## F Differentiating a function of a function (answers p 188)

$y = \sin(x^2 - 3)$ is an example of a function of a function.

If we let $u = x^2 - 3$, then $y = \sin u$. So $y$ is a function of $u$, which is itself a function of $x$.

The general case, where $u$ and $y$ are any functions, can be pictured like this:

Input $x \rightarrow u \rightarrow y$

Suppose $x$ is increased by a small quantity $\delta x$ and that, as a result, $u$ is increased by $\delta u$ and $y$ by $\delta y$.

The following relationship can be seen to be true by 'cancelling out' $\delta u$: $\dfrac{\delta y}{\delta x} = \dfrac{\delta y}{\delta u} \times \dfrac{\delta u}{\delta x}$

As $\delta x$ gets smaller and smaller, $\dfrac{\delta y}{\delta x}$ gets closer and closer to $\dfrac{dy}{dx}$, $\dfrac{\delta y}{\delta u}$ to $\dfrac{dy}{du}$ and $\dfrac{\delta u}{\delta x}$ to $\dfrac{du}{dx}$.

So we get the following relationship:

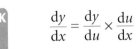

$$\frac{dy}{dx} = \frac{dy}{du} \times \frac{du}{dx}$$

This relationship is called the **chain rule**.

**F1** In the example at the top of this page, $y = \sin u$ where $u = x^2 - 3$.

    **(a)** Find $\dfrac{dy}{du}$.

    **(b)** Find $\dfrac{du}{dx}$.

    **(c)** Use the chain rule to show that $\dfrac{dy}{dx} = 2x \cos(x^2 - 3)$.

**F2** The function $y = \sin^2 x$ can be written as $y = u^2$, where $u = \sin x$.

    Find $\dfrac{dy}{dx}$.

**F3** The function $y = \sqrt{x^2 + 1}$ can be written as $y = u^{\frac{1}{2}}$, where $u = x^2 + 1$.

    Show that $\dfrac{dy}{dx} = \dfrac{x}{\sqrt{x^2 + 1}}$.

---

### Example 7

Find $\dfrac{dy}{dx}$ given that $y = \ln(1 + x^2)$.

### Solution

Let $u = 1 + x^2$, so that $y = \ln u$. So $\dfrac{du}{dx} = 2x$ and $\dfrac{dy}{du} = \dfrac{1}{u}$.

$$\frac{dy}{dx} = \frac{dy}{du} \times \frac{du}{dx} = \frac{1}{u} \times 2x = \frac{2x}{1 + x^2}$$

---

The simplest type of 'function of a function' is where the 'intermediate' function $u$ is a linear function, such as $u = 2x + 3$.

For this type, $\dfrac{du}{dx}$ is just a number.

After some practice you should find that you can do some of the working in your head, as shown in the next example.

---

### Example 8

Find $\dfrac{dy}{dx}$ given that $y = \sin(3x + 1)$.

### Solution

Full working:

Let $u = 3x + 1$, so $y = \sin u$.

$$\frac{dy}{dx} = \frac{dy}{du} \times \frac{du}{dx} = \cos u \times 3 = 3 \cos(3x + 1)$$

Working in head:

*Derivative of* $\sin$ *is* $\cos$.

*Derivative of* $3x + 1$ *is* 3.

So $\dfrac{dy}{dx} = 3 \cos(3x + 1)$

---

**F4** Find the derivative of each of these.

(a) $\cos 2x$      (b) $e^{-3x}$      (c) $\ln(6x + 1)$      (d) $\sqrt{5 - 2x}$

(e) $\dfrac{1}{3 + 4x}$      (f) $\sin(5x - 2)$      (g) $(3x - 2)^{\frac{2}{3}}$      (h) $\dfrac{1}{\sqrt{1 + 4x}}$

It is worth learning, as a commonly occurring special case, that

**K**    The derivative of $f(ax)$ is $af'(ax)$.

For example, the derivative of $\sin 4x$ is $4 \cos 4x$, the derivative of $e^{-5x}$ is $-5e^{-5x}$, and so on.

The chain rule can be extended.

For example, the function $y = \sqrt{\sin(x^2)}$ can be broken down as $y = \sqrt{u}$, $u = \sin v$, $v = x^2$.

The chain rule is then $\dfrac{dy}{dx} = \dfrac{dy}{du} \times \dfrac{du}{dv} \times \dfrac{dv}{dx}$.

**F5** Use the extended chain rule to differentiate $y = \sqrt{\sin(x^2)}$.

The chain rule (with one 'intermediate' function) can be expressed in function notation as: The derivative of $f(g(x))$ is $f'(g(x))\,g'(x)$.

### Exercise F (answers p 188)

**1** Differentiate these with respect to $x$.

(a) $\sin(3x - 2)$      (b) $\cos(5x + 1)$      (c) $\sin(3 - 2x)$      (d) $\cos\left(\frac{1}{2}x\right)$

(e) $\ln(3x + 1)$      (f) $\sqrt{5x - 1}$      (g) $(2x + 1)^7$      (h) $\tan(4x)$

(i) $(2x + 1)^{\frac{1}{3}}$      (j) $\tan(3x + 2)$      (k) $e^{5x - 2}$      (l) $\cos\left(1 - \frac{1}{2}x\right)$

**2** If $y = \cos^2 x$ then $y = u^2$ where $u = \cos x$.

Find $\dfrac{dy}{du}$ and $\dfrac{du}{dx}$ and use the chain rule to find $\dfrac{dy}{dx}$.

**3** If $y = \ln(\sin x)$ then $y = \ln u$ where $u = \sin x$.

Find $\dfrac{dy}{du}$ and $\dfrac{du}{dx}$ and use the chain rule to find $\dfrac{dy}{dx}$.

**4** Differentiate $y = e^{\sin x}$ by letting $u = \sin x$ and using the chain rule.

**5** Find $\dfrac{dy}{dx}$ given that

(a) $y = \sin(e^x)$    (b) $y = (\ln x)^2$    (c) $y = \tan^2 x$    (d) $y = (x^2 + 1)^5$

**6** (a) If $y = \operatorname{cosec} x = \dfrac{1}{\sin x}$, then $y = u^{-1}$ where $u = \sin x$.

Find $\dfrac{dy}{du}$ and $\dfrac{du}{dx}$ and use the chain rule to show that $\dfrac{dy}{dx} = -\dfrac{\cos x}{\sin^2 x} = -\operatorname{cosec} x \cot x$.

(b) If $y = \sec x = \dfrac{1}{\cos x}$, show that $\dfrac{dy}{dx} = \sec x \tan x$.

**7** Find $f'(x)$ given that

(a) $f(x) = e^{\tan x}$    (b) $f(x) = \sqrt{\ln x}$    (c) $f(x) = \dfrac{1}{\ln x}$    (d) $f(x) = \sin\left(\sqrt{x}\right)$

**8** Find $\dfrac{dy}{dx}$ given that

(a) $y = \ln(x^2 + 1)$    (b) $y = (\ln x)^2$    (c) $y = e^{x^2}$    (d) $y = e^{\tan x}$

(e) $y = \sin(1 - x^2)$    (f) $y = \sqrt{1 + x^2}$    (g) $y = \dfrac{1}{1 + x^2}$    (h) $y = \dfrac{1}{(1 + x^2)^3}$

**9** (a) Given that $y = \dfrac{1}{\sqrt{1 - x^2}}$, show that $\dfrac{dy}{dx} = \dfrac{x}{(1 - x^2)^{\frac{3}{2}}}$.

(b) Find the gradient of the graph of $y$ at the point where $x = 0.6$.

## G Selecting methods (answers p 189)

When you differentiate a function you need to decide which rule to apply:

Product rule        Quotient rule        Chain rule

The special case of the chain rule, where you have a function of $(ax + b)$, is very common and is worth learning separately:

**K**    Derivative of $f(ax + b) = af'(ax + b)$

**G1** Which rule would you use if you had to differentiate each of these?

(a) $\tan(2x - 1)$    (b) $\ln(\tan x)$    (c) $\dfrac{\ln x}{\tan x}$    (d) $\ln x \tan x$

You may need to use more than one of the rules.

For example, if $y = e^x \sin 3x$, then you can use the product rule with $u = e^x$ and $v = \sin 3x$. To use the product rule you need to find $\dfrac{du}{dx}$ and $\dfrac{dv}{dx}$.

Now $\sin 3x$ is itself a function of a function. Its derivative is $3\cos 3x$.

So we have $\dfrac{dy}{dx} = u\dfrac{dv}{dx} + v\dfrac{du}{dx} = e^x(3\cos 3x) + (\sin 3x)e^x = e^x(3\cos 3x + \sin 3x)$.

**G2** Given that $y = e^{2x}\sin x$, let $u = e^{2x}$ and $v = \sin x$.

    **(a)** Find $\dfrac{du}{dx}$ and $\dfrac{dv}{dx}$.        **(b)** Find $\dfrac{dy}{dx}$.

**G3** Given that $y = \dfrac{e^x}{\sin 4x}$, let $u = e^x$ and $v = \sin 4x$.

    Find $\dfrac{du}{dx}$ and $\dfrac{dv}{dx}$ and hence find $\dfrac{dy}{dx}$.

**G4** Given that $y = e^{2x}\cos 3x$, let $u = e^{2x}$ and $v = \cos 3x$.

    Find $\dfrac{du}{dx}$ and $\dfrac{dv}{dx}$ and hence find $\dfrac{dy}{dx}$.

For a function like $x^2e^x + 3\ln x$ you can use the product rule for the first term $x^2e^x$ and then add the derivative of the second term $3\ln x$.

**G5** Differentiate $x^2e^x + 3\ln x$.

Students sometimes have difficulty deciding when to use the product rule and when to use the chain rule.

    **G6** Differentiate      **(a)** $\sin(x^2 + 1)$      **(b)** $(x^2 + 1)\sin x$

---

## Example 9

Find the gradient of the graph of $y = x^2e^{-3x}$ at the point where $x = 1$.

## Solution

$y$ is the product of the two functions $x^2$ and $e^{-3x}$.

Let $u = x^2$ and $v = e^{-3x}$. Then $\dfrac{du}{dx} = 2x$ and $\dfrac{dv}{dx} = -3e^{-3x}$.

So $\dfrac{dy}{dx} = u\dfrac{dv}{dx} + v\dfrac{du}{dx} = x^2(-3e^{-3x}) + (e^{-3x})2x = e^{-3x}(-3x^2 + 2x)$.

When $x = 1$, $\dfrac{dy}{dx} = e^{-3}(-3 + 2) = -e^{-3}$.

---

## Exercise G (answers p 189)

**1** Find $\dfrac{dy}{dx}$ given that

(a) $y = x^2(e^x + 1)$  (b) $y = \ln(x^2 - 2)$  (c) $y = \ln(\cos x)$  (d) $y = \ln x \sin x$

(e) $y = \sin(\ln x)$  (f) $y = \dfrac{e^x}{5x + 1}$  (g) $y = \dfrac{e^{-x}}{2x + 1}$  (h) $y = \dfrac{e^{-2x}}{1 - x}$

**2** Find $f'(x)$ given that

(a) $f(x) = e^x \sin 3x$  (b) $f(x) = e^{-x} \cos 3x$  (c) $f(x) = e^{-2x} \tan x$

(d) $f(x) = \sin 3x \cos 2x$  (e) $f(x) = \tan(2 - 3x)$  (f) $f(x) = \dfrac{\ln x}{1 - 2x}$

**3 (a)** Differentiate $\dfrac{\sin 2x}{x}$ with respect to $x$.

**(b)** Show that the value of the gradient of the curve with equation $y = \dfrac{\sin 2x}{x}$ at the point where $x = \dfrac{\pi}{2}$ is $-\dfrac{4}{\pi}$.

**4** Find the gradient of each of these curves at the point where $x = 0$.

(a) $y = xe^{2x} + \sin x$  (b) $y = (2x + 1)e^{-x}$  (c) $y = \tan x - \sin 2x$

---

## Key points

- The derivative of $e^x$ is $e^x$.  (p 90)

- The derivative of $\ln x$ is $\dfrac{1}{x}$.  (p 91)

- $\dfrac{dy}{dx} = \dfrac{1}{\frac{dx}{dy}}$  (p 91)

- If $y = uv$, then $\dfrac{dy}{dx} = u\dfrac{dv}{dx} + v\dfrac{du}{dx}$ (product rule)  (p 93)

- If $y = \dfrac{u}{v}$, then $\dfrac{dy}{dx} = \dfrac{v\dfrac{du}{dx} - u\dfrac{dv}{dx}}{v^2}$ (quotient rule)  (p 96)

- The derivative of $\sin x$ is $\cos x$.
  The derivative of $\cos x$ is $-\sin x$.  (p 98)

- The derivative of $\tan x$ is $\sec^2 x$.  (p 99)

- $\dfrac{dy}{dx} = \dfrac{dy}{du} \times \dfrac{du}{dx}$ (chain rule)  (p 100)

- The derivative of $f(ax)$ is $af'(ax)$.
  The derivative of $f(ax + b)$ is $af'(ax + b)$.  (pp 101–102)

## Mixed questions (answers p 189)

**1** The volume of oil, $V\,\text{m}^3$, in a tank changes with time $t$ hours $(1 \le t \le T)$ according to the formula

$$V = 32 - 10\ln t$$

where $T$ represents the time when the tank is empty of oil.

(a) State the volume of oil in the tank when $t = 1$.

(b) Find the rate of change, in $\text{m}^3$ per hour, of the volume of oil in the tank at the time when $t = 8$, interpreting the sign of your answer.

(c) Determine the value of $T$.  AQA 2001

**2** Given that $f(x) = e^{3x} - \dfrac{2}{x}\ (x > 0)$,

(a) find $f'(x)$

(b) show that $f(x)$ is an increasing function

**3** Find the gradient of the curve $y = \dfrac{\tan x}{x + 2}$ at the point where $x = 0$.

**4** Differentiate these with respect to $x$.

(a) $\dfrac{e^{2x}}{x - 1}$  (b) $\ln(3x - 2)$  (c) $(3x - 2)\ln x$  (d) $(3x - 1)^4$

**5** A curve has equation

$$y = x^2 - 3x + \ln x + 2, \ x > 0$$

(a) (i) Find $\dfrac{dy}{dx}$.

(ii) Hence show that the gradient of the curve at the point where $x = 2$ is $\frac{3}{2}$.

(b) (i) Show that the $x$-coordinates of the stationary points of the curve satisfy the equation

$$2x^2 - 3x + 1 = 0$$

(ii) Hence find the coordinates of each of the stationary points.

(iii) Find $\dfrac{d^2y}{dx^2}$.

(iv) Find the value of $\dfrac{d^2y}{dx^2}$ at each of the stationary points.

(v) Hence show that the $y$-coordinate of the maximum point is $\frac{3}{4} - \ln 2$.  AQA 2002

**6** (a) Find the $x$-coordinates of the stationary points on the graph of $y = e^x(x^2 - 3x - 9)$.

(b) Determine the type of each stationary point.

**7** Show that the graphs of $y = x^2 - 5x$, $y = \dfrac{1}{x^2 - 5x}$ and $y = \ln(x^2 - 5x)$

all have a stationary point at the same value of $x$ and find this value of $x$.

## Test yourself (answers p 190)

**1** Find the coordinates of the point on the graph of $y = 5x - 4\ln x$ where the gradient is 3.

**2** Differentiate these with respect to $x$.

   **(a)** $\sin(3x - 2)$    **(b)** $e^{5x}$       **(c)** $\tan(4 - x)$       **(d)** $\ln(7 - 2x)$

**3** Differentiate these with respect to $x$.

   **(a)** $e^{-x}\sin x$    **(b)** $\dfrac{e^x}{\cos x}$    **(c)** $(x^2 - 7)^9$    **(d)** $\dfrac{x^2}{\tan x}$

**4** Find the gradient of the graph of $y = x\sin 2x$ at the point where $x = \dfrac{\pi}{4}$.

**5** It is given that $y = e^x(x^2 - 8)$.

   **(a)** Find $\dfrac{dy}{dx}$.

   **(b)** Find the values of $x$ for which the value of $y$ is stationary.

   **(c)** Show that $\dfrac{d^2y}{dx^2} = e^x(x^2 + 4x - 6)$.

   **(d)** Hence determine whether each of the two stationary values of $y$ is a maximum or a minimum.

**6** It is given that $y = \ln x - 2x^2 + 3, \; x > 0$.

   **(a)** Find $\dfrac{dy}{dx}$.

   **(b)** Verify that $y$ has a stationary value when $x = \frac{1}{2}$.

   **(c)** Find the value of $\dfrac{d^2y}{dx^2}$ when $x = \frac{1}{2}$.

   **(d)** Hence determine whether this stationary value is a maximum or a minimum.

AQA 2003

**7** Find $\dfrac{dy}{dx}$ for each of the following cases.

   **(a)** $y = e^{2x}\sin 3x$            **(b)** $y = (2x + 1)^5$       AQA 2001

**8** Given that $y = x^3\ln x$

   **(a) (i)** find $\dfrac{dy}{dx}$

      **(ii)** show that the curve has a stationary point at $x = e^{-\frac{1}{3}}$

      **(iii)** find the $y$-coordinate of the stationary point

   **(b) (i)** find $\dfrac{d^2y}{dx^2}$

      **(ii)** find the value of $\dfrac{d^2y}{dx^2}$ at the stationary point

      **(iii)** hence determine whether the stationary point is a maximum or a minimum

# 7 Integration

In this chapter you will learn how to

- integrate $e^x$, $\frac{1}{x}$, $\sin x$ and $\cos x$

- integrate by substitution and by parts

- find integrals of the forms $\int \dfrac{f'(x)}{f(x)}\,dx$, $\int \dfrac{1}{a^2+x^2}\,dx$, $\int \dfrac{1}{\sqrt{a^2-x^2}}\,dx$

---

### Key points from Core 1 and Core 2

- Integration is the reverse of differentiation.

- $\int x^n\,dx = \dfrac{x^{n+1}}{n+1} + c \quad (n \neq -1)$

- The definite integral $\int_a^b f(x)\,dx$ gives the area under the graph of $y = f(x)$ between $x = a$ and $x = b$.

  Areas below the $x$-axis are negative.

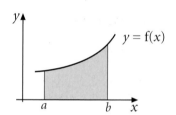

---

## A Integrating $e^x$, $\sin x$ and $\cos x$ (answers p 191)

The indefinite integrals of $e^x$, $\sin x$ and $\cos x$ can be found by 'reversing' the corresponding facts about their derivatives.

Because the derivative of $e^x$ is $e^x$, the indefinite integral of $e^x$ is $e^x + c$.

Because the derivative of $\sin x$ is $\cos x$, the indefinite integral of $\cos x$ is $\sin x + c$.

**A1** (a) Write down the derivative of $\cos x$.

　　(b) Hence write down the indefinite integral of $\sin x$.

**A2** Complete the calculation of each area below, giving exact values.

(a)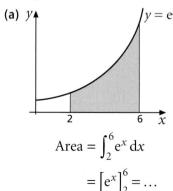

$$\text{Area} = \int_2^6 e^x\,dx$$
$$= \left[e^x\right]_2^6 = \dots$$

(b)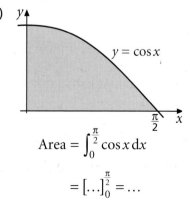

$$\text{Area} = \int_0^{\frac{\pi}{2}} \cos x\,dx$$
$$= \left[\dots\right]_0^{\frac{\pi}{2}} = \dots$$

The indefinite integrals of functions like $\sin 2x$, $e^{3x}$, and so on can be found by 'thinking backwards'.

**A3** (a) Write down the derivative of $\sin 2x$.

(b) Hence find the indefinite integral of      (i)   $2\cos 2x$      (ii)   $\cos 2x$

**A4** (a) Write down the derivative of $\cos 5x$.

(b) Hence find the indefinite integral of      (i)   $-5\sin 5x$      (ii)   $\sin 5x$

**A5** (a) Write down the derivative of $e^{2x}$.

(b) Hence find the indefinite integral of      (i)   $2e^{2x}$      (ii)   $e^{2x}$

The results obtained so far can be summarised as follows:

$$\int e^{ax}\,dx = \frac{1}{a}e^{ax} + c \qquad \int \cos ax\,dx = \frac{1}{a}\sin ax + c \qquad \int \sin ax\,dx = -\frac{1}{a}\cos ax + c$$

**A6** (a) Write down the indefinite integral of $e^{4x}$.

(b) Show that $\displaystyle\int_0^{0.5} e^{4x}\,dx = \frac{e^2 - 1}{4}$.

**A7** Find      (a) $\displaystyle\int_0^{0.1} e^{5x}\,dx$      (b) $\displaystyle\int_0^{\frac{\pi}{4}} \cos 2x\,dx$      (c) $\displaystyle\int_{\frac{\pi}{4}}^{\frac{\pi}{2}} \sin 2x\,dx$

---

**Example 1**

Find the area under the graph of $y = 5 + 2\sin 3x$ between $x = 0$ and $x = \frac{1}{6}\pi$.

**Solution**

$$\begin{aligned}
\text{Area} &= \int_0^{\frac{1}{6}\pi}(5 + 2\sin 3x)\,dx = \left[5x + 2\left(-\tfrac{1}{3}\cos 3x\right)\right]_0^{\frac{1}{6}\pi} \\
&= \left(\tfrac{5}{6}\pi - \tfrac{2}{3}\cos\tfrac{1}{2}\pi\right) - \left(5\times 0 - \tfrac{2}{3}\cos 0\right) \\
&= \left(\tfrac{5}{6}\pi - 0\right) - \left(0 - \tfrac{2}{3}\right) = \tfrac{5}{6}\pi + \tfrac{2}{3}
\end{aligned}$$

---

**Exercise A** (answers p 191)

**1** (a) Write down the indefinite integral of $e^{3x}$.

(b) Find

(i) $\displaystyle\int_0^1 e^{3x}\,dx$      (ii) $\displaystyle\int_0^2\left(e^{3x} - 1\right)dx$      (iii) $\displaystyle\int_1^2\left(e^{3x} - x\right)dx$

**2** (a) Write down the indefinite integral of $\cos 4x$.

(b) Find

(i) $\displaystyle\int_0^{\frac{1}{8}\pi}\cos 4x\,dx$      (ii) $\displaystyle\int_{-\frac{1}{8}\pi}^{\frac{1}{8}\pi}(1 - \cos 4x)\,dx$

**3** Find the following indefinite integrals.

(a) $\displaystyle\int(2\cos 3x - 5e^{2x})\,dx$      (b) $\displaystyle\int(4\cos 5x + 5\sin 4x)\,dx$      (c) $\displaystyle\int(e^{-x} + e^{-2x})\,dx$

**4** Find the following indefinite integrals.

(a) $\int (x^2 + e^{3x})\,dx$

(b) $\int (x - \sin 4x)\,dx$

(c) $\int \left(e^{-x} + \dfrac{1}{x^2}\right)dx$

(d) $\int \left(\sin 5x - \sqrt{x}\right)dx$

(e) $\int (e^{2x} + \sin 2x)\,dx$

(f) $\int \left(\cos 3x - \dfrac{1}{x^3}\right)dx$

**5** Find each of the following definite integrals.

(a) $\int_0^2 (3x - e^{3x})\,dx$

(b) $\int_0^\pi \left(x^2 + \sin\tfrac{1}{2}x\right)dx$

(c) $\int_{-\pi}^\pi \left(2 - 3\cos\tfrac{1}{2}x\right)dx$

(d) $\int_0^4 (e^{-2x} + 2x)\,dx$

(e) $\int_0^4 (x^3 - e^{-x})\,dx$

(f) $\int_0^{\frac{\pi}{2}} (2x - \sin 2x)\,dx$

**6** Find the area under the graph of $y = x^2 - e^{-2x}$ between $x = 1$ and $x = 3$.

**7** Find the area under the graph of $y = \sqrt{x} + e^{\frac{1}{2}x}$ between $x = 1$ and $x = 4$.

**8** Show that if $\int_0^k e^{-\frac{1}{4}x}\,dx = 1$ then $k = 4\ln\tfrac{4}{3}$.

## B Integrating $\dfrac{1}{x}$ (answers p 191)

At first sight it would appear that because the derivative of $\ln x$ is $\dfrac{1}{x}$, then the indefinite integral of $\dfrac{1}{x}$ should be $\ln x + c$.

However, $\ln x$ is defined only for positive values of $x$ and it looks as though there is no indefinite integral for $\dfrac{1}{x}$ when $x$ is negative.

But although $\ln x$ is not defined for negative $x$, $\ln(-x)$ is defined, because $-x$ is positive when $x$ is negative.

If $y = \ln(-x)$, then by the chain rule $\dfrac{dy}{dx} = -\dfrac{1}{-x} = \dfrac{1}{x}$.

So when $x$ is negative, the indefinite integral of $\dfrac{1}{x}$ is $\ln(-x) + c$.

This can be confirmed by finding areas under the graph of $y = \dfrac{1}{x}$.

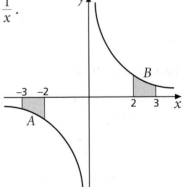

Area $A = \int_{-3}^{-2} \dfrac{1}{x}\,dx = \left[\ln(-x)\right]_{-3}^{-2} = \ln 2 - \ln 3$

Area $B = \int_2^3 \dfrac{1}{x}\,dx = \left[\ln x\right]_2^3 = \ln 3 - \ln 2$

As expected, $A = \ln 2 - \ln 3 = -(\ln 3 - \ln 2) = -B$.

The two statements $\int \dfrac{1}{x} dx = \ln x + c \qquad (x > 0)$

$$\int \dfrac{1}{x} dx = \ln(-x) + c \quad (x < 0)$$

can be combined into a single statement using the modulus function:

  $\int \dfrac{1}{x} dx = \ln|x| + c \quad (x \neq 0)$

Notice the restriction $x \neq 0$. It means that it is impossible to find the 'area' under $y = \dfrac{1}{x}$ between a negative and a positive value of $x$.

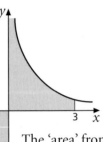

The 'area' from −2 to 3 is not defined as there is a discontinuity at $x = 0$.

**B1** Find

(a) $\displaystyle\int_1^5 \dfrac{1}{x} dx$    (b) $\displaystyle\int_{-4}^{-2} \dfrac{1}{x} dx$    (c) $\displaystyle\int_2^5 \left(3 + \dfrac{1}{x}\right) dx$

**B2** Find $\displaystyle\int \dfrac{1}{3x} dx$ by rewriting it as $\dfrac{1}{3}\displaystyle\int \dfrac{1}{x} dx$.

**B3** (a) Differentiate $\ln(2x + 1)$ using the chain rule.

(b) Hence show that $\displaystyle\int \dfrac{1}{2x + 1} dx = \tfrac{1}{2}\ln|2x + 1| + c$.

**B4** (a) Differentiate $\ln(5x - 2)$ using the chain rule.

(b) Hence find $\displaystyle\int \dfrac{1}{5x - 2} dx$.

Integrals of the form $\displaystyle\int \dfrac{1}{ax + b} dx$ can be found by 'thinking backwards' from $\ln(ax + b)$.

If you differentiate $\ln(ax + b)$, you get $\dfrac{a}{ax + b}$. It follows that

  $\displaystyle\int \dfrac{1}{ax + b} dx = \dfrac{1}{a}\ln|ax + b| + c$.

---

**Example 2**

Find $\displaystyle\int_2^5 \left(3 - \dfrac{2}{x}\right) dx$.

**Solution**

$$\int_2^5 \left(3 - \dfrac{2}{x}\right) dx = \left[3x - 2\ln|x|\right]_2^5$$

$$= (15 - 2\ln 5) - (6 - 2\ln 2)$$
$$= 9 - 2(\ln 5 - \ln 2)$$
$$= 9 - 2\ln \tfrac{5}{2} \qquad \textit{The last step uses the fact that } \ln a - \ln b = \ln \dfrac{a}{b}.$$

---

## Example 3

Find $\displaystyle\int_1^3 \frac{x^2+1}{x}\,dx$ .

### Solution

*First rewrite the expression as the sum of two separate fractions:* $\displaystyle\frac{x^2+1}{x} = \frac{x^2}{x} + \frac{1}{x} = x + \frac{1}{x}$

$$\int_1^3 \frac{x^2+1}{x}\,dx = \int_1^3\left(x+\frac{1}{x}\right)dx = \left[\tfrac{1}{2}x^2 + \ln|x|\right]_1^3$$

$$= \left(\tfrac{9}{2}+\ln 3\right)-\left(\tfrac{1}{2}+\ln 1\right) = 4+\ln 3$$

## Exercise B (answers p 191)

**1** Find the following indefinite integrals.

(a) $\displaystyle\int\left(1+x-\frac{1}{x}\right)dx$

(b) $\displaystyle\int\left(e^{2x}+\frac{2}{x}\right)dx$

(c) $\displaystyle\int\left(\sin 6x - \frac{1}{2x}\right)dx$

(d) $\displaystyle\int\left(\frac{1}{x}+\sqrt{x}\right)dx$

(e) $\displaystyle\int\left(\frac{1}{x}+\frac{1}{\sqrt{x}}\right)dx$

(f) $\displaystyle\int\left(\cos 4x + \frac{1}{4x}\right)dx$

(g) $\displaystyle\int\left(\frac{5}{x}+e^{-3x}\right)dx$

(h) $\displaystyle\int\left(1+\frac{1}{x}+\frac{1}{x^2}+\frac{1}{x^3}\right)dx$

(i) $\displaystyle\int\frac{1}{4x-1}\,dx$

**2 (a)** Find the exact value of the area enclosed by the curve with equation $y = \dfrac{4}{x}$, the x-axis and the lines $x = 2$ and $x = 6$.

**(b)** Show that the line $x = 2\sqrt{3}$ bisects this area.

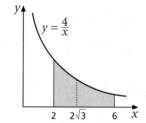

**3** Find the exact value of each of these definite integrals.

(a) $\displaystyle\int_3^9 \frac{1}{2x}\,dx$

(b) $\displaystyle\int_1^4\left(\sqrt{x}-\frac{1}{x}\right)dx$

(c) $\displaystyle\int_1^2\left(e^{-3x}-\frac{1}{3x}\right)dx$

(d) $\displaystyle\int_2^8\left(x^2+\frac{4}{x}\right)dx$

(e) $\displaystyle\int_4^9\left(\frac{1}{\sqrt{x}}-\frac{3}{2x}\right)dx$

(f) $\displaystyle\int_0^1 \frac{1}{3x+2}\,dx$

**4 (a)** Write $\dfrac{1+x}{x^2}$ as the sum of two fractions.

**(b)** Hence find $\displaystyle\int_1^3 \frac{1+x}{x^2}\,dx$ .

**5** Find $\displaystyle\int_1^3 \frac{1+x^2}{x^3}\,dx$ .

**6** The curve $y = 6 - \dfrac{2}{x}$ crosses the x-axis at the point $A$.

**(a)** Find the x-coordinate of $A$.

**(b)** Find the shaded area bounded by the curve, the x-axis and the line $x = 1$.

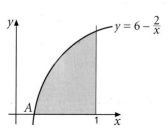

## C Integration by substitution (answers p 192)

The integral $\int 2x(x^2 + 1)^5 \, dx$ could be done by multiplying out $2x(x^2 + 1)^5$, but this would be very time-consuming.

It is easier to introduce a new variable $u$ such that $u = x^2 + 1$.

All the other parts of the integral, including $dx$, must now be rewritten in terms of $u$. We shall deal with $dx$ first.

By differentiating $u = x^2 + 1$ we get $\dfrac{du}{dx} = 2x$.

Up to now we have treated the symbol $\dfrac{du}{dx}$ as a single symbol, not as a quantity $du$ divided by a quantity $dx$.

But in the context of integration it is possible to write $\dfrac{du}{dx} = 2x$ as $du = 2x \, dx$. (The reason will appear later.)

The integral $\int 2x(x^2 + 1)^5 \, dx$ can be thought of as $\int (x^2 + 1)^5 \, 2x \, dx$.

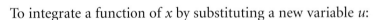

| | |
|---|---|
| Each part can now be expressed in terms of $u$. | $\int u^5 \, du$ |
| This integral is easy to do. | $= \frac{1}{6} u^6 + c$ |
| Rewrite the result in terms of $x$. | $= \frac{1}{6}(x^2 + 1)^6 + c$ |

The result can be checked by differentiation using the chain rule.

Let $y = \frac{1}{6}(x^2 + 1)^6 + c$.

Let $u = x^2 + 1$, so that $y = \frac{1}{6}u^6 + c$. Then $\dfrac{du}{dx} = 2x$ and $\dfrac{dy}{du} = u^5$.

So $\dfrac{dy}{dx} = \dfrac{dy}{du} \times \dfrac{du}{dx} = u^5 \times 2x = 2x(x^2 + 1)^5$.

The process of **integration by substitution** is based on the chain rule and this justifies rewriting $\dfrac{du}{dx} = 2x$ as $du = 2x \, dx$.

**K** To integrate a function of $x$ by substituting a new variable $u$:

(1) Find, by differentiation, the relationship between $du$ and $dx$.

(2) Rewrite the function and $dx$ in terms of of $u$ and $du$.

(3) Carry out the integration in terms of $u$.

(4) Rewrite the result in terms of $x$.

**C1** Follow the steps above to find $\int 3x^2(x^3 - 1) \, dx$ by using the substitution $u = x^3 - 1$.

**C2** Use the substitution $u = 5 - x^2$ to find $\int 2x(5 - x^2)^3 \, dx$.

Suppose we want to find $\int x(x^2 - 3)^4 \, dx$ using the substitution $u = x^2 - 3$.

Differentiating $u = x^2 - 3$ we get $\dfrac{du}{dx} = 2x$, from which $du = 2x \, dx$.

What appears in the integral is $x \, dx$, not $2x \, dx$.

However, this is easily dealt with: $\int x(x^2 - 3)^4 \, dx = \frac{1}{2}\int (x^2 - 3)^4 \, 2x \, dx = \frac{1}{2}\int u^4 \, du$

**C3** Complete the process above to find $\int x(x^2 - 3)^4 \, dx$.

**C4** Use the substitution $u = x^4 - 1$ to find $\int x^3(x^4 - 1)^3 \, dx$.

Sometimes the process of rewriting the function in terms of $u$ is not so simple.

In this integral, let $u = 2x + 1$.

$\dfrac{du}{dx} = 2$, so $du = 2 \, dx$.

Replace $(2x + 1)^5$ by $u^5$ and $2 \, dx$ by $du$. This still leaves $x$ to be replaced.

$u = 2x + 1 \implies x = \dfrac{u - 1}{2}$

$$\int 2x(2x + 1)^5 \, dx$$
$$= \int x(2x + 1)^5 \, 2 \, dx$$
$$= \int xu^5 \, du$$
$$= \int \left(\frac{u-1}{2}\right)u^5 \, du = \frac{1}{2}\int (u - 1)u^5 \, du$$
$$= \frac{1}{2}\int \left(u^6 - u^5\right) \, du$$

**C5** Complete the process above to find $\int 2x(2x + 1)^5 \, dx$.

**C6** Use the substitution $u = 3x - 2$ to find $\int 6x(3x - 2)^3 \, dx$.

**C7** Use the substitution $u = 2x + 3$ to find $\int x(2x + 3)^4 \, dx$.

---

### Example 4
Use the substitution $u = 1 - x^2$ to find $\int x\sqrt{1 - x^2} \, dx$.

### Solution
*First differentiate* $u = 1 - x^2$. $\dfrac{du}{dx} = -2x$, so $du = -2x \, dx$.

*Rearrange the integral so that* $-2x \, dx$ *appears in it.*

$$\int x\sqrt{1 - x^2} \, dx = -\frac{1}{2}\int \sqrt{1 - x^2}(-2x) \, dx$$
$$= -\frac{1}{2}\int \sqrt{u} \, du = -\frac{1}{2}\int u^{\frac{1}{2}} \, du$$
$$= -\frac{1}{2}\left(\frac{2}{3}u^{\frac{3}{2}}\right) + c = -\frac{1}{3}u^{\frac{3}{2}} + c$$

*Rewrite the result in terms of* $x$. $\qquad = -\frac{1}{3}\left(1 - x^2\right)^{\frac{3}{2}} + c$

---

**Exercise C** (answers p 192)

**1** Use the substitution $u = x^2 + 4$ to find $\int 2x(x^2 + 4)^3 \, dx$.

**2** Use the given substitution to find each of these indefinite integrals.

(a) $\int 3x^2(x^3 - 1)^4 dx \quad u = x^3 - 1$

(b) $\int x^2(x^3 - 1)^{-2} dx \quad u = x^3 - 1$

(c) $\int x\sqrt{x^2 - 4} \, dx \quad u = x^2 - 4$

(d) $\int x(2x^2 + 1)^5 \, dx \quad u = 2x^2 + 1$

**3** Use the given substitution to find each of these indefinite integrals.

(a) $\int 2x(2x - 3)^4 dx \quad u = 2x - 3$

(b) $\int x(2x + 1)^4 dx \quad u = 2x + 1$

(c) $\int x\sqrt{3x - 2} \, dx \quad u = 3x - 2$

(d) $\int \dfrac{5x}{5x - 2} \, dx \quad u = 5x - 2$

(e) $\int \dfrac{x}{4x + 1} \, dx \quad u = 4x + 1$

(f) $\int \dfrac{x}{(2x - 1)^3} \, dx \quad u = 2x - 1$

**4** Find each of the following indefinite integrals. Choose your own substitution.

(a) $\int 2x(x^2 + 3)^3 \, dx$

(b) $\int x\sqrt{x^2 + 5} \, dx$

(c) $\int x(6x + 5)^5 \, dx$

(d) $\int x(1 - 2x)^4 \, dx$

(e) $\int \dfrac{x}{\sqrt{x^2 - 1}} \, dx$

(f) $\int \dfrac{x}{\sqrt{x - 1}} \, dx$

# D Integrating $\dfrac{f'(x)}{f(x)}$ (answers p 192)

**D1** Use the substitution $u = x^2 + 1$ to find $\int \dfrac{2x}{x^2 + 1} \, dx$.

**D2** Use the substitution $u = x^3 - 1$ to find $\int \dfrac{3x^2}{x^3 - 1} \, dx$.

**D3** Use the substitution $u = x^4 + 3x^2 - 5$ to find $\int \dfrac{4x^3 + 6x}{x^4 + 3x^2 - 5} \, dx$.

In all three of the previous questions, the integral, in terms of $u$, comes out as $\ln|u| + c$. This happens because, in the function being integrated, the numerator is the derivative of the denominator.

In symbols, each integral above is of the form $\int \dfrac{f'(x)}{f(x)} \, dx$.

When you use the substitution $u = f(x)$, then $\dfrac{du}{dx} = f'(x)$ and so $du = f'(x) \, dx$.

So the integral becomes $\int \dfrac{1}{u} \, du$, which is $\ln|u| + c$ or, in terms of $x$, $\ln|f(x)| + c$.

$\int \dfrac{f'(x)}{f(x)} \, dx = \ln|f(x)| + c$

Sometimes it is not immediately obvious that a function to be integrated can be expressed in the form $\dfrac{f'(x)}{f(x)}$. A little ingenuity may be needed, as in the next example.

---

**Example 5**

Find $\displaystyle\int \frac{x^3}{x^4+1}\,dx$.

**Solution**

*The derivative of the denominator, $x^4 + 1$, is $4x^3$, so think of the numerator as $\frac{1}{4}(4x^3)$.*

$$\int \frac{x^3}{x^4+1}\,dx = \tfrac{1}{4}\int \frac{4x^3}{x^4+1}\,dx = \tfrac{1}{4}\ln|x^4+1| + c$$

---

**Exercise D** (answers p 192)

**1** Find each of these indefinite integrals.

(a) $\displaystyle\int \frac{3x^2}{x^3-1}\,dx$

(b) $\displaystyle\int \frac{2x+1}{x^2+x}\,dx$

(c) $\displaystyle\int \frac{x^4}{x^5+1}\,dx$

(d) $\displaystyle\int \frac{x-1}{x^2-2x}\,dx$

(e) $\displaystyle\int \frac{x+1}{2x^2+4x+1}\,dx$

(f) $\displaystyle\int \frac{e^x}{3e^x-1}\,dx$

**2 (a)** Find the indefinite integral $\displaystyle\int \frac{x}{4-x^2}\,dx$.

**(b)** Hence show that $\displaystyle\int_0^1 \frac{x}{4-x^2}\,dx = \tfrac{1}{2}\ln\left(\tfrac{4}{3}\right)$.

**3 (a)** Show that the area under the graph of $y = \dfrac{x}{x^2+1}$ between $x=0$ and $x=2$ is $\tfrac{1}{2}\ln 5$.

**(b)** Find the area under the graph of $y = \dfrac{x^2}{x^3+1}$ between $x=0$ and $x=2$.

**4 (a)** Express $\tan x$ in terms of $\sin x$ and $\cos x$.

**(b)** Explain why $\displaystyle\int \tan x\,dx = -\ln|\cos x| + c$.

**(c)** Find $\displaystyle\int \cot x\,dx$.

**5 (a)** Find $\displaystyle\int \frac{e^{3x}}{e^{3x}+1}\,dx$.

**(b)** Hence show that $\displaystyle\int_0^1 \frac{e^{3x}}{e^{3x}+1}\,dx = \tfrac{1}{3}\ln\left(\frac{e^3+1}{2}\right)$.

**6 (a)** Write down the derivative of $1 + \sqrt{x}$.

**(b)** Find $\displaystyle\int \frac{1}{\sqrt{x}\left(1+\sqrt{x}\right)}\,dx$.

## E Integration by parts (answers p 193)

Integration by parts is the name given to a method of integration that is based on using the product rule for differentiation 'backwards'. An example will make this clear.

Suppose we start with a function that is a product of two functions, for example $x \sin x$.

The derivative of $x \sin x$ can be found by the product rule by letting $u = x$ and $v = \sin x$.

So the derivative of $x \sin x = u \dfrac{dv}{dx} + v \dfrac{du}{dx} = x \cos x + \sin x$.

Because integration is the reverse of differentiation, it follows that

$$\int (x \cos x + \sin x) \, dx = x \sin x + c$$

Rewriting the integral in two parts, we get

$$\int x \cos x \, dx + \int \sin x \, dx = x \sin x + c$$

The second of these integrals we know already, so subtract it from both sides to get

$$\int x \cos x \, dx = x \sin x - \int \sin x \, dx + c$$
$$= x \sin x + \cos x + c$$

By starting with the product $x \sin x$ we have found the integral of $x \cos x$.

**E1** (a) By using the product rule to find the derivative of $x \cos x$, show that
$$\int (-x \sin x + \cos x) \, dx = x \cos x + c.$$

(b) Hence show that $\int x \sin x \, dx = \sin x - x \cos x + c.$

**E2** (a) By using the product rule to find the derivative of $x e^x$, show that
$$\int (x e^x + e^x) \, dx = x e^x + c.$$

(b) Hence show that $\int x e^x \, dx = x e^x - e^x + c.$

**E3** (a) By differentiating $x \sin 2x$, show that
$$\int (2x \cos 2x + \sin 2x) \, dx = x \sin 2x + c.$$

(b) Hence find $\int 2x \cos 2x \, dx.$

In the examples looked at so far, we started by differentiating a product and this led us to be able to find an integral.

However, in practice we start from an integral that we want to find and we don't know which product will lead us to it. We shall now see how the product idea can be used to find a given integral.

The general form of the product rule is:  derivative of $uv = u\dfrac{dv}{dx} + v\dfrac{du}{dx}$

Rewriting this in terms of integrals we get:  integral of $\left(u\dfrac{dv}{dx} + v\dfrac{du}{dx}\right) = uv + c$.

This can also be written as  $\displaystyle\int\left(u\dfrac{dv}{dx} + v\dfrac{du}{dx}\right)dx = uv + c$

or  $\displaystyle\int u\dfrac{dv}{dx}\,dx + \int v\dfrac{du}{dx}\,dx = uv + c$

Now suppose the first integral is the one we want to find and the second is one that we already know how to find. By subtracting the known one from both sides, we get the **formula for integration by parts:**

$$\int u\dfrac{dv}{dx}\,dx = uv - \int v\dfrac{du}{dx}\,dx + c$$

An example will show how the formula is used.

Suppose we want to find $\displaystyle\int x\cos 3x\,dx$.

Compare this with $\displaystyle\int u\dfrac{dv}{dx}\,dx$.

Let $u = x$ and $\dfrac{dv}{dx} = \cos 3x$.

Then $v = \tfrac{1}{3}\sin 3x$ ('$+\,c$' is not needed here.)

For the right-hand side of the formula we need $\dfrac{du}{dx}$.

Since $u = x$, $\dfrac{du}{dx} = 1$.

So applying the formula we get  $\displaystyle\int u\dfrac{dv}{dx}\,dx = uv - \int v\dfrac{du}{dx}\,dx + c$

$$= x\left(\tfrac{1}{3}\sin 3x\right) - \int\left(\tfrac{1}{3}\sin 3x\right)1\,dx + c$$

$$= \tfrac{1}{3}x\sin 3x + \tfrac{1}{9}\cos 3x + c$$

**E4** Find $\displaystyle\int x\sin 4x\,dx$ by integration by parts, letting $u = x$ and $\dfrac{dv}{dx} = \sin 4x$.

**E5** Find $\displaystyle\int xe^{4x}\,dx$ by integration by parts, letting $u = x$ and $\dfrac{dv}{dx} = e^{4x}$.

**E6** Find  (a) $\displaystyle\int x\cos 4x\,dx$  (b) $\displaystyle\int xe^{5x}\,dx$  (c) $\displaystyle\int xe^{-4x}\,dx$

**E7** What happens if you try to find $\displaystyle\int x\sin x\,dx$ by letting $u = \sin x$ and $\dfrac{dv}{dx} = x$?

**E8** (a) If you try to find $\displaystyle\int x\ln x\,dx$ by letting $u = x$ and $\dfrac{dv}{dx} = \ln x$, you come up against a difficulty. What is it?

(b) Try letting $u = \ln x$ and $\dfrac{dv}{dx} = x$.

When you are finding a definite integral using integration by parts, you can deal with the upper and lower limits of each part separately:

$$\int_a^b u\frac{dv}{dx}\,dx = [uv]_a^b - \int_a^b v\frac{du}{dx}\,dx$$

---

**Example 6**

Find $\int_0^2 xe^{3x}\,dx$.

**Solution**

Let $u = x$ and $\dfrac{dv}{dx} = e^{3x}$. So $v = \int e^{3x}\,dx = \tfrac{1}{3}e^{3x}$ and $\dfrac{du}{dx} = 1$.

$$\int_a^b u\frac{dv}{dx}\,dx = [uv]_a^b - \int_a^b v\frac{du}{dx}\,dx$$

$$\int_0^2 xe^{3x}\,dx = \left[x\left(\tfrac{1}{3}e^{3x}\right)\right]_0^2 - \int_0^2 \left(\tfrac{1}{3}e^{3x}\right)1\,dx$$

$$= \left(\tfrac{2}{3}e^6 - 0\right) - \tfrac{1}{3}\int_0^2 e^{3x}\,dx$$

$$= \tfrac{2}{3}e^6 - \tfrac{1}{3}\left[\tfrac{1}{3}e^{3x}\right]_0^2$$

$$= \tfrac{2}{3}e^6 - \tfrac{1}{9}\left(e^6 - 1\right) = \tfrac{1}{9}\left(6e^6 - e^6 + 1\right) = \tfrac{1}{9}\left(5e^6 + 1\right)$$

---

**Exercise E** (answers p 193)

**1** Find each of these indefinite integrals.

(a) $\int 2x\cos 7x\,dx$      (b) $\int 3xe^{6x}\,dx$      (c) $\int x\sin\tfrac{1}{2}x\,dx$

(d) $\int xe^{-x}\,dx$      (e) $\int xe^{-3x}\,dx$      (f) $\int xe^{-\frac{1}{2}x}\,dx$

**2** Find each of these definite integrals.

(a) $\int_0^{\frac{\pi}{2}} x\cos x\,dx$      (b) $\int_0^{\pi} x\sin x\,dx$      (c) $\int_0^4 xe^x\,dx$

(d) $\int_0^{\frac{\pi}{6}} x\sin 3x\,dx$      (e) $\int_0^1 2xe^{-x}\,dx$      (f) $\int_0^6 xe^{\frac{1}{2}x}\,dx$

**3** This diagram shows the graph of $y = x\sin 2x$.

(a) What are the exact values of the $x$-coordinates of the three points in the diagram where the curve intersects the $x$-axis?

(b) Find the area of each of the regions labelled $A$ and $B$.

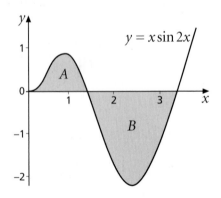

## F Two standard integrals (answers p 193)

When you were integrating by substitution (section C), you introduced a new variable $u$ defined in terms of $x$, for example $u = 2x - 1$, $u = x^2 + 1$, and so on.

It is sometimes better to use a substitution in which $x$ is defined in terms of $u$.

An example is $\int \dfrac{1}{1+x^2}\, dx$, which can be found by using the substitution $x = \tan u$.

From $x = \tan u$ it follows that $\dfrac{dx}{du} = \sec^2 u$, from which $dx = \sec^2 u\, du$.

But $1 + x^2 = 1 + \tan^2 u = \sec^2 u$, so the integral becomes $\int \dfrac{\sec^2 u}{\sec^2 u}\, du = \int 1\, du = u + c$.

This result now needs to be rewritten in terms of $x$.
From $x = \tan u$ it follows that $u = \tan^{-1} x$, so the final result is $\int \dfrac{1}{1+x^2}\, dx = \tan^{-1} x + c$.

**F1** Find $\int \dfrac{1}{9 + x^2}\, dx$ by following these steps.

    (a) Let $x = 3\tan u$. Find $\dfrac{dx}{du}$ and hence express $dx$ in terms of $du$.

    (b) Show that $9 + x^2 = 9\sec^2 u$.

    (c) Hence show that, in terms of $u$, the integral is $\frac{1}{3}u + c$.

    (d) Using the fact that $x = 3\tan u$, express $u$ in terms of $x$.

    (e) Hence write the result of the integration in terms of $x$.

**F2** Follow a similar sequence of steps to find $\int \dfrac{1}{25 + x^2}\, dx$ by using the substitution $x = 5\tan u$.

**F3** Find $\int \dfrac{1}{36 + x^2}\, dx$ by using the substitution $x = 6\tan u$.

The general rule that applies to all three integrals you have done is this:

$$\int \dfrac{1}{a^2 + x^2}\, dx = \dfrac{1}{a}\tan^{-1}\!\left(\dfrac{x}{a}\right) + c$$

This is an example of a 'standard integral'. It is in the formula book for the examination.

For example, you can find $\int \dfrac{1}{16 + x^2}\, dx$ by using the formula above with $a = 4$.

The result is $\frac{1}{4}\tan^{-1}\!\left(\dfrac{x}{4}\right) + c$.

**F4** (a) Find $\int \dfrac{1}{64 + x^2}\, dx$.

    (b) Hence find $\int_0^8 \dfrac{1}{64 + x^2}\, dx$.

Another standard integral is $\int \dfrac{1}{\sqrt{a^2 - x^2}} \, dx$. The next question shows how an example of this type is done by substitution.

**F5** Find $\int \dfrac{1}{\sqrt{9 - x^2}} \, dx$ by following these steps.

(a) Let $x = 3 \sin u$. Find $\dfrac{dx}{du}$ and hence express $dx$ in terms of $du$.

(b) Show that $\sqrt{9 - x^2} = 3 \cos u$.

(c) Hence show that, in terms of $u$, the integral is $u + c$.

(d) Using the fact that $x = 3 \sin u$, express $u$ in terms of $x$.

(e) Hence write the result of the integration in terms of $x$.

**F6** Find $\int \dfrac{1}{\sqrt{49 - x^2}} \, dx$ by using the substitution $x = 7 \sin u$.

The general rule for the integrals in F5 and F6 is

$$\int \frac{1}{\sqrt{a^2 - x^2}} \, dx = \sin^{-1}\left(\frac{x}{a}\right) + c$$

## Exercise F (answers p 193)

1  Find each of these integrals.

(a) $\int \dfrac{1}{\sqrt{4 - x^2}} \, dx$   (b) $\int \dfrac{1}{100 + x^2} \, dx$   (c) $\int \dfrac{1}{\sqrt{25 - x^2}} \, dx$   (d) $\int \dfrac{1}{81 + x^2} \, dx$

2  Show that $\displaystyle\int_0^3 \frac{1}{\sqrt{36 - x^2}} \, dx = \frac{\pi}{6}$.

3  (a) Find $\int \dfrac{1}{3 + x^2} \, dx$. $\left(\text{Hint: } 3 = \left(\sqrt{3}\right)^2\right)$

   (b) Hence show that $\displaystyle\int_0^3 \frac{1}{3 + x^2} \, dx = \frac{\pi\sqrt{3}}{9}$.

4  Find $\displaystyle\int_{-2}^{2} \frac{1}{\sqrt{16 - x^2}} \, dx$.

5  (a) By writing $\dfrac{1 + x}{1 + x^2}$ as $\dfrac{1}{1 + x^2} + \dfrac{x}{1 + x^2}$, find $\int \dfrac{1 + x}{1 + x^2} \, dx$.

   (b) Show that $\displaystyle\int_0^1 \frac{1 + x}{1 + x^2} \, dx = \frac{\pi}{4} + \tfrac{1}{2}\ln 2$.

6  Use the substitution $u = 3x$ to find $\int \dfrac{1}{1 + 9x^2} \, dx$.

7  Use the substitution $u = 5x$ to find $\int \dfrac{1}{\sqrt{1 - 25x^2}} \, dx$.

## Key points

- $\int e^{ax}\,dx = \dfrac{1}{a}e^{ax} + c$      $\int \cos ax\,dx = \dfrac{1}{a}\sin ax + c$      $\int \sin ax\,dx = -\dfrac{1}{a}\cos ax + c$    (p 108)

- $\int \dfrac{1}{x}\,dx = \ln|x| + c$    $(x \neq 0)$      $\int \dfrac{1}{ax+b}\,dx = \dfrac{1}{a}\ln|ax+b| + c$           (p 110)

- To integrate a function of $x$ by substituting a new variable $u$:
  
  (1) Find, by differentiation, the relationship between $du$ and $dx$.
  
  (2) Rewrite the function and $dx$ in terms of $u$ and $du$.
  
  (3) Carry out the integration in terms of $u$.
  
  (4) Rewrite the result in terms of $x$.           (p 112)

- $\int \dfrac{f'(x)}{f(x)}\,dx = \ln|f(x)| + c$           (p 114)

- $\int u\dfrac{dv}{dx}\,dx = uv - \int v\dfrac{du}{dx}\,dx + c$    $\int_a^b u\dfrac{dv}{dx}\,dx = \big[uv\big]_a^b - \int_a^b v\dfrac{du}{dx}\,dx$    (integration by parts)           (pp 117–118)

- $\int \dfrac{1}{a^2 + x^2}\,dx = \dfrac{1}{a}\tan^{-1}\!\left(\dfrac{x}{a}\right) + c$           (p 119)

- $\int \dfrac{1}{\sqrt{a^2 - x^2}}\,dx = \sin^{-1}\!\left(\dfrac{x}{a}\right) + c$           (p 120)

The following table should help you to decide which method of integration to use.

| Description | Examples | Method |
|---|---|---|
| The function is a sum of individual functions each of which you know how to integrate. | $\int\left(x^2 + \dfrac{2}{x} - e^{4x} + \cos 5x\right)dx$ | Integrate term by term. |
| The integral is one of the standard integrals. | $\int \dfrac{1}{9+x^2}\,dx$   $\int \dfrac{1}{\sqrt{4-x^2}}\,dx$ | Use the relevant formula. |
| The function is of the form $\dfrac{f'(x)}{f(x)}$ or can be rearranged into this form. | $\int \dfrac{x^2}{x^3-1}\,dx = \tfrac{1}{3}\int \dfrac{3x^2}{x^3-1}\,dx$ | Identify $f(x)$ to obtain $\ln|f(x)| + c$. |
| The function is a product of the form $xe^{ax}$, $x\cos ax$, $x\sin ax$, $x\ln x$ (or any of a similar type involving linear expressions, such as $(2x+3)e^{-4x}$, $(x+1)\cos 2x$, $x\sin(3x-1)$). | $\int x\sin 3x\,dx$ <br><br> $\int xe^{-2x}\,dx$ | Use integration by parts. |
| The function includes a function of a function, such as $(x^2+3)^5$, $\sqrt{2x-1}$, … | $\int x(x^2+3)^5\,dx$ <br><br> $\int \dfrac{x}{\sqrt{2x+1}}\,dx$ | Try substitution. (For the examples use $u = x^2 + 3$ $u = 2x + 1$) |

## Mixed questions (answers p 194)

1  *A* is the point on the graph of $y = \sin 2x$ where $x = \frac{5}{12}\pi$.

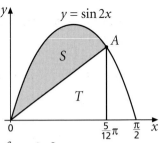

(a)  Explain why the area of the triangle labelled $T$ is $\frac{5}{48}\pi$.

(b)  Hence find the shaded area labelled $S$.

2  (a)  Draw a rough sketch of the curve with equation $y = 2e^{\frac{1}{2}x}$ for $x \geq 0$.

(b)  The curve crosses the line $y = 6$ at the point $A$.
Show that the $x$-coordinate of $A$ is $2\ln 3$.

(c)  Find the exact value of the area enclosed by the curve, the $y$-axis and the line $y = 6$.

3  Find the following indefinite integrals.

(a)  $\int \sin(3x - 1)\,dx$

(b)  $\int \frac{1}{\sqrt{2x-1}}\,dx$

(c)  $\int xe^{-2x}\,dx$

(d)  $\int \frac{x}{x^2 - 5}\,dx$

(e)  $\int x(x-2)^4\,dx$

(f)  $\int \frac{1}{49 + x^2}\,dx$

4  Find the following definite integrals.

(a)  $\int_4^9 \frac{x^{\frac{1}{2}}}{x^{\frac{3}{2}} - 1}\,dx$

(b)  $\int_0^2 \frac{1}{400 + x^2}\,dx$

(c)  $\int_0^\pi \sin\frac{1}{3}x\,dx$

(d)  $\int_0^4 \frac{1}{\sqrt{64 - x^2}}\,dx$

(e)  $\int_0^\pi \left(x + \sin\frac{1}{3}x\right)dx$

(f)  $\int_0^\pi x \sin\frac{1}{3}x\,dx$

5  The curve $y = e^x$ and the line $y = 2x + 1$ both pass
through $(0, 1)$ and intersect again at the point where $x = a$.

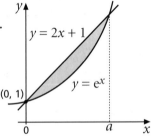

(a)  Write down the equation satisfied by $a$.

(b)  Show that the area enclosed between the line and the
curve is $a^2 - a$.

6  Find    (a)  $\int \frac{1}{4 + x^2}\,dx$    (b)  $\int \frac{x}{4 + x^2}\,dx$

7  Find    (a)  $\int \frac{1}{\sqrt{4 - x^2}}\,dx$    (b)  $\int \frac{x}{\sqrt{4 - x^2}}\,dx$

8  (a)  Find the $x$-coordinate of the point where the curve
$y = 2 + \frac{1}{x - 2}$ crosses the $x$-axis.

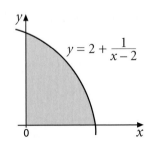

(b)  Find the area enclosed by the curve and the axes.

## Test yourself (answers p 194)

**1** Find the following indefinite integrals.

(a) $\int e^{6x}\,dx$        (b) $\int \cos \tfrac{1}{4}x\,dx$        (c) $\int \sin(2x+1)\,dx$

**2** Find the following definite integrals.

(a) $\int_1^3 \dfrac{6}{x}\,dx$        (b) $\int_0^{\frac{1}{2}} e^{-2x}\,dx$        (c) $\int_0^4 \dfrac{1}{3x+2}\,dx$

**3** Find $\displaystyle\int_1^2\left(e^{\frac{x}{2}}+\frac{1}{x}\right)dx$, giving your answer to three significant figures.        AQA 2002

**4** The diagram shows a sketch of the curve with equation $y = 4 - e^{2x}$ which crosses the $y$-axis at the point $A$ and the $x$-axis at the point $B\,(\ln 2, 0)$.

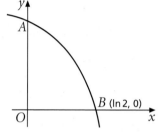

(a) Find the $y$-coordinate of $A$.

(b) (i) For the curve $y = 4 - e^{2x}$, find $\dfrac{dy}{dx}$.

    (ii) Find the gradient of the curve at $B$.

(c) The line $y = 2$ cuts the $y$-axis at the point $P$ and the curve at the point $Q$. $OPQR$ is a rectangle.

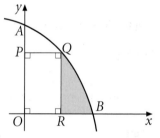

    (i) Find the exact value of the area of rectangle $OPQR$.

    (ii) Find $\int(4 - e^{2x})\,dx$.

    (iii) Find the area of the shaded region bounded by the curve, the $x$-axis and the line $QR$.
       Give your answer in the form $p\ln 2 + q$, where $p$ and $q$ are constants to be determined.

    (iv) Show that the region above $PQ$, bounded by the curve, the $y$-axis and the line $PQ$, is half the area of the shaded region.        AQA 2003

**5** Find the value of    (a) $\displaystyle\int_1^e\left(x-\frac{1}{x}\right)dx$        (b) $\displaystyle\int_0^{\frac{\pi}{4}}(\cos 2x + \sin 4x)\,dx$

**6** Find the value of    (a) $\displaystyle\int_0^{\frac{\pi}{6}}(x + \cos 3x)\,dx$        (b) $\displaystyle\int_0^{\frac{\pi}{6}} x\cos 3x\,dx$

**7** Find the value of    (a) $\displaystyle\int_1^2 \frac{2x+1}{x^2+x+1}\,dx$        (b) $\displaystyle\int_0^5 \frac{1}{\sqrt{100-x^2}}\,dx$

**8** Find the value of    (a) $\displaystyle\int_0^{0.2} x e^{5x}\,dx$        (b) $\displaystyle\int_0^{10} \frac{1}{100+x^2}\,dx$

# 8 Solids of revolution

In this chapter you will learn how to find the volume of a solid of revolution about the *x*- or *y*-axis.

## A Revolution about the *x*-axis (answers p 195)

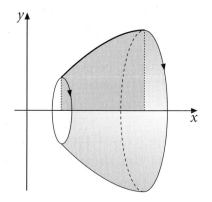

In this diagram the shaded region under a curve is rotated through a complete turn ($2\pi$ radians) about the *x*-axis to form a **solid of revolution**.

In this section you will learn how to calculate the volume of a solid of revolution when you know the equation of the curve.

The second diagram shows the volume $V$ up to the value $x$. The radius of the solid at this value is $y$.

If $x$ is increased by an amount $\delta x$, then $y$ is increased by $\delta y$ and $V$ is increased by $\delta V$.

The extra volume $\delta V$ consists of a slice of thickness $\delta x$, whose cross-sectional area varies from a circle of radius $y$ to a circle of radius $(y + \delta y)$.

The volume of the slice lies between $\pi y^2 \delta x$ and $\pi (y + \delta y)^2 \delta x$.

$$\pi y^2 \delta x < \delta V < \pi (y + \delta y)^2 \delta x$$

By dividing by $\delta x$, we get

$$\pi y^2 < \frac{\delta V}{\delta x} < \pi (y + \delta y)^2$$

Now suppose that $\delta x$ gets smaller and smaller.

Then $\delta y$ gets smaller and smaller and $\dfrac{\delta V}{\delta x}$ gets closer and closer to $\dfrac{dV}{dx}$, which is 'trapped' between $\pi y^2$ and a quantity that gets closer and closer to $\pi y^2$.

So $\dfrac{dV}{dx} = \pi y^2$ is equivalent to $V = \int \pi y^2 \, dx$.

To find the volume between two given values of $x$, you calculate a definite integral:

The volume of a solid of revolution about the *x*-axis between $x = a$ and $x = b$ is given by $\displaystyle\int_a^b \pi y^2 \, dx$.

**A1** A solid of revolution is formed by rotating about the $x$-axis the region under the line $y = \frac{1}{2}x$ between $x = 0$ and $x = 3$.

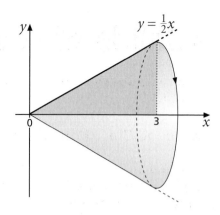

(a) What name is given to this solid of revolution?

(b) Express $y^2$ in terms of $x$.

(c) By substituting for $y^2$ in $\int_0^3 \pi y^2 \, dx$, find the volume of the solid of revolution.

**A2** The sloping line in this diagram goes through the point $(h, r)$. When the shaded area is rotated through $2\pi$ radians about the $x$-axis, the solid of revolution formed is a cone of base radius $r$ and height $h$.

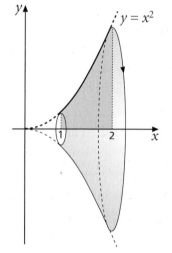

(a) Explain why the equation of the line is $y = \dfrac{r}{h}x$.

(b) By substituting for $y^2$ in $\int_0^h \pi y^2 \, dx$, show that the volume of the cone is $\frac{1}{3}\pi r^2 h$.

**A3** A solid of revolution is formed by rotating about the $x$-axis the region under the curve $y = x^2$ between $x = 1$ and $x = 2$.

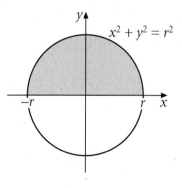

(a) Express $y^2$ in terms of $x$.

(b) Find the volume of the solid of revolution.

**A4** This diagram shows the circle of radius $r$ whose centre is at the origin. The equation of the circle is $x^2 + y^2 = r^2$, which can be written as $y^2 = r^2 - x^2$.

(a) What solid is formed when the shaded region is rotated through $2\pi$ radians about the $x$-axis?

(b) The volume of this solid is given by $\int_{-r}^{r} \pi y^2 \, dx$.

Using the fact that $y^2 = r^2 - x^2$, show that the volume of the solid of revolution is $\frac{4}{3}\pi r^3$.

The integration that you need to do in order to find the volume of a solid of revolution may require one of the techniques you met in the previous chapter.

---

### Example 1

The region under the curve $y = \sqrt{\dfrac{1+x}{x}}$ between $x = 1$ and $x = 4$ is rotated through $2\pi$ radians about the $x$-axis to form a solid of revolution. Find the volume of the solid.

### Solution

$$\int_1^4 \pi y^2 \, dx = \int_1^4 \pi\left(\frac{1+x}{x}\right) dx = \pi \int_1^4 \left(\frac{1}{x} + \frac{x}{x}\right) dx = \pi \int_1^4 \left(\frac{1}{x} + 1\right) dx$$

$$= \pi\left[\ln|x| + x\right]_1^4 = \pi\left((\ln 4 + 4) - (0 + 1)\right) = \pi(\ln 4 + 3)$$

---

### Example 2

The region under the curve $y = \sqrt{\dfrac{2x}{x^2 + 3}}$ between $x = 0$ and $x = 1$ is rotated through $2\pi$ radians about the $x$-axis to form a solid of revolution. Find the volume of the solid.

### Solution

$$\text{Volume} = \int_0^1 \pi y^2 \, dx = \pi \int_0^1 \frac{2x}{x^2 + 3} \, dx \qquad \left(\textit{This integral is of the form } \int \frac{f'(x)}{f(x)} \, dx.\right)$$

$$= \pi\left[\ln|x^2 + 3|\right]_0^1 = \pi(\ln 4 - \ln 3) = \pi \ln \tfrac{4}{3}$$

---

### Exercise A (answers p 195)

1  The region under the curve $y = \sqrt{x(4 - x)}$ between $x = 0$ and $x = 4$ is rotated through $2\pi$ radians about the $x$-axis.
   Find the volume of the solid of revolution formed.

2  The region under the curve $y = 1 - x^2$ between $x = 0$ and $x = 1$ is rotated through $2\pi$ radians about the $x$-axis.
   Find the volume of the solid of revolution formed.

3  Find the volume of the solid of revolution formed when the region enclosed by each of these curves and the $x$-axis, between the given values of $x$, is rotated through $2\pi$ radians about the $x$-axis.

   (a) $y = e^x$ from $x = 0$ to $x = 3$

   (b) $y = \dfrac{1}{x^2}$ from $x = 1$ to $x = 4$

   (c) $y = x + \dfrac{1}{x}$ from $x = 1$ to $x = 3$

   (d) $y = \sqrt{\sin 3x}$ from $x = 0$ to $x = \tfrac{1}{3}\pi$

   (e) $y = \sqrt{x \sin 2x}$ from $x = 0$ to $x = \tfrac{1}{2}\pi$

   (f) $y = \sqrt{xe^{-x}}$ from $x = 0$ to $x = 2$

   (g) $y = \dfrac{1}{\sqrt{1 + x^2}}$ from $x = 0$ to $x = 1$

   (h) $y = \sqrt{\dfrac{x}{x^2 + 1}}$ from $x = 0$ to $x = 3$

## B Revolution about the *y*-axis (answers p 195)

In this diagram the region between the curve and the *y*-axis is rotated about the *y*-axis to form a solid of revolution.

Because the roles of *x* and *y* are swapped, the volume this time is given by $V = \int \pi x^2 \, dy$.

The limits this time are the two values of *y* between which the region lies.

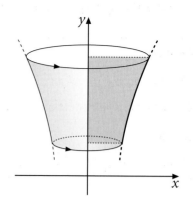

The volume of a solid of revolution about the *y*-axis between the lines $y = c$ and $y = d$ is given by $\int_c^d \pi x^2 \, dy$.

**B1** The curve in this diagram has the equation $y = x^2 + 1$. The shaded region is rotated about the *y*-axis to form a solid of revolution.

(a) Rearrange the equation of the curve in the form $x^2 = \ldots$

(b) Verify that when $x = 1$, $y = 2$, and when $x = 3$, $y = 10$.

(c) By evaluating $\int_2^{10} \pi x^2 \, dy$, find the volume of the solid.

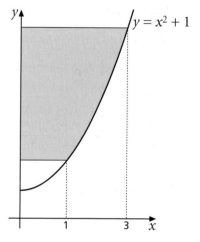

**B2** The curve in this diagram has the equation $y = \sqrt{x}$. Find the volume of the solid of revolution formed by rotating the region labelled $R$ through $2\pi$ radians about the *y*-axis.

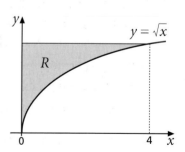

**B3** The region $R$ enclosed by the curve $y = \dfrac{1}{5 - x^2}$, the *y*-axis and the line $y = 1$ is rotated through $2\pi$ radians about the *y*-axis.

(a) Express $x^2$ in terms of *y*.

(b) Hence show that the volume of the solid of revolution formed is $\pi(4 - \ln 5)$.

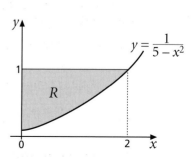

## Example 3

The curve in this diagram has the equation $y = \frac{1}{8}x^3$.
Find the volume of the solid of revolution formed by rotating
the region labelled $R$ through $2\pi$ radians about the $y$-axis.

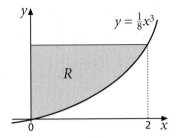

### Solution

*First express $x^2$ in terms of $y$.*

$y = \frac{1}{8}x^3 \implies 8y = x^3 \implies 2y^{\frac{1}{3}} = x \implies x^2 = 4y^{\frac{2}{3}}$

When $x = 0$, $y = 0$; when $x = 2$, $y = 1$.

$\text{Volume} = \int_0^1 \pi x^2 \, dy = \pi \int_0^1 4y^{\frac{2}{3}} \, dy = 4\pi \left[ \frac{3}{5}y^{\frac{5}{3}} \right]_0^1 = \frac{12}{5}\pi$

---

## Exercise B (answers p 195)

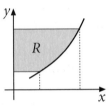

Each of the questions below refers to this diagram, in which the
curve has an equation of the form $y = f(x)$ and the region $R$
between two given values of $x$ is rotated $2\pi$ radians about the $y$-axis.

Find the volume of the solid of revolution in each case.

**1** $y = 1 + 3x$; $x = 0$, $x = 4$   **2** $y = 1 + 3x^2$; $x = 0$, $x = 2$

**3** $y = 1 - \frac{1}{4}x^2$; $x = 0$, $x = 2$   **4** $y = x^3$; $x = 0$, $x = 2$

**5** $y = x^3 - 1$; $x = 2$, $x = 4$   **6** $y = \ln x$; $x = 1$, $x = 2$

---

### Key points

- The volume of a solid of revolution about the $x$-axis between $x = a$ and $x = b$
  is given by $\int_a^b \pi y^2 \, dx$.   (p 124)

- The volume of a solid of revolution about the $y$-axis between $y = c$ and $y = d$
  is given by $\int_c^d \pi x^2 \, dy$.   (p 127)

---

## Mixed questions (answers p 195)

**1** The diagram shows the region $R$ bounded by
the curve $y = e^{\frac{1}{2}x}$, the axes and the line $x = 6$.

(a) Find the exact value of the area of $R$.

The region $R$ is rotated through $2\pi$ radians
about the $x$-axis.

(b) Find the exact value of the volume of the
solid of revolution formed.

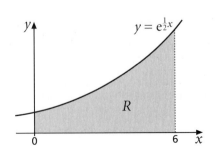

**2** The curve $y = e^{2x} - 3$ cuts the $y$-axis at $A$ and the $x$-axis at $B$.

    **(a)** Find the coordinates of $A$ and $B$ and sketch the curve between $A$ and $B$.

    **(b)** Find the area of the region $R$ enclosed by the curve and the axes.

    **(c)** The region $R$ enclosed by the curve and the axes is rotated $2\pi$ radians about the $x$-axis. Find the volume of the solid of revolution formed.

**3** Sketch the region enclosed by the curve $y = x^4$ between $(0, 0)$ and $(2, 16)$, the line $y = 16$ and the $y$-axis. Find the volume of the solid of revolution formed by rotating this region through $2\pi$ radians about the $y$-axis.

**4** The region $R$ bounded by the curve $y = x(x^3 + 1)^3$, the $x$-axis between 0 and 1, and the line $x = 1$, is rotated through $2\pi$ radians about the $x$-axis. Find the volume of the solid of revolution formed.

**5** The region $R$ bounded by the curve $y = x^{\frac{1}{2}}e^{3x}$, the $x$-axis and the lines $x = 1$ and $x = 4$ is rotated through $2\pi$ radians about the $x$-axis. Find the volume of the solid of revolution formed.

## Test yourself (answers p 195)

**1** The region enclosed by the curve $y = \dfrac{1}{x+1}$, the $x$-axis, and the lines $x = 1$ and $x = 4$ is rotated through $2\pi$ radians about the $x$-axis.

    Find the volume of the solid of revolution formed.

**2** The region $R$ is enclosed by the curve $y = 4 - x^2$ and the positive $x$- and $y$-axes. Find the volume of the solid of revolution formed when $R$ is rotated through $2\pi$ radians about

    **(a)** the $x$-axis             **(b)** the $y$-axis

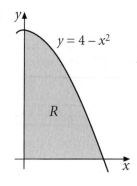

**3** This diagram shows the curve with equation

$$y = \frac{x}{\sqrt{x^3 + 3}}$$

The region $R$ bounded by the curve, the $x$-axis and the line $x = 2$ is rotated through $2\pi$ radians about the $x$-axis.

Find the exact value of the volume of the solid of revolution formed.

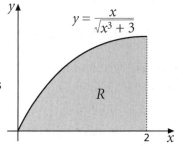

# 9 Numerical methods

In this chapter you will learn how to
- confirm that an equation has a solution between two values
- find an approximate solution to an equation using an iterative formula
- find the approximate area under a graph using the mid-ordinate rule or Simpson's rule

## A Locating roots (answers p 196)

**A1** Given the function $f(x) = 3 + x - x^2$, check that $f(2) = 1$ and $f(3) = -3$.

These values suggest that the graph of $y = 3 + x - x^2$ crosses the x-axis between $x = 2$ and $x = 3$. The value of $x$ where it does so is a solution of the equation $3 + x - x^2 = 0$.
So the fact that $f(x)$ changes from positive to negative between $x = 2$ and $x = 3$ tells us that there is a solution of the equation in that interval.

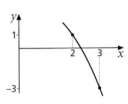

As this is a quadratic graph it was safe to assume that it continues without a break between $f(2)$ and $f(3)$.
But if it had been a function with a break as shown here, we could not deduce that it crosses the x-axis between $x = 2$ and $x = 3$. So we could not deduce that a solution of $f(x) = 0$ lies between those values.

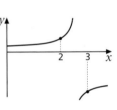

The function in the first diagram is **continuous**. The function in the second diagram is not continuous (it has a **discontinuity**) between $x = 2$ and $x = 3$.

Many functions (such as polynomials, $e^x$, $\sin x$) are continuous, but functions such as $\dfrac{1}{x-1}$ and $\tan x$ have discontinuities.

**K** For an equation of the form $f(x) = 0$, if $f(x_1)$ and $f(x_2)$ have opposite signs and $f(x)$ is continuous between $x_1$ and $x_2$, then a root (solution) of the equation lies between $x_1$ and $x_2$.

There could be more than one root between the two values of $x$, as this diagram shows.

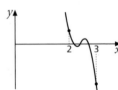

---

### Example 1
Show that the equation $\dfrac{x^3}{5} = x(x - 1)$ has a root between 3 and 4.

### Solution
*Rearrange the equation in the form* $f(x) = 0$.    $x^3 - 5x^2 + 5x = 0$

*$x^3 - 5x^2 + 5x$ is a polynomial so is continuous.*

When $x = 3$, the polynomial takes the value $3^3 - 5 \times 3^2 + 5 \times 3 = -3$, and when $x = 4$, it takes the value $4^3 - 5 \times 4^2 + 5 \times 4 = 4$.

The sign changes so the equation has a root between $x = 3$ and $x = 4$.

---

## Example 2

The graphs of $y = x$ and $y = \sqrt{x+1}$ are shown.

**(a)** Show that the $x$-coordinate of the point of intersection $P$ satisfies the equation $x^2 - x - 1 = 0$.

**(b)** Show that the equation in (a) has a root between 1 and 2.

### Solution

**(a)** *At P the y-value for each graph is the same.*

$$x = \sqrt{x+1}$$

*Square both sides.*

$$x^2 = x + 1$$

$$\Rightarrow x^2 - x - 1 = 0$$

**(b)** When $x = 1$, $x^2 - x - 1 = 1^2 - 1 - 1 = -1$

and when $x = 2$, $x^2 - x - 1 = 2^2 - 2 - 1 = 1$

The sign changes and the function $x^2 - x - 1$ is continuous, so there is a root between 1 and 2.

---

## Exercise A (answers p 196)

Remember to set your calculator to radians.

**1** Show that the equation $\ln x - 1 = 0$ has a root between 2 and 3.

**2** Show that the equation $e^x - 3x^2 = 0$ has roots between $-1$ and 0, between 0 and 1, and between 3 and 4.

**3 (a)** Show that the equation $\sin x - \dfrac{1}{x} = 0$ has a root between $-3$ and $-2$ and between 2 and 3.

**(b)** Does it have a root between $-1$ and 1? Give a reason for your answer.

**4** By rewriting the equation $\cos x = \ln x$ in the form $f(x) = 0$ show that it has at least one root between 1 and 2.

**5** By rewriting the equation $\sqrt{x} = x^2 - 2$ in a suitable form, show that it has at least one root between 1.8 and 1.9.

**6** The diagram shows the graphs of $y = x^3 - 10$ and $y = \dfrac{1}{x}$.

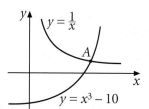

**(a)** Show that the $x$-coordinate of the point $A$ satisfies the equation $x^4 - 10x - 1 = 0$.

**(b)** Show that the $x$-coordinate of $A$ lies between 2 and 3.

**7** You are told that, for a given continuous function $f(x)$, $f(2)$ and $f(3)$ are both positive. Does it follow that $f(x) = 0$ has no root between 2 and 3? Give a reason.

**8** Show that the equation $x^4 - 2x^3 = 4$ has a root $\alpha$ between $-1.08985$ and $-1.08995$. Hence write the value of $\alpha$ to five significant figures.

## B Staircase and cobweb diagrams (answers p 196)

The equation $x^3 - 12x + 12 = 0$ can be written as $x^3 + 12 = 12x$ and hence as $\dfrac{x^3}{12} + 1 = x$.

This can be represented by two functions that we can graph: $\quad y = \dfrac{x^3}{12} + 1 \qquad (1)$

$$y = x \qquad (2)$$

The $x$-coordinate of a point of intersection of these two graphs is a root of
the original equation $x^3 - 12x + 12 = 0$.

**B1 (a)** On the same pair of axes, sketch the two graphs or plot them on a graph plotter.

**(b)** How many points of intersection are there?

**(c)** Confirm that there is a point of intersection between $x = 1$ and $x = 2$.

We are going to home in on this point of intersection, taking $x = 2$ as a starting value.

**B2** Confirm the following steps on your calculator.
Keep each result in your calculator ready for the next step.

Substituting $x = 2$ into $y = \dfrac{x^3}{12} + 1$
gives $y = 1.66\ldots$

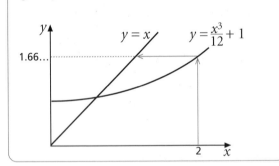

As the point marked ✪ is on $y = x$, its
coordinates are $(1.66\ldots, 1.66\ldots)$.
We shall use $1.66\ldots$ as our next value of $x$.

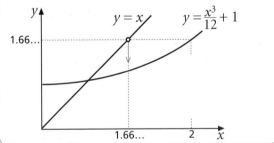

Substituting $x = 1.66\ldots$ into $y = \dfrac{x^3}{12} + 1$
gives $y = 1.38\ldots$

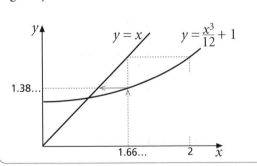

The point marked ✪ is $(1.38\ldots, 1.38\ldots)$.
We shall use $1.38\ldots$ as our next value of $x$.

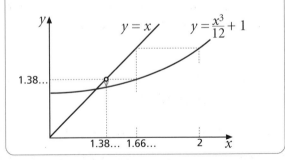

**B3** Substitute $x = 1.38\ldots$ from your calculator into $y = \dfrac{x^3}{12} + 1$.

Repeat the process a few times, each time substituting the value obtained for $y$
back into the equation as the value of $x$.

You should find that the values converge to 1.1157... This means that the graphs (1) and (2) intersect at (1.1157..., 1.1157...).

**B4** Verify by substitution that $x = 1.1157$ is an approximate solution to the original equation $x^3 - 12x + 12 = 0$.

The repeated substitution method can be represented by a 'staircase diagram'. Each vertical arrow shows a value of $x$ being input into the curved graph. The subsequent horizontal arrow shows the value of $y$ that is the output. Because the points marked ✗ are on the graph $y = x$, each output $y$-value becomes the next input $x$-value.

This is why we chose $y = x$ as one of the equations into which we arranged the original equation, $x^3 - 12x + 12 = 0$.

Repeatedly taking the output from an equation and making it the new input can be described by a **recurrence relation** (or **iterative formula**) as used for sequences in Core 2. The recurrence relation you have just been using is

$$x_1 = 2, \quad x_{n+1} = \frac{x_n^3}{12} + 1$$

We used $x = 2$ as the starting value because we knew a point of intersection lay between $x = 1$ and $x = 2$. Now we will try using $x = 1$ as the starting value.

**B5** Obtain the first few values from the recurrence relation $x_1 = 1$, $x_{n+1} = \frac{x_n^3}{12} + 1$. To what value do they converge?

You should find that starting with $x_1 = 1$ leads to the same limit as before, but here you are going up a staircase, not down.

With a recurrence relation it can take many steps for values to settle down to a required number of decimal places. A calculator with an ANS key helps. For example, for question B5, key $1 =$ (or 1 EXE) to enter the starting value. Without clearing, key ANS^3/12+1 then key $=$ (or EXE) as many times as required.

Alternatively you can use a spreadsheet, as here, or a similar facility on a graphic calculator.

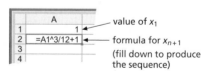

value of $x_1$

formula for $x_{n+1}$
(fill down to produce the sequence)

Using an iterative formula to solve an equation may not result in a staircase, as the following example shows.

**B6** Show that there is a solution of $e^{-x} - x = 0$ between $x = 0.2$ and $x = 1$.

The equation $e^{-x} - x = 0$ can be rewritten as $x = e^{-x}$ and hence can be solved by finding where the graphs $y = x$ and $y = e^{-x}$ intersect.

**B7** Starting with $x_1 = 0.2$, obtain the first few values from $x_{n+1} = e^{-x_n}$. What happens? Do the values approach a limit?

The situation in B7 is shown in the diagram.
Again each vertical arrow shows an $x$-value being input into
the curved graph, and the subsequent horizontal arrow shows
the $y$-value that is the output.
Points marked ✗ on the graph $y = x$ again turn each output value
into the next input.

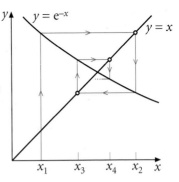

But the result is a 'cobweb', not a staircase, and although the values
get closer to a limit, they are alternately greater and less than it,
rather than to one side of it.

D  **B8 (a)** Trace each diagram and, starting from the $x_1$ marked, draw a staircase or cobweb
as appropriate. Make sure your first vertical line ends on the **curved** graph.

(i)

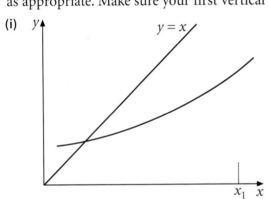

(ii)

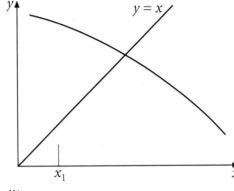

(iii)

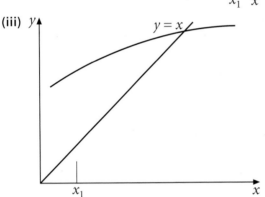

(iv)

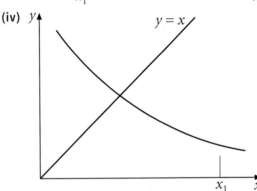

(b) What determines whether you get a staircase or a cobweb?

When an iterative formula of the form $x_{n+1} = f(x_n)$ converges to a limit,
the value of the limit is the $x$-coordinate of the point of intersection of the graphs of

$$y = f(x) \quad \text{and} \quad y = x$$

The limit is therefore a solution of the equation $f(x) = x$.

A staircase or cobweb diagram based on the graphs of $y = f(x)$ and $y = x$
illustrates the convergence.

Using an iterative formula to solve an equation is an example of a **numerical method**.
It is a useful approach when an equation cannot be solved entirely by algebra.

## Example 3

Find, to 3 d.p., the limit which the recurrence relation $x_1 = 3$, $x_{n+1} = 4 - \ln x_n$ approaches.

### Solution

*If you have an ANS facility, key  3 = (or 3 EXE)  then  4 − ln ANS  then repeated  = .*

$x_2 = 2.901...$, $x_3 = 2.934...$, $x_4 = 2.923...$; *after 7 iterations the values settle down to 2.9262...*

To 3 d.p. the limit is 2.926 .

## Example 4

(a) Using the iterative formula $x_{n+1} = \sqrt[3]{x_n + 1}$ with $x_1 = 1.5$, find $x_2$, $x_3$ and $x_4$ to 4 s.f.

(b) Given that the limit of of the sequence is $L$, show that $L$ satisfies
the equation $L^3 - L - 1 = 0$ .

### Solution

(a) *Write each value to 4 s.f., but keep the unrounded value in your calculator ready for
the next stage.*

$$x_2 = 1.357, \quad x_3 = 1.331, \quad x_4 = 1.326$$

(b) At the limit, $L = x_n = x_{n+1}$

Substituting into the iterative formula, $\qquad L = \sqrt[3]{L+1}$

Cube each side. $\qquad\qquad\qquad\qquad L^3 = L + 1$

$$\Rightarrow \quad L^3 - L - 1 = 0$$

## Example 5

(a) Show that the equation $x^3 - x^2 - 5x - 1 = 0$ can be rearranged into

$$x = \sqrt{\frac{5x+1}{x-1}}$$

(b) Use the rearranged form to write a recurrence relation for the purpose of
obtaining a solution to the original equation.

(c) With $x_1 = 3$, find to two decimal places the limit to which values from the
recurrence relation tend.

### Solution

(a)
$$x^3 - x^2 - 5x - 1 = 0$$
$$\Rightarrow \qquad x^3 - x^2 = 5x + 1$$
$$\Rightarrow \qquad x^2(x - 1) = 5x + 1$$

Dividing both sides by $x - 1$, $\qquad x^2 = \dfrac{5x+1}{x-1}$

Taking the positive square root of both sides, $\quad x = \sqrt{\dfrac{5x+1}{x-1}}$

(b) $x_{n+1} = \sqrt{\dfrac{5x_n + 1}{x_n - 1}}$

(c) Limit = 2.87 to 2 d.p.

**Exercise B** (answers p 197)

1 For each of these recurrence relations, find $x_2$, $x_3$ and $x_4$ to four decimal places.

(a) $x_1 = 1.4$, $x_{n+1} = \ln(x_n + 3)$     (b) $x_1 = 1.5$, $x_{n+1} = \sqrt{x_n + 1}$

(c) $x_1 = 0.5$, $x_{n+1} = 2 - \dfrac{x_n^3}{8}$     (d) $x_1 = 0.4$, $x_{n+1} = \dfrac{e^{x_n}}{4}$

2 Match each equation to a possible iterative formula.

(a) $x^2 - 8x + 1 = 0$

(b) $x^2 - 8x + 8 = 0$

(c) $x^2 - 8x - 1 = 0$

P $\boxed{x_{n+1} = \dfrac{1}{x_n} + 8}$

Q $\boxed{x_{n+1} = \sqrt{8x_n - 1}}$

R $\boxed{x_{n+1} = \dfrac{x_n^2}{8} + 1}$

3 Each of the iterative formulae below produces a sequence that converges to a limit. For each one,

    (i) find $x_2$, $x_3$ and $x_4$ to three decimal places and continue the sequence to obtain the limit correct to three decimal places

    (ii) write an equation in the form $f(x) = 0$ for which the formula provides an approximate solution

(a) $x_1 = 0.6$, $x_{n+1} = \cos(x_n)$     (b) $x_1 = 1.5$, $x_{n+1} = \dfrac{1}{x_n} + 1$

(c) $x_1 = 3$, $x_{n+1} = \frac{1}{3}(2^{x_n})$     (d) $x_1 = 0.1$, $x_{n+1} = \frac{1}{2}(1 - x_n^2)$

4 (a) A function is defined as $f(x) = x^3 + 2x - 1$.
    Show that there is a root $\alpha$ of $f(x) = 0$ between 0 and 1.

  (b) Show that $f(x) = 0$ can be rearranged as

$$x = \frac{1 - x^3}{2}$$

  (c) The root $\alpha$ is to be estimated using the iterative formula

$$x_{n+1} = \frac{1 - x_n^3}{2}$$

    Taking $x_1 = 0$, apply the formula enough times to obtain an approximation to $\alpha$ correct to three decimal places.

5 Each iterative formula below leads to a limit. Show that in each case the limit satisfies the equation $2x^2 - 5x + 1 = 0$.

(a) $x_{n+1} = \dfrac{1 + 2x_n^2}{5}$     (b) $x_{n+1} = \dfrac{1}{5 - 2x_n}$

(c) $x_{n+1} = \sqrt{\dfrac{5x_n - 1}{2}}$     (d) $x_{n+1} = \frac{1}{2}\left(5 - \dfrac{1}{x_n}\right)$

6 (a) An iterative formula is defined as follows.

$$x_{n+1} = \frac{1}{\sqrt[3]{x_n + 1}}$$

    Using $x_1 = 0.8$, find $x_2$, $x_3$ and $x_4$ to six decimal places.

  (b) Given that the limit of of the sequence is $k$, show that $k$ satisfies the equation $k^4 + k^3 - 1 = 0$.

**7** The graphs of $y = \sin x + \frac{1}{2}$ and $y = x$ are shown sketched.

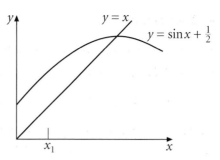

Trace the sketch and draw a cobweb or staircase diagram to show the convergence of the recurrence relation
$$x_1 = 0.5, \quad x_{n+1} = \sin x_n + \frac{1}{2}$$

**8 (a)** What, to the nearest integer, is the solution to $x^3 = 10$?

**(b)** Show that the equation can be arranged into the form $x = \sqrt{\dfrac{10}{x}}$.

Using the corresponding iterative formula with your answer to part (a) as the starting value, obtain the solution to $x^3 = 10$ to three decimal places.

**(c)** Show that $x^3 = 10$ can also be arranged into $x = \sqrt{\sqrt{10x}}$.

Using the new corresponding iterative formula with the same starting value, obtain the positive solution to $x^3 = 10$ to three decimal places.

**(d)** Which formula gives the solution more quickly?

**9 (a)** By sketching appropriate graphs and substituting suitable integer values of $x$, find an interval that contains the root of
$$x^2 - 1 = 6\sqrt{x}$$

**(b)** Show that $x = \sqrt{6\sqrt{x} + 1}$ is a rearrangement of this equation.

**(c)** Choosing a suitable starting value, solve the equation by an iterative method, giving your answer to three decimal places.

**10 (a)** Show that $x^3 + x^2 - 3x - 1 = 0$ can be rearranged as
$$x = \sqrt{\dfrac{3x + 1}{x + 1}}$$

**(b)** The equation $x^3 + x^2 - 3x - 1 = 0$ has only one positive root $\alpha$.

The iteration formula $x_{n+1} = \sqrt{\dfrac{3x_n + 1}{x_n + 1}}$ may be used to find an approximation to $\alpha$.

Taking $x_1 = 3$, find to four decimal places the values of $x_2$, $x_3$ and $x_4$.

**(c)** Giving your reasons, write down a value of $x_1$ for which the iteration formula above does not produce a valid value for $x_2$.

**\*11 (a)** For each of these recurrence relations, find $x_2, x_3, x_4, x_5$.

**(i)** $x_1 = 2, \quad x_{n+1} = x_n^3 - 1$      **(ii)** $x_1 = 0.4, \quad x_{n+1} = \dfrac{1}{x_n^2}$

**(b)** What happens?

**(c)** In each case, carefully draw a staircase or cobweb diagram to show the situation.

**(d)** What feature of the curved graphs in your diagrams results in a limit not being approached?

## C The mid-ordinate rule (answers p 198)

In Core 2 you used the trapezium rule to find an approximate
area under the graph of a function that you could not integrate.
The method treats the area under the curve as the sum of
the areas of several trapeziums of equal width.
It uses the ordinates $y_0, y_1, \ldots$, which are the lengths of
the sides of the trapeziums.

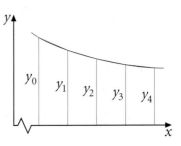

The total area is given by

$\frac{1}{2} \times$ width of strip $\times$ (sum of end ordinates + twice sum of 'interior' ordinates)

An alternative method is the **mid-ordinate rule**, in which the
area is treated as the sum of several rectangles of equal width.
The height of each rectangle is the value of the function halfway
across the rectangle. So the ordinates to be calculated are those
shown dotted (the **mid-ordinates**).

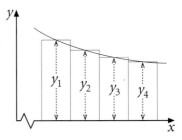

So the total area is given by

width of strip $\times y_1$ + width of strip $\times y_2$ + ...

= width of strip $\times (y_1 + y_2 + \ldots)$

This gives the mid-ordinate rule:

**K**     Area = width of strip $\times$ sum of mid-ordinates

---

### Example 6

(a) Sketch the graph of $\ln x$ for $2 \le x \le 5$.

(b) Use the mid-ordinate rule with 6 strips to calculate an approximation to $\int_2^5 \ln x \, dx$ to 3 s.f.

### Solution

(a) The sketch is shown on the right.

(b) The width of each strip is $\frac{5-2}{6} = 0.5$.

    *Work to a greater accuracy than required in the answer.*

    This table gives the positions of the mid-ordinates
    and their values.

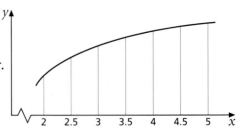

| $x$ | 2.25 | 2.75 | 3.25 | 3.75 | 4.25 | 4.75 |
|---|---|---|---|---|---|---|
| $y$ | 0.811 | 1.012 | 1.179 | 1.322 | 1.447 | 1.558 |

Approximate area = width of strip $\times$ sum of mid-ordinates

$= 0.5 \times (0.811 + 1.012 + 1.179 + 1.322 + 1.447 + 1.558) = 3.66$ to 3 s.f.

---

The trapezium and mid-ordinate rules are examples of **numerical integration**.
Numerical integration allows you to find the value of a definite integral that
you could not deal with using any of the calculus methods you have met so far.

**D** **C1** Here is a close-up of the top of the first strip in example 6.

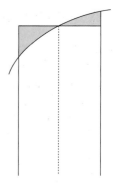

(a) By considering the two shaded regions, can you tell whether the area of the rectangle is greater or less than the corresponding area under the actual curve?

(b) Is the approximate result for $\int_2^5 \ln x \, dx$ an overestimate or an underestimate?

An estimate using the mid-ordinate rule can be improved by using a larger number of narrower strips. It is easy to do this using a spreadsheet.

### Exercise C (answers p 198)

**1** (a) Use the mid-ordinate rule, with strips 0.2 units wide, to estimate the area under the graph of $\cos^{-1} x$ from $x = 0$ to $x = 1$.

(b) By reducing the width of strip to 0.1 units, calculate a better estimate.

**2** Use the mid-ordinate rule to find an approximation to each of these integrals, using the number of strips stated in each case. Give your answers to 3 s.f.

(a) $\int_2^5 \dfrac{1}{x} \, dx$ (6 strips)

(b) $\int_1^3 x \ln x \, dx$ (4 strips)

(c) $\int_0^3 x \sin x \, dx$ (6 strips)

(d) $\int_{-2}^2 \dfrac{1}{e^x + 1} \, dx$ (4 strips)

**3** The diagram shows part of the graph of $y = 1 - x \cos x$.

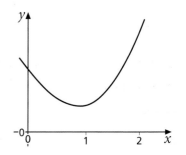

(a) Use the mid-ordinate rule with 4 strips to calculate an approximation to $\int_0^2 (1 - x \cos x) \, dx$.

(b) State, with a reason, whether your result is an overestimate or underestimate.

**4** A curve has the equation $y = \sqrt{4x - x^2}$.

(a) Sketch the curve. Explain why it lies entirely above the $x$-axis and state where it meets the $x$-axis.

(b) Use the mid-ordinate rule with 8 strips to estimate the area bounded by the curve and the $x$-axis. Give your answer to three significant figures.

**\*5** Investigate the following hypotheses. Try to justify any conclusions.

(A) In cases where the trapezium rule rule gives an underestimate, the mid-ordinate rule gives an overestimate, and vice versa.

(B) In any given case, the magnitude of the error using the mid-ordinate rule is less than that using the trapezium rule.

# D Simpson's rule (answers p 199)

You have seen how errors arise from treating the area under a curved graph as a series of trapeziums or rectangles. If, instead, you could fit a smooth graph whose function you could integrate, the errors should be much smaller.

In fact you can always fit a quadratic graph to three points, and we will do so for P, Q, R, which define two strips of equal width as shown.

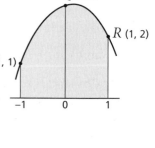

Let the equation of the quadratic be $y = ax^2 + bx + c$.
We need to find the values $a, b, c$.

| | | |
|---|---|---|
| Substitute the values of $x$ and $y$ at point P. | $1 = a - b + c$ | (1) |
| Substitute similarly for point Q ... | $3 = c$ | (2) |
| ... and for point R. | $2 = a + b + c$ | (3) |
| Substitute the value of $c$ from (2) into (1). | $1 = a - b + 3$ | (1A) |
| Substitute the value of $c$ into (3). | $2 = a + b + 3$ | (3A) |
| Add (1A) and (3A). | $3 = 2a + 6$ | $\Rightarrow a = -\frac{3}{2}$ |
| Subtract (1A) from (3A). | $1 = 2b$ | $\Rightarrow b = \frac{1}{2}$ |

So the quadratic through P, Q, R is $y = -\frac{3}{2}x^2 + \frac{1}{2}x + 3$.

So the shaded area is given by $\int_{-1}^{1}\left(-\frac{3}{2}x^2 + \frac{1}{2}x + 3\right)dx$ .

**D1** By evaluating the integral, show that the area under the quadratic graph through P, Q, R is 5 square units.

It would be too much to do all this work for each section of a curved graph. Instead a formula for the area is needed and it can be obtained as follows.

Consider the three points S, T, U, with coordinates $(-h, y_S)$, $(0, y_T)$, $(h, y_U)$. These define two strips of width $h$.

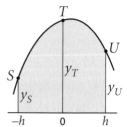

With $y = ax^2 + bx + c$ as the equation of the graph through the three points, we can again use simultaneous equations to find expressions for $a$, $b$ and $c$ in terms of the given coordinates.

| | | |
|---|---|---|
| Put each point's coordinates into the quadratic. | $y_S = ah^2 - bh + c$ | (1) |
| | $y_T = c$ | (2) |
| | $y_U = ah^2 + bh + c$ | (3) |
| Replace $c$ by $y_T$ (from (2)) in equation (1). | $y_S = ah^2 - bh + y_T$ | (1A) |
| Replace $c$ by $y_T$ in (3). | $y_U = ah^2 + bh + y_T$ | (3A) |
| Add (1A) and (3A). | $y_S + y_U = 2ah^2 + 2y_T$ | |
| $\Rightarrow$ | $a = \dfrac{y_S - 2y_T + y_U}{2h^2}$ | |

You could find an expression for $b$ at this point but, as you will see, it is not needed.

The shaded area is given by $\int_{-h}^{h}\left(ax^2 + bx + c\right)dx = \left[\dfrac{ax^3}{3} + \dfrac{bx^2}{2} + cx\right]_{-h}^{h}$

$$= \left(\dfrac{ah^3}{3} + \dfrac{bh^2}{2} + ch\right) - \left(-\dfrac{ah^3}{3} + \dfrac{bh^2}{2} - ch\right)$$

$$= \tfrac{2}{3}ah^3 + 2ch$$

Substituting the expressions for $a$ and $c$, the shaded area is $\tfrac{2}{3}\left(\dfrac{y_S - 2y_T + y_U}{2h^2}\right)h^3 + 2y_T h$

**D2** Show that this expression for the area simplifies to $\tfrac{1}{3}h(y_S + 4y_T + y_U)$.

The shaded shape could be translated any distance in the $x$-direction without its area changing, so the formula applies for any pair of strips, each of width $h$, with the given $y$-ordinates. Conventionally the $y$-ordinates are identified by numbers, so the formula becomes

$\tfrac{1}{3}h(y_0 + 4y_1 + y_2)$

**D3** Substitute the values for the points $P$, $Q$, $R$ on the opposite page into this formula and check that you get the area referred to in question D1.

**D4** Apply the formula to a section of a curve through $(1, 1.5)$, $(3, 1.3)$ and $(5, 2.3)$, remembering first to work out the value of $h$.

Here a given area (shown grey) has been divided into three pairs of strips. The formula is applied separately to each pair (so a separate quadratic is fitted to each of the three sections).

Notice how positive and negative errors tend to compensate for one another.

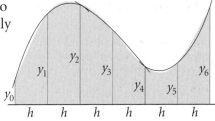

The total area here is $\tfrac{1}{3}h(y_0 + 4y_1 + y_2) + \tfrac{1}{3}h(y_2 + 4y_3 + y_4) + \tfrac{1}{3}h(y_4 + 4y_5 + y_6)$.

Notice that $y_2$ is shared by two neighbouring pairs of strips, so appears twice – as does $y_4$. So the area can be written as $\tfrac{1}{3}h(y_0 + 4y_1 + 2y_2 + 4y_3 + 2y_4 + 4y_5 + y_6)$ or as

**K** $\tfrac{1}{3}h($sum of end ordinates $+ 4\times$sum of odd ordinates $+ 2\times$sum of remaining even ordinates$)$

This is known as **Simpson's rule**. Any number of **pairs** of strips may be used.

---

**Example 7**

Use Simpson's rule with 8 strips to calculate an approximation to $\int_{5}^{7} x\cos x\,dx$.

**Solution**

Using 8 strips means the width of each strip is $\dfrac{7-5}{8} = 0.25$.

| $x$ | 5.00 | 5.25 | 5.50 | 5.75 | 6.00 | 6.25 | 6.50 | 6.75 | 7.00 |
|---|---|---|---|---|---|---|---|---|---|
| $y$ | 1.42 | 2.69 | 3.90 | 4.95 | 5.76 | 6.25 | 6.35 | 6.03 | 5.28 |

Approximate area

$= \tfrac{1}{3}\times 0.25\times [1.42 + 5.28 + 4\times(2.69 + 4.95 + 6.25 + 6.03) + 2\times(3.90 + 5.76 + 6.35)] = 9.9$

---

**Exercise D** (answers p 199)

**1 (a)** Use Simpson's rule, with strips 0.6 units wide, to estimate to 3 s.f. the area under the graph of $y = x \cos x$ from $x = 0$ to $x = 1.2$.

**(b)** Use strips 0.1 units wide to calculate a better estimate.

**2** Use Simpson's rule to find an approximation to each of these integrals, using the number of strips stated in each case. Give your answers to 3 s.f.

**(a)** $\int_1^4 \dfrac{e^x}{x}\, dx$ (6 strips)    **(b)** $\int_0^{0.6} \sqrt{1 - x^2}\, dx$ (6 strips)    **(c)** $\int_0^{\frac{\pi}{2}} \dfrac{1}{1 + \cos x}\, dx$ (4 strips)

**3 (a)** Using calculus methods, evaluate $\int_0^3 \dfrac{2x}{x^2 + 1}\, dx$.

**(b)** Using the same number of strips in each case, find an approximate value for the integral using

**(i)** the trapezium rule   **(ii)** the mid-ordinate rule   **(iii)** Simpson's rule

**(c)** Which method gives the closest approximation to your result in (a)?

---

## Key points

- For an equation of the form $f(x) = 0$, if $f(x_1)$ and $f(x_2)$ have opposite signs and $f(x)$ is continuous between $x_1$ and $x_2$, then a root (solution) of the equation lies between $x_1$ and $x_2$. (p 130)

- If an iterative formula of the form $x_{n+1} = f(x_n)$ converges to a limit, the value of the limit is the $x$-coordinate of the point of intersection of the graphs of

    $y = f(x)$ and $y = x$

  The limit is therefore a solution of the equation $f(x) = x$.

  A staircase or cobweb diagram based on the graphs of $y = f(x)$ and $y = x$ illustrates the convergence.

  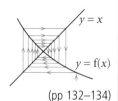

  (pp 132–134)

- The mid-ordinate rule gives an approximation to the area under a graph. The area is divided into strips of equal width. The value of the function halfway across each strip (the mid-ordinate) is calculated.

    Area = width of strip × sum of mid-ordinates    (p 138)

- Simpson's rule gives a more accurate approximation to the area under a graph. An **even** number of strips of equal width are used. The ordinates $y_0, y_1, y_2, \ldots$ are the values of the function on the vertical edges of the strips. The area is given by

    $\frac{1}{3}h($sum of end ordinates $+ 4 \times$ sum of odd ordinates $+ 2 \times$ sum of remaining even ordinates$)$    (p 141)

  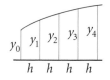

## Mixed questions (answers p 200)

**1** The diagram shows the graphs of $y = x^2 + 1$ and $y = \dfrac{1}{x}$ for $x > 0$. The graphs intersect at the point $P$.

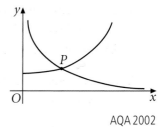

(a) Show that the $x$-coordinate of $P$ satisfies the equation
$$x^3 + x - 1 = 0$$

(b) Show that the $x$-coordinate of $P$ lies between $0.6$ and $0.7$.

AQA 2002

**2** (a) The diagram shows the graph of $y = \sin^{-1} x$.
Write down the coordinates of the end-points $A$ and $B$.

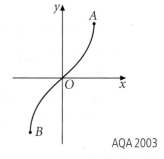

(b) Use the mid-ordinate rule, with 5 strips of equal width, to estimate the value of $\displaystyle\int_0^1 \sin^{-1} x \, dx$.
Give your answer to three decimal places.

AQA 2003

**3** (a) Without using a calculator, show that the equation $x^3 - 12 = 0$ has a root in the interval $2 \le x \le 4$.

(b) (i) Show that the equation $x = \dfrac{3x}{4} + \dfrac{3}{x^2}$ can be arranged to give the equation
$$x^3 - 12 = 0$$

(ii) Use the iterative formula $x_{n+1} = \dfrac{3x_n}{4} + \dfrac{3}{x_n{}^2}$, starting with $x_1 = 4$,
to find the values of $x_2$, $x_3$ and $x_4$, giving your answers to two decimal places.

(iii) The graphs of $y = \dfrac{3x}{4} + \dfrac{3}{x^2}$ and $y = x$ are shown below.

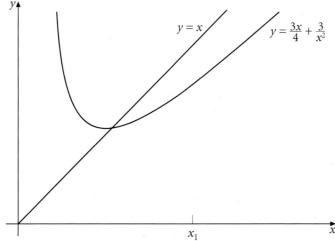

Trace the graphs and draw a staircase diagram to show the convergence of the sequence $x_1, x_2, x_3, \ldots$

(iv) Write down the **exact** value of the limit of this sequence.

**4 (a)** Sketch the following graphs on the same pair of axes. There is no need to find any points of intersection with the $x$-axis.
$$y = 1.5 - e^{-x} \qquad\qquad y = \sqrt{x}$$

**(b)** A function g is defined as $g(x) = e^{-x} + \sqrt{x} - 1.5$.
Explain how your graphs show that $g(x) = 0$ has only one solution.

**(c)** Show that the solution of $g(x) = 0$ lies between $x = 1.7$ and $x = 1.8$.

**(d)** The equation $g(x) = 0$ may be solved by means of the iterative formula $x_{n+1} = (1.5 - e^{-x_n})^2$.

Starting with $x_1 = 1.7$ find an approximate solution, to three decimal places, to the equation $g(x) = 0$.

**5** The diagram shows a sketch of the graph of $y = e^{2x} + 2x^{-1}$ for $x > 0$.

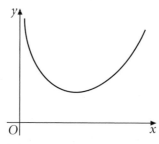

**(a)** Find $\dfrac{dy}{dx}$.

**(b)** Show that, at the stationary point on the graph, $x^2 e^{2x} = 1$.

**(c)** Deduce that, at the stationary point, $xe^x = 1$ and hence $\ln x + x = 0$.

**(d)** Show that the equation $\ln x + x = 0$ has a root between 0.5 and 0.6.

**(e)** Find $\displaystyle\int (e^{2x} + 2x^{-1})\,dx$. 

AQA 2004

**6** The diagram shows a sketch of the curve $y = x\cos x,\ 0 \le x \le \dfrac{\pi}{2}$.
The maximum point is $M$.

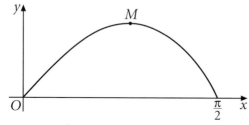

**(a) (i)** Find $\dfrac{dy}{dx}$.

**(ii)** Show that the $x$-coordinate of $M$ satisfies the equation $x = \tan^{-1}\dfrac{1}{x}$.

**(iii)** It is estimated that the relevant root of the above equation is approximately 0.9.
Use the iterative formula
$$x_{n+1} = \tan^{-1}\dfrac{1}{x_n}$$
starting with $x_1 = 0.9$, to obtain the root correct to two decimal places.

**(b)** Find the area of the region bounded by the curve and the $x$-axis. 

AQA 2003

## Test yourself (answers p 201)

1  Show that the equation $\sqrt{x} = 2\ln x$ has a root between 2 and 2.1.

2  The graphs of $y = e^{-x}$ and $y = x$ are shown sketched.

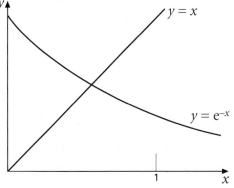

(a) Trace the sketch and draw a cobweb or staircase diagram to show the convergence of the recurrence relation

$$x_1 = 1, \ x_{n+1} = e^{-x_n}$$

(b) Find the limit to which the sequence tends, to 2 d.p.

3  A sequence is defined by $x_{n+1} = \sqrt{x_n + 12}, \ x_1 = 2$.

(a) Find the values of $x_2, x_3$ and $x_4$, giving your answers to three decimal places.

(b) Given that the limit of the sequence is $L$,

(i)  show that $L$ must satisfy the equation $L^2 - L - 12 = 0$.

(ii) find the value of $L$.

(c) The graphs of $y = \sqrt{x+12}$ and $y = x$ are sketched below.
On a copy of the sketch, draw a cobweb or staircase diagram to show how convergence takes place.

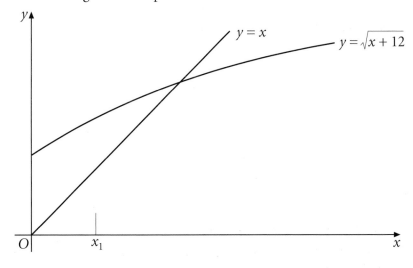

AQA 2004

4  Using the mid-ordinate rule with strips of width 0.5, obtain an approximation for $\int_{0.5}^{2.5} \dfrac{3}{e^{3x} - 1} \, dx$, giving your answer to two decimal places.

5  Use Simpson's rule with 4 strips to find an approximation for $\int_{-1}^{1} \sqrt{\cos x} \, dx$ to 2 d.p.

# 10 Proof

## A Introducing proof (answers p 201)

Most mathematicians would agree that proof is at the heart of mathematics.
A proof uses known truths and logical argument to show that a statement is
true and, once the statement has been proved this way, its truth is certain.

A proof may do more than show the truth of a statement: it may reveal
something that gives a better understanding of **why** the statement is true.
Many mathematics teachers think that proof is important, not just to
establish certainty but to **explain**, helping students to develop a stronger and
deeper understanding of ideas and techniques.

A proof must be valid; but whether or not a person finds it convincing
depends to a large extent on their mathematical knowledge and understanding:
what convinces one person may not convince another.

**D** **A1** How would you convince a 10-year-old child that when you add any two
odd numbers together you always get an even number?

How would you respond to the question in a mathematics examination
'Prove that the sum of any two odd numbers is always an even number'?

**A2** Here are three responses to the question
'Prove that $x^2 - 1 = (x + 1)(x - 1)$ for all values of $x$.'

Comment on each response.

**Response 1**

When $x = 1$,     $x^2 - 1 = 1^2 - 1 = 0$
$(x + 1)(x - 1) = (1 + 1)(1 - 1) = 2 \times 0 = 0$

When $x = 2$,     $x^2 - 1 = 2^2 - 1 = 3$
$(x + 1)(x - 1) = (2 + 1)(2 - 1) = 3 \times 1 = 3$

When $x = 3$,     $x^2 - 1 = 3^2 - 1 = 8$
$(x + 1)(x - 1) = (3 + 1)(3 - 1) = 4 \times 2 = 8$

When $x = 4$,     $x^2 - 1 = 4^2 - 1 = 15$
$(x + 1)(x - 1) = (4 + 1)(4 - 1) = 5 \times 3 = 15$

... and so on.

**Response 2**

$(x + 1)(x - 1) = (x \times x) + (x \times -1) + (1 \times x) + (1 \times -1)$
$= x^2 - x + x - 1$
$= x^2 - 1$

**Response 3**

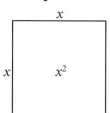 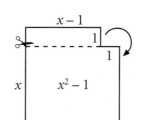 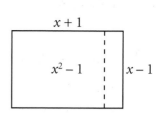

$x^2 - 1 = (x + 1)(x - 1)$ is true for **all** values of $x$ and so is an example of an **identity**.

Hence we can use the **identity symbol** $\equiv$ to write it as $x^2 - 1 \equiv (x + 1)(x - 1)$.

## B Disproof by counterexample

A **conjecture** is a statement that has not yet been proved true or false.

It is sometimes straightforward to prove a conjecture is false.
For example, we can show that the conjecture 'All multiples of 3 are odd' is false by producing one multiple of 3 that is even, for example 6. This is called a **counterexample** and only one counterexample is needed to prove a conjecture is false.

---

### Example 1

By finding a suitable counterexample, prove that the conjecture below is false.

$$a^3 + b^3 \equiv (a + b)^3$$

### Solution

When $a = 4$ and $b = 1$, then $\quad a^3 + b^3 = 4^3 + 1^3 = 64 + 1 = 65$

and $\quad (a + b)^3 = (4 + 1)^3 = 5^3 = 125$

Clearly $65 \neq 125$, a counterexample that shows the conjecture is false.

---

### Exercise B (answers p 202)

Prove that each of these conjectures is false by finding a suitable counterexample.

**1** All prime numbers are odd.

**2** $\dfrac{\cos(3\theta)}{3} \equiv \cos\theta$

**3** The product of two odd numbers is always a multiple of 3.

**4** $\cos(-\theta) \equiv -\cos\theta$

**5** $\sin(2\theta) \equiv 2\sin\theta$

**6** For all real values of $x$, $x^2 \geq x$.

**7** $(a + b)^2 \equiv a^2 + b^2$

**8** The function $f(x) = \operatorname{cosec} x$ is defined for all real values of $x$.

**9** The product of two different irrational numbers is always irrational.

**10** $\sin A + \sin B \equiv \sin(A + B)$

**11** $\sqrt{x + y} \equiv \sqrt{x} + \sqrt{y}$

**12** $\dfrac{1}{2\cos x} = 2\sec x$ for all values of $x$ for which $\cos x \neq 0$.

**13** $e^{2x} \equiv e^x + e^2$

**14** For all positive real values of $A$ and $B$, $\ln(AB) = \ln A \ln B$.

**15** For all real values of $x$, $|x + 2| < 3 \Rightarrow |x| < 1$.

**16** For all real values of $x$ and $y$, $x^2 > y^2 \Rightarrow x > y$.

## C Constructing a proof (answers p 202)

Students often find producing a mathematical proof extremely difficult.
They find it hard to know where to start or else get stuck in the middle.
Sometimes they can follow a proof that someone else has produced but
feel that they could never have constructed it for themselves.

The truth is that many published proofs are the polished result of a
messy process that has involved many dead-ends. The final proof may look
effortless and elegant but does not reveal the work involved in constructing it.
Most people only feel confident about proof after a lot of experience of
proving things in a variety of mathematical contexts.

Consider this conjecture.　　For all odd numbers $n$, $n^2 - 1$ is divisible by 8.

The following shows how one person proved the conjecture true.

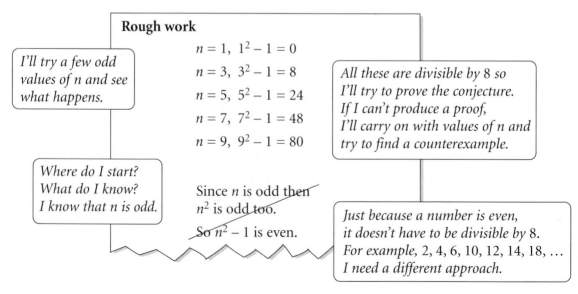

*All odd numbers can be written as $2 \times$ some number + 1. For example, $11 = 2 \times 5 + 1$.*

*So I can write n as $2k + 1$.*

$$n = 2k + 1$$
$$\text{so } n^2 = (2k + 1)^2$$
$$= 4k^2 + 4k + 1$$
$$\text{so } n^2 - 1 = 4k^2 + 4k$$
$$= 4k(k + 1)$$

*Clearly this is divisible by 4 but I need to show it is divisible by 8. I'll factorise and see if that helps.*

*If I could show that $k(k + 1)$ was even then the number would be the product of 4 and an even number, which is divisible by 8. But I see that $k$ and $k + 1$ are consecutive integers so one of them must be even and hence the product must be even. I think I'm there!*

---

**Final proof**

As $n$ is odd there is some integer $k$ such that $n = 2k + 1$.

So $n^2 - 1 = (2k + 1)^2 - 1$
$$= 4k^2 + 4k + 1 - 1$$
$$= 4k^2 + 4k$$
$$= 4k(k + 1)$$

Since $k$ and $k + 1$ are consecutive integers, one of them must be even, so the product $k(k + 1)$ is even too.

So $4k(k + 1)$ is the product of 4 and an even number.
Hence $4k(k + 1)$ is divisible by 8.

So for all odd $n$, $n^2 - 1$ is divisible by 8.

---

**C1** What mathematical experience, skills and knowledge do you think a reader needs to be convinced by the above proof?

**C2** One of these conjectures is true and one of them is false.

• For all odd numbers $n$, $n^2 + 3$ is divisible by 4.

• For all odd numbers $n$, $n^2 + 5$ is divisible by 3.

Decide which conjecture is true and prove it.

## D Direct proof

The proof outlined in section C is an example of a direct proof: it starts with what is known and proceeds, by a sequence of logical steps, to the conclusion.

Most of the proofs that you construct as part of your A2 studies are of this type.

### Example 2

Prove $\cos\theta\cot\theta + \sin\theta \equiv \operatorname{cosec}\theta$ and find any values for which the identity is not defined.

### Solution

*Use the identity* $\cot\theta \equiv \dfrac{\cos\theta}{\sin\theta}$.

$$\cos\theta\cot\theta + \sin\theta \equiv \cos\theta \times \frac{\cos\theta}{\sin\theta} + \sin\theta$$

$$\equiv \frac{\cos^2\theta}{\sin\theta} + \sin\theta$$

*Write* $\sin\theta$ *as* $\dfrac{\sin^2\theta}{\sin\theta}$.

$$\equiv \frac{\cos^2\theta}{\sin\theta} + \frac{\sin^2\theta}{\sin\theta}$$

*Add.*

$$\equiv \frac{\cos^2\theta + \sin^2\theta}{\sin\theta}$$

*Use the identity* $\cos^2\theta + \sin^2\theta \equiv 1$.

$$\equiv \frac{1}{\sin\theta}$$

$$\equiv \operatorname{cosec}\theta$$

The identity is not defined for any values that give 0 on a denominator.

$\cot\theta \equiv \dfrac{\cos\theta}{\sin\theta}$ and $\operatorname{cosec}\theta \equiv \dfrac{1}{\sin\theta}$.

The denominator $\sin\theta$ is 0 for $\theta = 0, \pm\pi, \pm2\pi, \pm3\pi, \ldots$

So the identity is not defined for $\theta = 0, \pm\pi, \pm2\pi, \pm3\pi, \ldots$

### Example 3

Show that the cube of any even number is divisible by 8.

### Solution

Any even number can be written as $2k$ for some integer $k$.

The cube of this number is $(2k)^3$ which is equivalent to $8k^3$.

Since $k$ is an integer then $k^3$ is an integer too and so $8k^3$ must be divisible by 8.

Hence the cube of any even number is divisible by 8.

### Exercise D (answers p 203)

Prove each of these.

**1** The area of a trapezium is $\frac{1}{2}h(a + b)$, where $h$ is the distance between the parallel edges and $a$ and $b$ are the lengths of the parallel edges.

**2** The sum of any two consecutive odd numbers is a multiple of 4.

**3** $\cos^2\theta + \sin^2\theta \equiv 1$

**4** The sum of the first $n$ odd numbers is $n^2$.

**5** For any four consecutive integers, the difference between the product of the last two and the product of the first two of these numbers is equal to their sum.

**6** The graphs of $y = |\sin x \cos x + 1|$ and $y = \sin x \cos x + 1$ are identical.

**7** $\sin\theta\tan\theta \equiv \sec\theta - \cos\theta$

**8 (a)** If $f(x) = \left(1 - \frac{1}{2}x^2\right)\cos x + x\sin x$ then $f'(x) = \frac{1}{2}x^2\sin x$.
   **(b)** Hence write down the indefinite integral $\int x^2\sin x\,dx$.

**9** The product of four consecutive integers is always 1 less than a perfect square.

**\*10** $\dfrac{\tan^2 A + \cos^2 A}{\sin A + \sec A} \equiv \sec A - \sin A$

**\*11** $k^3 - k$ is divisible by 6 for all integers $k$.

**\*12** $9^n - 1$ is a multiple of 8 for any positive integer $n$.

**\*13** If $p$ is a prime number such that $p > 3$, then $p^2 - 1$ is a multiple of 24.

## E Proof by contradiction

For this method of proof, assume that what you want to prove is in fact false and try to derive a logical contradiction.

One of the best known proofs of this kind is shown below.

**Proof by contradiction that $\sqrt{2}$ is irrational**

Assume that $\sqrt{2}$ is rational.

Then there must exist integers $p$ and $q$ such that $\sqrt{2} = \dfrac{p}{q}$ in its simplest form.

$$\sqrt{2} = \frac{p}{q}$$
$$\Rightarrow \quad 2 = \frac{p^2}{q^2}$$
$$\Rightarrow \quad p^2 = 2q^2$$

So $p^2$ is even and therefore $p$ is even too.

If $p$ is even then there exists an integer $k$ such that $p = 2k$ and so $p^2 = (2k)^2 = 4k^2$.

Hence $2q^2 = 4k^2$ which gives $q^2 = 2k^2$ and so $q^2$ is even and therefore $q$ is even too.

But if both $p$ and $q$ are even, then $\dfrac{p}{q}$ is not in its simplest form and our original assumption was false.

We conclude that $\sqrt{2}$ is irrational.

One of the first known proofs by contradiction is Euclid's proof that there are infinitely many prime numbers. It is considered to be one of the most elegant proofs in mathematics.

**Proof by contradiction that there are infinitely many primes**

Assume that there are a finite number of primes.

Let $p_1 = 2, p_2 = 3, p_3 = 5, p_4 = 7, \ldots$ be the primes in ascending order and let $p_n$ be the largest.

Now consider the integer $N$ which is one more than the product of all the primes:

$$N = p_1 p_2 p_3 p_4 \cdots p_n + 1$$

This number is not divisible by any of the primes $p_1, p_2, p_3, \ldots p_n$ as division by each leaves a remainder of 1. Hence $N$ is divisible by a prime larger than $p_n$ or is itself prime.

This contradicts the assumption that $p_n$ is the largest prime.

Hence our original assumption is false and there must be infinitely many primes.

---

### Example 4

Prove that the equation $x^3 = 99x + 1$ has no integer solutions.

### Solution

Assume that the equation $x^3 = 99x + 1$ does have at least one integer solution and call it $k$. Hence $k^3 = 99k + 1$.

Now $k$ is either even or odd.

If $k$ is even then $k^3$ is even and $99k + 1$ is odd which is not possible.
If $k$ is odd then $k^3$ is odd and $99k + 1$ is even which is not possible either.

In both cases we have a contradiction.
Hence our original assumption is false and the equation $x^3 = 99x + 1$ has no integer solutions.

---

### Exercise E (answers p 205)

**1** Prove each of these by contradiction.

    **(a)** $\sqrt[3]{2}$ is irrational

    **(b)** $x^4 = 45x + 1$ has no integer solutions.

    **(c)** There are no pairs of positive integers $x$ and $y$ such that $x^2 - y^2 = 10$.

**2** A teacher calls Jo and Raj to the front of the class and shows them two £5 notes and a £50 note.
She asks them to shut their eyes and raise a hand over their head.
The teacher places a £5 note in each of their hands.
She hides the £50 note and tells them to open their eyes.

Each can then see the other's note but not their own.

The teacher explains that the first person to say which note is in their own hand and prove it will win the £50 note.

After a few minutes silence, Jo proves that she must be holding a £5 note.
How do you think she did it?

## F Convincing but flawed

A proof must be convincing, but not all arguments that look convincing are valid proofs.

**Exercise F** (answers p 205)

Explain what is wrong with each of the following arguments.

**1 Statement**    $2 = 1$

  **Argument**    Suppose that    $a = b$

             Hence         $a^2 = ab$

             $\Rightarrow$       $a^2 + a^2 = ab + a^2$

             $\Rightarrow$         $2a^2 = ab + a^2$

             $\Rightarrow$     $2a^2 - 2ab = ab + a^2 - 2ab$

             $\Rightarrow$     $2a^2 - 2ab = a^2 - ab$

             $\Rightarrow$     $2(a^2 - ab) = a^2 - ab$

             and dividing both sides by $(a^2 - ab)$ gives $2 = 1$ as required.

**2 Statement**    The sum of any two numbers is even.

  **Argument**    Let $n$ represent any number.

             Then the sum of any two numbers is $n + n$ which is $2n$.

             $2n$ is even so the sum of any two numbers is even.

**3 Statement**    $0 = 2$

  **Argument**    We know that  $\cos^2 \theta + \sin^2 \theta \equiv 1$

             Hence                $\cos^2 \theta \equiv 1 - \sin^2 \theta$

             $\Rightarrow$            $\cos \theta \equiv \sqrt{1 - \sin^2 \theta}$

             $\Rightarrow$     $1 + \cos \theta \equiv 1 + \sqrt{1 - \sin^2 \theta}$

             Now this is true for all values of $\theta$, so substitute $\theta = \pi$ to obtain

                      $1 + \cos \pi = 1 + \sqrt{1 - \sin^2 \pi}$

             $\Rightarrow$       $1 + -1 = 1 + \sqrt{1 - 0^2}$

             $\Rightarrow$           $0 = 2$

**4 Statement**    $n^2 - n + 41$ is prime for any positive integer $n$.

  **Argument**    I have tested the statement for numbers 1 to 30 and $n^2 - n + 41$ always produced a prime number.

**5 Statement**   The diagram below is produced by joining each vertex of a square to the mid-point of each edge.

The shape *ABCDEFGH* is a regular octagon.

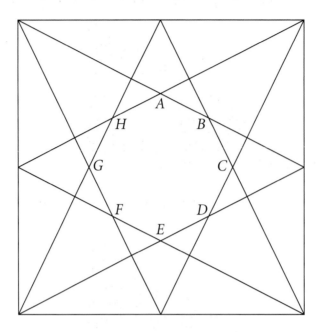

**Argument**   The whole figure is symmetrical about the lines *AE*, *BF*, *CG* and *DH* so all the edges of *ABCDEFGH* are equal. Hence the shape is a regular octagon.

**6 Statement**   The maximum number of regions that can be formed in a circle by drawing all possible chords between $n$ points on the circumference is $2^{n-1}$.

**Argument**

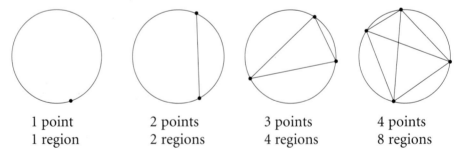

| 1 point | 2 points | 3 points | 4 points |
| 1 region | 2 regions | 4 regions | 8 regions |

Clearly, the pattern continues, doubling each time. So we are looking for the $n$th term of the geometric sequence 1, 2, 4, 8, …, which is $2^{n-1}$.

**7 Statement**    This black shape ■ has an area of 0 square units.

**Argument**    Two right-angled triangles, three rectangles and a square are arranged to make a right-angled triangle with an area of $\frac{1}{2}(13 \times 8) = 52$ square units.

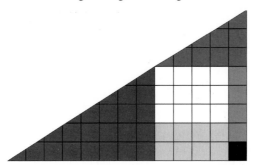

The same pieces are arranged to make another triangle with the same area.

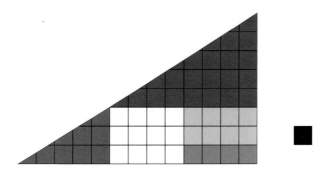

However, the black shape is left over.
So the black shape has an area of 0 square units.

## Test yourself (answers p 206)

**1** Find counterexamples to show that the following conjectures are false.

(a) $\cos(A - B) \equiv \cos A - \cos B$

(b) All even numbers greater than 2 can be expressed as the sum of two primes in only one way.

**2** Prove each of these.

(a) For any four consecutive integers, the difference between the product of the first and last and the product of the middle two of these integers is always 2.

(b) $(\tan\theta + \cot\theta)^2 \equiv \sec^2\theta + \text{cosec}^2\theta$

(c) The sum of any three consecutive multiples of 4 is a multiple of 12.

(d) When $a$ is positive, $\ln a^3 - \ln a^2 - \ln a \equiv 0$.

# Answers

## 1 Functions

### A What is a function? (p 6)

**A1** (a) P: $y = x^2$, Q: $x^2 + y^2 = 25$, R: $y^2 = x$, S: $y = \sqrt{x}$

(b) $y = x^2$: $y = 16$, $y^2 = x$: $y = 2$ and $y = -2$
$x^2 + y^2 = 25$: $y = 3$ and $y = -3$, $y = \sqrt{x}$: $y = 2$

**A2** $y^2 - x^2 = 0$, $y^4 = x$

**A3** No, you cannot find the square root of a negative number.

**A4** (a) $A(r) = 100 - \pi r^2$    (b) 71.73

(c) $0 \le r \le 5$

**A5** (a) 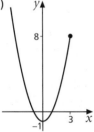    (b)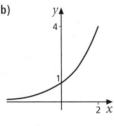

(c) 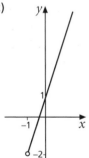    (d)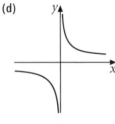

**A6**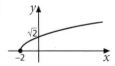

### Exercise A (p 9)

**1** (a) P    (b) W    (c) V    (d) Q    (e) U

(f) S    (g) R    (h) T

**2** (a) 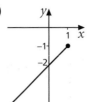    (b)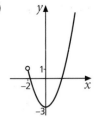

(c) 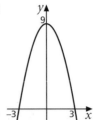    (d)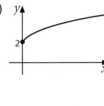

(e) 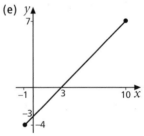    (f)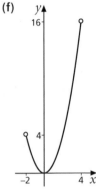

**3** (a) (i) $\frac{1}{5}$ or 0.2    (ii) 1

(iii) $\frac{1}{3}$ or 0.333...    (iv) $-\frac{1}{2}$ or −0.5

(b) −3

### B Many–one and one–one functions (p 10)

**B1** (a) $x = 9$    (b) $x = 2, -2$    (c) $x = 3$

**B2** An explanation such as:
The line $y = 1$ cuts the graph in three places showing that there are three different values of $x$ for which $f(x) = 1$. Hence g is not one–one.

**B3** (a) $f(1) = 0$, $f(0) = 0$, $f(-1) = 0$    (b) No

**B4** (a) Many–one    (b) One–one

(c) One–one    (d) Many–one

**Exercise B** (p 11)

**1 (a)**

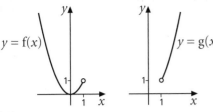

**(b)** g

**2 (a)** $t = -2, 0$

**(b)** $f(t) = 3 \Rightarrow t^2 + 2t = 3$

$\Rightarrow t^2 + 2t - 3 = 0$

$\Rightarrow (t + 3)(t - 1) = 0$

If $t$ can take any value then this equation has two solutions $t = -3$ and $t = 1$. However, only one of these is in the domain of f, so the equation has only one solution, $t = 1$.

**3 (a)** $\sin 0 = 0$, $\sin \pi = 0$

**(b)** $\pi$ and 0 are two different values for $\theta$ in the domain of g, both of which give the same value for $g(\theta)$. Hence the function g is many–one.

**(c)** $\dfrac{\pi}{6} < \theta < \dfrac{5\pi}{6}$

**4** h is one–one.

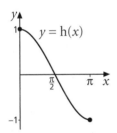

From the graph $y = h(x)$, each output can be obtained from only one input. Hence h is one–one.

**5 (a)** The area of the large square is $12^2 = 144 \, \text{cm}^2$.
The area of the small square is $x^2 \, \text{cm}^2$.
Hence the shaded area in $\text{cm}^2$ is $144 - x^2$.

**(b)** $0 \leq x \leq 6\sqrt{2}$

**(c) (i)**

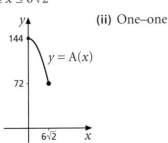

**(ii)** One–one

**(d)** $x = 2\sqrt{11} = 6.63$ (to 2 d.p.)

**6 (a)** In $\text{cm}^2$, the area of the base is
$(10 - 2x)(20 - 2x) = 200 - 60x + 4x^2$.
The height of the box is $x \, \text{cm}$ so the volume is
$x(200 - 60x + 4x^2) = 4x^3 - 60x^2 + 200x$.

**(b)** $0 \leq x \leq 5$, $0 \leq x < 5$, $0 < x \leq 5$ or $0 < x < 5$

**(c)** One explanation is:
The expression $4x^3 - 60x^2 + 200x$ equals 0 when $x = 0$ or 5 and is positive for all values in between. Hence the graph of $y = V(x)$ is above the x-axis for all these values, increasing to its maximum and decreasing back to the x-axis. Hence there must be two values of $x$ that lead to each value of $V(x)$ (except for the maximum value) so the function is many–one.

**(d)** We need to solve the equation
$4x^3 - 60x^2 + 200x = 144$
$\Rightarrow 4x^3 - 60x^2 + 200x - 144 = 0$
When $x = 1$, $4x^3 - 60x^2 + 200x - 144 = 0$, so, by the factor theorem, $(x - 1)$ is a factor of $4x^3 - 60x^2 + 200x - 144$.
Factorising gives $(x - 1)(4x^2 - 56x + 144) = 0$
$\Rightarrow 4(x - 1)(x^2 - 14x + 36) = 0$. The solutions to $x^2 - 14x + 36 = 0$ are $x = 3.39$ and $x = 10.61$ (to 2 d.p.). 10.61 is not in the domain of V so the only solutions in the domain of V are $x = 1$ and $x = 3.39$ (to 2 d.p.). Both values will give the manufacturer a box with the required volume though $x = 1$ will give a very shallow box.

## C The range of a function

**Exercise C** (p 13)

**1 (a)**

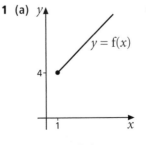

Range: $f(x) \geq 4$

**(b)**

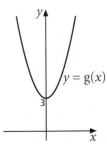

Range: $g(x) \geq 3$

**(c)**

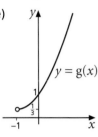

$y = h(x)$

Range: $h(x) \le 1$

**(d)**

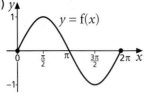

$y = f(x)$

Range: $-1 \le f(x) \le 1$

**(e)**

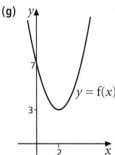

$y = g(x)$

Range: $g(x) > \frac{1}{3}$

**(f)**

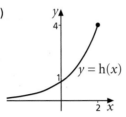

$y = h(x)$

Range: $0 < h(x) \le 4$

**(g)**

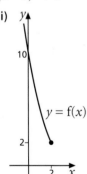

$y = f(x)$

Range: $f(x) \ge 3$

**(h)**

$y = g(x)$

Range: $g(x) \ge -1$

**2 (a)** $(x - 3)^2 + 1$

**(b) (i)**

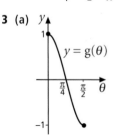

$y = f(x)$

**(ii)** $f(x) \ge 2$

**3 (a)**

$y = g(\theta)$

**(b)** $-1 \le g(\theta) \le 1$

**4 (a)** $f(x) \ge 5$

**(b)** 3 is not in the range so the equation has no solution.

**5 (a)** One way to show that h is many–one is to find two different input values that give the same output. For example, $h(-1) = 0$ and $h(5) = 0$ so the function is many–one.

**(b)** $-9 \le h(x) \le 7$

**6 (a) (i)** $x = 3$ **(ii)** $x = 1$ **(iii)** $x = \frac{1}{2}$ **(iv)** $x = -1$

**(b)** For $h(x)$ to be 2, it would have to be the case that $\frac{1}{x} = 0$ and this is not possible.

**(c)** $h(x) \in \mathbb{R}$, $h(x) \ne 2$

**7 (a)** $f(x) \in \mathbb{R}$, $f(x) \ne -5$

**(b)** $f(x) \in \mathbb{R}$, $f(x) \ne 3$

**8**

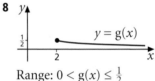

$y = g(x)$

Range: $0 < g(x) \le \frac{1}{2}$

**9** $0 < f(t) < 4$

**10 (a)** $x = \frac{1}{4}$ **(b)** $0 < g(x) \le 3$

## D Composite functions (p 14)

**D1 (a)** 517 **(b)** £55

**(c) (i)** £56.36 **(ii)** £180.44 **(iii)** £428.60

**D2** 97.72

**D3 (a)** $gf(x) = 0.4136x + 15$ **(b)** £242.48

**D4 (a) (i)** 6 **(ii)** −16 **(iii)** −26

**(b) (i)** $32 - 3x^2$

**(ii)** $10 - (3x + 2)^2$ or $6 - 12x - 9x^2$

**(iii)** $9x + 8$

### Exercise D (p 16)

**1 (a) (i)** 49 **(ii)** 13 **(iii)** 22

**(b)** $3x^2 + 1$

**(c)** $fg(x) = (3x + 1)^2 = 9x^2 + 6x + 1$

**(d) (i)** $9x + 4$ **(ii)** −5 **(iii)** $x = 5$

**2** **(a)** $fg(x) = 2x^3 + 3$, $gf(x) = (2x + 3)^3$

**(b)** $fg(x) = \left(\dfrac{1}{x+1}\right)^2$, $gf(x) = \dfrac{1}{x^2+1}$

**(c)** $fg(x) = 17 - 3x$, $gf(x) = 3 - 3x$

**(d)** $fg(x) = 1 - (1 - 2x)^2$ or $4x - 4x^2$ or $4x(1 - x)$, $gf(x) = 2x^2 - 1$

**3** $\frac{3}{2}$ or $1\frac{1}{2}$

**4** $x = 5$

**5** **(a)** $-9$

**(b)** gf cannot be formed as there are negative values in the range of f for which the square roots cannot be found.

**6** $x = 2$

**7** **(a)** $\frac{1}{3}$ or 33.3% (to the nearest 0.1%)

**(b)** $20\,°C$

**(c)** $\frac{1}{3} \le P(c) \le \frac{3}{5}$

**(d)** 45.5% (to the nearest 0.1%)

**(e)** $Pf(t) = 1 - \dfrac{10}{\frac{5}{9}(t - 32)}$ or $1 - \dfrac{18}{t - 32}$ or $\dfrac{t - 50}{t - 32}$

**(f)** $72\,°F$

**(g)** $59 \le t \le 77$

## E Inverse functions (p 17)

**E1** **(a)** $gf(5) = 5$, $fg(5) = 5$

**(b)** $gf(-3) = -3$, $fg(-3) = -3$

**(c)** $gf(x) = x$

**E2** **(a)** **(i)** $f(7) = 3 \times 7 - 1 = 21 - 1 = 20$

**(ii)** 7

**(b)** C: $f^{-1}(x) = \dfrac{x+1}{3}$

**E3** **(a)** $\dfrac{x-3}{4}$ or $\frac{1}{4}(x - 3)$

**(b)** $5(x - 3)$ or $5x - 15$

**(c)** $\frac{1}{2}x + 7$ or $\frac{1}{2}(x + 14)$

**E4** **(a)** $10 - x$ **(b)** $-x$ **(c)** $\dfrac{1}{x}$

**E5** A: $f(x) = x^2 - 5$, $-3 \le x \le 3$

**E6** **(a)** **(i)** 2 **(ii)** 5 **(iii)** 6 **(iv)** $-2$

**(b)** 10 is not in the range of g so $g^{-1}(10)$ cannot be found.

**(c)** $-1 \le x \le 4$ or $-1 \le y \le 4$

**(d)** $-2 \le g^{-1}(x) \le 6$ or $-2 \le g^{-1}(y) \le 6$

**(e)**

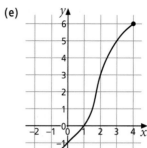

**E7** **(a)** **(i), (iv)**

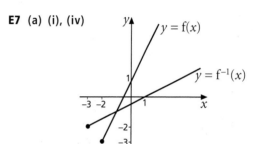

**(ii)** $\frac{1}{2}(x - 1)$ or $\frac{1}{2}x - \frac{1}{2}$ **(iii)** $x \ge -3$

**(b)** **(i), (iv)**

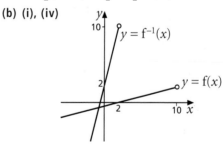

**(ii)** $4x + 2$ or $4(x + \frac{1}{2})$ **(iii)** $x < 2$

**(c)** **(i), (iv)**

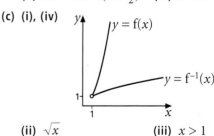

**(ii)** $\sqrt{x}$ **(iii)** $x > 1$

**(d) (i), (iv)**

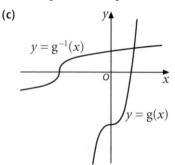

(ii) $(x-1)^{\frac{1}{3}}$ or $= \sqrt[3]{x-1}$   (iii) $1 \le x \le 9$

### Exercise E (p 20)

**1** $\frac{1}{5}(x-1)$ or $\frac{1}{5}x - \frac{1}{5}$

**2 (a)** $4(x+3)$ or $4x + 12$

   **(b)** Domain: $-3 \le x \le 1$, range: $0 \le g^{-1}(x) \le 16$

**3 (a)** $\frac{9}{5}t + 32$   **(b)** $t \ge -273$   **(c)** $-94\,°F$

**4** f has no inverse as it is not one–one (for example $f(1) = f(-1)$)

**5 (a)** $\frac{1}{3}(2-x)$ or $\frac{2}{3} - \frac{1}{3}x$   **(b)** $x < 2$   **(c)** $x = \frac{1}{2}$

**6 (a)** $\sqrt{x+5} + 2$   **(b)** $x > -5$

**7 (a)** $(x+3)^2 + 1$   **(b)** $\sqrt{x-1} - 3$

**8 (a)** $(x-2)^2$, $x \ge 2$

   **(b)** $(x+5)^{\frac{1}{3}}$ or $\sqrt[3]{x+5}$, $x \in \mathbb{R}$

   **(c)** $\dfrac{2-3x}{x}$ or $\dfrac{2}{x} - 3$, $0 < x < \frac{2}{3}$

   **(d)** $\dfrac{5}{x+4}$, $x < -4$

**9 (a)** $a = \frac{2}{3}$, $b = 1$

   **(b)**               **(c)** $-\frac{1}{3} < x \le \frac{2}{3}$

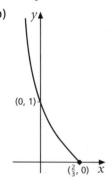

---

**10** $y = \dfrac{2x+3}{x-2} \Rightarrow y(x-2) = 2x + 3$ where $x \ne 2$

Expanding brackets gives

$yx - 2y = 2x + 3 \Rightarrow yx - 2x = 2y + 3 \Rightarrow$

$x(y-2) = 2y + 3 \Rightarrow x = \dfrac{2y+3}{y-2}$, where $y \ne 2$

So $f^{-1}(x) = \dfrac{2x+3}{x-2} = f(x)$ for $x \in \mathbb{R}$, $x \ne 2$

### Test yourself (p 22)

**1 (a)** $x > \frac{4}{3}$

   **(b)** $fg(x) = 17 - 3x^3$ which is of the form $p + qx^3$ with $p = 17$ and $q = -3$

   **(c)**

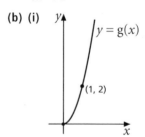

   **(d)** $(x+4)^{\frac{1}{3}}$ or $\sqrt[3]{x+4}$

**2 (a)** $\dfrac{1}{8x^6 + 1}$

   **(b) (i)**

   **(ii)** $g(x) \ge 0$   **(iii)** $x = 3$

   **(c)** $x \ge 0$   **(d)** $0, \frac{1}{2}$

**3** $G_2$ does not represent a function as each $x$-value to the left of the vertex of the graph gives rise to two different $y$-values.

**4 (a) (i)** 2　　　　　　　　**(ii)** $f(x) \geq 2$

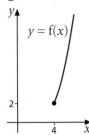

**(b)** $f(x) = 1$ has no solution as 1 is not in the range of f.

**(c)** $\sqrt{x-1} + 3$

**5 (a)** 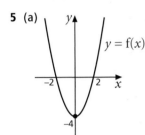　　　　**(b)** $f(x) \geq -4$

**(c)** The function g is not one–one, for example $f(2) = f(-2) = 0$ so two different inputs lead to the same output.

**6 (a)** $\dfrac{2}{6 - x^2}$

**(b) (i)** 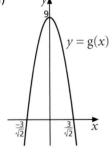　　**(ii)** $g(x) \leq 9$

**(c) (i)** $x = \pm 2$

**(ii)** The function g is not one–one: the solution to part (i) shows that $g(2) = g(-2) = 1$ so two different inputs lead to the same output.

**(d) (i)** $\dfrac{4 - 3x}{x}$ or $\dfrac{4}{x} - 3$　　**(ii)** $x = 1$

**7 (a)** $f(x) \geq 3$　　　**(b)** 2　　　　**(c)** $x = 5, -1$

---

## A Introducing the modulus function

### Exercise A (p 24)

**1 (a)** 4　　**(b)** 2　　**(c)** 6　　**(d)** 6

**2 (a)** 1　　**(b)** 1　　**(c)** 3　　**(d)** 9　　**(e)** 9

**3 (a)** 2　　**(b)** 3　　**(c)** 6　　**(d)** 7　　**(e)** $2\frac{1}{2}$

**4 (a)** 4　　**(b)** 4　　**(c)** 5　　**(d)** 1　　**(e)** 11

**5 (a)** 2　　**(b)** 4　　**(c)** 1　　**(d)** 6　　**(e)** 0

## B Graphs (p 25)

**B1 (a)** The values in the second row of the table are 3, 2, 1, 0, 1, 2, 3.

**(b) (i)** $\frac{1}{2}$　　　　**(ii)** $\frac{3}{4}$　　　　**(iii)** 2.25

**(c)**

**B2 (a)** The values in the second row of the table are 2, 1, 0, 1, 2, 3, 4.

**(b)**

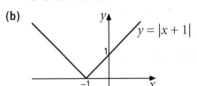

**B3 (a)**

| $x$ | –3 | –2 | –1 | 0 | 1 | 2 | 3 |
|---|---|---|---|---|---|---|---|
| $\left|x^2 - 4\right|$ | 5 | 0 | 3 | 4 | 3 | 0 | 5 |

**(b)**

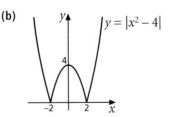

**B4 (a)** C　**(b)** B　**(c)** F　**(d)** E　**(e)** A　**(f)** D

**B5** One explanation is that $2 - x = -(x - 2)$, so $|2 - x| = |-(x - 2)| = |x - 2|$ and so the graphs are the same.

## Exercise B (p 27)

**1 (a)**

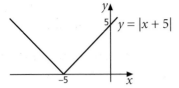
$y = |x + 5|$

**(b)**

$y = |3x - 5|$

**(c)**

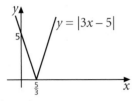
$y = |2x + 8|$

**2 (a)**

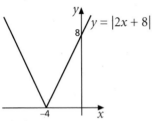
$y = |x^2 - 1|$

**(b)**

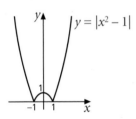
$y = |x^2 - x|$

**(c)**

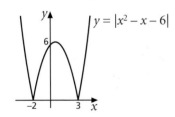
$y = |x^2 - x - 6|$

**3** One explanation is that $x^2 - 9 = -(9 - x^2)$, so $|x^2 - 9| = |-(9 - x^2)| = |9 - x^2|$ and so the graphs are the same.

**4**

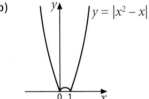
$y = |f(x)|$

**5**

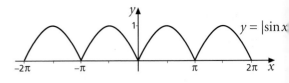
$y = |\sin x|$

**6**

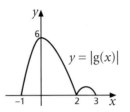
$y = |g(x)|$

**7**

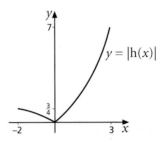
$y = |h(x)|$

**8**

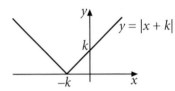
$y = |x + k|$

**9 (a)** $y = |x - 3|$    **(b)** $y = |2x - 6|$    **(c)** $y = |4x + 4$

## C Equations and inequalities (p 28)

**C1** $|-4 + 1| = |-3| = 3$
Another solution is $x = 2$.

**C2 (a)** $x = 1, -9$    **(b)** $x = 6, -4$    **(c)** $x = -2, -4$
**(d)** $x = -6$

**C3** $|x + 2|$ is greater than or equal to 0 for all values of $x$. So $|x + 2|$ is never negative.

**C4 (a)** $x = 1, -4$    **(b)** $x = \frac{1}{3}, -1$    **(c)** $x = \frac{1}{2}, 4\frac{1}{2}$

**C5** There is no solution as can be seen by drawing the graphs of $y = |3x + 2|$ and $y = x$ and observing that they do not intersect.

**C6 (a)**

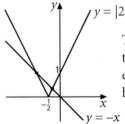
$y = |2x + 1|$
$y = -x$

The graphs intersect at two points, showing the equation $|2x + 1| = -x$ has two solutions.

**(b)** $x = -1, -\frac{1}{3}$

**C7** $x = \frac{4}{3}, 6$

**C8 (a)**

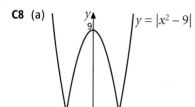

**(b) (i)** 4  **(ii)** 0  **(iii)** 2

**(c)** $x = \pm 4, \pm \sqrt{2}$

**C9 (a)**

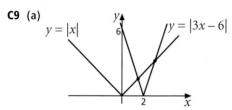

**(b)** $x = 3, 1\frac{1}{2}$  **(c)** $1\frac{1}{2} < x < 3$

**C10**

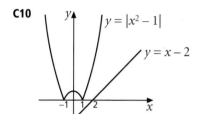

There is no solution to $|x^2 - 1| = x - 2$ as can be seen by drawing the graphs of $y = |x^2 - 1|$ and $y = x - 2$ and observing that they do not intersect.

**C11** $x \le -1$ and $x \ge \frac{1}{2}$

**C12** $x = \pm 3$

### Exercise C (p 31)

**1 (a)** $x = 3, -15$  **(b)** $x = 5\frac{1}{2}, -4\frac{1}{2}$  **(c)** $x = 4, -4$

**(d)** $x = \pm\sqrt{3}, \pm 1$  **(e)** $x = \pm\dfrac{3}{\sqrt{2}}$  **(f)** $x = -1, 3$

**2 (a)** $3 < x < 7$  **(b)** $x \le -\frac{5}{3}$ and $x \ge -1$

**3 (a)**

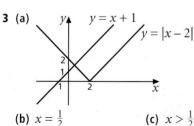

**(b)** $x = \frac{1}{2}$  **(c)** $x > \frac{1}{2}$

**4 (a)** $x = 3, \frac{1}{5}$  **(b)** $x = -4, 2$

**(c)** $x = -1, 2$  **(d)** $x = -1, 0, 1$

**(e)** $x = -2, 3$  **(f)** $x = 4, -1 - \sqrt{11}$

**5 (a)** The diagram below shows the graphs of $y = |x + 4|$ and $y = |x - 1|$.

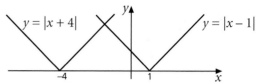

The left-hand segments are parallel as are the right-hand segments. Hence there is only the one solution to $|x + 4| = |x - 1|$.

**(b)** $x \ge -1\frac{1}{2}$

**6 (a)** $x = -\frac{2}{3}, 4$  **(b)** $x = 1\frac{1}{2}$  **(c)** $x = -2, -1$

**7 (a)** $x \ge -\frac{1}{2}$  **(b)** $-2 < x < 2$

**(c)** $x > 9$  **(d)** $x \le 2\frac{2}{3}, x \ge 12$

**(e)** $-3 < x < 4$  **(f)** $x \le -3, x \ge 2$

**8 (a)**

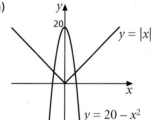

**(b)** $x = \pm 4$

**9 (a)**

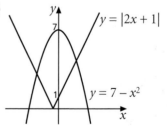

**(b)** $-2 < x < \sqrt{7} - 1$

**10** $-2 - \sqrt{6} < x < 1 - \sqrt{11}, -2 + \sqrt{6} < x < 1 + \sqrt{11}$

## D Further graphs and equations (p 32)

**D1 (a)** $f(4) = 7, f(-1) = 4$

**(b)** B

**(c)** $f(x) \ge 3$

**(d)** An explanation such as: '1 is not in the range of f' or 'f$(x) = 1 \Rightarrow |x| = -2$ which is not possible'.

**(e)** $x = -2, 2$

**D2 (a)** A  **(b)** $x = -3, 5$

**D3**

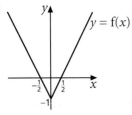

**D4 (a)**

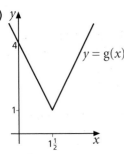

**(b)** An explanation such as '0 is not in the range of g' or 'g$(x) = 0 \Rightarrow |2x - 3| = -1$ which is not possible'.

**(c)** $x = -2, 5$

**D5 (a)** f$(1) = -3$, f$(-2) = 0$  **(b)** C

**(c)** f$(x) \leq 0$

**D6**

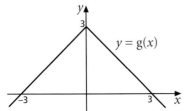

**D7 (a)**

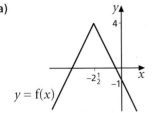

**(b)** f$(x) \leq 4$

**D8 (a)** fg$(x) = 6 - |x - 2|$, gf$(x) = |4 - x|$

**(b)**

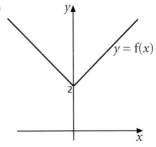

**Exercise D** (p 35)

**1 (a)**

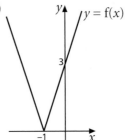

Range: f$(x) \geq 2$

**(b)**

Range: f$(x) \geq 0$

**(c)**

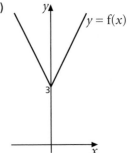

Range: f$(x) \geq 3$

**(d)**

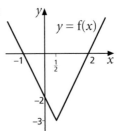

Range: f$(x) \geq -3$

**(e)**

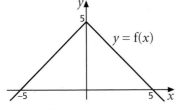

Range: $f(x) \leq 5$

**(f)**

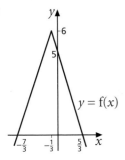

Range: $f(x) \leq 6$

**2 (a)** $x = -6, 10$     **(b)** $x = -1, 3$     **(c)** $x = 2$

**3 (a)** $x = -6, 1$

**(b)** An explanation such as '9 is not in the range of f' or 'f$(x) = 9 \Rightarrow |2x + 5| = -1$ which is not possible'.

**(c)** $x \leq -5\frac{1}{2}, x \geq \frac{1}{2}$

**4 (a)** $x = 2, 3$

**(b)** The diagram below shows the graphs of $y = 1 + |3x - 7|$ and $y = x - 2$. There are no points of intersection and hence no solutions to the equation $1 + |3x - 7| = x - 2$.

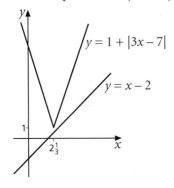

**5** $x < -\frac{1}{2}, x > 1$

**6** $x < 3$

**7 (a)**

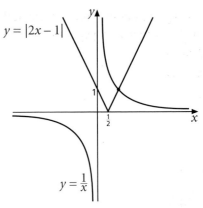

**(b)** There is only one point of intersection and hence only one solution to the equation $|2x - 1| = \frac{1}{x}$.
Multiplying each side by $x$ gives us $x|2x - 1| = 1$ and hence there is only one solution to this equation too. The solution is $x = 1$.

**8** f is not one–one because, for example, $f(3) = f(-3)$ so f has no inverse.

**9 (a)** $fg(x) = |(x + 2)^2 - 3| = |x^2 + 4x + 1|$
$gf(x) = |x^2 - 3| + 2$

**(b)**

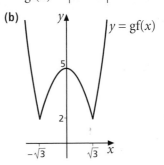

**10 (a)** $x = -9, 7$         **(b)** $x > 1$

**11 (a)**

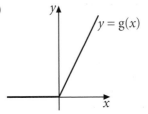

**(b)** $x = 5$

**12** $x = -2, 2, \frac{1}{2}(\sqrt{17} - 1), \frac{1}{2}(1 - \sqrt{17})$

**13 (a)**

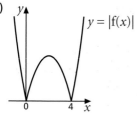

**(b)**

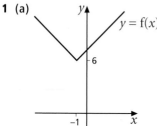

## Test yourself (p 37)

**1 (a)**

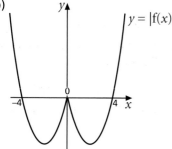

Range: $f(x) \geq 6$

**(b)** 17        **(c)** $x = -5, 3$

**2 (a)**

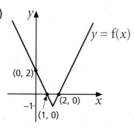

**(b)** $f(x) \geq -1$      **(c)** $x = \frac{2}{3}, 4$

**3 (a) (i)**

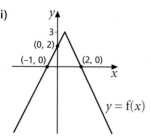

**(ii)** The maximum value of $f(x)$ is 3 so $f(x) = 4$ has no real roots.

**(b)** $f(x) \leq 3$

**(c)** $x = -2, \frac{4}{3}; \quad x < -2, x > \frac{4}{3}$

**4** $x = \frac{2}{3}$

**5 (a)**

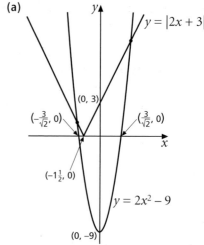

**(b)** The graphs show that there are two points of intersection, so the equation has two roots: $x = \frac{1}{2}\left(-1 - \sqrt{13}\right)$ and $x = 3$.

**6** $-4 < x < 0$

**7 (a)**

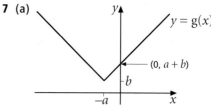

**(b)** $g(x) \geq b$      **(c)** $a = 2, b = 6$

# 3 Transforming graphs

## A Single transformations: revision (p 38)

**A1** For a stretch of scale factor $\frac{1}{2}$ in the $x$-direction, replace $x$ by $2x$ to obtain $y = (2x)^2 + 1 = 4x^2 + 1$.

**A2** Let $(x_1, y_1)$ be a point on $y = f(x)$ and let $(x_2, y_2)$ be its image on the translated curve.
Then $(x_2, y_2) = (x_1 + a, y_1)$, giving $x_1 = x_2 - a$ and $y_1 = y_2$. We know that $y_1 = f(x_1)$, so it must be true that $y_2 = f(x_2 - a)$ and so $y = f(x - a)$ is the equation of the image.

**A3** $y = |x - 3|$

**A4** $y = f(x) + a$

**A5** $y = 3^x + 5$

**A6** (a) $y = -f(x)$          (b) $y = f(-x)$

**A7** $y = x^2 - x$

### Exercise A (p 41)

**1** (a) A stretch of factor 3 in the $y$-direction
   (b) A stretch of factor $\frac{1}{3}$ in the $x$-direction
   (c) A stretch of factor $\frac{1}{3}$ in the $y$-direction
   (d) A stretch of factor 3 in the $x$-direction

**2** $y = 2x^3$

**3** (a) $f(5x) = (5x)^2 - (5x) = 25x^2 - 5x$
   (b) A stretch of factor $\frac{1}{5}$ in the $x$-direction
   (c)

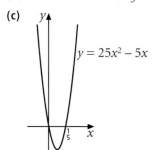
$y = 25x^2 - 5x$

**4** (a) A translation of $\begin{bmatrix} 0 \\ 3 \end{bmatrix}$   (b) A translation of $\begin{bmatrix} -3 \\ 0 \end{bmatrix}$

   (c) A translation of $\begin{bmatrix} 0 \\ -3 \end{bmatrix}$   (d) A translation of $\begin{bmatrix} 3 \\ 0 \end{bmatrix}$

**5** A translation of $\begin{bmatrix} -90 \\ 0 \end{bmatrix}$

**6** (a) $f(x - 4) = (x - 4)^2 + (x - 4)$
      $= x^2 - 8x + 16 + x - 4 = x^2 - 7x + 12$
   (b) A translation of $\begin{bmatrix} 4 \\ 0 \end{bmatrix}$

**7** $y = x^3 - 3x^2 - x + 3$

**8** (a) $y = (-x)^4 + (-x)^2 = x^4 + x^2$
   (b) The equation remains the same so the $y$-axis must be a line of symmetry.

**9** (a) (i) $y = 5^{x+1}$          (ii) $y = 5 \times 5^x$
   (b) $5 \times 5^x = 5^1 \times 5^x = 5^{x+1}$ so the images are the same.

## B Combining transformations (p 42)

**B1**

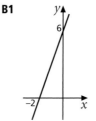

The equation is $y = 3x + 6$.

**B2** (a) $y = -x - 1$          (b) $y = -x + 1$

**B3** The stretch transforms $y = x^2$ to $\frac{1}{3}y = x^2$ or $y = 3x^2$. The translation transforms $y = 3x^2$ to $y + 5 = 3x^2$ which is $y = 3x^2 - 5$.

**B4** (a) $y = -x^2 - 1$          (b) $y = 2(x - 5)^2$
   (c) $y = (x + 3)^2 - 2$        (d) $y = -6x^2$

**B5** (a) A translation of $\begin{bmatrix} -1 \\ 0 \end{bmatrix}$ and a stretch of factor $\frac{1}{2}$ in the $y$-direction (the order doesn't matter)
   (b) A reflection in the $x$-axis followed by a translation of $\begin{bmatrix} 0 \\ 7 \end{bmatrix}$ (or a translation of $\begin{bmatrix} 0 \\ -7 \end{bmatrix}$ followed by a reflection in the $x$-axis)

**B6** B: $y = 3f(x - 1)$

**B7** B: $y = f\left(-\frac{1}{2}x\right)$

**Exercise B** (p 45)

**1**  $y = (x-1)^2 + 5$  or  $y = x^2 - 2x + 6$

**2**  $y = \frac{1}{8}x^3 - 2$

**3** (a)  $y = 2|x-3|$

(b)

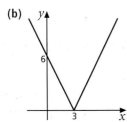

**4** (a) A translation of $\begin{bmatrix} 1 \\ 0 \end{bmatrix}$ and a stretch of factor $\frac{1}{2}$ in the $y$-direction (the order doesn't matter)

(b) A translation of $\begin{bmatrix} 0 \\ -5 \end{bmatrix}$ and a stretch of factor $\frac{1}{3}$ in the $x$-direction (the order doesn't matter)

(c) A translation of $\begin{bmatrix} -1 \\ 0 \end{bmatrix}$ and a translation of $\begin{bmatrix} 0 \\ 3 \end{bmatrix}$ (the order doesn't matter)

**5** (a) A stretch of factor $\frac{1}{4}$ in the $x$-direction and a stretch of factor 2 in the $y$-direction (the order doesn't matter)

(b) A translation of $\begin{bmatrix} -1 \\ 0 \end{bmatrix}$ and a stretch of factor 3 in the $y$-direction (the order doesn't matter)

(c) A translation of $\begin{bmatrix} 2 \\ 0 \end{bmatrix}$ and a stretch of factor $\frac{1}{4}$ in the $y$-direction (the order doesn't matter)

**6**

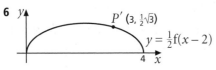

$P'\ (3, \frac{1}{2}\sqrt{3})$

$y = \frac{1}{2}f(x-2)$

**7** (a) $\frac{1}{2}f(x-4) = \frac{1}{2}(x-4)^2 = \frac{1}{2}(x^2 - 8x + 16)$
$= \frac{1}{2}x^2 - 4x + 8$

(b) A translation of $\begin{bmatrix} 4 \\ 0 \end{bmatrix}$ and a stretch of factor $\frac{1}{2}$ in the $y$-direction (the order doesn't matter)

**8**

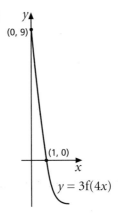

(0, 9)

(1, 0)

$y = 3f(4x)$

**9**

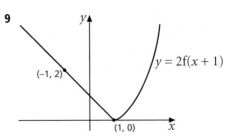

$y = 2f(x+1)$

(−1, 2)

(1, 0)

**10** The image of $(0, p)$ is $(0, p+3)$.
The image of $(q, 0)$ is $(4q, 3)$.

**11**

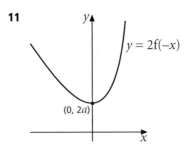

$y = 2f(-x)$

(0, 2a)

**C  Order of transformations** (p 46)

**C1** (a)

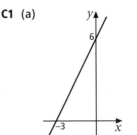

6

−3

The equation is $y = 2x + 6$.

(b) $y = 2x + 3$      (c) No

**C2 (a)**

The equation is $y = (x + 2)^2$.

**(b)** $y = (x - 2)^2$

The equations of the final images are different.

**C3 (a)** $y = -(x - 1)^2$      **(b)** $y = -(x - 1)^2$

**(c)** An explanation such as:

The reflection replaces $y$ by $-y$ and the translation replaces $x$ by $(x - 1)$.

These are independent of each other so the order they are done in does not matter.

**C4 (a)** $y = (-x + 1)^2$

**(b)** $y = (-x - 1)^2$   or   $y = (x + 1)^2$

**(c)** No

**C5 (a) (i)** A translation of $\begin{bmatrix} 4 \\ 0 \end{bmatrix}$ replaces $x$ by $x - 4$

so $y = |x|$ maps on to $y = |x - 4|$.

A stretch of factor 2 in the $x$-direction replaces $x$ by $\frac{1}{2}x$ and so $y = |x - 4|$ maps on to $y = |\frac{1}{2}x - 4|$.

**(ii)**

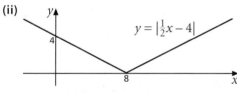

$y = |\frac{1}{2}x - 4|$

**(b)** $y = |\frac{1}{2}x - 2|$

**Exercise C** (p 49)

**1 (a)** $y = 5x^2 - 10$

**(b)** $y = 5x^2 - 2$

The equations of the final images are different.

**2** A reflection in the $y$-axis replaces $x$ by $-x$ and so $y = 3^x$ maps to $y = 3^{-x}$.

A translation of $\begin{bmatrix} 5 \\ 0 \end{bmatrix}$ replaces $x$ by $x - 5$ and so $y = 3^{-x}$ maps to $y = 3^{-(x - 5)}$, which is equivalent to $y = 3^{5 - x}$.

**3 (a)** $y = \frac{1}{2}f(x) - 3$      **(b)** $y = -f(x) - 4$

**(c)** $y = f(4x + 1)$        **(d)** $y = f(-x + 4)$

**4 (a)** $y = f(kx - a)$

**(b)** A translation of $\begin{bmatrix} 5 \\ 0 \end{bmatrix}$ followed by a stretch of factor $\frac{1}{3}$ in the $x$-direction

**5** A translation of $\begin{bmatrix} 9 \\ 0 \end{bmatrix}$ followed by a stretch of factor $\frac{1}{2}$ in the $x$-direction (or a stretch factor of $\frac{1}{2}$ in the $x$-direction followed by a translation of $\begin{bmatrix} 4\frac{1}{2} \\ 0 \end{bmatrix}$)

**6** An explanation such as:

The stretch replaces $y$ by $\frac{1}{2}y$ and the translation replaces $x$ by $(x - 3)$. These are independent of each other so the order they are done in does not matter. Either order will result in the image $y = 2f(x - 3)$.

**7 (a)** $y = kf(x) + a$

**(b)** A stretch of factor 3 in the $y$-direction followed by a translation of $\begin{bmatrix} 0 \\ -5 \end{bmatrix}$

**8 (a)** A stretch of factor $\frac{1}{3}$ in the $y$-direction followed by a translation of $\begin{bmatrix} 0 \\ 1 \end{bmatrix}$ (or a translation of $\begin{bmatrix} 0 \\ 3 \end{bmatrix}$ followed by a stretch of factor $\frac{1}{3}$ in the $y$-direction)

**(b)** A reflection in the $x$-axis followed by a translation of $\begin{bmatrix} 0 \\ 5 \end{bmatrix}$ (or a translation of $\begin{bmatrix} 0 \\ -5 \end{bmatrix}$ followed by a reflection in the $x$-axis)

**(c)** A translation of $\begin{bmatrix} 8 \\ 0 \end{bmatrix}$ followed by a stretch of factor $\frac{1}{2}$ in the $x$-direction (or a stretch of factor $\frac{1}{2}$ in the $x$-direction followed by a translation of $\begin{bmatrix} 4 \\ 0 \end{bmatrix}$)

**(d)** A stretch of factor 3 in the $y$-direction followed by a translation of $\begin{bmatrix} 0 \\ -6 \end{bmatrix}$ (or a translation of $\begin{bmatrix} 0 \\ -2 \end{bmatrix}$ followed by a stretch of factor 3 in the $y$-direction)

**(e)** A translation of $\begin{bmatrix} -4 \\ 0 \end{bmatrix}$ followed by a stretch of factor 2 in the $x$-direction (or a stretch of factor 2 in the $x$-direction followed by a translation of $\begin{bmatrix} -8 \\ 0 \end{bmatrix}$)

**(f)** A reflection in the $y$-axis followed by a translation of $\begin{bmatrix} 3 \\ 0 \end{bmatrix}$ (or a translation of $\begin{bmatrix} -3 \\ 0 \end{bmatrix}$ followed by a reflection in the $y$-axis)

**9 (a) (i)** $y = 2f(x) + 10$    **(ii)** $y = 2f(x) + 10$

    **(b)** Since the images are the same the combinations of transformations are equivalent.

**10 (a) (i)** $y = -f(x) - 2$    **(ii)** $y = -f(x) - 2$

    **(b)** Since the images are the same the combinations of transformations are equivalent.

**11 (a)** A stretch of factor 3 in the $x$-direction replaces $x$ by $\frac{1}{3}x$ and a stretch of factor $1\frac{1}{2}$ or $\frac{3}{2}$ in the $y$-direction replaces $y$ by $\frac{2}{3}y$, so $x^2 + y^2 = 1$ maps on to $(\frac{1}{3}x)^2 + (\frac{2}{3}y)^2 = 1$, which is equivalent to $\frac{1}{9}x^2 + \frac{4}{9}y^2 = 1$ or $x^2 + 4y^2 = 9$.

A translation of $\begin{bmatrix} -1 \\ 2 \end{bmatrix}$ replaces $x$ by $x + 1$ and $y$ by $y - 2$, so $x^2 + 4y^2 = 9$ maps on to $(x + 1)^2 + 4(y - 2)^2 = 9$, which is equivalent to $x^2 + 2x + 1 + 4y^2 - 16y + 16 = 9$ or $x^2 + 4y^2 + 2x - 16y + 8 = 0$.

    **(b)**

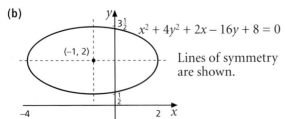

$x^2 + 4y^2 + 2x - 16y + 8 = 0$

Lines of symmetry are shown.

    **(c)** $x = -1$ and $y = 2$

## Test yourself (p 51)

**1** A stretch of factor $\frac{1}{2}$ in the $y$-direction and a translation of $\begin{bmatrix} -1 \\ 0 \end{bmatrix}$ (the order doesn't matter)

**2 (a)** A stretch of factor 4 in the $y$-direction and a translation of $\begin{bmatrix} 3 \\ 0 \end{bmatrix}$ (the order doesn't matter)

    **(b)**

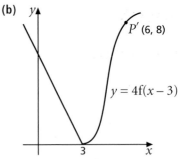

$P'$ (6, 8)

$y = 4f(x - 3)$

**3** A stretch of factor 4 in the $y$-direction and a reflection in the $y$-axis (the order doesn't matter)

**4 (a)** A stretch of factor 2 in the $y$-direction and a stretch of factor $\frac{1}{3}$ in the $x$-direction (the order doesn't matter)

    **(b)**

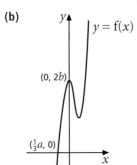

$y = f(x)$

(0, 2$b$)

($\frac{1}{3}a$, 0)

**5** $y = 2x^2 - 6$

**6 (a)** A stretch of factor 3 in the $y$-direction followed by a translation of $\begin{bmatrix} 0 \\ 4 \end{bmatrix}$ (or a translation of $\begin{bmatrix} 0 \\ \frac{4}{3} \end{bmatrix}$ followed by a stretch of factor 3 in the $y$-direction)

    **(b)** A reflection in the $y$-axis and a translation of $\begin{bmatrix} 0 \\ -7 \end{bmatrix}$ (the order doesn't matter)

    **(c)** A translation of $\begin{bmatrix} 3 \\ 0 \end{bmatrix}$ followed by a stretch of factor $\frac{1}{5}$ in the $x$-direction (or a stretch of factor $\frac{1}{5}$ in the $x$-direction followed by a translation of $\begin{bmatrix} \frac{3}{5} \\ 0 \end{bmatrix}$)

**7** $y = -f(x) + 6$

# 4 Trigonometry

## A Inverse circular functions (p 52)

**A1**

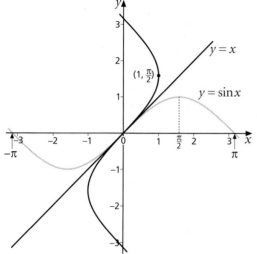

**A2** No, because it is a one–many mapping, so not a function.

**A3** f(x) and h(x).

**A4** $-1 \leq x \leq 1$

**A5** (a) 30°  (b) 45°  (c) 0°  (d) −90°

**A6** (a) $\mathbb{R}$

(b), (c)

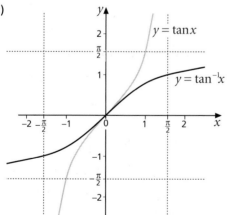

(d) Domain is $x \in \mathbb{R}$; range is $-1 \leq y \leq 1$.

## Exercise A (p 54)

**1** (a), (b)

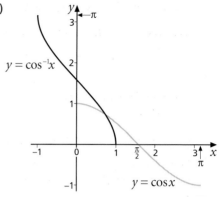

(c) Domain: $-1 \leq x \leq 1$; range: $0 \leq y \leq \pi$.

**2** (a) $\theta° = 60°$  (b) $\theta° = 120°$ and 240°  (c) 120°

**3** (a) 180°  (b) 30°  (c) 90°  (d) −60°

**4** (a) 0  (b) $\dfrac{2\pi}{3}$  (c) $-\dfrac{\pi}{4}$  (d) $-\dfrac{\pi}{3}$

(e) $\dfrac{\pi}{2}$  (f) 0  (g) $\dfrac{3\pi}{4}$  (h) $-\dfrac{\pi}{6}$

**5** (a) $x = \dfrac{1}{\sqrt{2}}$  (b) $x = \dfrac{1}{2}$

(c) $x = -\dfrac{1}{\sqrt{2}}$  (d) No solution

**6** (a) (i) $\dfrac{1}{2}$  (ii) 1  (iii) $\dfrac{\sqrt{3}}{2}$  (iv) $-\dfrac{1}{2}$

(b) Yes

**7** (a) (i) $\dfrac{\pi}{6}$  (ii) $\dfrac{\pi}{6}$  (iii) $-\dfrac{\pi}{6}$  (iv) $\dfrac{\pi}{6}$

(b) No

**8** (a) C  (b) $-1 \leq f(x) \leq 1$

(c) Domain: $-1 \leq x \leq 1$
range: $-\dfrac{\pi}{4} \leq f^{-1}(x) \leq \dfrac{\pi}{4}$

**9** (a) $y = \frac{1}{2} \sin^{-1} x$

(b) A confirmation by graphing

## B Sec, cosec and cot (p 55)

**B1** (a) $\dfrac{1}{\sqrt{2}}$  (b) $\sqrt{2}$

**B2** (a) $\dfrac{2}{\sqrt{3}}$  (b) 2  (c) 1  (d) $\sqrt{2}$

**B3** (a) 1  (b) −1  (c) $\sqrt{2}$  (d) −2

**B4** (a) 1  (b) $\sqrt{3}$  (c) $-\dfrac{1}{\sqrt{3}}$  (d) 1

**B5 (a)** You cannot; it is $1 \div 0$.

**(b)** Two other values of $x$ which have $\sin x = 0$, such as $\pi$ or $2\pi$

**(c)** $x = 0, \pm\pi, \pm2\pi, \pm3\pi, \pm4\pi, \ldots$

**B6 (a)** Three values of $x$ which have $\cos x = 0$, such as $\dfrac{\pi}{2}, \dfrac{3\pi}{2}, \dfrac{5\pi}{2}$

**(b)** $x = \pm\dfrac{\pi}{2}, \pm\dfrac{3\pi}{2}, \pm\dfrac{5\pi}{2}, \pm\dfrac{7\pi}{2}, \ldots$

**B7 (a)**

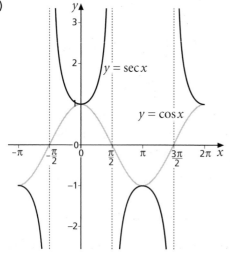

**(b)** $x \in \mathbb{R}, x \neq \pm\dfrac{\pi}{2}, \pm\dfrac{3\pi}{2}, \pm\dfrac{5\pi}{2}, \ldots$

**(c)** $y \in \mathbb{R}, y \leq -1$ and $y \geq 1$

**(d)** $2\pi$

**B8 (a), (b)**

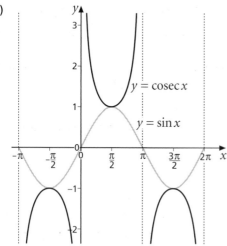

**(c)** Domain: $x \in \mathbb{R}, x \neq 0, \pm\pi, \pm2\pi, \pm3\pi, \ldots$
range: $x \in \mathbb{R}, x \leq -1$ and $x \geq 1$

**(d)** $2\pi$

**B9**  $\sin^2 x + \cos^2 x = 1$

$\Rightarrow \dfrac{\sin^2 x}{\sin^2 x} + \dfrac{\cos^2 x}{\sin^2 x} = \dfrac{1}{\sin^2 x}$

$\Rightarrow 1 + \cot^2 x = \operatorname{cosec}^2 x$

**Exercise B** (p 57)

**1 (a), (b)**

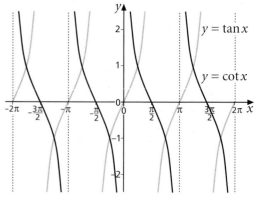

**(c)** Domain: $x \in \mathbb{R}, x \neq 0, \pm\pi, \pm2\pi, \pm3\pi, \ldots$
range: $x \in \mathbb{R}$

**(d)** $\pi$

**2 (a)** $\dfrac{2}{\sqrt{3}}$  **(b)** $\dfrac{1}{\sqrt{3}}$  **(c)** 2  **(d)** $-\dfrac{2}{\sqrt{3}}$

**3 (a)** $\sec x$  **(b)** 1  **(c)** 1  **(d)** $\tan x$

**4 (a)** $\cot\theta$  **(b)** $\cot\theta$  **(c)** $\operatorname{cosec} x$  **(d)** $\cot x$

**5 (a)** $\sin^3 x$  **(b)** 1

**6 (a)** $\tan\theta + \cot\theta = \tan\theta + \dfrac{1}{\tan\theta} = \dfrac{\sin\theta}{\cos\theta} + \dfrac{\cos\theta}{\sin\theta}$

$= \dfrac{\sin^2\theta + \cos^2\theta}{\cos\theta \sin\theta} = \dfrac{1}{\cos\theta \sin\theta}$

$= \dfrac{1}{\cos\theta} \times \dfrac{1}{\sin\theta} = \sec\theta \operatorname{cosec}\theta$

**(b)** $\cot\theta \sec\theta = \dfrac{\cos\theta}{\sin\theta} \times \dfrac{1}{\cos\theta} = \dfrac{1}{\sin\theta} = \operatorname{cosec}\theta$

**7 (a)** $\cot^2 x$  **(b)** $\tan^2 x$  **(c)** $-\cot x$

**8**  $\operatorname{cosec}^2 x = 1 + \cot^2 x$

$\Rightarrow \operatorname{cosec}^2 x - \cot^2 x = 1$

$\Rightarrow (\operatorname{cosec} x + \cot x)(\operatorname{cosec} x - \cot x) = 1$

$\Rightarrow \operatorname{cosec} x + \cot x = \dfrac{1}{\operatorname{cosec} x - \cot x}$

**9 (a)** $\frac{3}{5}$  **(b)** $\frac{4}{3}$  **(c)** $\frac{5}{3}$  **(d)** $\frac{5}{4}$

**10 (a)** $-\frac{5}{12}$  **(b)** $-\frac{12}{13}$  **(c)** $\frac{5}{13}$  **(d)** $\frac{13}{5}$

**11 (a)** 1     **(b)** $\dfrac{1}{\sqrt{2}}$ or $-\dfrac{1}{\sqrt{2}}$

**(c)** $\dfrac{1}{\sqrt{2}}$ or $-\dfrac{1}{\sqrt{2}}$     **(d)** $\sqrt{2}$ or $-\sqrt{2}$

## C Solving equations (p 58)

**C1** $\tan^2 x + \sec x = 1 \Rightarrow \dfrac{\sin^2 x}{\cos^2 x} + \dfrac{1}{\cos x} = 1$

$\Rightarrow \sin^2 x + \cos x = \cos^2 x$

$\Rightarrow (1 - \cos^2 x) + \cos x = \cos^2 x$

$\Rightarrow 2\cos^2 x - \cos x - 1 = 0$

$\Rightarrow (2\cos x + 1)(\cos x - 1) = 0$

$\Rightarrow \cos x = -\tfrac{1}{2}$ or 1

$\Rightarrow x = \dfrac{2\pi}{3}$ or $\dfrac{4\pi}{3}$ or $x = 0$ or $2\pi$

**Exercise C** (p 59)

**1 (a)** $\theta° = 45°$ or $315°$

**(b)** $\theta° = 45°, 135°, 225°$ or $315°$

**2** $\theta° = -162°$ or $18°$

**3 (a)** $x = \dfrac{\pi}{4}$ or $\dfrac{5\pi}{4}$     **(b)** $x = \dfrac{\pi}{2}$

**(c)** $x = \dfrac{\pi}{2}$ or $\dfrac{3\pi}{2}$     **(d)** $\dfrac{\pi}{3}, \dfrac{2\pi}{3}, \dfrac{4\pi}{3}$ or $\dfrac{5\pi}{3}$

**4 (a)** $x = -1.23$ or $1.23$

**(b)** $x = -1.91, -1.23, 1.23$ or $1.91$

**(c)** $x = 0.34$ or $2.80$

**(d)** $x = -2.03$ or $1.11$

**5 (a)** $\sec^2 x + \tan x = 3$

$\Rightarrow (1 + \tan^2 x) + \tan x = 3$

$\Rightarrow \tan^2 x + \tan x - 2 = 0$

**(b)** $(\tan x - 1)(\tan x + 2)$

**(c)** $x = \dfrac{\pi}{4}$ (0.79), $-\dfrac{3\pi}{4}$ (−2.36), −1.11 or 2.03

**6** $\theta = -\dfrac{\pi}{2}$

**7** $x = 1.2$ or $5.1$

**8** $x = 45.0°$ or $56.3°$

**9 (a)** $\theta° = 78.69°, 153.43°, 258.69°$ or $333.43°$

**(b)** $\theta° = 14.04°, 135.00°, 194.04°$ or $315.00°$

**10** There is no solution $\left(\text{note that } x = \dfrac{\pi}{2} \text{ is not a}\right.$ solution, since neither $\sec x$ nor $\tan x$ is defined for $x = \dfrac{\pi}{2}\Big)$.

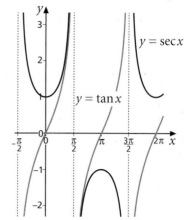

$y = \sec x$ and $y = \tan x$ do not intersect, and share the same asymptotes.

**11** $A$ (0.90, 0.79) and $B$ (5.38, −0.79)

## D Transforming graphs (p 60)

**D1 (a)** A stretch in the $y$-direction, scale factor $\tfrac{1}{3}$; a reflection in the $x$- or $y$-axis (order unimportant)

**(b)** A stretch in the $x$-direction, scale factor $\tfrac{1}{2}$; a translation of $\begin{bmatrix} 0 \\ 3 \end{bmatrix}$ (order unimportant)

**(c)** A reflection in the $x$- or $y$-axis; a translation of $\begin{bmatrix} 0 \\ 3 \end{bmatrix}$ (order unimportant)

**D2 (a) (i)** $y = \cos \tfrac{1}{4}x + 2$    **(ii)** $y = 2\cos(x - 1)$

**(iii)** $y = 2\cos \tfrac{1}{3}x$

**(b) (i)**

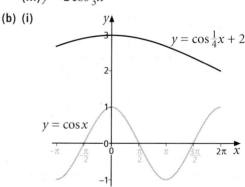

**(ii)**

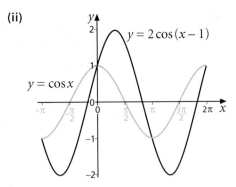

$y = 2\cos(x - 1)$

$y = \cos x$

**(iii)**

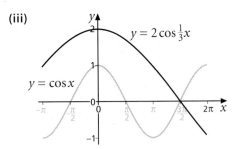

$y = 2\cos\frac{1}{3}x$

$y = \cos x$

**D3** There are other possibilities besides those described here.

(a) (i) A stretch in the $y$-direction, scale factor $\frac{1}{2}$; then a translation of $\begin{bmatrix} \frac{\pi}{4} \\ 0 \end{bmatrix}$ (or vice versa)

(ii) $y = \frac{1}{2}\sin\left(x - \frac{\pi}{4}\right)$

(b) (i) A reflection in the $x$-axis; then a translation of $\begin{bmatrix} -\frac{\pi}{6} \\ 0 \end{bmatrix}$ (or vice versa)

(ii) $y = -\sin\left(x + \frac{\pi}{6}\right)$

(c) (i) A stretch in the $y$-direction, scale factor 2; then a stretch in the $x$-direction, scale factor $\frac{1}{3}$ (or vice versa)

(ii) $y = 2\sin 3x$

(d) (i) A stretch in the $x$-direction, scale factor 2; then a translation of $\begin{bmatrix} 0 \\ 1 \end{bmatrix}$

(ii) $y = \left(\sin\frac{1}{2}x\right) + 1$

**Exercise D** (p 63)

Where transformations have to be identified from given graphs there are alternative answers to those provided here.

**1** (a) A stretch in the $x$-direction, scale factor $\frac{1}{4}$; $y = \cos 4x$

(b) A translation of $\begin{bmatrix} 0 \\ -1 \end{bmatrix}$; $y = (\cos x) - 1$

(c) A translation of $\begin{bmatrix} \frac{\pi}{2} \\ 0 \end{bmatrix}$; $y = \cos\left(x - \frac{\pi}{2}\right)$

(d) A stretch in the $x$-direction, scale factor 4; $y = \cos\frac{1}{4}x$

**2** (a) (i) $y = \left(\tan\frac{1}{2}x\right) - 1$ (ii) $y = \tan(-2x)$

(iii) $y = -\tan(x - 1)$ (iv) $y = \tan(-x) + 1$

(b) (i)

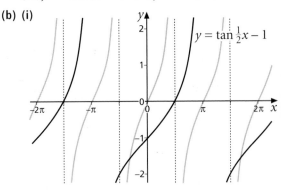

$y = \tan\frac{1}{2}x - 1$

(ii)

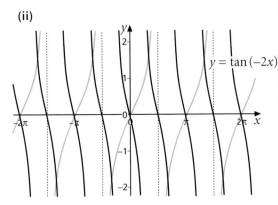

$y = \tan(-2x)$

(iii)

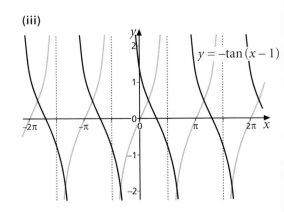

$y = -\tan(x - 1)$

**(iv)**

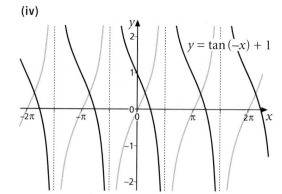

$y = \tan(-x) + 1$

**(b)**

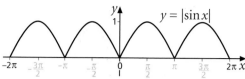

$y = |\sin x|$

**(c)**

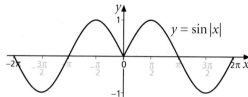

$y = \sin|x|$

**3 (a)** $\left(\dfrac{5\pi}{12}, 1\right)$

**(b)** $y = 2\sin\left(x - \dfrac{\pi}{4}\right)$

**(c)** When $x = \dfrac{5\pi}{12}$, $2\sin\left(x - \dfrac{\pi}{4}\right) = 2\sin\left(\dfrac{5\pi}{12} - \dfrac{\pi}{4}\right)$

$= 2\sin\left(\dfrac{\pi}{6}\right) = 1$; the image of $A$ fits.

**4 (a) (i)** A stretch in the $x$-direction, scale factor $\frac{1}{2}$, then a stretch in the $y$-direction scale factor $\frac{1}{2}$ (or vice versa).

**(ii)** $y = \frac{1}{2}\cos 2x$

**(b) (i)** A stretch in the $x$-direction, scale factor 2, then a translation by $\begin{bmatrix} 0 \\ -1 \end{bmatrix}$ (or vice versa)

**(ii)** $y = \left(\cos \frac{1}{2}x\right) - 1$

**(c) (i)** A stretch in the $y$-direction, scale factor $1\frac{1}{2}$, then a translation by $\begin{bmatrix} -\dfrac{\pi}{3} \\ 0 \end{bmatrix}$ (or vice versa)

**(ii)** $y = 1.5\cos\left(x + \dfrac{\pi}{3}\right)$

**(d) (i)** A translation by $\begin{bmatrix} 0.5 \\ 0 \end{bmatrix}$ then a translation by $\begin{bmatrix} 0 \\ -0.25 \end{bmatrix}$ (or vice versa).

**(ii)** $y = \cos(x - 0.5) - 0.25$

**5 (a)**

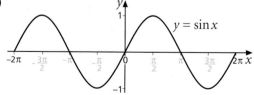

$y = \sin x$

**6 (a), (b)**

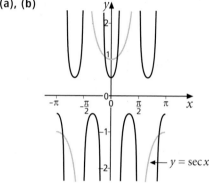

$y = \sec x$

**(c)** $y = \frac{1}{2}\sec 3x$

**7 (a)** Maxima $\left(-\dfrac{2\pi}{3}, 1\right)$, $(0, 1)$, $\left(\dfrac{2\pi}{3}, 1\right)$;

minima $(-\pi, -1)$, $\left(-\dfrac{\pi}{3}, -1\right)$, $\left(\dfrac{\pi}{3}, -1\right)$, $(\pi, -1)$

**(b)**

$y = |\cos 3x|$

**(c)** $x = -\pi, -\dfrac{2\pi}{3}, -\dfrac{\pi}{3}, 0, \dfrac{\pi}{3}, \dfrac{2\pi}{3}$ and $\pi$

**8 (a)** $y = 2\sin^{-1}(x - 1)$

**(b)**

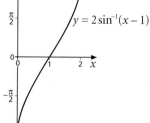

$y = 2\sin^{-1}(x - 1)$

**9 (a)** $-1 \leq f(x) \leq 1$

**(b)** Domain: $-1 \leq x \leq 1$; range: $-\pi \leq f^{-1}(x) \leq \pi$

**(c)** $y = 2\sin^{-1}x$

**(d)** $fg(x) = \sin\frac{1}{2}|x|$

**(e)**

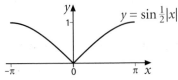

$y = \sin\frac{1}{2}|x|$

**10 (a)**

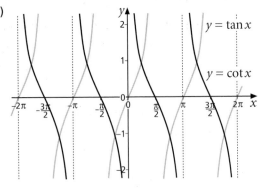

$y = \tan x$

$y = \cot x$

**(b)** Transform $y = \cot x$ by, for example, a reflection in the $y$-axis, followed by a translation of $\begin{bmatrix} -\dfrac{\pi}{2} \\ 0 \end{bmatrix}$

**(c)** $y = \cot\left(-x + \dfrac{\pi}{2}\right)$

**(d)** $y = \cot\left(-x + \dfrac{\pi}{2}\right) = \cot\left(\dfrac{\pi}{2} - x\right)$

$= \dfrac{1}{\tan\left(\dfrac{\pi}{2} - x\right)} = \dfrac{1}{\left(\dfrac{\sin\left(\dfrac{\pi}{2} - x\right)}{\cos\left(\dfrac{\pi}{2} - x\right)}\right)}$

$= \dfrac{1}{\left(\dfrac{\cos x}{\sin x}\right)} = \dfrac{\sin x}{\cos x} = \tan x$

## E Order of transformations (p 66)

**E1 (a)**

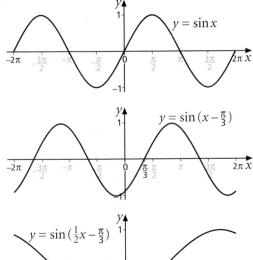

$y = \sin x$

$y = \sin\left(x - \dfrac{\pi}{3}\right)$

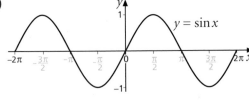

$y = \sin\left(\dfrac{1}{2}x - \dfrac{\pi}{3}\right)$

**(b)** $y = \sin\left(\dfrac{1}{2}x - \dfrac{\pi}{3}\right)$

**E2** Transform by a stretch, scale factor $\dfrac{1}{2}$, in the $x$-direction, followed by a translation by $\begin{bmatrix} -\dfrac{1}{2} \\ 0 \end{bmatrix}$

**E3 (a)** $y = \left(\dfrac{1}{3}\sin x\right) + 1$

**(b)**

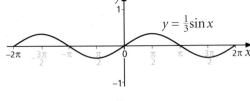

$y = \sin x$

$y = \dfrac{1}{3}\sin x$

$y = \left(\dfrac{1}{3}\sin x\right) + 1$

**Exercise E** (p 67)

**1** (a) $y = \cos 2(x - 3)$     (b) $y = \cos(2x - 3)$

**2** (a) $y = \tan(-x - 3)$     (b) $y = \tan\left(-\frac{1}{2}x\right)$

    (c) $y = \tan 2(x - 3)$     (d) $y = \tan\left(\frac{1}{3}x + 1\right)$

    (e) $y = \tan{-(x - 2)}$

**3** (a) $\frac{1}{2}(y + 1) = \cos x$ or $y = 2\cos x - 1$

    (b) $-y - 2 = \cos x$ or $y = -\cos x - 2$

    (c) $-(y - 3) = \cos x$ or $y = -\cos x + 3$

    (d) $3y + 3 = \cos x$ or $y = \frac{1}{3}\cos x - 1$

    (e) $-\frac{1}{5}y = \cos x$ or $y = -5\cos x$

**4** (a) (i) A translation by $\begin{bmatrix} 1 \\ 0 \end{bmatrix}$ followed by a stretch in the $\theta$-direction, factor $\frac{1}{3}$

      (ii) A stretch in the $\theta$-direction, factor $\frac{1}{2}$, followed by a translation by $\begin{bmatrix} 3 \\ 0 \end{bmatrix}$

      (iii) A stretch in the $y$-direction, factor 2, followed by a translation by $\begin{bmatrix} 0 \\ 1 \end{bmatrix}$

      (iv) A translation by $\begin{bmatrix} 0 \\ -1 \end{bmatrix}$ followed by a stretch in the $y$-direction, factor $\frac{1}{2}$

(b) (i)

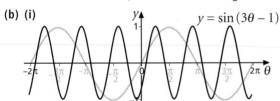

$y = \sin(3\theta - 1)$

(ii)

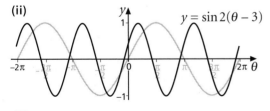

$y = \sin 2(\theta - 3)$

(iii)

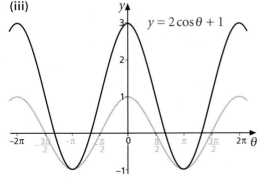

$y = 2\cos\theta + 1$

(iv)

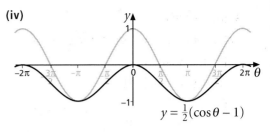

$y = \frac{1}{2}(\cos\theta - 1)$

**5** (a) A reflection in the $x$-axis, followed by a translation of $\begin{bmatrix} 0 \\ 1 \end{bmatrix}$; $y = -\cos x + 1$

    (b) A translation of $\begin{bmatrix} 0 \\ 1 \end{bmatrix}$ followed by a stretch in the $y$-direction, factor 0.75; $y = 0.75(\cos x + 1)$

    (c) A stretch in the $x$-direction, factor $\frac{1}{2}$, followed by a translation of $\begin{bmatrix} \frac{\pi}{4} \\ 0 \end{bmatrix}$; $y = \cos 2\left(x - \frac{\pi}{4}\right)$

    (d) A stretch in the $x$-direction, factor 2, followed by a translation of $\begin{bmatrix} -\pi \\ 0 \end{bmatrix}$; $y = \cos\frac{1}{2}(x + \pi)$

**6** (a)

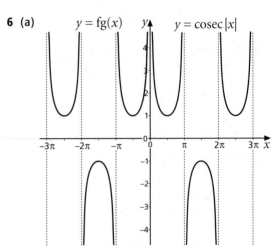

$y = fg(x)$     $y = \operatorname{cosec}|x|$

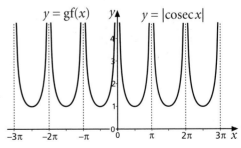

$y = gf(x)$     $y = |\operatorname{cosec} x|$

    (b) No       (c) $-\pi < x < \pi$ $(x \neq 0)$

## Test yourself (p 70)

**1 (a)** $\dfrac{\pi}{6}$    **(b)** $\dfrac{\pi}{6}$    **(c)** $\dfrac{5\pi}{6}$    **(d)** $\dfrac{2\pi}{3}$

**2 (a)** 2    **(b)** $\sqrt{2}$    **(c)** $\dfrac{1}{\sqrt{3}}$    **(d)** 2

**3 (a)** $\operatorname{cosec} x$   **(b)** $-\tan^2 x$   **(c)** $\operatorname{cosec}^2 x$

**4** $x = \dfrac{\pi}{2}, \dfrac{3\pi}{4}, \dfrac{3\pi}{2}, \dfrac{7\pi}{4}$

**5** $x = 200°$ or $340°$

**6 (a)** A reflection in the $y$-axis, followed by a stretch in the $y$-direction, factor 2 (or vice versa)

**(b)** A stretch in the $x$-direction, factor $\frac{1}{2}$, followed by a translation by $\begin{bmatrix} 0 \\ 1 \end{bmatrix}$ (or vice versa)

**(c)** A reflection in the $x$-axis, followed by a stretch in the $x$-direction, factor 2 (or vice versa)

**(d)** A reflection in the $x$-axis, followed by a translation by $\begin{bmatrix} 0 \\ 2 \end{bmatrix}$

**7 (a)** $y = \left(\sin \frac{1}{4}x\right) + 2$    **(b)** $y = 2\sin(-x)$

**(c)** $y = -\sin(x + 1)$

**8 (a)** $x = -1.47$ or $-0.10$ (to 2 d.p.)

**(b) (i)**

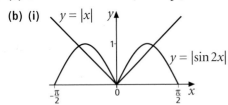

**(ii)** 3 times

**9 (a) (i)** A stretch in the $x$-direction, factor 2, followed by a stretch in the $y$-direction, factor $\frac{1}{2}$ (or vice versa)

**(ii)** $y = \frac{1}{2} \sin \frac{1}{2}x$

**(b) (i)** A stretch in the $x$-direction, factor $\frac{3}{2}$, followed by a stretch in the $y$-direction, factor $\frac{3}{2}$ (or vice versa)

**(ii)** $y = \frac{3}{2} \sin \frac{2}{3}x$

**10 (a)** $y = -\sin x + 1$    **(b)** $y = -(\sin x + 1)$

**(c)** $y = \sin 3(x - 2)$    **(d)** $y = \sin(3x - 2)$

**11 (a)** A translation by $\begin{bmatrix} -1 \\ 0 \end{bmatrix}$ followed by a stretch in the $x$-direction, factor 2

**(b)** A stretch in the $x$-direction, factor $\frac{1}{3}$, followed by a translation by $\begin{bmatrix} 2 \\ 0 \end{bmatrix}$

**(c)** A translation by $\begin{bmatrix} 0 \\ -3 \end{bmatrix}$ followed by a stretch in the $y$-direction, factor 2

**12 (a) (i)** A stretch in the $x$-direction, factor $\frac{1}{2}$

**(ii)** $x = \dfrac{\pi}{2}$

**(b) (i)** Range: $-1 \le f(x) \le 1$

**(ii)** Domain of $f^{-1}(x)$: $-1 \le x \le 1$
range of $f^{-1}(x)$: $0 \le f^{-1}(x) \le \dfrac{\pi}{2}$

**(iii)**

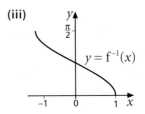

**(c) (i)** $gf(x) = |\cos 2x|$

**(ii)**

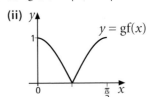

# 5 Natural logarithms and $e^x$

## A Introducing e (p 72)

**A1**  £2.00

**A2**  After six months the amount will be
£1.00×1.5 = £1.50. After another six months it
will be £1.50×1.5 = £2.25.

**A3**  After the first calculation the amount in pounds
will be $1 \times 1\frac{1}{3}$. After the second calculation the
amount in pounds will be $1 \times 1\frac{1}{3} \times 1\frac{1}{3} = \left(1\frac{1}{3}\right)^2$.
After the third and final calculation the amount
in pounds will be $\left(1\frac{1}{3}\right)^3 = \left(1 + \frac{1}{3}\right)^3$ as required.
This amount is £2.37 to the nearest penny.

**A4**  (a)  After the first calculation the amount in
pounds will be $1 \times \left(1 + \frac{1}{n}\right)$. After the second
calculation the amount in pounds will be
$\left(1 + \frac{1}{n}\right)^2$ and so on. After the $n$th and final
calculation the amount in pounds will be
$\left(1 + \frac{1}{n}\right)^n$ as required.

(b)  £2.70 to the nearest penny

(c)  Comments such as:
The amount increases but at a slower and
slower rate. The amount appears to converge
to a limit of £2.72.

**A5**  (a)  A sketch of $y = \left(1 + \frac{1}{x}\right)^x$ is

(b)  2.718

**A6**  (a)  $f(3) = \frac{1}{0!} + \frac{1}{1!} + \frac{1}{2!} + \frac{1}{3!}$
$= \frac{1}{1} + \frac{1}{1} + \frac{1}{2} + \frac{1}{6} = 2\frac{2}{3}$

(b)  (i)  2.716 667    (ii)  2.718 279
(iii) 2.718 282    (iv) 2.718 282

(c)  They are all very close and f(10) and f(15)
agree to six decimal places.

## Exercise A (p 73)

**1**  (a) F    (b) T    (c) T    (d) T    (e) T
(f) T    (g) F    (h) T    (i) T    (j) T
(k) F    (l) T

**2**  (a) 7.3891        (b) 0.0498        (c) 1.6487
(d) 0.7788        (e) 0.6796

**3**  C, A, D, B

## B Natural logarithms (p 73)

**B1**  (a)  1.95                (b)  0.69

**B2**  (a)  0.693 147
(b)  $e^{\ln 2} = e^{0.693\,147} = 1.999\,999\,639\ldots \approx 2$

**B3**  4

**B4**  (a)  4.000                (b)  1.4

**B5**  (a)  $x = 2.3026$          (b)  $x = 0.9163$
(c)  $x = -0.6931$          (d)  $x = -2.3026$

**B6**  $e^x$ is positive for all $x$ so no value for $x$ exists such
that $e^x = -5$.

**B7**  (a)  $e^{-3}$                (b)  −3

**B8**  (a) 5    (b) 1    (c) −2    (d) 0.5    (e) 0

**B9**  No value for $x$ exists such that $e^x = -2$ so $\ln(-2)$
does not exist.

**B10**  $2\ln 3 + 5\ln 2 = \ln 3^2 + \ln 2^5 = \ln 9 + \ln 32$
$= \ln(9 \times 32) = \ln 288$ as required

**B11**  (a)  $\ln 6$    (b)  $\ln 2$    (c)  $\ln 36$    (d)  $\ln 128$

**B12**  (a)  1.609 438
(b)  (i)  3.2        (ii)  2.6        (iii)  −0.6

**B13**  $\ln(8e^2) = \ln 8 + \ln e^2 = \ln 2^3 + 2 = 2 + 3\ln 2$ as
required

## Exercise B (p 76)

**1**  (a)  $x = 1.099$    (b)  $x = 1.386$    (c)  $x = 1.253$
(d)  $x = 1.996$    (e)  $x = -0.536$    (f)  $x = 4.159$
(g)  $x = 0.101$    (h)  $x = 0.564$    (i)  $x = -4$

**2**  (a)  (i)  11        (ii)  132        (iii)  88106
(b)  Just over 4.8 hours

**3** **(a)** 5 mg

**(b) (i)** 4.09 mg     **(ii)** 1.84 mg     **(iii)** 0.04 mg

**(c)** Just over 31 hours

**4** One method is to solve the equation $e^{3x-2} = 5$ directly as follows.

$$e^{3x-2} = 5 \Rightarrow 3x - 2 = \ln 5$$
$$\Rightarrow \quad 3x = \ln 5 + 2$$
$$\Rightarrow \quad x = \tfrac{1}{3}(\ln 5 + 2) \text{ as required}$$

**5** **(a)** $x = \tfrac{1}{2}(\ln 5 - 1)$    **(b)** $x = \tfrac{4}{3}$    **(c)** $x = 2(1 - \ln 4)$

**6** **(a)** $\ln \tfrac{1}{2} = \ln 2^{-1} = -\ln 2$

**(b)** $e^{-\ln 4} = e^{\ln 4^{-1}} = e^{\ln \tfrac{1}{4}} = \tfrac{1}{4}$ or $e^{-\ln 4} = \dfrac{1}{e^{\ln 4}} = \tfrac{1}{4}$

**7** $x = \tfrac{1}{2}\ln 3$

**8** $x = \tfrac{1}{5}\ln 6 \left(\text{or} -\tfrac{1}{5}\ln \tfrac{1}{6}\right)$

**9** **(a)** $x = 54.598$    **(b)** $x = 0.025$    **(c)** $x = 5.294$

**(d)** $x = 0.822$    **(e)** $x = 3.741$    **(f)** $x = 2.096$

**10** One method is to solve the equation $\ln(4x - 1) = 2$ directly as follows.

$$\ln(4x - 1) = 2 \Rightarrow 4x - 1 = e^2$$
$$\Rightarrow \quad 4x = e^2 + 1$$
$$\Rightarrow \quad x = \tfrac{1}{4}(e^2 + 1) \text{ as required}$$

**11** **(a)** $x = \tfrac{1}{4}e^5$    **(b)** $x = e^{-2} + 1$    **(c)** $x = \tfrac{1}{2}(e - 3)$

**12** **(a)** $\ln(x^3)$    **(b)** $\ln(20x)$    **(c)** $\ln(x^2)$

**(d)** $\ln(25x)$    **(e)** $\ln\left(\tfrac{1}{2}x\right)$    **(f)** $\ln \dfrac{3}{x}$

**13** **(a)** $x = \tfrac{1}{5}e^2$    **(b)** $x = 3e$    **(c)** $x = \sqrt{\tfrac{1}{2}e^3}$

**(d)** $x = \tfrac{1}{40}$    **(e)** $x = \tfrac{1}{2}e^5 - 1$    **(f)** $x = 5 - 4e$

**14** **(a)**
$$\ln(x + 2) + \ln x = \ln 8$$
$$\Rightarrow \quad \ln(x(x + 2)) = \ln 8$$
$$\Rightarrow \quad x^2 + 2x = 8$$
$$\Rightarrow \quad x^2 + 2x - 8 = 0$$
so $x$ must be a solution of this equation.

**(b)** The two solutions are $x = 2$ and $x = -4$. Only $x = 2$ is a solution of $\ln(x + 2) + \ln x = \ln 8$ as $\ln x$ is not defined for a negative number.

**15** **(a)** $x = \tfrac{3}{4}$    **(b)** $x = 2$    **(c)** $x = 1, 5$    **(d)** $x = \tfrac{3}{5}$

**16** **(a)**
$$e^{2x} - 4e^x + 3 = 0$$
$$\Rightarrow \quad (e^x)^2 - 4(e^x) + 3 = 0$$
$$\Rightarrow \quad y^2 - 4y + 3 = 0 \text{ where } y = e^x$$

**(b)** $x = 0, \ln 3$

**17** **(a)** $x = 0, \ln 5$    **(b)** $x = \ln 2$    **(c)** $x = \ln 4$

**18** $x = 2 + \sqrt{3}, 2 - \sqrt{3}$

**19** **(a)** $x = \ln\left(\tfrac{2}{3}\right)$    **(b)** $x = \ln 3 - 1$    **(c)** $x = \ln 4, 0$

## C Graphs (p 78)

**C1** $y > 0$

**C2** $x > 0$

**C3** **(a)**

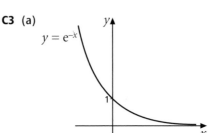

**(b)**

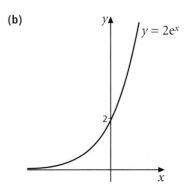

**(c)**

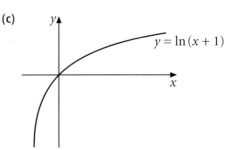

**(d)**

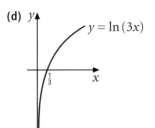

**C4** **(a)** $f(x) > 0$      **(b)** $f(x) > 0$

**(c)** $f(x) \in \mathbb{R}$      **(d)** $f(x) \in \mathbb{R}$

**Exercise C** (p 80)

**1 (a)** 6

**(b)**

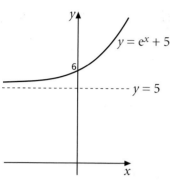

$y = e^x + 5$

$y = 5$

6

**(c)** $f(x) > 5$

**2**

$(0, e^5)$

$y = e^{x+5}$

**3** A stretch in the $x$-direction of factor 3

**4 (a)** A translation of $\begin{bmatrix} 0 \\ -1 \end{bmatrix}$

**(b)** $y = 0 \Rightarrow \ln x - 1 = 0 \Rightarrow \ln x = 1 \Rightarrow x = e^1 = e$.
So the graph meets the $x$-axis at $(e, 0)$.

**5 (a)**

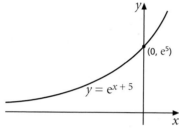

$(e^3, 0)$

$y = \ln x - 3$

**(b)**

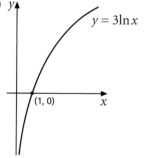

$y = 3\ln x$

$(1, 0)$

**(c)**

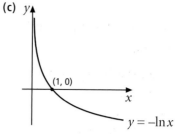

$(1, 0)$

$y = -\ln x$

**(d)**

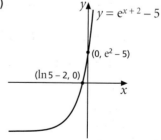

$y = 1 - \ln x$

$(e, 0)$

**6** A reflection in the $y$-axis and a stretch of factor 5 in the $y$-direction (or vice versa)

**7**

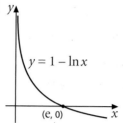

$(-\ln 4, 0)$

$(0, -3)$

$y = e^{-x} - 4$

**8 (a)** $-4$

**(b)**

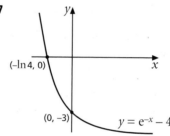

$y = e^{x+2} - 5$

$(0, e^2 - 5)$

$(\ln 5 - 2, 0)$

**(c)** $y = -5$

**(d)** $f(x) > -5$

**(e)** $x = \ln 6 - 2$

**9** (a) A translation of $\begin{bmatrix} -2 \\ 0 \end{bmatrix}$

(b) $x = -2$

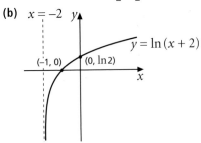
$y = \ln(x + 2)$
$(-1, 0)$  $(0, \ln 2)$

**10** (a) 1

(b) $f(x) = 0 \Rightarrow 2e^{-x} - 1 = 0$
$\Rightarrow e^{-x} = \frac{1}{2}$
$\Rightarrow -x = \ln \frac{1}{2} = \ln 2^{-1} = -\ln 2$
$\Rightarrow x = \ln 2$

(c) $f(x) > -1$

(d) $x = -\ln 2 \left( \text{or } \ln \frac{1}{2} \right)$

**11** (a) $p = 3, q = \frac{1}{2}(e^{-3} - 1)$    (b) $x = -\frac{1}{2}$

(c) $x = \frac{1}{2}(e^{-5} - 1)$

**12**

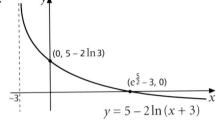
$(0, 5 - 2\ln 3)$
$(e^{\frac{5}{2}} - 3, 0)$
$-3$
$y = 5 - 2\ln(x + 3)$

**13** (a)

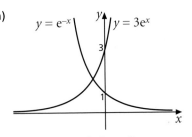
$y = e^{-x}$    $y = 3e^x$
3
1

(b) (i)
$3e^x = e^{-x}$
$\Rightarrow 3e^x \times e^x = e^{-x} \times e^x$
$\Rightarrow 3e^{2x} = 1$
$\Rightarrow e^{2x} = \frac{1}{3}$
so $x$ must be a root of this equation.

(ii) $x = -0.5493$ (to 4 s.f.)

**14** (a)

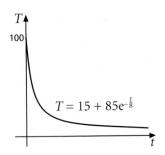
$T$
100
$T = 15 + 85e^{-\frac{t}{8}}$
$t$

(b) About 10 minutes

**15** (a) 2

(b) (i) 4.39    (ii) 0.28    (iii) 2.95

(c) $x = \ln 3$

(d)

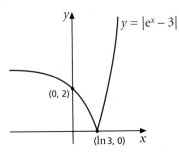
$y = |e^x - 3|$
$(0, 2)$
$(\ln 3, 0)$  $x$

(e) $f(x) \geq 0$

(f) The line $y = 1$ cuts the graph above in two places, so the equation $f(x) = 1$ has two solutions; $x = \ln 4, \ln 2$

(g) $x = \ln 8$

**16** (a) $g(3) = g(1) = 0$

(b)

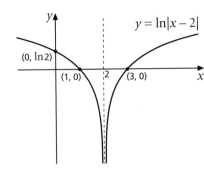
$y = \ln|x - 2|$
$(0, \ln 2)$
$(1, 0)$  $2$  $(3, 0)$  $x$

(c) $x = 2 + e^3, 2 - e^3$

## D Inverses

### Exercise D (p 84)

**1** (a) $\frac{1}{2}\ln x$    (b) $\ln x - 2$    (c) $\ln(x - 2)$

(d) $\ln\left(\frac{1}{2}x\right)$    (e) $2 - \ln x$    (f) $-\ln(x + 2)$

**2 (a)** $\frac{1}{5}e^x$  **(b)** $e^x - 5$  **(c)** $e^{x-5}$

**(d)** $e^{\frac{1}{5}x}$  **(e)** $5e^x$  **(f)** $e^{\frac{1}{5}(x+1)}$

**3 (a)** $f(x) > 2$  **(b)** $\ln(x-2) + 1$

**(c)** Domain: $x > 2$; range: $f^{-1}(x) \in \mathbb{R}$

**(d)**

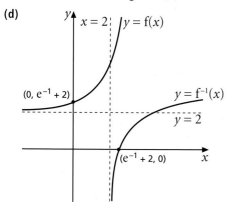

**4 (a) (i)** $e^{x+2} - 1$

**(ii)** The solution is $g^{-1}(7)$, which is $e^9 - 1$.

**(b)** Domain: $x \in \mathbb{R}$; range: $g^{-1}(x) > -1$

**5 (a)** $\ln\left(\frac{1}{2}(x-3)\right)$

**(b) (i)** $x > 3$

**(ii)** 1 is not in the domain of $f^{-1}$ so $f(x) = 1$ has no solution.

**6 (a)** $\frac{1}{2}e^x + 2$

**(b)**

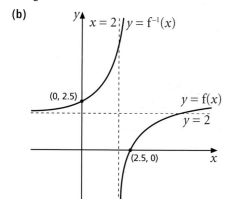

**7 (a)** $3e^2$  **(b)** $-\ln\left(\frac{1}{3}x\right)$

**(c)** Domain: $0 < x \le 3e^2$; range: $f^{-1}(x) \ge -2$

**8 (a)** $t = -\dfrac{10}{3}\ln\left(\dfrac{V}{14\,000}\right)$  **(b)** 2008

## Mixed questions (p 85)

**1 (a) (i)** $(0, 5)$  **(ii)** $f(x) > 0$  **(iii)** $\frac{5}{6}$

**(b) (i)** $gf(x) = g(5e^{-x}) = 5e^{-x} + 10 = 5(e^{-x} + 2)$

**(ii)** $gf(x) > 10$

**(iii)**

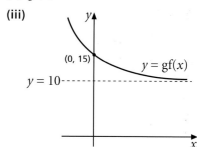

**(iv)**
$$gf(x) = 11$$
$$\Rightarrow \quad 5(e^{-x} + 2) = 11$$
$$\Rightarrow \quad e^{-x} + 2 = \tfrac{11}{5}$$
$$\Rightarrow \quad e^{-x} = \tfrac{1}{5}$$
$$\Rightarrow \quad \frac{1}{e^x} = \tfrac{1}{5}$$
$$\Rightarrow \quad e^x = 5$$
$$\Rightarrow \quad x = \ln 5$$

**(c) (i)** $15\,°\mathrm{C}$  **(ii)** 1.6 minutes

**2 (a)**  **(b)** $x > \ln 3$

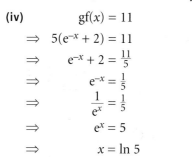

**3 (a)** $2(e^x + 3)$  **(b)** 4

**(c)** $gf(x) = 4e^{2\ln\left(\frac{1}{2}x - 3\right)}$
$$= 4e^{\ln\left(\frac{1}{2}x - 3\right)^2}$$
$$= 4\left(\tfrac{1}{2}x - 3\right)^2$$
$$= \left(2\left(\tfrac{1}{2}x - 3\right)\right)^2$$
$$= (x - 6)^2 \text{ as required}$$

**4 (a)** 184.73

**(b)** A translation of $\begin{bmatrix} 0 \\ 1 \end{bmatrix}$

**(c)** $e^{x-1}$

**(d)** $fg(x) = 1 + \ln(ex)^2$
$$= 1 + 2\ln(ex)$$
$$= 1 + 2(\ln e + \ln x)$$
$$= 1 + 2(1 + \ln x)$$
$$= 3 + 2\ln x \text{ as required}$$

**(e)**

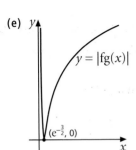
$y = |fg(x)|$
$(e^{-\frac{3}{2}}, 0)$

**5 (a)** 52.5

**(b)**

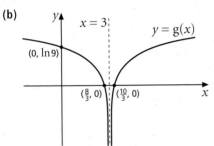
$x = 3$
$y = g(x)$
$(0, \ln 9)$
$(\frac{8}{3}, 0)$ $(\frac{10}{3}, 0)$

## Test yourself (p 86)

**1 (a)** $\ln p + \ln q$  **(b)** $3\ln p + 2\ln q$
  **(c)** $2\ln p - \ln q$  **(d)** $\ln p - \frac{1}{2}\ln q$

**2 (a)** $1$  **(b)** $\frac{1}{4}\ln x$

**(c)**

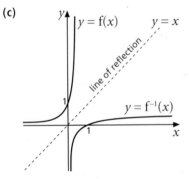
$y = f(x)$  $y = x$
line of reflection
$y = f^{-1}(x)$

**(d)**

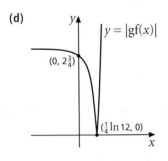
$y = |gf(x)|$
$(0, 2\frac{3}{4})$
$(\frac{1}{4}\ln 12, 0)$

**3 (a)** A stretch of factor $\frac{1}{3}$ in the $x$-direction

  **(b)** A translation of $\begin{bmatrix} 3 \\ 0 \end{bmatrix}$

  **(c)** A reflection in $y = x$

**4** $y = \frac{1}{3}(5e^2 - 2)$

**5 (a)**

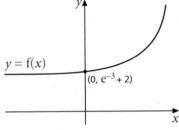
$y = f(x)$
$(0, e^{-3} + 2)$

  **(b)** $f(x) > 2$
  **(c)** $x = \ln 5 + 3$
  **(d)** $\ln(x - 2) + 3$ with domain $x > 2$

**6 (a) (i)** Reflection in the line $y = x$

  **(ii)**

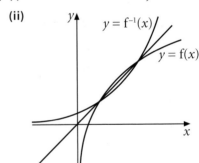
$y = f^{-1}(x)$
$y = f(x)$

  **(b) (i)** A stretch of factor 3 in the $y$-direction
  **(ii)** $e^{\frac{1}{3}x}$

**7 (a)** Reflection in the $y$-axis followed by a stretch
    of factor 2 in the $y$-direction (or vice versa)

  **(b)**

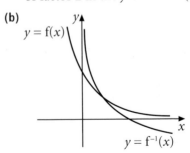
$y = f(x)$
$y = f^{-1}(x)$

  **(c)** $-\ln\left(\frac{1}{2}x\right)$
  **(d)** Domain: $x > 0$; range: $f^{-1}(x) \in \mathbb{R}$
  **(e)** 1.4 hours (to 1 d.p.)

**8 (a)** $\frac{1}{2}(5 - e^x)$  **(b)** $x \in \mathbb{R}$

# 6 Differentiation

## A Exponential functions (p 88)

**A1** (a) $\dfrac{2^h - 1}{h - 0} = \dfrac{2^h - 1}{h}$

(b) 0.7177

(c) 0.7053, 0.6956, 0.6934, 0.6932

(d) 0.69

**A2** 1.161, 1.105, 1.099, 1.099

The gradient is approximately 1.1.

**A3** The results are 1.0517..., 1.0050..., 1.0005...

**A4** (a) $\dfrac{e^{p+h} - e^p}{h} = \dfrac{e^p e^h - e^p}{h} = \dfrac{e^p(e^h - 1)}{h}$

(b) We already know that $\dfrac{e^h - 1}{h}$ approaches 1, and so the value of this expression gets closer and closer to $e^p \times 1 = e^p$.
The gradient of $y = e^x$ at $x = p$ is $e^p$.

**A5** (a) $3e^x$  (b) $5e^x + 4$

(c) $2e^x - 2x$  (d) $e^x - \dfrac{2}{x^2}$

**A6** $e^2 e^x = e^{x + 2}$

### Exercise A (p 90)

**1** (a) $e^x - 5$  (b) $2x + 4e^x$

(c) $e^x - \dfrac{3}{2\sqrt{x}}$  (d) $3e^x + 3x^2$

**2** (a) $2e^x + 2x^{-3}$  (b) $6e^x - \dfrac{1}{x^2}$

(c) $\frac{3}{2}x^{\frac{1}{2}} + 2e^x$  (d) $-\frac{1}{2}x^{-\frac{3}{2}} + 2e^x$

**3** (a) $\dfrac{dy}{dx} = e^x - 3$

(b) When $x = \ln 3$, $\dfrac{dy}{dx} = e^{\ln 3} - 3 = 3 - 3 = 0$

(c) $y = e^{\ln 3} - 3\ln 3$
$= 3 - 3\ln 3$
$= -0.296$

(d) $\dfrac{d^2 y}{dx^2} = e^x$

(e) 3

(f) Minimum, as $\dfrac{d^2 y}{dx^2}$ is positive

**4** $f'(x) = e^x + \dfrac{3}{x^4}$; $e^x$ and $\dfrac{3}{x^4}$ are always positive, so the gradient of $f(x)$ is always positive.

## B The derivative of ln x (p 91)

**B1** (a) $\dfrac{1}{x} + 2x$  (b) $\dfrac{1}{x} - \dfrac{1}{2\sqrt{x}}$

(c) $\dfrac{1}{x} + 5e^x$  (d) $-\dfrac{1}{x^2} - \dfrac{1}{x}$

**B2** $\ln ab = \ln a + \ln b$ so $\ln 3x = \ln 3 + \ln x$
The derivative of $\ln 3 + \ln x$ is
$0 + \dfrac{1}{x} = \dfrac{1}{x}$ ($\ln 3$ is a constant).

**B3** (a) $\ln 5x^2 = \ln 5 + \ln x + \ln x = \ln 5 + 2\ln x$;
$\dfrac{d}{dx}(\ln 5 + 2\ln x) = 0 + \dfrac{2}{x} = \dfrac{2}{x}$

(b) (i) $\dfrac{3}{x}$  (ii) $\dfrac{1}{2x}$  (iii) $-\dfrac{3}{x}$  (iv) $-\dfrac{1}{x}$

### Exercise B (p 92)

**1** (a) $2x + \dfrac{1}{x}$  (b) $\dfrac{3}{x} - 3x^2$

(c) $\dfrac{1}{2\sqrt{x}} - \dfrac{2}{x}$  (d) $\dfrac{1}{x} + e^x$

**2** $\ln 7 + 3\ln x$; $\dfrac{3}{x}$

**3** (a) $\dfrac{2}{x}$  (b) $\dfrac{5}{x}$  (c) $\dfrac{1}{2x}$  (d) $\dfrac{3}{2x}$

**4** $\ln 3 - 2\ln x$; $-\dfrac{2}{x}$

**5** (a) $e^x + \dfrac{3}{x}$  (b) $-\dfrac{1}{x}$

(c) $\dfrac{2}{3x}$  (d) $-\frac{1}{2}x^{-\frac{3}{2}} - \frac{1}{2}x^{-1}$

**6** (a) $\dfrac{dy}{dx} = \dfrac{1}{x} - 1$; at $x = 1$, $\dfrac{dy}{dx} = 0$

(b) $\dfrac{d^2 y}{dx^2} = -\dfrac{1}{x^2} \le 0$

**7** $\left(\frac{1}{2}, \frac{1}{16} - \frac{1}{4}\ln\frac{1}{2}\right)$; minimum

## C Differentiating a product of functions (p 93)

**C1** (a) $6x^2 + 2x$

(b) $2x \times 2 = 4x$, not $6x^2 + 2x$

**C2** $y + \delta y = (u + \delta u)(v + \delta v)$
$= uv + u\delta v + v\delta u + \delta u\delta v$
$= y + u\delta v + v\delta u + \delta u\delta v$
$\delta y = u\delta v + v\delta u + \delta u\delta v$

**C3** $\dfrac{du}{dx} = 2x, \dfrac{dv}{dx} = 2; 6x^2 + 2x$

**C4** (a) $f'(x) = 3x^2, g'(x) = 2x; 5x^4 - 9x^2$
(b) $f(x)g(x) = x^5 - 3x^3; 5x^4 - 9x^2$

**C5** $3x^2 e^x + x^3 e^x$

**C6** $4x^3 \ln x + x^3 = x^3(4\ln x + 1)$

**C7** (a) $(x^2 - x - 3)e^x$ (b) $(2x - 3)\ln x + x - 3$
(c) $x^{-\frac{1}{2}}\left(\frac{1}{2}\ln x + 1\right)$

**Exercise C** (p 95)

**1** (a) $(5 + x)e^x x^4$ (b) $\left(\frac{1}{2}x^{-\frac{1}{2}} + x^{\frac{1}{2}}\right)e^x$
(c) $x(2\ln x + 1)$ (d) $3e^x(x + 1)$
(e) $e^x\left(\ln x + \dfrac{1}{x}\right)$ (f) $e^x \sqrt[3]{x}\left(\dfrac{1}{3x} + 1\right)$
(g) $\dfrac{1 - 2\ln x}{x^3}$ (h) $e^x x^{-3}(x - 2)$

**2** (a) $e^x(2x + 5)$
(b) $4\ln x + 4 - \dfrac{1}{x}$
(c) $e^x(x + 1)^2$
(d) $\dfrac{1}{\sqrt{x}}\left(\frac{1}{2}\ln x + 1\right) - \dfrac{1}{x}$
(e) $e^x\left(1 - \dfrac{1}{x} + \dfrac{1}{x^2}\right)$
(f) $e^x\left(x + 1 + \dfrac{1}{x} + \ln x\right)$

**3** (a) $e^x(x^3 + 4x^2 + 2x)$
(b) $(3x^2 + x^3)e^x; (2x + x^2)e^x; e^x(x^3 + 4x^2 + 2x)$
(c) $(3x^2 + 2x)\ln x + x^2 + x$

**4** (a) $\dfrac{dy}{dx} = e^x(1 + x)$
(b) At $x = -1$, $\dfrac{dy}{dx} = 0$
(c) $y = -\dfrac{1}{e}$
(d) $\dfrac{d^2y}{dx^2} = e^x(2 + x)$; minimum

**5** (a) $e^x(x^2 - 5x + 6)$
(b) $e^x(x - 2)(x - 3)$
(c) $x = 2, x = 3$
(d) $f''(x) = e^x(x^2 - 3x + 1)$
At $x = 2$, $f(x)$ is a maximum.
At $x = 3$, $f(x)$ is a minimum.

**6** (a) $\dfrac{dy}{dx} = \ln x + 1$; at $x = e$, $\dfrac{dy}{dx} = 2$,
so the gradient is 2
(b) At $x = \dfrac{1}{e}$, $\dfrac{dy}{dx} = -1 + 1 = 0$
(c) $\dfrac{d^2y}{dx^2} = \dfrac{1}{x}$; positive at $x = \dfrac{1}{e}$

**7** (a) $\dfrac{dy}{dx} = x^2 \times \dfrac{1}{x} + \ln x \times 2x$
$= x + 2x\ln x$
$= x(1 + 2\ln x)$
(b) $x(1 + 2\ln x) = 0$ at a stationary point
$\Rightarrow x = 0$ or $1 + 2\ln x = 0$
$y$ is not defined when $x = 0$
so use $1 + 2\ln x = 0$
$\Rightarrow \qquad 2\ln x = -1$
$\Rightarrow \qquad \ln x = -0.5$
$\Rightarrow \qquad x = e^{-0.5}$
(c) Minimum

**D Differentiating a quotient** (p 96)

**D1** (a) $\dfrac{x^2 + 2x}{(x + 1)^2}$ (b) $\dfrac{-2x^3 - 1}{(x^3 - 1)^2}$
(c) $\dfrac{1 - \ln x}{x^2}$ (d) $\dfrac{e^x(x - 2)}{(x - 1)^2}$

**Exercise D** (p 97)

**1** (a) $\dfrac{2x^2 + 6x}{(2x + 3)^2}$ (b) $\dfrac{2x^3 - 3x^2}{(x - 1)^2}$
(c) $\dfrac{1 - x^2}{(x^2 + 1)^2}$ (d) $\dfrac{2 - 2x^2}{(x^2 + x + 1)^2}$
(e) $\dfrac{2x - x^2}{(x^2 - x + 1)^2}$ (f) $\dfrac{-4x^3 - 1}{(2x^3 - 1)^2}$
(g) $\dfrac{2x - x^4}{(x^3 + 1)^2}$ (h) $\dfrac{-x^4 + 8x^2 + 2x + 5}{(x^3 + 5x + 1)^2}$

**2 (a), (b)** $e^x\left(\dfrac{1}{x^2} - \dfrac{2}{x^3}\right)$

**3 (a)** $\dfrac{xe^x}{(x+1)^2}$

**(b)** $\dfrac{e^x(x-1)^2}{(x^2+1)^2}$

**(c)** $\dfrac{2x + 2xe^x - x^2 e^x}{(e^x+1)^2}$

**(d)** $\dfrac{x - 1 - x\ln x}{x(x-1)^2}$

**(e)** $\dfrac{x^2(1 - 2\ln x) + 1}{x(x^2+1)^2}$

**(f)** $\dfrac{e^x(x\ln x - 1)}{x(\ln x)^2}$

**4 (a)** $\dfrac{dy}{dx} = \dfrac{(x+1)\times 1 - x\times 1}{(x+1)^2}$

$= \dfrac{1}{(x+1)^2}$

**(b)** $\dfrac{1}{(x+1)^2} = 0$ has no solution.

**5 (a)** $f'(x) = \dfrac{(x^2+3)\times 1 - (x+1)\times 2x}{(x^2+3)^2}$

$= \dfrac{x^2 + 3 - 2x^2 - 2x}{(x^2+3)^2}$

$= \dfrac{-(x^2 + 2x - 3)}{(x^2+3)^2}$

$= \dfrac{-(x-1)(x+3)}{(x^2+3)^2}$

**(b)** $x = 1, x = -3$

**6** $x = 2, x = -2$

**7** $(3, e^3)$

**8 (a) (i)** $\dfrac{1 - \ln x}{x^2}$     **(ii)** $\dfrac{2\ln x - 3}{x^3}$

**(b)** $\left(e, \dfrac{1}{e}\right)$

**(c)** Maximum

**9** $\dfrac{dy}{dx} = \dfrac{\ln x \times 2x - x^2 \times \dfrac{1}{x}}{(\ln x)^2}$

$= \dfrac{2x\ln x - x}{(\ln x)^2}$

At a stationary point $\dfrac{dy}{dx} = 0$

so the numerator must be 0.

$$2x\ln x - x = 0$$
$$x(2\ln x - 1) = 0$$

$y$ is not defined for $x = 0$

so use   $2\ln x - 1 = 0$

$\Rightarrow$           $2\ln x = 1$

$\Rightarrow$           $\ln x = 0.5$

$\Rightarrow$           $x = e^{0.5}$

When $x = e^{0.5}$, $y = \dfrac{(e^{0.5})^2}{\ln e^{0.5}}$

$= \dfrac{e}{0.5}$

$= 2e$

## E Differentiating sin *x*, cos *x* and tan *x* (p 98)

**E1** 0.9983, 1.0000, 1.0000; the gradient appears to be 1.

**E2 (a)** 0, −1, 0, 1

**(b)**

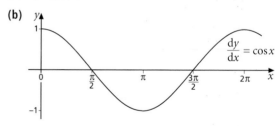

**E3**

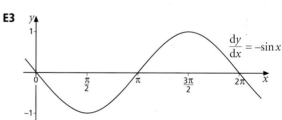

**E4 (a)** $\cos x + 3 + 2x$     **(b)** $\tfrac{1}{2}x^{-\frac{1}{2}} + \sin x$

**(c)** $3e^x + 4\cos x$     **(d)** $\dfrac{5}{x} + 2\sin x$

**E5 (a)** $\dfrac{dy}{dx} = \dfrac{\cos x \times \cos x - \sin x \times (-\sin x)}{(\cos x)^2}$

$= \dfrac{\cos^2 x + \sin^2 x}{\cos^2 x}$

**(b)** Since $\cos^2 x + \sin^2 x = 1$

$\dfrac{dy}{dx} = \dfrac{1}{\cos^2 x} = \left(\dfrac{1}{\cos x}\right)^2 = \sec^2 x$

**E6** It tends to infinity; the graph of $y = \tan x$ has a vertical asymptote.

### Exercise E (p 99)

**1 (a)** $\cos x - \sin x$     **(b)** $\cos x - 2x$

**(c)** $3\cos x + 2\sin x$     **(d)** $1 + 2\sec^2 x$

**2 (a)** $3\cos x - 3x\sin x$     **(b)** $-\dfrac{1}{x^2}(x\sin x + \cos x)$

**(c)** $\dfrac{1}{x^3}(x\cos x - 2\sin x)$     **(d)** $e^x(\sec^2 x + \tan x)$

**3** $f'(x) = \dfrac{x \times \cos x - \sin x \times 1}{x^2}$

$= \dfrac{\cos x}{x} - \dfrac{\sin x}{x^2}$

**4 (a)** $f'(x) = 3\cos x - 4\sin x$

**(b)** $0 = 3\cos x - 4\sin x$

$\Rightarrow \tan x = \frac{3}{4}$

$x = 0.644, 3.785$

**5** $f'(x) = \dfrac{x^2 \times (-\sin x) - \cos x \times 2x}{(x^2)^2}$

$= -\dfrac{\sin x}{x^2} - \dfrac{2\cos x}{x^3}$

$f'\left(\dfrac{\pi}{2}\right) = -\dfrac{1}{\left(\dfrac{\pi}{2}\right)^2} - 0$

$= -\dfrac{4}{\pi^2}$

**6** $0, 2\pi$

**7** $\dfrac{dy}{dx} = \dfrac{\sin x \times (-\sin x) - \cos x \times \cos x}{\sin^2 x}$

$= \dfrac{-(\sin^2 x + \cos^2 x)}{\sin^2 x}$

$= -\dfrac{1}{\sin^2 x}$

$= -\csc^2 x$

## F Differentiating a function of a function (p 100)

**F1 (a)** $\cos u$     **(b)** $2x$

**(c)** $\dfrac{dy}{dx} = \dfrac{dy}{du} \times \dfrac{du}{dx} = \cos u \times 2x = 2x\cos(x^2 - 3)$

**F2** $2\sin x\cos x$

**F3** $\dfrac{dy}{dx} = \dfrac{dy}{du} \times \dfrac{du}{dx} = \frac{1}{2}u^{-\frac{1}{2}} \times 2x$

$= x(x^2 + 1)^{-\frac{1}{2}}$

$= \dfrac{x}{\sqrt{x^2 + 1}}$

**F4 (a)** $-2\sin 2x$     **(b)** $-3e^{-3x}$

**(c)** $\dfrac{6}{6x + 1}$     **(d)** $\dfrac{-1}{\sqrt{5 - 2x}}$

**(e)** $\dfrac{-4}{(3 + 4x)^2}$     **(f)** $5\cos(5x - 2)$

**(g)** $2(3x - 2)^{-\frac{1}{3}}$     **(h)** $-2(1 + 4x)^{-\frac{3}{2}}$

**F5** $\dfrac{x\cos x^2}{\sqrt{\sin x^2}}$

### Exercise F (p 101)

**1 (a)** $3\cos(3x - 2)$     **(b)** $-5\sin(5x + 1)$

**(c)** $-2\cos(3 - 2x)$     **(d)** $-\frac{1}{2}\sin\frac{1}{2}x$

**(e)** $\dfrac{3}{3x + 1}$     **(f)** $\dfrac{5}{2\sqrt{5x - 1}}$

**(g)** $14(2x + 1)^6$     **(h)** $4\sec^2 4x$

**(i)** $\frac{2}{3}(2x + 1)^{-\frac{2}{3}}$     **(j)** $3\sec^2(3x + 2)$

**(k)** $5e^{5x - 2}$     **(l)** $\frac{1}{2}\sin(1 - \frac{1}{2}x)$

**2** $\dfrac{dy}{du} = 2u, \dfrac{du}{dx} = -\sin x, \dfrac{dy}{dx} = -2\sin x\cos x$

**3** $\dfrac{dy}{du} = \dfrac{1}{u}, \dfrac{du}{dx} = \cos x, \dfrac{dy}{dx} = \cot x$

**4** $e^{\sin x}\cos x$

**5 (a)** $e^x\cos(e^x)$     **(b)** $\dfrac{2\ln x}{x}$

**(c)** $2\tan x\sec^2 x$     **(d)** $10x(x^2 + 1)^4$

**6 (a)** $\dfrac{dy}{du} = -u^{-2}, \dfrac{du}{dx} = \cos x, \dfrac{dy}{dx} = -\dfrac{\cos x}{\sin^2 x}$

$= -\csc x\cot x$

**(b)** $\dfrac{dy}{du} = -u^{-2}, \dfrac{du}{dx} = -\sin x, \dfrac{dy}{dx} = \dfrac{\sin x}{\cos^2 x}$

$= \sec x\tan x$

**7 (a)** $e^{\tan x} \sec^2 x$
**(b)** $\dfrac{1}{2x\sqrt{\ln x}}$

**(c)** $\dfrac{-1}{x(\ln x)^2}$
**(d)** $\dfrac{\cos(\sqrt{x})}{2\sqrt{x}}$

**8 (a)** $\dfrac{2x}{x^2+1}$
**(b)** $\dfrac{2\ln x}{x}$

**(c)** $2x\,e^{x^2}$
**(d)** $e^{\tan x}\sec^2 x$

**(e)** $-2x\cos(1-x^2)$
**(f)** $\dfrac{x}{\sqrt{1+x^2}}$

**(g)** $\dfrac{-2x}{\left(1+x^2\right)^2}$
**(h)** $\dfrac{-6x}{\left(1+x^2\right)^4}$

**9 (a)** Let $u = 1 - x^2$ so $y = u^{-\frac{1}{2}}$

$$\frac{dy}{dx} = \frac{dy}{du} \times \frac{du}{dx}$$

$$= -\tfrac{1}{2}u^{-\frac{3}{2}}(-2x)$$

$$= \frac{x}{\left(1-x^2\right)^{\frac{3}{2}}}$$

**(b)** 1.171 (to 4 s.f.)

## G Selecting methods (p 102)

**G1 (a)** Chain rule
**(b)** Chain rule

**(c)** Quotient rule
**(d)** Product rule

**G2 (a)** $\dfrac{du}{dx} = 2e^{2x},\ \dfrac{dv}{dx} = \cos x$

**(b)** $\dfrac{dy}{dx} = e^{2x}\cos x + 2e^{2x}\sin x$

**G3** $\dfrac{du}{dx} = e^x,\ \dfrac{dv}{dx} = 4\cos 4x,\ \dfrac{dy}{dx} = \dfrac{e^x(\sin 4x - 4\cos 4x)}{\sin^2 4x}$

**G4** $\dfrac{du}{dx} = 2e^{2x},\ \dfrac{dv}{dx} = -3\sin 3x,$

$\dfrac{dy}{dx} = e^{2x}(2\cos 3x - 3\sin 3x)$

**G5** $2xe^x + x^2 e^x + \dfrac{3}{x}$

**G6 (a)** $2x\cos(x^2+1)$
**(b)** $(x^2+1)\cos x + 2x\sin x$

### Exercise G (p 104)

**1 (a)** $x^2 e^x + 2xe^x + 2x$
**(b)** $\dfrac{2x}{x^2-2}$

**(c)** $-\tan x$
**(d)** $\dfrac{\sin x}{x} + \ln x \cos x$

**(e)** $\dfrac{1}{x}\cos(\ln x)$
**(f)** $\dfrac{e^x(5x-4)}{(5x+1)^2}$

**(g)** $\dfrac{-e^{-x}(2x+3)}{(2x+1)^2}$
**(h)** $\dfrac{e^{-2x}(2x-1)}{(1-x)^2}$

**2 (a)** $e^x \sin 3x + 3e^x \cos 3x$

**(b)** $-e^{-x}(\cos 3x + 3\sin 3x)$

**(c)** $e^{-2x}(\sec^2 x - 2\tan x)$

**(d)** $3\cos 3x \cos 2x - 2\sin 3x \sin 2x$

**(e)** $-3\sec^2(2-3x)$

**(f)** $\dfrac{2\ln x + \dfrac{1}{x} - 2}{(1-2x)^2}$

**3 (a)** $\dfrac{2x\cos 2x - \sin 2x}{x^2}$

**(b)** Substituting $x = \dfrac{\pi}{2}$,

$$\frac{dy}{dx} = \frac{\pi(-1) - 0}{\left(\dfrac{\pi}{2}\right)^2}$$

$$= -\pi\left(\frac{2}{\pi}\right)^2$$

$$= -\frac{4}{\pi}$$

**4 (a)** 2
**(b)** 1
**(c)** −1

## Mixed questions (p 105)

**1 (a)** $32\,\text{m}^3$

**(b)** $-1.25\,\text{m}^3/\text{h}$; the amount of oil is decreasing

**(c)** $T = 24.53$

**2 (a)** $f'(x) = 3e^{3x} + \dfrac{2}{x^2}$

**(b)** $e^{3x}$ and $\dfrac{2}{x^2}$ are always positive, so $f'(x) > 0$ and $f(x)$ is increasing.

**3** $\dfrac{1}{2}$

**4 (a)** $\dfrac{e^{2x}(2x-3)}{(x-1)^2}$
**(b)** $\dfrac{3}{3x-2}$

**(c)** $3\ln x + 3 - \dfrac{2}{x}$
**(d)** $12(3x-1)^3$

**5 (a) (i)** $\dfrac{dy}{dx} = 2x - 3 + \dfrac{1}{x}$

**(ii)** When $x = 2$, $\dfrac{dy}{dx} = 4 - 3 + \frac{1}{2} = \frac{3}{2}$

**(b) (i)** $2x - 3 + \dfrac{1}{x} = 0$

$2x^2 - 3x + 1 = 0$

**(ii)** $(0.5, 0.0569)$, $(1, 0)$

**(iii)** $\dfrac{d^2y}{dx^2} = 2 - \dfrac{1}{x^2}$

**(iv)** $-2$, $1$

**(v)** At the maximum point $\dfrac{d^2y}{dx^2}$ is negative, so the turning point with $x = 0.5$ is the maximum. The exact value of $y$ at this point is

$0.5^2 - 3(0.5) + \ln 0.5 + 2$

$= \frac{3}{4} + \ln \frac{1}{2}$

$= \frac{3}{4} - \ln 2$

**6 (a)** $x = 4$, $x = -3$

**(b)** $x = 4$ is a minimum; $x = -3$ is a maximum.

**7** $\dfrac{dy}{dx} = 2x - 5$, $\dfrac{dy}{dx} = \dfrac{5 - 2x}{\left(x^2 - 5x\right)^2}$ and $\dfrac{dy}{dx} = \dfrac{2x - 5}{x^2 - 5x}$

are all zero when $2x - 5 = 0$; hence $x = 2.5$

## Test yourself (p 106)

**1** $(2, 10 - \ln 16) = (2, 7.227)$

**2 (a)** $3 \cos (3x - 2)$     **(b)** $5e^{5x}$

**(c)** $-\sec^2 (4 - x)$     **(d)** $\dfrac{2}{2x - 7}$

**3 (a)** $e^{-x}(\cos x - \sin x)$     **(b)** $\dfrac{e^x(1 + \tan x)}{\cos x}$

**(c)** $18x(x^2 - 7)^8$     **(d)** $\dfrac{2x \sin x \cos x - x^2}{\sin^2 x}$

**4** $1$

**5 (a)** $e^x(x^2 + 2x - 8)$

**(b)** $x = 2$, $x = -4$

**(c)** $\dfrac{d^2y}{dx^2} = e^x(2x + 2) + (x^2 + 2x - 8)e^x$

$= e^x(x^2 + 4x - 6)$

**(d)** $x = 2$ is a minimum; $x = -4$ is a maximum.

**6 (a)** $\dfrac{dy}{dx} = \dfrac{1}{x} - 4x$

**(b)** When $x = \frac{1}{2}$, $\dfrac{dy}{dx} = \dfrac{1}{\frac{1}{2}} - 4\left(\frac{1}{2}\right)$

$= 2 - 2 = 0$

so there is a stationary value when $x = \frac{1}{2}$.

**(c)** $-8$

**(d)** Maximum

**7 (a)** $e^{2x}(2 \sin 3x + 3 \cos 3x)$

**(b)** $10(2x + 1)^4$

**8 (a) (i)** $x^2(3 \ln x + 1)$

**(ii)** When $x = e^{-\frac{1}{3}}$, $\dfrac{dy}{dx} = \left(e^{-\frac{1}{3}}\right)^2\left(3 \ln e^{-\frac{1}{3}} + 1\right)$

$= \left(e^{-\frac{1}{3}}\right)^2\left(\ln\left(e^{-\frac{1}{3}}\right)^3 + 1\right)$

$= \left(e^{-\frac{1}{3}}\right)^2\left(\ln e^{-1} + 1\right)$

$= \left(e^{-\frac{1}{3}}\right)^2(-1 + 1)$

$= 0$

So there is a stationary value at $x = e^{-\frac{1}{3}}$.

**(iii)** $-\dfrac{1}{3e}$

**(b) (i)** $x(6 \ln x + 5)$

**(ii)** $3e^{-\frac{1}{3}}$

**(iii)** Minimum

# 7 Integration

## A Integrating $e^x$, $\sin x$ and $\cos x$ (p 107)

**A1** (a) $-\sin x$  (b) $-\cos x + c$

**A2** (a) $e^6 - e^2$  (b) $\left[\sin x\right]_0^{\frac{\pi}{2}} = 1$

**A3** (a) $2\cos 2x$

(b) (i) $\sin 2x + c$  (ii) $\frac{1}{2}\sin 2x + c$

**A4** (a) $-5\sin 5x$

(b) (i) $\cos 5x + c$  (ii) $-\frac{1}{5}\cos 5x + c$

**A5** (a) $2e^{2x}$

(b) (i) $e^{2x} + c$  (ii) $\frac{1}{2}e^{2x} + c$

**A6** (a) $\frac{1}{4}e^{4x} + c$

(b) $\int_0^{0.5} e^{4x}\,dx = \left[\frac{1}{4}e^{4x}\right]_0^{0.5} = \frac{1}{4}e^2 - \frac{1}{4}e^0 = \frac{e^2 - 1}{4}$

**A7** (a) $\frac{1}{5}(e^{0.5} - 1)$  (b) $\frac{1}{2}$  (c) $\frac{1}{2}$

### Exercise A (p 108)

**1** (a) $\frac{1}{3}e^{3x} + c$

(b) (i) $\frac{1}{3}(e^3 - 1)$  (ii) $\frac{1}{3}e^6 - \frac{7}{3}$

(iii) $\frac{1}{3}(e^6 - e^3) - \frac{3}{2}$

**2** (a) $\frac{1}{4}\sin 4x + c$

(b) (i) $\frac{1}{4}$  (ii) $\frac{1}{4}\pi - \frac{1}{2}$

**3** (a) $\frac{2}{3}\sin 3x - \frac{5}{2}e^{2x} + c$  (b) $\frac{4}{5}\sin 5x - \frac{5}{4}\cos 4x + c$

(c) $-e^{-x} - \frac{1}{2}e^{-2x} + c$

**4** (a) $\frac{1}{3}x^3 + \frac{1}{3}e^{3x} + c$  (b) $\frac{1}{2}x^2 + \frac{1}{4}\cos 4x + c$

(c) $-e^{-x} - \frac{1}{x} + c$  (d) $-\frac{1}{5}\cos 5x - \frac{2}{3}x^{\frac{3}{2}} + c$

(e) $\frac{1}{2}e^{2x} - \frac{1}{2}\cos 2x + c$  (f) $\frac{1}{3}\sin 3x + \frac{1}{2x^2} + c$

**5** (a) $\left[\frac{3}{2}x^2 - \frac{1}{3}e^{3x}\right]_0^2 = \frac{19}{3} - \frac{1}{3}e^6$

(b) $\left[\frac{1}{3}x^3 - 2\cos\frac{1}{2}x\right]_0^{\pi} = \frac{1}{3}\pi^3 + 2$

(c) $\left[2x - 6\sin\frac{1}{2}x\right]_{-\pi}^{\pi} = 4\pi - 12$

(d) $\left[-\frac{1}{2}e^{-2x} + x^2\right]_0^4 = \frac{33}{2} - \frac{1}{2}e^{-8}$

(e) $\left[\frac{1}{4}x^4 + e^{-x}\right]_0^4 = 63 + e^{-4}$

(f) $\left[x^2 + \frac{1}{2}\cos 2x\right]_0^{\frac{\pi}{2}} = \frac{1}{4}\pi^2 - 1$

**6** $\frac{26}{3} + \frac{1}{2}(e^{-6} - e^{-2})$

**7** $\frac{14}{3} + 2e^2 - 2e^{\frac{1}{2}}$

**8** $\int_0^k e^{-\frac{1}{4}x}\,dx = 1 \Rightarrow \left[-4e^{-\frac{1}{4}x}\right]_0^k = 1$

$\Rightarrow -4e^{-\frac{1}{4}k} + 4 = 1$

$\Rightarrow 4e^{-\frac{1}{4}k} = 3$

$\Rightarrow e^{-\frac{1}{4}k} = \frac{3}{4}$

$\Rightarrow \ln\left(e^{-\frac{1}{4}k}\right) = \ln\frac{3}{4}$

$\Rightarrow -\frac{1}{4}k = \ln\frac{3}{4}$

$\Rightarrow k = -4\ln\frac{3}{4}$

$\Rightarrow k = 4\ln\frac{4}{3}$

## B Integrating $\frac{1}{x}$ (p 109)

**B1** (a) $\ln 5$  (b) $\ln\frac{1}{2}$  (c) $9 + \ln\frac{5}{2}$

**B2** $\frac{1}{3}\ln|x| + c$

**B3** (a) $\dfrac{2}{2x + 1}$

(b) $\int \dfrac{1}{2x + 1}\,dx = \frac{1}{2}\int \dfrac{2}{2x + 1}\,dx$
$= \frac{1}{2}\ln|2x + 1| + c \quad \left(x \neq -\frac{1}{2}\right)$

**B4** (a) $\dfrac{5}{5x - 2}$  (b) $\frac{1}{5}\ln|5x - 2| + c \quad \left(x \neq \frac{2}{5}\right)$

### Exercise B (p 111)

**1** (a) $x + \frac{1}{2}x^2 - \ln|x| + c$

(b) $\frac{1}{2}e^{2x} + 2\ln|x| + c$

(c) $-\frac{1}{6}\cos 6x - \frac{1}{2}\ln|x| + c$

(d) $\ln|x| + \frac{2}{3}x^{\frac{3}{2}} + c$

(e) $\ln|x| + 2\sqrt{x} + c$

(f) $\frac{1}{4}\sin 4x + \frac{1}{4}\ln|x| + c$

(g) $5\ln|x| - \frac{1}{3}e^{-3x} + c$

(h) $x + \ln|x| - \frac{1}{x} - \frac{1}{2x^2} + c$

(i) $\frac{1}{4}\ln|4x - 1| + c$

**2** (a) $4\ln 3$

(b) $\int_2^{2\sqrt{3}} \frac{4}{x}\,dx = 4\ln\sqrt{3} = 2\ln 3$
$= $ half the area in part (a) as required

**3** (a) $\frac{1}{2}\ln 3$

(b) $\frac{14}{3} - \ln 4$

(c) $\frac{1}{3}(e^{-3} - e^{-6} - \ln 2)$

(d) $168 + 4\ln 4$

(e) $2 + 3\ln\frac{2}{3}$ or $2 - 3\ln\frac{3}{2}$

(f) $\frac{1}{3}\ln\frac{5}{2}$

4 (a) $\dfrac{1}{x^2} + \dfrac{1}{x}$　　　　　(b) $\frac{2}{3} + \ln 3$

5 $\frac{4}{9} + \ln 3$

6 (a) $\frac{1}{3}$　　　　　　　　　(b) $4 - 2\ln 3$

## C Integration by substitution (p 112)

C1 $\frac{1}{2}(x^3 - 1)^2 + c$

C2 $-\frac{1}{4}(5 - x^2)^4 + c$

C3 $\frac{1}{10}(x^2 - 3)^5 + c$

C4 $\frac{1}{16}(x^4 - 1)^4 + c$

C5 $\frac{1}{14}(2x + 1)^7 - \frac{1}{12}(2x + 1)^6 + c$

C6 $\frac{2}{15}(3x - 2)^5 + \frac{1}{3}(3x - 2)^4 + c$

C7 $\frac{1}{24}(2x + 3)^6 - \frac{3}{20}(2x + 3)^5 + c$

### Exercise C (p 114)

1 $\frac{1}{4}(x^2 + 4)^4 + c$

2 (a) $\frac{1}{5}(x^3 - 1)^5 + c$　　　(b) $-\dfrac{1}{3(x^3 - 1)} + c$

(c) $\frac{1}{3}(x^2 - 4)^{\frac{3}{2}} + c$　　　(d) $\frac{1}{24}(2x^2 + 1)^6 + c$

3 (a) $\frac{1}{12}(2x - 3)^6 + \frac{3}{10}(2x - 3)^5 + c$

(b) $\frac{1}{24}(2x + 1)^6 - \frac{1}{20}(2x + 1)^5 + c$

(c) $\frac{2}{45}(3x - 2)^{\frac{5}{2}} + \frac{4}{27}(3x - 2)^{\frac{3}{2}} + c$

(d) $\frac{1}{5}(5x - 2) + \frac{2}{5}\ln|5x - 2| + c$

(e) $\frac{1}{16}(4x + 1) - \frac{1}{16}\ln|4x + 1| + c$

(f) $-\frac{1}{4}(2x - 1)^{-1} - \frac{1}{8}(2x - 1)^{-2} + c$

4 (a) $u = x^2 + 3$, $\frac{1}{4}(x^2 + 3)^4 + c$

(b) $u = x^2 + 5$, $\frac{1}{3}(x^2 + 5)^{\frac{3}{2}} + c$

(c) $u = 6x + 5$, $\frac{1}{252}(6x + 5)^7 - \frac{5}{216}(6x + 5)^6 + c$

(d) $u = 1 - 2x$, $\frac{1}{24}(1 - 2x)^6 - \frac{1}{20}(1 - 2x)^5 + c$

(e) $u = x^2 - 1$, $\sqrt{x^2 - 1} + c$

(f) $u = x - 1$, $\frac{2}{3}(x - 1)^{\frac{3}{2}} + 2(x - 1)^{\frac{1}{2}} + c$

## D Integrating $\dfrac{f'(x)}{f(x)}$ (p 114)

D1 $\ln|x^2 + 1| + c$

D2 $\ln|x^3 - 1| + c$

D3 $\ln|x^4 + 3x^2 - 5| + c$

### Exercise D (p 115)

1 (a) $\ln|x^3 - 1| + c$

(b) $\ln|x^2 + x| + c$

(c) $\frac{1}{5}\ln|x^5 + 1| + c$

(d) $\frac{1}{2}\ln|x^2 - 2x| + c$

(e) $\frac{1}{4}\ln|2x^2 + 4x + 1| + c$

(f) $\frac{1}{3}\ln|3e^x - 1| + c$

2 (a) $-\frac{1}{2}\ln|4 - x^2| + c$

(b) $\left[-\frac{1}{2}\ln|4 - x^2|\right]_0^1 = -\frac{1}{2}\ln 3 + \frac{1}{2}\ln 4 = \frac{1}{2}\ln\left(\frac{4}{3}\right)$

3 (a) Area required
$$= \int_0^2 \frac{x}{x^2 + 1}\,dx = \frac{1}{2}\int_0^2 \frac{2x}{x^2 + 1}\,dx = \left[\frac{1}{2}\ln|x^2 + 1|\right]_0^2$$
$$= \frac{1}{2}\ln 5$$

(b) $\frac{1}{3}\ln 9$

4 (a) $\dfrac{\sin x}{\cos x}$

(b) The derivative of $\cos x$ is $-\sin x$, so we have
$-\dfrac{f'(x)}{f(x)}$ where $f(x) = \cos x$.

(c) $\ln|\sin x| + c$

5 (a) $\frac{1}{3}\ln|e^{3x} + 1| + c$

(b) $\int_0^1 \dfrac{e^{3x}}{e^{3x} + 1}\,dx = \left[\frac{1}{3}\ln|e^{3x} + 1|\right]_0^1$
$= \frac{1}{3}\ln(e^3 + 1) - \frac{1}{3}\ln(e^0 + 1)$
$= \frac{1}{3}(\ln(e^3 + 1) - \ln 2)$
$= \frac{1}{3}\ln\left(\dfrac{e^3 + 1}{2}\right)$

6 (a) $\dfrac{1}{2\sqrt{x}}$　　　　　(b) $2\ln|1 + \sqrt{x}| + c$

## E Integration by parts (p 116)

**E1 (a)** The derivative of $x\cos x$ is $-x\sin x + \cos x$
so $\int(-x\sin x + \cos x)\,dx = x\cos x + c$.

**(b)** $\int x\sin x\,dx = \int\cos x\,dx - x\cos x - c$
$= \sin x - x\cos x + c$

Note that as $c$ is an arbitrary constant, we can choose that it be added rather than subtracted without altering its effect.

**E2 (a)** The derivative of $xe^x$ is $xe^x + e^x$
so $\int(xe^x + e^x)\,dx = xe^x + c$.

**(b)** $\int xe^x\,dx = xe^x - \int e^x\,dx + c$
$= xe^x - e^x + c$

**E3 (a)** The derivative of $x\sin 2x$ is $2x\cos 2x + \sin 2x$
so $\int(2x\cos 2x + \sin 2x)\,dx = x\sin 2x + c$.

**(b)** $\int 2x\cos 2x\,dx = x\sin 2x - \int\sin 2x\,dx + c$
$= x\sin 2x + \tfrac{1}{2}\cos 2x + c$

**E4** $-\tfrac{1}{4}x\cos 4x + \tfrac{1}{16}\sin 4x + c$

**E5** $\tfrac{1}{4}xe^{4x} - \tfrac{1}{16}e^{4x} + c$

**E6 (a)** $\tfrac{1}{4}x\sin 4x + \tfrac{1}{16}\cos 4x + c$

**(b)** $\tfrac{1}{5}xe^{5x} - \tfrac{1}{25}e^{5x} + c$

**(c)** $-\tfrac{1}{4}xe^{-4x} - \tfrac{1}{16}e^{-4x} + c$

**E7** The integral to be found is harder than the original, not easier.

**E8 (a)** We do not yet know how to integrate $\ln x$.

**(b)** $\tfrac{1}{2}x^2\ln x - \tfrac{1}{4}x^2 + c$

### Exercise E (p 118)

**1 (a)** $\tfrac{2}{7}x\sin 7x + \tfrac{2}{49}\cos 7x + c$

**(b)** $\tfrac{1}{2}xe^{6x} - \tfrac{1}{12}e^{6x} + c$

**(c)** $-2x\cos\tfrac{1}{2}x + 4\sin\tfrac{1}{2}x + c$

**(d)** $-xe^{-x} - e^{-x} + c$

**(e)** $-\tfrac{1}{3}xe^{-3x} - \tfrac{1}{9}e^{-3x} + c$

**(f)** $-2xe^{-\frac{1}{2}x} - 4e^{-\frac{1}{2}x} + c$

**2 (a)** $\dfrac{\pi}{2} - 1$     **(b)** $\pi$     **(c)** $3e^4 + 1$

**(d)** $\tfrac{1}{9}$     **(e)** $2 - \dfrac{4}{e}$     **(f)** $8e^3 + 4$

**3 (a)** $0, \dfrac{\pi}{2}, \pi$     **(b)** $A = \dfrac{\pi}{4},\ B = -\tfrac{3}{4}\pi$

## F Two standard integrals (p 119)

**F1 (a)** $\dfrac{dx}{du} = 3\sec^2 u,\ dx = 3\sec^2 u\,du$

**(b)** $9 + x^2 = 9 + 9\tan^2 u$
$= 9(1 + \tan^2 u)$
$= 9\sec^2 u$

**(c)** $\int\dfrac{1}{9+x^2}\,dx = \int\dfrac{3\sec^2 u}{9\sec^2 u}\,du = \int\tfrac{1}{3}\,du = \tfrac{1}{3}u + c$

**(d)** $u = \tan^{-1}\dfrac{x}{3}$

**(e)** $\tfrac{1}{3}\tan^{-1}\left(\dfrac{x}{3}\right) + c$

**F2** $\tfrac{1}{5}\tan^{-1}\left(\dfrac{x}{5}\right) + c$

**F3** $\tfrac{1}{6}\tan^{-1}\left(\dfrac{x}{6}\right) + c$

**F4 (a)** $\tfrac{1}{8}\tan^{-1}\left(\dfrac{x}{8}\right) + c$     **(b)** $\dfrac{\pi}{32}$

**F5 (a)** $\dfrac{dx}{du} = 3\cos u,\ dx = 3\cos u\,du$

**(b)** $\sqrt{9 - x^2} = \sqrt{9 - 9\sin^2 u}$
$= 3\sqrt{1 - \sin^2 u}$
$= 3\cos u$

**(c)** $\int\dfrac{1}{\sqrt{9-x^2}}\,dx = \int\dfrac{3\cos u}{3\cos u}\,du = \int 1\,du = u + c$

**(d)** $u = \sin^{-1}\dfrac{x}{3}$

**(e)** $\sin^{-1}\left(\dfrac{x}{3}\right) + c$

**F6** $\sin^{-1}\left(\dfrac{x}{7}\right) + c$

### Exercise F (p 120)

**1 (a)** $\sin^{-1}\left(\dfrac{x}{2}\right) + c$     **(b)** $\tfrac{1}{10}\tan^{-1}\left(\dfrac{x}{10}\right) + c$

**(c)** $\sin^{-1}\left(\dfrac{x}{5}\right) + c$     **(d)** $\tfrac{1}{9}\tan^{-1}\left(\dfrac{x}{9}\right) + c$

**2** $\displaystyle\int_0^3\dfrac{1}{\sqrt{36-x^2}}\,dx = \left[\sin^{-1}\dfrac{x}{6}\right]_0^3 = \sin^{-1}\tfrac{1}{2} = \dfrac{\pi}{6}$

**3 (a)** $\dfrac{1}{\sqrt{3}}\tan^{-1}\left(\dfrac{x}{\sqrt{3}}\right) + c$

**(b)** $\displaystyle\int_0^3\dfrac{1}{3+x^2}\,dx = \left[\dfrac{1}{\sqrt{3}}\tan^{-1}\dfrac{x}{\sqrt{3}}\right]_0^3 = \dfrac{1}{\sqrt{3}}\tan^{-1}\sqrt{3}$

$= \dfrac{1}{\sqrt{3}}\dfrac{\pi}{3} = \dfrac{\pi\sqrt{3}}{9}$

**4** $\dfrac{\pi}{3}$

**5 (a)** $\tan^{-1}x + \frac{1}{2}\ln|1 + x^2| + c$

**(b)** $\displaystyle\int_0^1 \dfrac{1+x}{1+x^2}\,dx = \left[\tan^{-1}x + \frac{1}{2}\ln|1 + x^2|\right]_0^1$

$= \tan^{-1}1 + \frac{1}{2}\ln 2 - \tan^{-1}0 - \frac{1}{2}\ln 1$

$= \dfrac{\pi}{4} + \frac{1}{2}\ln 2$

**6** $\frac{1}{3}\tan^{-1}3x + c$

**7** $\frac{1}{5}\sin^{-1}5x + c$

## Mixed questions (p 122)

**1 (a)** Area $= \frac{1}{2}$ base $\times$ height $= \frac{1}{2} \times \frac{5}{12}\pi \times \sin\frac{5}{6}\pi$

$= \dfrac{5}{48}\pi$

**(b)** $\dfrac{\sqrt{3}}{4} + \frac{1}{2} - \frac{5}{48}\pi$

**2 (a)**

**(b)** At $A$, $y = 2e^{\frac{1}{2}x} = 6 \Rightarrow e^{\frac{1}{2}x} = 3 \Rightarrow \frac{1}{2}x = \ln 3$
$\Rightarrow x = 2\ln 3$

**(c)** $12\ln 3 - 8$

**3 (a)** $-\frac{1}{3}\cos(3x - 1) + c$

**(b)** $\sqrt{2x - 1} + c$

**(c)** $-\frac{1}{2}xe^{-2x} - \frac{1}{4}e^{-2x} + c$

**(d)** $\frac{1}{2}\ln|x^2 - 5| + c$

**(e)** $\frac{1}{6}(x - 2)^6 + \frac{2}{5}(x - 2)^5 + c$

**(f)** $\frac{1}{7}\tan^{-1}\left(\dfrac{x}{7}\right) + c$

**4 (a)** $\frac{2}{3}\ln\frac{26}{7}$     **(b)** $\frac{1}{20}\tan^{-1}\frac{1}{10}$     **(c)** $\frac{3}{2}$

**(d)** $\dfrac{\pi}{6}$     **(e)** $\dfrac{\pi^2}{2} + \frac{3}{2}$     **(f)** $-\frac{3}{2}\pi + \dfrac{9\sqrt{3}}{2}$

**5 (a)** $e^a = 2a + 1$

**(b)** Area under $y = 2x + 1$ is $a^2 + a$
(using trapezium formula)
Area under $y = e^x$ is $e^a - 1 = 2a$
(using integration)
Area required $= a^2 - a$

**6 (a)** $\frac{1}{2}\tan^{-1}\left(\dfrac{x}{2}\right) + c$     **(b)** $\frac{1}{2}\ln|4 + x^2| + c$

**7 (a)** $\sin^{-1}\left(\dfrac{x}{2}\right) + c$     **(b)** $-\sqrt{4 - x^2} + c$

**8 (a)** $\frac{3}{2}$     **(b)** $3 - 2\ln 2$

## Test yourself (p 123)

**1 (a)** $\frac{1}{6}e^{6x} + c$     **(b)** $4\sin\frac{1}{4}x + c$
**(c)** $-\frac{1}{2}\cos(2x + 1) + c$

**2 (a)** $6\ln 3$     **(b)** $\frac{1}{2}\left(1 - \dfrac{1}{e}\right)$     **(c)** $\frac{1}{3}\ln 7$

**3** $2.83$

**4 (a)** $3$

**(b) (i)** $-2e^{2x}$     **(ii)** $-8$
**(c) (i)** $\ln 2$
    **(ii)** $4x - \frac{1}{2}e^{2x} + c$
    **(iii)** $2\ln 2 - 1$
    **(iv)** Required area
$= \displaystyle\int_0^{\ln\sqrt{2}}\left(4 - e^{2x}\right)dx - \text{area of } OPQR$
$= \left[4x - \frac{1}{2}e^{2x}\right]_0^{\ln\sqrt{2}} - \ln 2$
$= 4\ln\sqrt{2} - \frac{1}{2}e^{2\ln\sqrt{2}} + \frac{1}{2} - \ln 2 = \ln 2 - \frac{1}{2}$
$= \text{half the area of the shaded region}$

**5 (a)** $\frac{1}{2}e^2 - \frac{3}{2}$     **(b)** $1$

**6 (a)** $\dfrac{\pi^2}{72} + \frac{1}{3}$     **(b)** $\dfrac{\pi}{18} - \frac{1}{9}$

**7 (a)** $\ln\frac{7}{3}$     **(b)** $\dfrac{\pi}{6}$

**8 (a)** $\frac{1}{25}$     **(b)** $\dfrac{\pi}{40}$

# 8 Solids of revolution

## A Revolution about the *x*-axis (p 124)

**A1** (a) Cone     (b) $y^2 = \frac{1}{4}x^2$     (c) $\frac{9}{4}\pi$

**A2** (a) The gradient is $\frac{r}{h}$ and the $y$-intercept is 0.

(b) $\displaystyle\int_0^h \pi y^2 \, dx = \int_0^h \frac{\pi r^2}{h^2} x^2 \, dx$

$\displaystyle = \left[\frac{\pi r^2}{3h^2} x^3\right]_0^h$

$\displaystyle = \frac{\pi r^2 h^3}{3h^2} - 0$

$\displaystyle = \frac{1}{3}\pi r^2 h$

**A3** (a) $y^2 = x^4$       (b) $\frac{31}{5}\pi$

**A4** (a) Sphere

(b) $\displaystyle\int_{-r}^r \pi y^2 \, dx = \int_{-r}^r \pi(r^2 - x^2)\,dx = \left[\pi r^2 x - \frac{1}{3}\pi x^3\right]_{-r}^r$

$\displaystyle = \frac{4}{3}\pi r^3$

### Exercise A (p 126)

**1** $\frac{32}{3}\pi$

**2** $\frac{8}{15}\pi$

**3** (a) $\frac{\pi}{2}(e^6 - 1)$    (b) $\frac{21}{64}\pi$    (c) $\frac{40}{3}\pi$

(d) $\frac{2}{3}\pi$    (e) $\frac{\pi^2}{4}$    (f) $\pi\left(1 - \frac{3}{e^2}\right)$

(g) $\frac{\pi^2}{4}$    (h) $\frac{\pi}{2}\ln 10$

## B Revolution about the *y*-axis (p 127)

**B1** (a) $x^2 = y - 1$

(b) When $x = 1$, $y = 1^2 + 1 = 2$
When $x = 3$, $y = 3^2 + 1 = 10$

(c) $40\pi$

**B2** $\frac{32}{5}\pi$

**B3** (a) $x^2 = 5 - \frac{1}{y}$

(b) $V = \displaystyle\int_{0.2}^1 \pi x^2 \, dy = \pi\int_{0.2}^1 \left(5 - \frac{1}{y}\right)dy$

$= \pi\left[5y - \ln|y|\right]_{0.2}^1 = \pi(4 - \ln 5)$

### Exercise B (p 128)

**1** $64\pi$

**2** $24\pi$

**3** $2\pi$

**4** $\frac{96}{5}\pi$

**5** $\frac{2976}{5}\pi$

**6** $\frac{3}{2}\pi$

### Mixed questions (p 128)

**1** (a) $2(e^3 - 1)$      (b) $\pi(e^6 - 1)$

**2** (a) $A = (0, -2)$, $B = \left(\frac{1}{2}\ln 3, 0\right)$

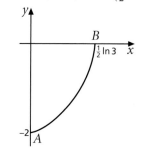

(b) $1 - \frac{3}{2}\ln 3$      (c) $\pi\left(\frac{9}{2}\ln 3 - 4\right)$

**3**

Volume $= \frac{127}{21}\pi$

**4** $\frac{127}{21}\pi$

**5** $\pi\left(\frac{23}{36}e^{24} - \frac{5}{36}e^6\right)$

### Test yourself (p 129)

**1** $\frac{3}{10}\pi$

**2** (a) $\frac{256}{15}\pi$      (b) $8\pi$

**3** $\frac{\pi}{3}\ln\frac{11}{3}$

# 9 Numerical methods

## A Locating roots (p 130)

**A1** $f(2) = 3 + 2 - 2^2 = 1$
$f(3) = 3 + 3 - 3^2 = -3$

### Exercise A (p 131)

**1** $\ln 2 - 1 = -0.307$
$\ln 3 - 1 = 0.099$
The sign changes and $\ln x$ is continuous for $x > 0$
so there is a root between 2 and 3.

**2** $e^x$ and $x^2$ are continuous.
$e^{-1} - 3 \times (-1)^2 = -2.632$
$e^0 - 3 \times 0^2 = 1$
$e^1 - 3 \times 1^2 = -0.282$
$e^3 - 3 \times 3^2 = -6.914$
$e^4 - 3 \times 4^2 = 6.598$
The sign changes between $-1$ and 0, between
0 and 1, and between 3 and 4, so there are roots in
these intervals.

**3** (a) $\sin(-3) - \frac{1}{-3} = 0.192$
$\sin(-2) - \frac{1}{-2} = -0.409$
$\sin 2 - \frac{1}{2} = 0.409$
$\sin 3 - \frac{1}{3} = -0.192$

The sign changes between $-3$ and $-2$, and
between 2 and 3, and $\sin x$ and $\frac{1}{x}$ are both
continuous in these intervals. So there are
roots in these intervals.

(b) $\frac{1}{x}$ has a discontinuity at $x = 0$, so although
there is a change of sign this does not indicate
a root. Sketching indicates there is in fact no
root.

**4** $\cos x - \ln x = 0$
$\cos 1 - \ln 1 = 0.540$
$\cos 2 - \ln 2 = -1.109$
The sign changes and the function is continuous
between 1 and 2 so there is a root in this interval.

**5** $x^2 - \sqrt{x} - 2 = 0$
$1.8^2 - \sqrt{1.8} - 2 = -0.102$
$1.9^2 - \sqrt{1.9} - 2 = 0.232$
The sign changes and the function is continuous
between 1.8 and 1.9 so there is at least one root in
this interval.

**6** (a) At $A$, $\quad x^3 - 10 = \dfrac{1}{x}$
$\Rightarrow \quad x^4 - 10x = 1$
$\Rightarrow x^4 - 10x - 1 = 0$

(b) $2^4 - 10 \times 2 - 1 = -5$
$3^4 - 10 \times 3 - 1 = 50$
The sign changes between $x = 2$ and $x = 3$ and
$x^4 - 10x - 1$ is continuous in this interval so
there is a root in this interval. Hence the
$x$-coordinate of $A$ lies between 2 and 3.

**7** No, it is possible that over the interval $f(x)$ falls
below 0 then returns to a positive value, giving
two roots in the interval. (In general, there must
be no roots or an even number of roots.)

**8** Rearranging, $x^4 - 2x^3 - 4 = 0$
$(-1.089\,85)^4 - 2 \times (-1.089\,85)^3 - 4 = -0.000\,206$
$(-1.089\,95)^4 - 2 \times (-1.089\,95)^3 - 4 = 0.001\,024$
The sign changes and the function is continuous,
so there is a root $\alpha$ in this interval.
To 5 s.f., $\alpha = -1.0899$

## B Staircase and cobweb diagrams (p 132)

**B1** (a)

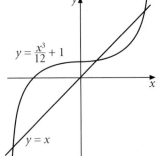

(b) 3

(c) This may be confirmed on the graph plotter
or by testing for a root between 1 and 2 in
$x^3 - 12x + 12 = 0$:
$1^3 - 12 \times 1 + 12 = 1$
$2^3 - 12 \times 2 + 12 = -4$
So there is a root between $x = 1$ and $x = 2$.

**B2** Confirmation of the values shown

**B3** The values are 1.22…, 1.15…, 1.12…, converging on 1.1157… after 10 iterations.

**B4** Substituting $x = 1.1157$ into the cubic gives 0.000 408, which is close to zero.

**B5** $x_2 = 1.083…, x_3 = 1.105…, x_4 = 1.112…$, converging to 1.1157 after 7 iterations

**B6** $e^{-0.2} - 0.2 = 0.619$
$e^{-1} - 1 = -0.632$
The sign changes and $e^{-x}$ is continuous so there is a solution between $x = 0.2$ and $x = 1$.

**B7** $x_2 = 0.81…, x_3 = 0.44…, x_4 = 0.64…, x_5 = 0.52…$
The values zigzag up and down but do eventually approach the limit 0.567…

**B8** (a)

(i) 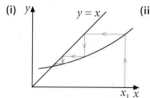 (ii)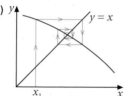

(iii) (iv)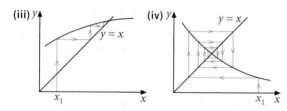

(b) The curves with a positive gradient give a staircase. The curves with a negative gradient give a cobweb.

### Exercise B (p 136)

**1** (a) $x_2 = 1.4816, x_3 = 1.5000, x_4 = 1.5041$
(b) $x_2 = 1.5811, x_3 = 1.6066, x_4 = 1.6145$
(c) $x_2 = 1.9844, x_3 = 1.0233, x_4 = 1.8661$
(d) $x_2 = 0.3730, x_3 = 0.3630, x_4 = 0.3594$

**2** (a) Q      (b) R      (c) P

**3** (a) (i) $x_2 = 0.825, x_3 = 0.678, x_4 = 0.779$
limit = 0.739
(ii) $x - \cos x = 0$ (or an equivalent equation)

(b) (i) $x_2 = 1.667, x_3 = 1.600, x_4 = 1.625$
limit = 1.618
(ii) $x^2 - x - 1 = 0$ (or an equivalent)

(c) (i) $x_2 = 2.667, x_3 = 2.117, x_4 = 1.446$
limit = 0.458
(ii) $3x - 2^x = 0$ (or an equivalent)

(d) (i) $x_2 = 0.495, x_3 = 0.377, x_4 = 0.429$
limit = 0.414
(ii) $x^2 + 2x - 1 = 0$ (or an equivalent)

**4** (a) $f(0) = -1, f(1) = 2$
The sign changes and $f(x)$ is continuous so there is a root between 0 and 1.
(b) $x^3 + 2x - 1 = 0$
$\Rightarrow \qquad 2x = 1 - x^3$
$\Rightarrow \qquad x = \dfrac{1 - x^3}{2}$
(c) 0.453

**5** In each case if $x$ is the limit $x_n = x_{n+1} = x$. Hence:

(a) $x = \dfrac{1 + 2x^2}{5}$
$\Rightarrow \qquad 5x = 1 + 2x^2$
$\Rightarrow \quad 2x^2 - 5x + 1 = 0$

(b) $x = \dfrac{1}{5 - 2x}$
$\Rightarrow \qquad (5 - 2x)x = 1$
$\Rightarrow \qquad 5x - 2x^2 = 1$
$\Rightarrow \quad 2x^2 - 5x + 1 = 0$

(c) $x = \sqrt{\dfrac{5x - 1}{2}}$
$\Rightarrow \qquad x^2 = \dfrac{5x - 1}{2}$
$\Rightarrow \qquad 2x^2 = 5x - 1$
$\Rightarrow \quad 2x^2 - 5x + 1 = 0$

(d) $x = \frac{1}{2}\left(5 - \dfrac{1}{x}\right)$
$\Rightarrow \qquad 2x = 5 - \dfrac{1}{x}$
$\Rightarrow \qquad 2x^2 = 5x - 1$
$\Rightarrow \quad 2x^2 - 5x + 1 = 0$

**6** (a) $x_2 = 0.822\,071, x_3 = 0.818\,738, x_4 = 0.819\,238$
(b) At the limit, $x_n = x_{n+1} = k$ so $k = \dfrac{1}{\sqrt[3]{k+1}}$,
which can be rearranged to give $k^4 + k^3 - 1 = 0$.

**7**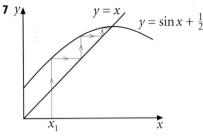

**8 (a)** 2

**(b)** $x^3 = 10$

$\Rightarrow x^2 = \dfrac{10}{x} \quad (x \neq 0)$

So $x = \sqrt{\dfrac{10}{x}}$ (taking the positive square root)

The formula is $x_{n+1} = \sqrt{\dfrac{10}{x_n}}$.

$x = 2.154$

**(c)** $x^3 = 10$

$\Rightarrow x^4 = 10x$

So $x^2 = \sqrt{10x}$ (taking the positive square root)

So $x = \sqrt{\sqrt{10x}}$ (again the positive square root)

The formula is $x_{n+1} = \sqrt{\sqrt{10x_n}}$.

**(d)** The second one is quicker.

**9 (a)** For example:

(graph with points (4, 15), (4, 12), (3, 10.39), (3, 8), curves $y = 6\sqrt{x}$ and $y = x^2 - 1$)

**(b)** $x^2 - 1 = 6\sqrt{x}$

$\Rightarrow x^2 = 6\sqrt{x} + 1$

So $x = \sqrt{6\sqrt{x} + 1}$
(taking the positive square root)

**(c)** 3.495

**10 (a)** $x^3 + x^2 - 3x - 1 = 0$

$\Rightarrow x^2(x + 1) = 3x + 1$

$\Rightarrow x^2 = \dfrac{3x+1}{x+1}$

$x = \sqrt{\dfrac{3x+1}{x+1}}$

**(b)** $x_2 = 1.5811$, $x_3 = 1.4917$, $x_4 = 1.4823$

**(c)** Either of the following:

When $x_1 = -1$, $x + 1 = 0$ so $\dfrac{3x+1}{x+1}$ is not defined.

For $-1 < x_1 < -\frac{1}{3}$, $\dfrac{3x+1}{x+1}$ is negative so there is no real square root of it.

**11 (a) (i)** $x_2 = 7$, $x_3 = 342$, $x_4 = 40\,001\,687$,
$x_5 \approx 6.4 \times 10^{22}$

**(ii)** $x_2 = 6.25$, $x_3 = 0.0256$, $x_4 \approx 1526$,
$x_5 \approx 4.29 \times 10^{-7}$

**(b)** In neither case does the sequence converge. In (i) the values become ever more rapidly larger. In (ii) the outputs oscillate between ever larger and ever smaller values.

**(c) (i)**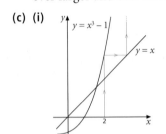

**(ii)**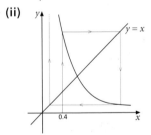

**(d)** In both cases the problem arises where the curved graph is too steep, namely $|\text{gradient}| > 1$.

## C The mid-ordinate rule (p 138)

**C1 (a)** Greater  **(b)** An overestimate

**Exercise C** (p 139)

**1 (a)** 1.0061  **(b)** 1.0023

**2 (a)** 0.914  **(b)** 2.93  **(c)** 3.14  **(d)** 2.00

**3 (a)** 1.563

**(b)** An underestimate; by considering the shaded regions, the area of the rectangle is less than the corresponding area under the curve.

This is true of all strips below a 'valley' curve.

**4 (a)**

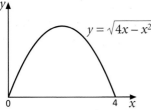

It lies entirely above the $x$-axis because of the positive square root in the curve's equation. It meets the $x$-axis at $x = 0$ and $x = 4$.

**(b)** 6.37

**5** Both hypotheses hold for smooth curves.
Considering (A), the diagram for question C1 showed that the mid-ordinate rule gives overestimates for 'hill' curves.

This diagram shows that the trapezium rule gives underestimates for 'hill' curves.

(A) can be similarly justified for the 'valley' curves.

(B) can be supported by numerical exploration. The following outline proof applies to a 'valley' curve.

Shaded area $E_t$ = error from the trapezium rule

Arc $MB$ is obtained by rotating arc $AM$ 180° about mid-point $M$.

Area under curve $AMB$ = area of rectangle.

So shaded area $E_m$ = error from mid-point rule.

Area of $\triangle ABC = E_t + E_m$ (1)

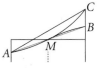

Area of $\triangle MBC = \frac{1}{2}$ area of $\triangle ABC$ (2)
(same base $BC$, half the perpendicular height)

$E_m <$ area of $\triangle MBC$ (3)
So, using (2) above,
$E_m < \frac{1}{2}$ area $\triangle ABC$
So, using (1), $E_m < E_t$, as required.

A similar proof can be developed for a 'hill' curve.

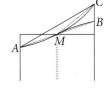

**D Simpson's rule** (p 140)

**D1** $\left[-\frac{3}{2}\left(\frac{x^3}{3}\right) + \frac{1}{2}\left(\frac{x^2}{2}\right) + 3x\right]_{-1}^{1}$

$= \left[-\frac{x^3}{2} + \frac{x^2}{4} + 3x\right]_{-1}^{1}$

$= \left(-\frac{1}{2} + \frac{1}{4} + 3\right) - \left(\frac{1}{2} + \frac{1}{4} - 3\right)$

$= 5$

**D2** The expression $= \frac{1}{3}(y_S - 2y_T + y_U)h + 2y_T h$

$= \frac{1}{3}y_S h + \frac{4}{3}y_T h + \frac{1}{3}y_U h$

$= \frac{1}{3}h(y_S + 4y_T + y_U)$

**D3** $\frac{1}{3} \times 1 \times (1 + 4 \times 3 + 2) = 5$

**D4** 6 square units

**Exercise D** (p 142)

**1 (a)** 0.483 **(b)** 0.481

**2 (a)** 17.7 **(b)** 0.562 **(c)** 1.00

**3** For these answers, given to 4 s.f., 6 strips have been used.

**(a)** 2.303

**(b) (i)** 2.256 **(ii)** 2.326 **(iii)** 2.308

**(c)** Simpson's rule

## Mixed questions (p 143)

**1 (a)** At $P$, $\quad x^2 + 1 = \dfrac{1}{x}$

$\Rightarrow \qquad x^3 + x = 1$

$\Rightarrow \quad x^3 + x - 1 = 0$

**(b)** $0.6^3 + 0.6 - 1 = -0.184$

$0.7^3 + 0.7 - 1 = 0.043$

$x^3 + x - 1$ is continuous so there is a root between 0.6 and 0.7.

**2 (a)** $A\left(1, \dfrac{\pi}{2}\right)$, $B\left(-1, -\dfrac{\pi}{2}\right)$    **(b)** 0.565

**3 (a)** $2^3 - 12 = -4$

$4^3 - 12 = 52$

The sign changes and the function is continuous, so there is a root in the interval.

**(b) (i)** $\qquad x = \dfrac{3x}{4} + \dfrac{3}{x^2}$

$\Rightarrow \qquad x^3 = \dfrac{3x^3}{4} + 3$

$\Rightarrow \qquad 4x^3 = 3x^3 + 12$

$\Rightarrow x^3 - 12 = 0$

**(ii)** $x_2 = 3.19$, $x_3 = 2.69$, $x_4 = 2.43$

**(iii)**

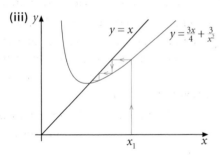

**(iv)** $\sqrt[3]{12}$

**4 (a)**

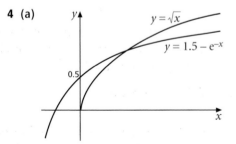

**(b)** $e^{-x} + \sqrt{x} - 1.5 = 0$ is the condition for the intersection of $y = \sqrt{x}$ and $y = 1.5 - e^{-x}$.

$y = 1.5 - e^{-x}$ has $y = 1.5$ as an asymptote but $y = \sqrt{x}$ continues to increase indefinitely, so the point of intersection shown is the only one.

**(c)** $e^{-1.7} + \sqrt{1.7} - 1.5 = -0.0134\ldots$

$e^{-1.8} + \sqrt{1.8} - 1.5 = 0.0069\ldots$

The sign changes and the function is continuous, so there is a root in the interval.

**(d)** 1.766

**5 (a)** $2e^{2x} - 2x^{-2}$

**(b)** At the stationary point,

$2e^{2x} - 2x^{-2} = 0$

$\Rightarrow \qquad 2e^{2x} = 2x^{-2}$

$\Rightarrow \qquad 2e^{2x} = \dfrac{2}{x^2}$

$\Rightarrow \qquad e^{2x} = \dfrac{1}{x^2}$

$\Rightarrow \qquad x^2 e^{2x} = 1$

**(c)** Taking the positive square root of both sides,

$xe^x = 1$

Taking logs of both sides,

$\ln x + x \ln e = \ln 1$

$\ln x + x = 0$

**(d)** $\ln 0.5 + 0.5 = -0.193\ldots$

$\ln 0.6 + 0.6 = 0.089\ldots$

The sign changes and the function is continuous, so there is a root in the interval.

**(e)** $\frac{1}{2}e^{2x} + 2 \ln x + c$

**6 (a) (i)** $\cos x - x \sin x$

**(ii)** At a maximum $\dfrac{dy}{dx} = 0$

$\cos x - x \sin x = 0$

$x \sin x = \cos x$

$x \dfrac{\sin x}{\cos x} = 1$

$\dfrac{\sin x}{\cos x} = \dfrac{1}{x}$

$\tan x = \dfrac{1}{x}$

$x = \tan^{-1} \dfrac{1}{x}$ as required

**(iii)** 0.86

**(b)** $\dfrac{\pi}{2} - 1$

**1** The equation can be rearranged as

$$\sqrt{x} - 2\ln x = 0$$
$$\sqrt{2} - 2\ln 2 = 0.0279\ldots$$
$$\sqrt{2.1} - 2\ln 2.1 = -0.0347\ldots$$

The sign changes and the function is continuous so there is a root in the interval.

**2 (a)**

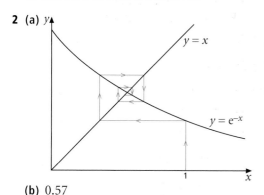

**(b)** 0.57

**3 (a)** $x_2 = 3.742$, $x_3 = 3.968$, $x_4 = 3.996$

**(b) (i)** At the limit, $L = x_n = x_{n+1}$

Substituting in the recurrence formula,

$$L = \sqrt{L + 12}$$
$$\Rightarrow \qquad L^2 = L + 12$$
$$\Rightarrow \quad L^2 - L - 12 = 0$$

**(ii)** 4

**(c)**

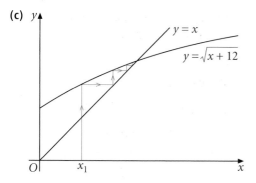

**4** 0.22

**5** 1.83

# 10 Proof

## A Introducing proof (p 146)

**A1** With a 10-year-old child you might start by showing that an odd number of counters can be arranged in two equal rows with one counter left over. Then use a particular case such as 7 + 5, which can be represented by

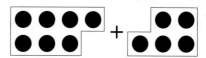

Since there are two odd numbers then the two 'left over' counters fit together so that there are two equal rows and hence an even number, which in this case is 12.

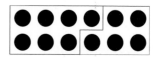

Since you will be able to produce pictures like this for any two odd numbers then you will always get an even number when you add two odd numbers.

In a mathematics examination, a briefer algebraic argument that does not appeal to pictures is more appropriate. It has the advantage that it shows that the statement is valid both for positive and for negative numbers.

Any two odd numbers can be written as $2k + 1$ and $2m + 1$ where $k$ and $m$ are integers.

The sum is
$$(2k + 1) + (2m + 1) = 2k + 2m + 2$$
$$= 2(k + m + 1)$$

Since $k + m + 1$ is an integer then $2(k + m + 1)$ is an even number and so the sum of any two odd numbers is always an even number.

**A2** Some possible comments are

**Response 1**
After trying a few examples like this, it is difficult to believe that you will be able to find one where the identity will not hold true. However, no matter how far you go, this argument will not constitute a proof as it doesn't show that the identity is true for all values of $x$.

## Response 2

This is a valid proof that shows the identity is true for all values of $x$. It relies on the distributive law that $a(b + c) = ab + ac$ for all real numbers. Whether or not you find this proof convincing will depend on your knowledge and experience of expanding brackets and simplifying algebraic expressions.

## Response 3

This does not require as much knowledge of how to manipulate algebraic expressions and some may find the visual argument more convincing. An accompanying commentary that explains what is going on would possibly make things clearer.

Its main disadvantage is that it shows that the identity is valid for positive numbers greater than 1 whereas response 2 shows the identity is valid for all values of $x$.

## B Disproof by counterexample

### Exercise B (p 147)

1 There is only one possible counterexample and that is 2, the only even prime number.

2 Almost any value of $\theta$ gives a counterexample. The simplest is $\theta = 0$ as
$$\frac{\cos(3 \times 0)}{3} = \frac{\cos 0}{3} = \frac{1}{3} \text{ but } \cos 0 = 1.$$

3 A counterexample is given by 1 and 5, whose product is 5 which is not a multiple of 3.

4 The simplest counterexample is with $\theta = 0$ as
$\cos(-0) = \cos 0 = 1$ but $-\cos 0 = -1$.

5 A counterexample is given by $\theta = \dfrac{\pi}{2}$ as
$$\sin\left(2 \times \frac{\pi}{2}\right) = \sin \pi = 0 \text{ but } 2 \sin\left(\frac{\pi}{2}\right) = 2.$$

6 A counterexample is with $x = \frac{1}{2}$ as $x^2 = \left(\frac{1}{2}\right)^2 = \frac{1}{4}$ and $\frac{1}{4}$ is smaller than $\frac{1}{2}$.

7 Almost any pair of values gives a counterexample. The simplest is $a = 1$, $b = 1$ as
$(1 + 1)^2 = 2^2 = 4$ but $1^2 + 1^2 = 1 + 1 = 2$.

8 The simplest counterexample is with $x = 0$ as
$$\operatorname{cosec} 0 = \frac{1}{\sin 0} = \frac{1}{0} \text{ and this is not defined.}$$

9 A counterexample is given by the irrational numbers $\sqrt{2}$ and $\sqrt{8}$ as $\sqrt{2} \times \sqrt{8} = \sqrt{16} = 4$ which is rational.

10 Almost any pair of values gives a counterexample. One pair is $A = \dfrac{\pi}{2}$, $B = \dfrac{\pi}{2}$ as
$$\sin \frac{\pi}{2} + \sin \frac{\pi}{2} = 1 + 1 = 2$$
$$\text{but } \sin\left(\frac{\pi}{2} + \frac{\pi}{2}\right) = \sin \pi = 0.$$

11 Almost any pair of values gives a counterexample. One pair is $x = 9$, $y = 16$ as
$\sqrt{9 + 16} = \sqrt{25} = 5$ but $\sqrt{9} + \sqrt{16} = 3 + 4 = 7$.

12 Any value of $x$ gives a counterexample. The simplest is $x = 0$ as
$$\frac{1}{2 \cos 0} = \frac{1}{2} \text{ but } 2 \sec 0 = \frac{2}{\cos 0} = 2.$$

13 Almost any value of $x$ gives a counterexample. The simplest is $x = 0$ as
$e^{(2 \times 0)} = e^0 = 1$ but $e^0 + e^2 = 1 + e^2$.

14 Almost any pair of values gives a counterexample. One pair is $A = 1$, $B = e$ as
$\ln(1 \times e) = \ln e = 1$ but $\ln 1 \times \ln e = 0 \times 1 = 0$.

15 A counterexample is given by $x = -4$ as
$|-4 + 2| = |-2| = 2$ which is less than 3 but $|-4| = 4$ which is not less than 1.

16 A counterexample is given by $x = -4$, $y = 1$ as
$(-4)^2 = 16$ which is greater than $1^2 = 1$ but $-4$ is less than 1.

## C Constructing a proof (p 148)

C1 Some experience of using the fact that an odd number can be written in the form $2k + 1$ for some integer $k$ will be helpful (though not necessary). You would need to be able to square a simple linear expression ($2k + 1$ in this case) and factorise a simple expression ($4k^2 + 4k$). You also need to know that the product of an even number and a multiple of 4 will be a multiple of 8.

**C2** The first conjecture is true (a counterexample for the second conjecture is that 3 is odd but $3^2 + 5 = 14$ which is not divisible by 3).

Proof:

If $n$ is odd then there is some integer $k$ such that $n = 2k + 1$.

So $n^2 + 3 = (2k + 1)^2 + 3$
$$= 4k^2 + 4k + 1 + 3$$
$$= 4k^2 + 4k + 4$$
$$= 4(k^2 + k + 1)$$

and since $k$ is an integer, $k^2 + k + 1$ is an integer so $4(k^2 + k + 1)$ is a multiple of 4.

Hence, for all odd numbers $n$, $n^2 + 3$ is divisible by 4.

## D  Direct proof

### Exercise D (p 150)

Each of these is just one possible proof.

**1** A trapezium $PQRS$ is shown below with the appropriate lengths labelled $a$, $b$ and $h$.
The mid-point of $QR$ is labelled $O$.

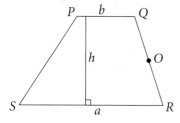

A rotation of 180° about $O$ gives the shape $PS'P'S$.

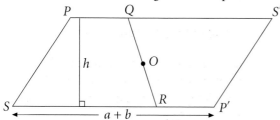

The length of $SP'$ is $a + b$. The shape $PS'P'S$ is a parallelogram as its opposite angles are equal.
Hence its area is base × height = $h(a + b)$.

Now the area of trapezium $PQRS$ is half this area and so is $\frac{1}{2}h(a + b)$.

**2** Any odd number can be written as $2k + 1$ where $k$ is some integer. Hence the next odd integer is $2k + 1 + 2 = 2k + 3$.
The sum is $(2k + 1) + (2k + 3) = 4k + 4$
$= 4(k + 1)$ which is a multiple of 4.

**3** $\cos\theta$ and $\sin\theta$ can be defined as the $x$- and $y$-coordinates of the point $P$ on the unit circle with centre $(0, 0)$, where $\theta$ is measured anticlockwise from the positive $x$-axis.

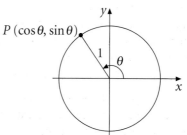

The equation of the circle is $x^2 + y^2 = 1$ so substituting for $x$ and $y$ gives $\cos^2\theta + \sin^2\theta = 1$.

**4** The $n$th odd number is $2n - 1$.
So the sum $S$ of the first $n$ odd numbers can be written as
$S = 1 + 3 + 5 + 7 + \dots + (2n - 3) + (2n - 1)$.
Reversing this sum gives
$S = (2n - 1) + (2n - 3) + \dots + 7 + 5 + 3 + 1$.
Adding the first term from each series gives
$1 + (2n - 1) = 2n$.
Adding the second terms gives $3 + (2n - 3) = 2n$ and so on, giving $n$ pairs of terms that each add to give $2n$. So $2S = 2n \times n = 2n^2$ which gives $S = n^2$ as required.

**5** Four consecutive integers can be written as $k, k + 1, k + 2$ and $k + 3$ for some integer $k$.

The product of the last two integers is $(k + 2)(k + 3) = k^2 + 5k + 6$ and the product of the first two is $k(k + 1) = k^2 + k$.

The difference is $(k^2 + 5k + 6) - (k^2 + k) = 4k + 6$.

The sum of the four integers is $k + k + 1 + k + 2 + k + 3 = 4k + 6$ which is the same as the difference, as required.

**6** The values of both $\sin\theta$ and $\cos\theta$ are between $-1$ and 1 inclusive. Hence the lowest possible value of $\sin\theta\cos\theta$ is $1\times-1 = -1$. So for all values of $\theta$, the lowest possible value of $\sin\theta\cos\theta + 1$ is 0. So the graph of $y = \sin\theta\cos\theta + 1$ does not dip below the horizontal axis at any point and so the graph of $y = |\sin\theta\cos\theta + 1|$ is identical.

**7** $\sin\theta\tan\theta \equiv \sin\theta \times \dfrac{\sin\theta}{\cos\theta}$

$\equiv \dfrac{\sin^2\theta}{\cos\theta}$

$\equiv \dfrac{1-\cos^2\theta}{\cos\theta}$

$\equiv \dfrac{1}{\cos\theta} - \dfrac{\cos^2\theta}{\cos\theta}$

$\equiv \sec\theta - \cos\theta$ as required

**8 (a)** Differentiating $\left(1 - \frac{1}{2}x^2\right)\cos x + x\sin x$ by using the product rule for each term gives
$\left(1 - \frac{1}{2}x^2\right)(-\sin x) - x\cos x + x\cos x + \sin x$
$= \frac{1}{2}x^2\sin x$ as required.

**(b)** $\int x^2 \sin x\,dx = 2 \times \int \frac{1}{2}x^2 \sin x\,dx$
$= 2 \times \left(\left(1 - \frac{1}{2}x^2\right)\cos x + x\sin x\right) + c$
$= (2 - x^2)\cos x + 2x\sin x + c$

**9** Four consecutive integers can be written as $k, k+1, k+2$ and $k+3$ for some integer $k$.

The product of these integers is
$k(k+1)(k+2)(k+3) = (k^2 + k)(k^2 + 5k + 6)$
$= k^4 + 5k^3 + 6k^2 + k^3 + 5k^2 + 6k$
$= k^4 + 6k^3 + 11k^2 + 6k$

Now the perfect square $(k^2 + 3k + 1)^2$
is $(k^2 + 3k + 1)(k^2 + 3k + 1)$
$= k^4 + 3k^3 + k^2 + 3k^3 + 9k^2 + 3k + k^2 + 3k + 1$
$= k^4 + 6k^3 + 11k^2 + 6k + 1$ which is one more than the expression above.

Hence the product of four consecutive integers is one less than a perfect square.

**10** $\dfrac{\tan^2 A + \cos^2 A}{\sin A + \sec A} \equiv \dfrac{\sec^2 A - 1 + \cos^2 A}{\sin A + \sec A}$

$\equiv \dfrac{\sec^2 A - (1 - \cos^2 A)}{\sin A + \sec A}$

$\equiv \dfrac{\sec^2 A - \sin^2 A}{\sin A + \sec A}$

$\equiv \dfrac{(\sec A - \sin A)(\sec A + \sin A)}{\sin A + \sec A}$

$\equiv \sec A - \sin A$ as required

**11** $k^3 - k = k(k^2 - 1) = k(k+1)(k-1)$
$= (k-1)k(k+1)$ which is the product of three consecutive integers (as $k$ is an integer).

In any set of three consecutive integers, at least one is divisible by 2 and one is divisible by 3.

Hence the product is divisible by 6 as required.

**12** $9^n - 1 = 3^{2n} - 1 = (3^n - 1)(3^n + 1)$.
Now $3^n$ is odd for all $n$ so both $3^n - 1$ and $3^n + 1$ are even.
$3^n - 1 + 2 = 3^n + 1$ so $3^n - 1$ and $3^n + 1$ are consecutive even numbers. In any pair of consecutive even numbers, one must be a multiple of 4. So the product $(3^n - 1)(3^n + 1)$ is the product of an even number and a multiple of 4. Hence the product is a multiple of 8 as required.

**13** $p^2 - 1 = (p-1)(p+1)$

$p - 1, p$ and $p + 1$ are three consecutive integers so one of them must be a multiple of 3. Now $p$ is a prime greater than 3 so $p$ is not a multiple of 3. Hence either $p - 1$ or $p + 1$ is a multiple of 3 and so the product $p^2 - 1$ is a multiple of 3.

Also, $p$ is a prime greater than 2 so $p$ must be odd. Hence there exists an integer $k$ so that $p = 2k + 1$ and $p^2 - 1 = (p-1)(p+1)$
$= 2k(2k + 2) = 4k(k + 1)$.
Now, since $k$ and $k + 1$ are consecutive integers, one of them must be even and so $k(k+1)$ is even. So $4k(k+1)$ is the product of 4 and an even number and so is a multiple of 8.

Since $p^2 - 1$ is a multiple of 3 and of 8 (and 3 and 8 have no common factor except 1) then $p^2 - 1$ is a multiple of $3\times8 = 24$.

## E Proof by contradiction

### Exercise E (p 152)

**1 (a)** Assume that $\sqrt[3]{2}$ is rational. Then there must exist integers $p$ and $q$ such that $\sqrt[3]{2} = \frac{p}{q}$ in its simplest form.

$\sqrt[3]{2} = \frac{p}{q} \implies p^3 = 2q^3$.

So $p^3$ is even and therefore $p$ is even too.

If $p$ is even then there exists an integer $k$ such that $p = 2k$ and so $p^3 = (2k)^3 = 8k^3$.

Hence, $2q^3 = 8k^3$ which gives $q^3 = 4k^3$ and so $q^3$ is even and therefore $q$ is even too.

But, if both $p$ and $q$ are even, then $\frac{p}{q}$ is not in its simplest form and our original assumption was false.

We conclude that $\sqrt[3]{2}$ is not rational.

**(b)** Assume that the equation $x^4 = 45x + 1$ does have at least one integer solution and call it $k$. Hence $k^4 = 45k + 1$.

Now $k$ is either even or odd.

If $k$ is even then $k^4$ is even and $45k + 1$ is odd so $k^4 \neq 45k + 1$.

If $k$ is odd then $k^4$ is odd and $45k + 1$ is even so again $k^4 \neq 45k + 1$.

Hence our original assumption is false and the equation $x^4 = 45x + 1$ has no integer solutions.

**(c)** Assume that there is at least one pair of positive integers $x$, $y$ such that $x^2 - y^2 = 10$.

Now $x^2 - y^2 \equiv (x - y)(x + y)$.

If $x$ and $y$ are both even, then both $(x - y)$ and $(x + y)$ are even so the product $(x - y)(x + y)$ is a multiple of 4.

If $x$ and $y$ are both odd, then both $(x - y)$ and $(x + y)$ are even so the product $(x - y)(x + y)$ is a multiple of 4.

If $x$ is even and $y$ is odd (or vice versa), then both $(x - y)$ and $(x + y)$ are odd so the product $(x - y)(x + y)$ is odd.

Each of these contradicts our original assumption that $x^2 - y^2 = 10$.

Hence no such integers exist.

**2** Jo must have reasoned something like this. 'If I have the £50 note, then Raj would now be looking at it and he would say straight away that he had a £5 note. He isn't saying anything so I cannot have the £50 note. Hence I must have a £5 note.'

## F Convincing but flawed

### Exercise F (p 153)

**1** As $a = b$, then $a^2 - ab = a^2 - a^2 = 0$.
So the last step is equivalent to dividing by 0 which is impossible (for example, we know that $1 \times 0 = 2 \times 0$ but this does not imply that $1 = 2$) and leads to the contradiction.

**2** $n + n$ represents the sum of two identical numbers which is indeed even but, if the numbers are different, then you need two different letters such as $m$ and $n$ to represent the two different numbers. You cannot conclude that $m + n$ is even.

**3** The mistake here is on line 3.
The expression on the right-hand side should be $\pm\sqrt{1 - \sin^2\theta}$ to include both the positive and negative square roots. This would give
$1 + \cos\pi = 1 \pm \sqrt{1 - \sin^2\pi}$ on line 6 which does not lead to a contradiction as
$1 + \cos\pi = 1 - \sqrt{1 - \sin^2\pi}$ is true.

**4** The mistake here is to assume that, if a statement is true for many cases, then it will be true for all cases. It is clear, for example, that when $n = 41$, the expression is equivalent to $41^2$ which is not prime.

**5** The mistake here is to assume that, if the sides of a polygon are all equal, then it will have equal angles (clearly not true in the case of a rhombus that is not a square for example). It also, on first glance, looks like a regular octagon. However, we can use symmetry and trigonometry to show that $\angle A = \angle C = \angle E = \angle G \approx 126.9°$ and $\angle B = \angle D = \angle F = \angle H \approx 143.1°$.

**6** The mistake here is to assume that a pattern will continue in the obvious way. Here 5 points gives 16 regions (following the doubling pattern) but 6 points gives 31 regions (not the expected 32).

The maximum number of regions is in fact $\frac{1}{24}(n^4 - 6n^3 + 23n^2 - 18n + 24)$.

(For those who would like to try proving this, a proof can be obtained using Euler's formula for connected networks that can be drawn on the surface of a sphere.)

**7** The mistake here is to assume that the large shapes are in fact triangles. Consider the smaller triangle at the top of the first shape. The gradient of the hypotenuse is $\frac{3}{5} = 0.6$. However, the gradient of the hypotenuse of the larger triangle is $\frac{5}{8} = 0.625$. As the gradients are close the lines look as though they form the hypotenuse of a large right-angled triangle but they don't. The large shape is in fact a convex quadrilateral.

The second shape is not a triangle for the same reasons and is in fact a concave quadrilateral with a smaller area than the first quadrilateral.

The area of the black shape is the difference between their areas.

## Test yourself (p 155)

**1 (a)** Almost any pair of values gives a counterexample.

One pair is $A = \frac{\pi}{2}, B = \frac{\pi}{2}$ as

$\cos\left(\frac{\pi}{2} - \frac{\pi}{2}\right) = \cos 0 = 1$ but

$\cos\frac{\pi}{2} - \cos\frac{\pi}{2} = 0 - 0 = 0.$

**(b)** The smallest counterexample is the even number 10 as it can be expressed as the sum of two primes in two different ways, $3 + 7$ and $5 + 5$.

**2 (a)** Four consecutive integers can be written as $k, k + 1, k + 2$ and $k + 3$ for some integer $k$.

The product of the first and last integers is $k(k + 3) = k^2 + 3k$ and the product of the middle two is $(k + 1)(k + 2) = k^2 + 3k + 2$. The difference is $(k^2 + 3k + 2) - (k^2 + 3k) = 2$ as required.

**(b)** $(\tan\theta + \cot\theta)^2 \equiv \tan^2\theta + \cot^2\theta + 2\tan\theta\cot\theta$
$\equiv \tan^2\theta + \cot^2\theta + 2$
$\equiv (\tan^2\theta + 1) + (\cot^2\theta + 1)$
$\equiv \sec^2\theta + \csc^2\theta$

**(c)** Three consecutive multiples of 4 can be written as $4k$, $4k + 4$ and $4k + 8$ for some integer $k$.

The sum is $4k + 4k + 4 + 4k + 8 = 12k + 12$ $= 12(k + 1)$ which is a multiple of 12.

**(d)** $\ln a^3 - \ln a^2 - \ln a$
$\equiv 3\ln a - 2\ln a - \ln a$
$\equiv 0$ as required.

# Index

Brilliant Activities for

# Grammar and Punctuation, Year 2

## Activities for Developing and Reinforcing Key Language Skills

**Irene Yates**

**Brilliant**
PUBLICATIONS

This set of books is dedicated to the memory of Miss Hannah Gamage and to the children of St. Philip Neri with St. Bede's Catholic Primary School, Mansfield.

● ● ● ● ● ● ● ● ● ● ● ● ● ● ● ● ● ● ● ● ● ● ●

We hope you and your pupils enjoy using the ideas in this book. Brilliant Publications publishes many other books to help primary school teachers. To find out more details on all of our titles, including those listed below, please log onto our website: www.brilliantpublications.co.uk.

Other books in the **Brilliant Activities for Grammar and Punctuation Series**

| | Printed ISBN | e-pdf ISBN |
|---|---|---|
| Year 1 | 978-1-78317-125-5 | 978-1-78317-132-3 |
| Year 3 | 978-1-78317-127-9 | 978-1-78317-134-7 |
| Year 4 | 978-1-78317-128-6 | 978-1-78317-135-4 |
| Year 5 | 978-1-78317-129-3 | 978-1-78317-136-1 |
| Year 6 | 978-1-78317-130-9 | 978-1-78317-137-8 |

**Brilliant Activities for Creative Writing Series**
| Year 1 | 978-0-85747-463-6 |
|---|---|
| Year 2 | 978-0-85747-464-3 |
| Year 3 | 978-0-85747-465-0 |
| Year 4 | 978-0-85747-466-7 |
| Year 5 | 978-0-85747-467-4 |
| Year 6 | 978-0-85747-468-1 |

**Brilliant Activities for Reading Comprehension Series**
| Year 1 | 978-1-78317-070-8 |
|---|---|
| Year 2 | 978-1-78317-071-5 |
| Year 3 | 978-1-78317-072-2 |
| Year 4 | 978-1-78317-073-9 |
| Year 5 | 978-1-78317-074-6 |
| Year 6 | 978-1-78317-075-3 |

Published by Brilliant Publications
Unit 10
Sparrow Hall Farm
Edlesborough
Dunstable
Bedfordshire
LU6 2ES, UK

Email: info@brilliantpublications.co.uk
Website: www.brilliantpublications.co.uk
Tel: 01525 222292

The name Brilliant Publications and the logo are registered trademarks.

Written by Irene Yates
Illustrated by Molly Sage
Front cover illustration by Brilliant Publications

© Text Irene Yates 2015
© Design Brilliant Publications 2015

Printed ISBN 978-1-78317-126-2
e-pdf ISBN 978-1-78317-133-0

First printed and published in the UK in 2015

The right of Irene Yates to be identified as the author of this work has been asserted by herself in accordance with the Copyright, Designs and Patents Act 1988.

# Contents

# Introduction

The **Brilliant Activities for Grammar and Punctuation** series is designed to introduce and reinforce grammatical concepts in line with the National Curriculum Programmes of Study.

The rules of grammar and punctuation are not always easy to access and absorb – or even to teach. It is difficult for children to make the leap from speaking and writing to talking about speaking and writing and to think in the abstract about the words of the language. The ability or readiness to do this requires a certain way of thinking and, for the most part, repetition is the key.

The sheets for this series are all written to add to the children's understanding of these fairly abstract ideas. They aim to improve children's ability to use English effectively and accurately in their own writing and speaking.

The sheets contain oral as well as written contexts because grammar and punctuation are not just about writing. Sometimes the way children have learned to speak is not always grammatically correct but it is the way of speaking that they own. We always have to be aware of instances of regional or familial language and make the point that what we are teaching is what is known universally as 'correct' speech without deprecating the children's own patterns of speech.

The children should always be encouraged to discuss what it is they are learning, to ask questions and to make observations. All of this discussion will help them to understand how the English language works.

The sheets are designed to be structured but flexible so that they can be used to introduce a concept, as stand-alones or as follow-ons. The activities on the sheets can be used as templates to create lots more for practice and reinforcement purposes.

Each book aims to offer:
* groundwork for the introduction of new concepts.
* a range of relevant activities
* ideas for continuation
* opportunity for reinforcement
* simple and clear definition of concepts and terms
* opportunities for assessing learning
* clear information to teachers.

Grammar and punctuation can sometimes be a hard grind, but nothing feels so good to a teacher as a pupil, eyes shining, saying, 'Oh, I get that now!' Once they 'get' a concept they never lose it and you can watch it become functional in their writing and, hopefully, hear it become functional in their speaking.

# Links to the curriculum

· · · · · · · · · · · · · · · · · · · · · · · · · · · · · · · · · · · · · · · · · · · · · · · · · · · · · · · ·

The activity sheets in this series of books will help children to develop their knowledge of Grammar and Punctuation as set out in the Programmes of Study and Appendix 2 of the 2014 National Curriculum for England.

Each book focuses on the concepts to be introduced during that relevant year. Where appropriate, content from previous years is revisited to consolidate knowledge and build on children's understanding.

# Tell me about it

Fill in the blanks.

Make a list of the ten nouns:

1. _____
2. _____
3. _____
4. _____
5. _____
6. _____
7. _____
8. _____
9. _____
10. _____

Today we've caught the cat behaving badly!

e _ e _       e _ r _

n _ _ _

f _ _ _

b _ _ _ _

w _ _ _ _ _

c _ _

t _ _ _

l _ _

p _ _

Make noun phrases by adding an article (a, an or the) and an adjective – the first one shows you how.

1.  <u>cat</u>        <u>a black cat</u>
2.  _____        _____
3.  _____        _____
4.  _____        _____
5.  _____        _____
6.  _____        _____

Remember:
Noun phrases expand the noun and make a sentence more interesting.

---

**Tell the cat's story using as many of your noun phrases as you can.**

---

*Talk through lots of adjectives so that children try to be more adventurous with them than sticking to just colour or size.*

**Brilliant Activities for Grammar and Punctuation, Year 2**
© Irene Yates and Brilliant Publications

# Add an adjective challenge

Competition time! With a friend, read the nouns in the shaded boxes. Talk about different adjectives for them.

Compete with a friend to find five different adjectives for each noun.

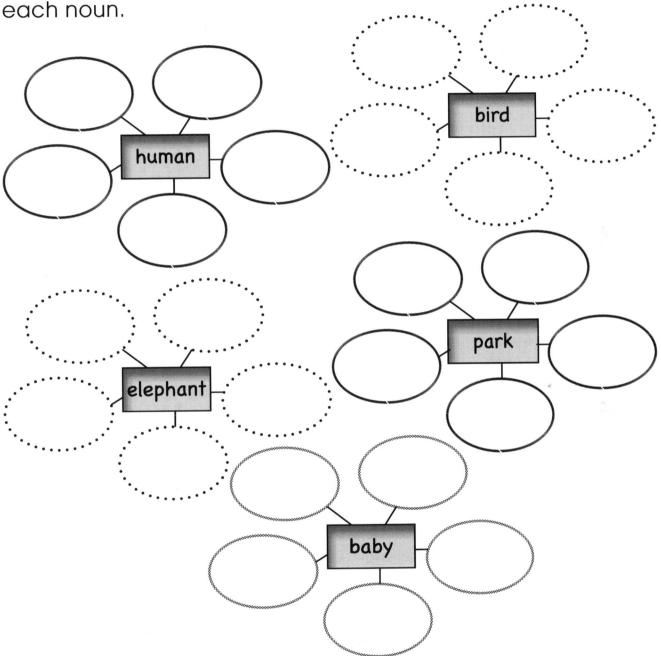

## Give each other two more nouns and five minutes to find five adjectives for each.

*Give one point for each adjective and five points for each appropriate adjective no other pupil has thought of. And the winner is…?*

# Crazy capitals

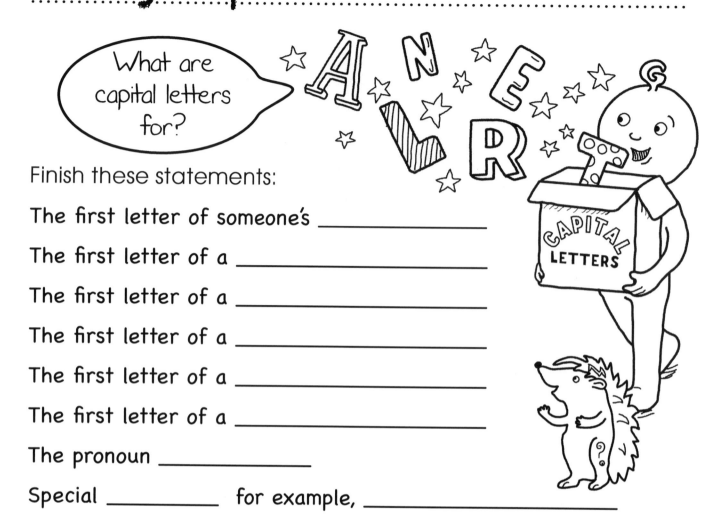

What are capital letters for?

Finish these statements:

The first letter of someone's _____

The first letter of a _____

The first letter of a _____

The first letter of a _____

The first letter of a _____

The first letter of a _____

The pronoun _____

Special _____ for example, _____

Circle the words that should start with a capital letter:

| | | | |
|---|---|---|---|
| horse | telephone | key | judy |
| table | christmas | joshua | bucket |
| april | monday | fire | keiron |
| bike | penguin | shrek | africa |
| london | holiday | december | |

## Test each other. How many countries can you think of?

*Reinforce the rules for capital letters before working on the sheet.*

**Brilliant Activities for Grammar and Punctuation, Year 2**
© Irene Yates and Brilliant Publications

# Using full stops

Do you know that people used to write without any gaps between the words and without punctuation?

welltheydidandthisiswhattheir
writinglookedlikeanditwashardtoread

Then they found that leaving gaps between the words and adding punctuation marks were really useful. Full stops are used at the end of every sentence that isn't a question or an exclamation.

The paragraph below doesn't make sense. Can you put in the full stops? Don't forget to start each new sentence with a

_____ _____ .

he ran fast along the dusty path his feet hurt and he had lost his hat he could not see anyone and he was scared suddenly there was his mum she waved at him and shouted his name then he knew everything would be all right

---

**Tell each other what you think the story might be about. Try to notice where you pause, in talking, for a full stop.**

---

*Read through the passage together two or three times without leaving pauses for full stops. The children should be able to recognise where they need to be.*

# What's a question mark for?

> We know that sentences that are statements end with a full stop.

> If a sentence is a question, then the full stop is replaced with a question mark (?).

A question sentence might be just one word:

**Why?**   or   **How?**

Do you know the others?

| ? | ? | ? | ? |
|---|---|---|---|
| _____ | _____ | _____ | _____ |

Can you add one word to each of these groups of words to turn them into questions? Of course you can! Write them out again.

1. Where you live:   Where do you live?
2. What your name: _____
3. You like pizza: _____
4. You friendly: _____
5. It rain: _____
6. Scored the goal: _____
7. Much will it cost: _____
8. Has happened: _____

> **How many questions can you ask each other in five minutes? For each one, give yourself a question mark. The one who has the most wins. Tip: don't answer the questions or you'll use up your time!**

*Do lots of talking – making statements – asking questions. Point out the way intonation changes on questions.*

**Brilliant Activities for Grammar and Punctuation, Year 2**
© Irene Yates and Brilliant Publications

# Verb search

Find the right verb to complete the sentences, then find the verbs in the wordsearch.

Verbs are action words - things that we can do.

| c | a | t | c | h | x | t |
|---|---|---|---|---|---|---|
| l | y | u | j | d | o | q |
| i | s | r | u | n | o | p |
| m | n | n | m | r | i | g |
| b | v | m | p | i | h | w |
| z | k | l | e | d | j | u |
| d | a | n | c | e | r | f |

We can _____ trees.

We can _____ bikes.

We can _____ in puddles.

We can _____ fast.

We can _____ on one foot

We can _____ cartwheels.

We can _____ balls.

We can _____ wheelies.

We can _____ joyfully.

You are looking for:

**climb, do, run, dance, jump, catch, turn, hop, ride**.

---

**Talk about all the physically active things that you do.
Make some into a verb search puzzle like this.**

---

*Talk through the sentences. Take suggestions for the words before the children do the wordsearch.*

# What did you do?

Verbs tell us what we are doing or what we did. Use a verb to write a short sentence under each picture.

## In a group of four, take turns to perform active verbs for the others to guess.

*Have lots of talk about the pictures with children suggesting lots of different sentences before they complete the sheet.*

**Brilliant Activities for Grammar and Punctuation, Year 2**
© Irene Yates and Brilliant Publications

# Being verbs

An important verb is the being verb. This tells us who or what people or things are.

We use the verb **is** when we talk about one person or one thing, and the verb **are** when talking about two or more people or things.

Complete these sentences using the verb **is** or **are**:

What _____ your name?

Who _____ these people?

_____ we going home yet?

Hamsters _____ good pets to have.

The hamster _____ escaping.

Sarah and Joe _____ trying to catch him.

The teacher _____ not happy.

Who _____ taking the pet home?

> **Say the beginning of a sentence with 'is' or 'are' for your partner to complete. Take turns.**

*Go round the classroom, asking each child to verbalise an **is** or **are** sentence to describe your environment.*

# I have but he has ...

We say 'she has a sister' but 'I have a brother' and 'they have two children'.

Complete these sentences using the verb 'has' or 'have'.

Ali _____ two cats.

Ellie and Ethan _____ a big dog.

Do you _____ any pets?

I _____ many friends.

The mice _____ lots of food to eat

The book _____ a red cover.

We _____ a big classroom.

My teacher _____ curly hair.

**Say the beginning of a sentence with 'has' or 'have' for your partner to complete. Take turns.**

*Go round the classroom, asking each child to verbalise a **have** or **has** sentence about something they or someone else owns.*

**Brilliant Activities for Grammar and Punctuation, Year 2**
© Irene Yates and Brilliant Publications

# Thinking and feeling verbs

Not all verbs are about actions you can do and see. Some are about thinking and feeling.

I really **like** riding my bike.
I **thought** I saw a snowman.
He **hated** going on the train.
Sophie really **wanted** to go out.
I cleaned my teeth but Mum didn't **believe** me.

Write six sentences of your own that use thinking and feeling, not action, verbs.

1. _____

2. _____

3. _____

4. _____

5. _____

6. _____

Here are some thinking and feeling verbs you could use.

| to see | to need | to dislike | to think | to want |
|--------|---------|-----------|----------|---------|
| to love | to believe | to hate | to like | to feel |

**Think up five sentences together that use the verb 'to belong'.**

*Have lots of talk about **non-doing** verbs opposed to **doing** verbs. Also discuss **to be** and **to have**.*

# Is it now?

Verbs are the most important part of a sentence because, not only do they tell you what is happening, they also they tell you when. A verb can show you that the action is taking place now. This is called the present tense.

Use the present tense of the verbs in brackets to write what is happening in each picture.

(score)
The boy is <u>scoring a goal</u>.

(jump)
The girl _____

(leap)
The frog _____

(sing)
The children _____

(chase)
The dog _____

(sleep)
The cat _____

## In pairs, one performs an action, one gives a sentence to describe what is happening. Take turns.

*Go through lots of verbs verbally before they complete the sheet.*

**Brilliant Activities for Grammar and Punctuation, Year 2**
© Irene Yates and Brilliant Publications

# Was it yesterday?

Verbs can show that the action has taken place in the past. This is called the past tense.

We played Olympics last Saturday.

I won gold.

It was magic!

Use the **past tense** to put in verbs to finish this story:

Last week we _____ into town on the bus. It _____ with rain. Everyone _____ wet and fed up. My dad _____ to sing on the bus. He _____ really loud. People _____ _____ at him. Then, suddenly, the bus driver _____ to sing as well. And then somebody else _____ in. Then the old lady next to me _____ singing. All the people on the bus _____ _____ and _____. Then a rainbow _____ in the sky. Everybody _____.

My dad _____ **so** embarrassing!

> ## Tell each other about a time in the past when someone embarrassed you.

*Verbalise the story first. Encourage children to provide lots of suggestions for what the verbs might be. Talk about how sometimes a verb is two words, eg 'were staring'.*

# Simple sentences

Simple sentences are made up of one clause. They have a verb and they make sense on their own. The verb (doing word) has a subject, which is the person or thing doing the action. Like this:

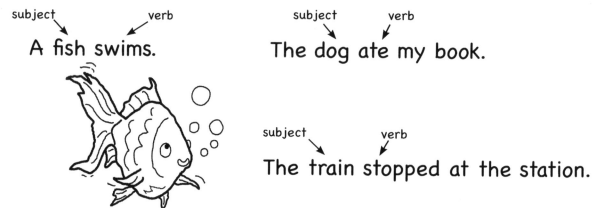

subject      verb

A fish swims.

subject      verb

The dog ate my book.

subject      verb

The train stopped at the station.

Write simple sentences for these pictures:

**Working in pairs, one chooses the subject and the verb, eg 'dog – eats' and the other completes the sentence. Make your sentences funny.**

*Discuss the pattern of simple sentences with the subject coming before the verb and the verb being in different tenses.*

# What is it?

Fill in the nouns. The first letters reading downwards tell you what a group of words containing a verb is called. What else does the answer need besides a verb?

A _____ _____ and a _____ _____.

Make your own puzzle together for the word that means the ABC. Talk about the nouns you can use before you start.

*Recap on 'noun' and 'verb'. Explain how the puzzle works. Complete the puzzle then children spend time talking and making their own alphabet puzzle.*

# Noisy verbs

If pigs (noun) grunt (verb), do you know which noises other animals make? Choose ten verbs from the box and write a sentence for each one. The first one is done for you.

What is a lion's favourite letter?

Rrrrrr ! Tee hee.

Choose from:

barks
neighs
roars
cackles
croaks
hisses
quacks
bleats
hoots
bellows
shouts
brays
buzzes
yawns
ticks

1. An owl hoots.

2. _____

3. _____

4. _____

5. _____

6. _____

7. _____

8. _____

9. _____

10. _____

## Have a contest – can you think of any more animals and their sounds that are not on this page?

*Go through all the suggested verbs to begin with; also make sure the children can identify the animals and have a stab at their sounds. There are five sounds too many – can they suggest what subjects might make these sounds?*

**Brilliant Activities for Grammar and Punctuation, Year 2**
© Irene Yates and Brilliant Publications

# What's a vowel?

There are 26 letters in the alphabet. Five of them are called vowels. These are sounds that you make in your throat and not with your lips or tongue. Practise these sounds:

## a e i o u

Fill in the missing vowels from these words. The pictures around the page will help you.

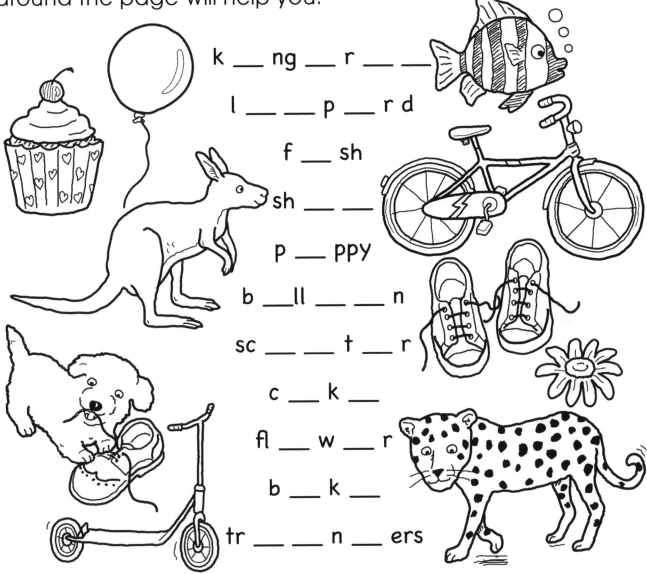

k __ ng __ r __ __

l __ __ p __ r d

f __ sh

sh __ __ __

p __ ppy

b __ ll __ __ n

sc __ __ t __ r

c __ k __

fl __ w __ r

b __ k __

tr __ __ n __ ers

---

**Take turns to name as many things you can see in your room that begin with a vowel.**

---

*Have lots of fun going through all the different sounds that the vowels make. The children should be able to touch their throats gently to feel where the sound comes from.*

# What's a consonant?

There are 26 letters in the alphabet. Five of them are the vowels: a e i o u. The rest are called consonants. These are letter sounds you make by shaping your tongue and your lips.

Make these sounds:

b c d f g h j k l m n p q r s t v w x y z

In English, nearly all words have vowels and consonants. Using the code breaker below, you can make lots of new words without any vowels in them:

| code letter | b | c | d | e | f | g | h | i | j | k | l | m | n | o | p | q | r | s | t | u | v | w | x | y | z | a |
|---|---|---|---|---|---|---|---|---|---|---|---|---|---|---|---|---|---|---|---|---|---|---|---|---|---|---|
| answer | a | b | c | d | e | f | g | h | i | j | k | l | m | n | o | p | q | r | s | t | u | v | w | x | y | z |

Work out what these code letter words mean?

dblf          cfmm          mph          hjsm

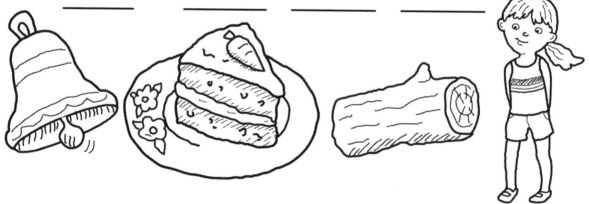

Make up some words of your own, using only consonants from this code.

## Try to say the words from the code puzzle.
## Think of some other short words, take out the vowels and try to say the words.

*Have fun exaggerating how lips and tongue movements make the different sounds of consonants. Let the children watch each other and themselves in mirrors.*

**Brilliant Activities for Grammar and Punctuation, Year 2**
© Irene Yates and Brilliant Publications

Exclamation marks (!) tell us to express a strong emotion.

An exclamation mark can show fear, anger, pain and danger.

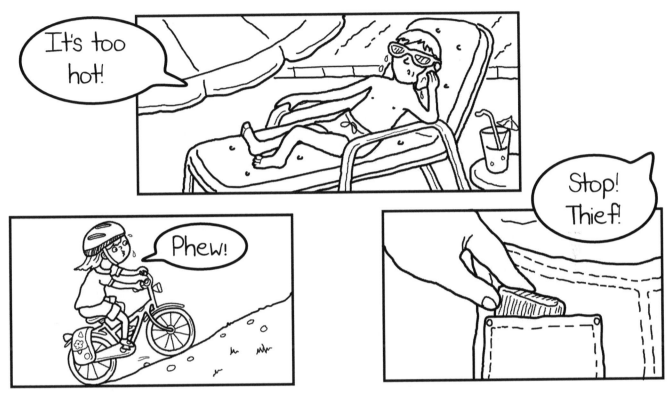

Draw or suggest pictures for these exclamations.

**Tell the story of one of the pictures you have drawn.**

*Make it clear to the children that one exclamation mark is enough per exclamation. They don't need two or three.*

# Wow! She said

Look at these pictures. Write some sentences for each one, making sure you use some exclamation marks.

Ouch!    Danger!    Wow!    Help!    Yuck!    Don't!

Stop!    Eeek!    Done it!

**When have you ever said something that would have an exclamation mark if it was written down? Swap stories.**

*Remind children what an exclamation mark is for. Verbalise some sentences to make little stories before writing.*

**Brilliant Activities for Grammar and Punctuation, Year 2**
© Irene Yates and Brilliant Publications

# Add a suffix

You can change words by adding bits at the end. An end bit is called a **suffix**. You can change all these adjectives and verbs into nouns by adding either 'er' or 'ness.'

Draw lines from the word to the right suffix. Be careful because some of the words could use both. You don't want any suffixes left over.

| | |
|---|---|
| sad | er |
| kind | ness |
| teach | ness |
| work | er |
| sing | er |
| tired | er |
| stiff | ness |
| paint | ness |
| ill | er |
| read | ness |

## Choose four verbs each and see what happens if you add 'er'.

*Discuss how 'er' and 'ness' can change words into nouns. The children need to do the words that can only end with one of the suffixes first, then work out the others.*

# More add-ons

Here is another suffix to try out. It is 'ful'.

You can add 'ful' to some words to make an adjective like this:

Someone who **wishes** for lots of things is wish**ful**.

Someone who takes lots of care over things
is __ __ __ __ ful.

Someone who never tells a fib
is __ __ __ __ __ ful.

Someone who is frightened
is __ __ __ __ ful.

What did the lamp say when it got turned off?

Something that is brightly coloured
is __ __ __ __ __ __ ful.

Somewhere that is calm and quiet
is __ __ __ __ __ ful.

How delightful! Tee hee.

Someone who is crying is __ __ __ __ ful.

Something that you can use is __ __ __ ful.

Someone who can't remember things is __ __ __ __ __ __ ful.

Make sentences for:

   painful    powerful    bagful   hurtful     restful

> **How many adjectives ending with 'ful' can you think of to describe each other?**

*Talk through the concept of suffix and adjective. Verbalise all the sentences and words before children complete the task.*

**Brilliant Activities for Grammar and Punctuation, Year 2**
© Irene Yates and Brilliant Publications

# Less is more

Another suffix you can add to words to turn them into adjectives is 'less'. Like this:

The puppy had no <u>home</u>. He was <u>home**less**</u>.

Fill in the missing words. Use the words in the box below.

The girl ran out of breath. She was _____.

The teacher thought she would never get to the end of the marking. It was _____.

Jimmy was not afraid of anything. He was _____.

Gran couldn't think what to say. She was _____.

The park was a wide, open space without trees. It was _____.

The nurse said the needle wouldn't hurt. It would be _____.

The invention didn't work. It was _____.

Dad couldn't help. He said he was _____.

Sophie took no care over her homework. She was _____.

They couldn't reach the bottom of the well. It was _____.

| | | | | |
|---|---|---|---|---|
| end | breath | fear | tree | speech |
| bottom | pain | help | care | use |

**Make up and tell each other a story about one of the sentences, using the adjective formed by adding 'less'.**

*Read the sentences together; go through the words shown. Talk about other words that can take the suffix 'less'.*

# When one + one equals one

**Compound** words happen when you add one word to another word to make a new word, like this:

| | | | | | |
|---|---|---|---|---|---|
| skate | + | board | = | skateboard |

| | | | | | |
|---|---|---|---|---|---|
| moon | + | light | = | |

| | | | | | |
|---|---|---|---|---|---|
| butter | + | | = | butterfly |

| | | | | |
|---|---|---|---|---|
| home | + | | = | homework |
| | + | ball | = | football |
| rattle | + | snake | = | |
| sun | + | flower | = | |
| spear | + | | = | spearmint |
| | + | hopper | = | grasshopper |
| with | + | out | = | |

Think of compound words for these words:

| | | | | |
|---|---|---|---|---|
| snow | no | be | dish | some |
| after | selves | ground | port | prints |

## Read a piece of text aloud, picking out all the compound words that come up.

*Have lots of talk about this. The children use compound words all the time without knowing it. Get them to de-construct some of their normal, natural vocabulary until they have really internalised the idea.*

**Brilliant Activities for Grammar and Punctuation, Year 2**
© Irene Yates and Brilliant Publications

# Commas are useful

A comma is used to separate words in a list that are not joined by the words 'and' or 'or'. Like this:

Saturday and Sunday come after Monday, Tuesday, Wednesday, Thursday and Friday because the week days need a rest.

Put commas in these question sentences:

What are Mars Jupiter Saturn Uranus Neptune and Pluto?

What kind of food are peas cabbage broccoli sprouts and spinach?

If my birthday is not in January February March May June July August September October November or December, which month is it in?

Ants bees beetles bugs dragonflies and earwigs are all what?

Tyrannosaurus Rex Stegosaurus Brachiosaurus Diceratops and Diplodocus were all kinds of what?

> **How many things in a list can you say without pausing (where the commas would be) without losing your breath? Who goes on longest wins.**

*Talk about making lists in a sentence structure – this is where the comma is used. What other ways of listing can the children think of? Turn bullet point lists into sentence lists using commas.*

# Commas in Lists

Commas are used in lists to separate words that are not joined by 'and' or 'or'. Like this:

For my lunch I had a burger, chips, peas and half a tomato.

Add a list with commas to complete these sentences:

My friends are _____

The foods I like best are _____

The books I have read are _____

The games I like to play are _____

My favourite animals are _____

At school we do _____

> **Think up a new kind of list each and talk it through, pausing where the commas should go.**

*Verbalise the beginning of the sentences and what the children may add before they begin the writing task. Remind them of the comma rule and to check that they have put commas into their lists.*

**Brilliant Activities for Grammar and Punctuation, Year 2**
© Irene Yates and Brilliant Publications

# Make it smaller

When you make something smaller, you **contract** it. This happens with words quite often. We use **contractions** to fit two words together and make them sound like one. When we write them down we use an apostrophe, which is like an upside-down comma (') to show we've missed out some letters. Like this:

Instead of saying I am going

we say I'm going

Instead of saying she has got measles

we say she's got measles

What do you think these contractions are for?

I've ___I have___  I'd _____

who's _____  she'd _____

hasn't _____  he's _____

shouldn't _____  haven't _____

you've _____  it's _____

Write the contractions:

would not _wouldn't_  we have _____

were not _____  they are _____

you had _____  they had _____

I cannot _____  he is _____

> ## Discuss something you have done together. Every time you use a contraction, write it down. Which one do you use most?

*Have lots of talking – changing the words verbally before even thinking of writing. A normal conversation/discussion with half the group talking and the other half spotting the contractions will help to consolidate the concept.*

# More apostrophes

The apostrophe mark (') has not one, but two jobs.

It shows contractions for one job, but its second job is to show that something belongs to someone (or someone belongs to something!),

Like this:

The puppy belongs to Izzy
The biscuits belong to the puppy.

It is Izzy's puppy.
They are the puppy's biscuits.

Try these:

That is the grandad of Ben.

       That is _____ grandad.

Where is the book that belongs to Henry?

       Where is _____ book?

The burger is for Dad.

       It is _____ burger.

Does the rabbit belong to Emma?

       Is it _____ rabbit?

Today is the brthday of Jack.

       Today is _____ .

> **Swap sentences beginning: Dad's ... Mum's ... Jamie's ... Tina's ... The dog's... The cat's... The elephant's ... The lizard's ...**

*Practise aloud forming sentences without apostrophes for belonging before going through the task together.*

**Brilliant Activities for Grammar and Punctuation, Year 2**
© Irene Yates and Brilliant Publications

# Apostrophe challenge

These sentences use apostrophes in two ways: to show that something belongs to someone (or something) and to show a contraction.

Can you write the sentences?

That is the brother of Dad.

_____ _____ brother.

Where is the bike that belongs to Kirsten?

_____ _____ bike?

The hamster belongs to this group.

_____ this _____ hamster.

The flowers were bought
for my mum.

_____ ____ _____ flowers.

Make up a sentence of your
own that uses apostrophes in two different ways.

_____

_____

## How many different contractions can you think of? Use a reading book to help

*Practise aloud forming sentences without apostrophes for belonging and without contractions before going through the task together.*

# Adjectives get better

We know that adjectives are the words we use to describe things or people or places or feelings (or anything we want to describe). Like this:

      red        dull        small      smelly

Sometimes we add the suffixes 'er' and 'est' to compare one thing with another or others, like this:

    This tree is tall.      This tree is taller.      This tree is the tallest.

We call these 'comparative adjectives'. Complete this table:

| | | |
|---|---|---|
| nice | | |
| | | brightest |
| | darker | |
| high | | |
| | | finest |
| | quieter | |
| small | | |
| | kinder | |
| | | coldest |
| cool | | |

Can you do this trick one?

| | | |
|---|---|---|
| good | | |

---

**Challenge each other. One gives an adjective, the other tries to answer with the comparatives that go with it. Take turns.**

---

*Talk through as many comparative adjectives as the children can think of, but don't write them all down at this point because spelling rules apply to many that will make for confusion.*

**Brilliant Activities for Grammar and Punctuation, Year 2**
© Irene Yates and Brilliant Publications

# Bigger and better sentences

See if you can use the suffixes 'er' and 'est' to finish off the sentences below.

The first one shows you how.

**My dad is <u>bigger</u> than your dad but Jon's dad is the <u>biggest</u>.**

My car is faster than your skateboard but _____

_____

A bike is smaller than _____

An drum is louder than _____

My gran in older than _____

My brother is younger than _____

Tigers are _____

A mouse is _____

A castle is _____

A sunflower _____

## How do these words work?

| good | bad | many | far |
|------|-----|------|-----|

*Reinforce how comparative adjectives work through talk. Go through the sentences for ideas before the children complete the task.*

# About adverbs

An adverb is a word that adds meaning to a verb, an adjective or another adverb. In a sentence it tells us when, where or how. Like this:

We went to a party <u>yesterday</u>. (when)
Put it over <u>there</u>. (where)
He drank the juice <u>quickly</u>. (how)

You can turn lots of adjectives into adverbs just by adding 'ly'. Like this:

slow    +   **ly**   =   slowly
quick   +   **ly**   =   quickly
neat    +   **ly**   =   neatly

Try these:

The children sang _____. (sweet)

They all played together _____. (quiet)

The snail moved very _____. (slow)

The boy called out _____. (cheerful)

The girl climbed the ladder _____. (daring)

The teacher spoke _____. (calm)

He unwrapped the present _____. (eager)

They went to the moon _____. (bold)

---

**Swap as many 'ly' words as you can think of. Do they tell you when, where, how or which?**

---

*Talk through as many when, where and how adverbs the children can think of. Practise aloud forming sentences using them.*

**Brilliant Activities for Grammar and Punctuation, Year 2**
© Irene Yates and Brilliant Publications

# Linking

Link these pairs of sentences. Choose from:

| and | but | when | so | that |
|-----|-----|------|-----|------|

It was freezing cold _____ Sophie wore her gloves.

Harry was happy _____ he was going on holiday.

Lucy went to the park _____ went on the swings.

The boy waited for his friend _____ he didn't turn up.

Jack saw Sophie _____ he was at the shops.

**In pairs: one suggests a linking word, the other makes up a linked sentence. Take turns.**

*Have children finish sentences orally, eg: we laughed when …, I can't come because…, Ice is cold but…. Point out the linking words. Take suggestions and examples before reading through the activity together.*

# Conjunctions

Choose conjunctions from the box to link these pairs of sentences:

| before | if | because | until | unless |
|--------|-----|---------|-------|--------|

The kittens will wake up _____ we make a noise.

Josh hadn't been out Saturday _____ he had watched a film instead.

Tamsin cleaned her teeth _____ she went to bed.

We waited _____ the train came.

Dad said I'd get no pocket money _____ I cleaned my room.

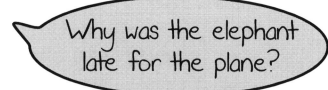

Why was the elephant late for the plane?

Because he forgot his trunk! Tee hee.

**In pairs, one starts a sentence, the other adds a link word and ends the sentence.**

*Make up a group story orally, using as many new linking words as the children can think of.*

**Brilliant Activities for Grammar and Punctuation, Year 2**
© Irene Yates and Brilliant Publications

# Which order?

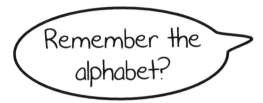
Remember the alphabet?

A B C D E F G H I J K L M N
O P Q R S T U V W X Y Z

a b c d e f g h i j k l m n
o p q r s t u v w x y z

Make sure you know the correct order.

We put words into alphabetical order by looking at their first letter (the initial letter), and then putting the words in the order of that first letter, like this:

**shoe, cat, kitten, gloves, apple =**

**apple    cat    gloves    kitten    shoe**

Can you arrange these sets of words into alphabetical order? Of course you can!

| head | lamp | kick | August |
|------|------|------|--------|
| | | | |
| Jack | men | food | brick |
| | | | |
| coat | ice | ear | grass |

**Work out which letters in the above lists haven't got a word. Decide on a word for each and put them in alphabetical order together. Make notes if you need to.**

*Get the children to recite the alphabet frequently so that they learn it by rote. Show them that there doesn't have to be a word beginning with all 26 letters to be able to use alphabetical order.*

# More about alphabetical order

When we are putting words into order and some of them begin with the same first (initial) letter, we use the second letter to arrange them, like this:

**beef**    **bath**    **blow**    **box**    **bird**    **bring**

They all begin with 'b' so we have to look at the second letter and put these into alphabetical order, like this:

**bath**    **beef**    **bird**    **blow**    **box**    **bring**

See if you can arrange these sets of words into alphabetical order.

ate    angel    actor    again    army    ape

---

end    excite    edge    ear    elbow    empty

---

fun    frog    fool    field    face    fly

---

or    owl    over    obey    oats    others

---

## Arrange the names of the people in your class in alphabetical order. Make notes if you need to.

*It's important to get this concept across clearly as it's the foundation to all dictionary work. If the children can take it further – to the third letter – encourage and help them.*

**Brilliant Activities for Grammar and Punctuation, Year 2**
© Irene Yates and Brilliant Publications

# Match the family

Write the vowels here

Do you remember the vowels?

___ ___ ___ ___ ___

All the nouns in the first box are grown-up animals. The ones in the second are their babies. But which is which? And just to make it more of a challenge, we've taken out the vowels. Can you put them back?

| | | |
|---|---|---|
| d __ g | h __ n | l __ __ n |
| g __ __ s __ | sh __ __ p | h __ rs __ |
| c __ t | __ wl | g __ __ t |

| | | |
|---|---|---|
| c __ b | c __ lf | p __ ppy |
| ch __ ck | g __ sl __ ng | __ wl __ t |
| k __ d | f __ __ l | k __ tt __ n |

Here's a list of some family members without vowels. Can you complete them?

f __ th __ r          m __ th __ r          br __ th __ r

s __ st __ r          __ __ nt          __ ncl __

c __ __ s __ n          gr __ ndm __ th __ r

n __ ph __ w          n __ __ c __

gr __ ndf __ th __ r

# What can you draw?

Use these noun phrases to draw a picture of a creature.

| | |
|---|---|
| one long neck | three pointed wings |
| a big head | frightening claws |
| huge teeth | a flicking tongue |
| a scary face | a spotted body |
| six legs | hairy feet |

four arms          a curly tail

My creation is called a _____ .

Make up some noun phrases to describe another creature and have a friend to draw it.

## Tell a story about your creature. Where does it come from? How does it move? What does it want?

*Let the children have some fun with this. Before they begin the task ask the children to point out the nouns and adjectives in the noun phrases.*

**Brilliant Activities for Grammar and Punctuation, Year 2**
© Irene Yates and Brilliant Publications

# Sort these sentences!

A <u>statement sentence</u> starts with a _____ _____ and ends with a _____ _____ , like this:

    Carrots are good for your eyes.

A <u>question sentence</u> starts with a _____ _____ and ends with a _____ _____ , like this:

    What's your name?

An <u>exclamation sentence</u> starts with a _____ _____ and ends with an _____ _____ , like this:

    Surprise, surprise!

And a <u>command sentence</u> starts with a _____ _____ and usually ends with an exclamation mark, like this:

## How many situations can you think of where people give commands? What are they?

*Go through the different kinds of sentences given above and take verbal examples of each from the children before they complete the task.*

# Here's a story

Here's a story for you to read. Whoops! All the sentences are in the wrong order. Time for you to put them right!

Phew! He tried to reach the dog. A man who was passing got hold of his collar. Sam was walking by the pond. He pulled him out. The dog jumped in the water after the duck. His dog was running beside him. A duck swam by. Sam screamed.

Write the story and draw a picture.

_____

_____

_____

_____

_____

_____

_____

_____

_____

**With a friend, talk about what might happen next.**

*Read the jumbled up story chorally. Let the children discuss the story before starting the task, to reinforce their reading of the sentences.*

**Brilliant Activities for Grammar and Punctuation, Year 2**
© Irene Yates and Brilliant Publications

# Not alphabetical order! (1)

> Not everything is put into alphabetical order. There are other ways of ordering things as well.

Sometimes things are in time order, like this:

**Spring**        **Summer**        **Autumn**        **Winter**

Put the days of the week in order:

_____

_____

Put the months of the year in order:

_____          _____

_____          _____

_____          _____

_____          _____

_____          _____

_____          _____

## Think of some more ways of ordering things. Do a list verbally together.

*Choose one of the lists when all the activities are completed and ask the children to put them into alphabetical order and compare them.*

# Not alphabetical order! (2)

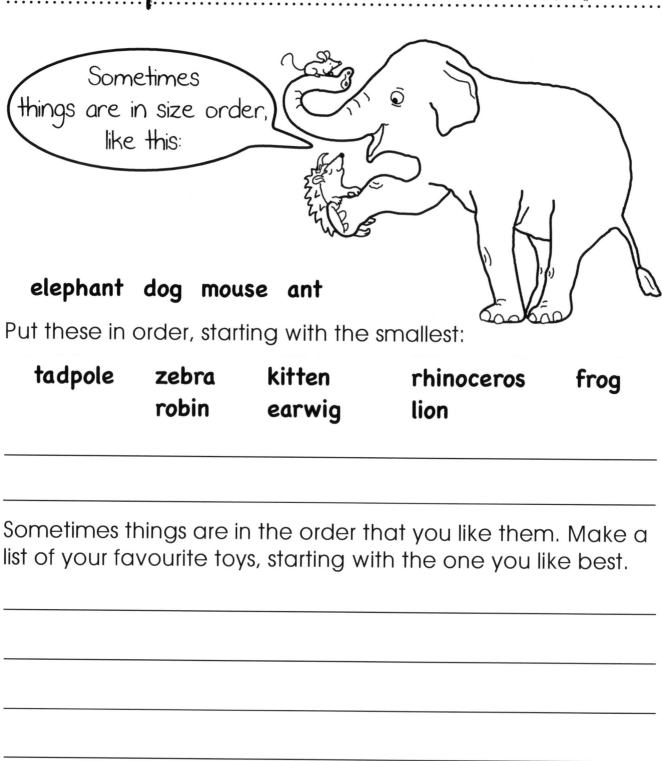

Sometimes things are in size order, like this:

**elephant dog mouse ant**

Put these in order, starting with the smallest:

**tadpole    zebra    kitten    rhinoceros    frog
robin    earwig    lion**

_____

_____

Sometimes things are in the order that you like them. Make a list of your favourite toys, starting with the one you like best.

_____

_____

_____

_____

_____

**Brilliant Activities for Grammar and Punctuation, Year 2**
© Irene Yates and Brilliant Publications

# Getting the words in order

A sentence wouldn't make sense if its words were in the wrong order, like this:

trees. oak on grow Acorns

Of course, it should be:     **Acorns grow on oak trees.**

Put these words in the right order to make proper sentences.

**us give Hens eggs.**

_____

**prickly have Hedgehogs spines.**

_____

**is called young kitten. cat a A**

_____

**milk. us give Cows**

_____

**flowing London river the The through Thames. is**

_____

**do nuts. Monkeys like really**

_____

**robin's nest. five There eggs were the in**

_____

> **Take turns to think of a sentence. Try to say the words in the wrong order. Can your friend guess what you mean?**

*Read through the words chorally. Let the children discuss the order they think they should be in before completing the task.*

# Cut and stick

You need a comic, a magazine or a newsletter.

Look for these kinds of words, cut and stick them to this page.

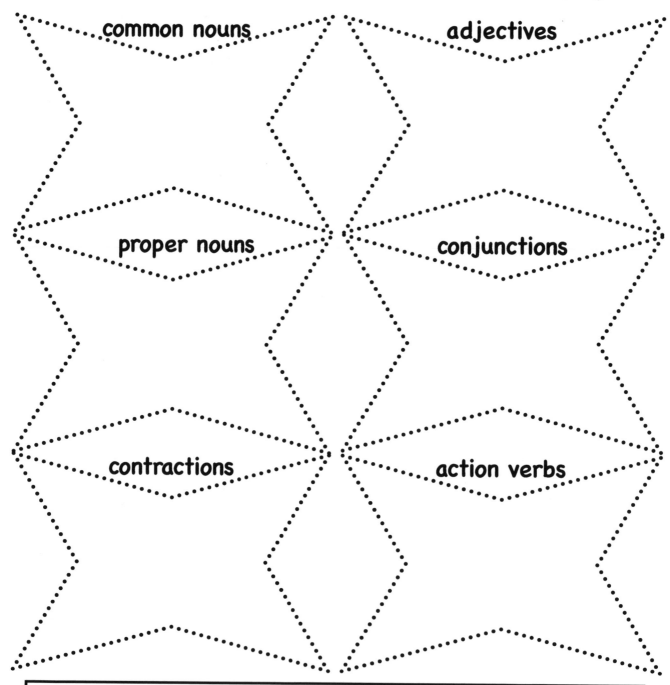

common nouns

adjectives

proper nouns

conjunctions

contractions

action verbs

**With a partner discuss exactly what each of the groups are before you start.**

*Let the children have a free rein to do this task, talking, chatting and exploring together. Check their collections verbally in small group situations.*

**Brilliant Activities for Grammar and Punctuation, Year 2**
© Irene Yates and Brilliant Publications

# Assessment checklist

| Name | 1 | 2 | 3 |
|---|---|---|---|
| **Can understand and use the following terminology:** | | | |
| Noun | | | |
| Noun phrase | | | |
| Statement | | | |
| Question | | | |
| Exclamation | | | |
| Command | | | |
| Compound | | | |
| Suffix | | | |
| Adjective | | | |
| Adverb | | | |
| Verb | | | |
| Tense (past, present) | | | |
| Apostrophe | | | |
| Comma | | | |
| **Understands and is able to:** | | | |
| Create noun phrases, use an article (a, an, the), an adjective and a noun | | | |
| Identify proper nouns and punctuate correctly | | | |
| Identify and use action verbs | | | |
| Identify and use being and having verbs correctly | | | |
| Identify and use thinking and feeling verbs | | | |
| Identify present and past tense of verbs and use them correctly | | | |
| Create simple sentences using a subject and verb | | | |
| Create new words by adding the suffixes 'er', 'ness', 'ful' and 'less'. | | | |
| Create compound words | | | |
| Understand and use comparative adjectives | | | |
| Use adverbs to show how, when or where | | | |
| Use conjunctions as linking words | | | |
| Identify and write questions, statements, exclamations and commands | | | |
| Punctuate sentences using a capital letter and full stop, question mark or exclamation mark | | | |
| Use commas in lists | | | |
| Use apostrophes for contractions | | | |
| Use apostrophes for possession | | | |
| Order words alphabetically to second place | | | |
| Identify vowels and consonants | | | |

# Answers

## Tell me about it (pg 6)

**Cat**, eyes, ears, tail, leg, paw, water, bowl, fish, nose.

## Crazy Capitals (pg 8)

Capital letters are used for the first letter of someone's name, for days of the week, months, towns, cities, countries, oceans, specific buildings (eg, Buckingham Palace), The pronoun **I**. Also for holidays such as Diwali, Christmas etc.

Judy, Christmas, Joshua, Shrek, April, Monday, Keiran, Africa, London, December.

## Using full stops (pg 9)

… capital letter.

He ran fast along the dusty path. His feet hurt and he had lost his hat. He could not see anyone and he was scared. Suddenly there was his mum. She waved at him and shouted his name. Then he knew everything would be all right.

## What's a question mark for? (pg 10)

When?, Where?, Who?, What?

What is your name? Do you like pizza? Are you friends? Will it rain? Who scored the goal? How much will it cost? What has happened?

## Verb search (pg 11)

climb trees, ride bikes, jump in puddles, run fast, hop on one foot, turn cartwheels, catch balls, do wheelies, dance joyfully.

## Being verbs (pg 13)

**is** your name; **are** these people; **Are** we going; **are** good pets; **is** escaping; **are** trying to catch; teacher **is** not happy; Who **is** taking the pet … .

## I have but he has … (pg 14)

Ali has; Ellie and Ethan have; Do you have; I have; The mice have; The book has; We have; My teacher has.

## Is it now? (pg 16)

(jumps) The girl is jumping; (leaps) The frog is leaping; (sing) The children are singing; (chase) The dog is chasing; (sleep) The cat is sleeping. Both the present tense (jump) and the continuous present tense (is jumping) can be used here.

## Was it yesterday? (pg 17)

Note: Other past tense verbs could be used, provided they make sense. Last week we **went** into town on the bus. It **poured** with rain. Everyone **was** wet and fed up. My dad **began** to sing on the bus. He **sang** really loud. People **were staring** at him. Then, suddenly, the bus driver **began** to sing as well. And then somebody else **joined** in. Then the old lady next to me **started** singing. All the people **were smiling** and **laughing**. Then a rainbow **appeared** in the sky. Everybody **cheered**. My dad **was** so embarrassing!

## What is it? (pg 19)

capital letter, full stop

sun, eyes, nuts, tree, eagle, nail, cat, eggs. (sentence).

## What's a vowel? (pg 21)

k**a**ngar**oo**, l**eo**p**a**rd, f**i**sh, sh**oe**, p**u**ppy, b**a**ll**oo**n, sc**oo**t**e**r, c**a**ke, fl**o**w**e**r, b**i**ke, tr**ai**n**e**rs.

## What's a consonant? (pg 22)

cake, bell, log, girl

## Add a suffix (pg 25)

sad**ness**, kind**ness**, teach**er**, work**er**, sing**er**, tired**ness**, stiff**ness**, paint**er**, ill**ness**, read**er**.

## More add-ons (pg 26)

care**ful**, truth**ful**, fear**ful**, colour**ful**, peace**ful**, tear**ful**, use**ful**, forget**ful**.

## Less is more (pg 27)

breath**less**, end**less**, fear**less**, speech**less**, tree**less**, pain**less**, use**less**, help**less**, care**less**, bottom**less**.

## When one + one equals one (pg 28)

moonlight, fly, work, foot, rattlesnake, sunflower, mint, grass, without.

**Brilliant Activities for Grammar and Punctuation, Year 2**
© Irene Yates and Brilliant Publications

## Commas are useful (pg 29)

What are Mars, Jupiter, Saturn, Uranus, Neptune and Pluto?

What kind of food are peas, cabbage, broccoli, sprouts and spinach?

If my birthday is not in January, February, March, May, June, July, August, September, October, November or December, which month is it in?

Ants, bees, beetles, bugs, dragonflies and earwigs are all what?

Tyrannosaurus Rex, Stegosaurus, Brachiosaurus, Diceratops and Diplodocus were all kinds of what?

## Make it smaller (pg 31)

I have, who has, has not, should not, you have, I had, she had, he has, have not, it is. Wouldn't, weren't, you'd, I can't, we've, they're, they'd, he's.

## More apostrophes (pg 32)

That is Ben's grandad. Where is Henry's book? It is Dad's burger. Is it Emma's rabbit? Today is Jack's birthday.

## Apostrophe challenge (pg 33)

That's Dad's brother. Where's Kirsten's bike? It's this group's hamster. They're my Mum's flowers.

## Adjectives get better (pg 34)

| nice | nicer | nicest |
|------|-------|--------|
| bright | brighter | brightest |
| dark | darker | darkest |
| high | higher | highest |
| fine | finer | finest |
| quiet | quieter | quietest |
| small | smaller | smallest |
| kind | kinder | kindest |
| cold | colder | coldest |
| cool | cooler | coolest |
| good | better | best |

## About adverbs (pg 36)

sweetly, quietly, slowly, cheerfully, daringly, calmly, eagerly, boldly.

## Linking (pg 37)

It was freezing cold **so** Sophie wore her gloves.
Harry was happy **that** he was going on holiday.
Lucy went to the park **and** went on the swings.
The boy waited for his friend **but** he didn't turn up.
Jack saw Sophie **when** he was at the shops.

## Conjunctions (pg 38)

The kittens will wake up **if** we make a noise.
Josh hadn't been out Saturday **because** he had watched a film instead. Tamsin cleaned her teeth **before** she went to bed. We waited **until** the train came. Dad said I'd get no pocket money **unless** I cleaned my room.

## Which order (pg 39)

August, head, kick, lamp; brick, food, Jack, men; coat, ear, grass, ice.

## More about alphabetical order (pg 40)

actor, again, angel, ape, army, ate
ear, edge, elbow, empty, end, excite
face, field, fly, fool, frog, fun
oats, obey, or, others, over, owl.

## Match the family (pg 41)

dog, hen, lion, goose, sheep, horse, cat, owl, goat.
cub, calf, puppy, chick, gosling, owlet, kid, foal, kitten, father, mother, brother, sister, aunt, uncle, cousin, grandmother, nephew, niece, grandfather.

## Sort these sentences (pg 43)

Capital letter, full stop. Capital letter, question mark. Capital letter, exclamation mark. Capital letter.

## Here's a story (pg 44)

Sam was walking by the pond. His dog was running beside him. A duck swam by. The dog jumped in the water after the duck. Sam screamed. He tried to reach the dog. A man who was passing got hold of his collar. He pulled him out. Phew!

## Not alphabetical order! (1) (pg 45)

Monday, Tuesday, Wednesday, Thursday, Friday, Saturday, Sunday.

January, February, March, April, May, June, July, August, September, October, November, December.

## Not alphabetical order! (2) (pg 46)

earwig, tadpole, frog, robin, kitten, lion, zebra, rhinoceros.

## Getting the words in order (pg 47)

Hens give us eggs.
Hedgehogs have prickly spines.
A young cat is called a kitten.
Cows give us milk.
The river flowing through London is the Thames.
Monkeys really do like nuts.
There were five eggs in the robin's nest.

# IMAGES

## —*OF*—

# BRISTOL

VICTORIAN PHOTOGRAPHERS
AT WORK 1850–1910

*James Belsey & David Harrison*

**R**

REDCLIFFE

# CONTENTS

First published in 1987 by Redcliffe Press Ltd., Bristol

© text: James Belsey and David Harrison, 1987

ISBN 0 948265 26 4

Typesetting by Dorchester Typesetting Group (Bristol).
Designed by Jem Southam & Christopher Binding.
Printed by Redwood Burn Ltd., Trowbridge.

Acknowledgements:  *The authors thank the following for their invaluable assistance in the planning and compilation of this book: Martyn Heighton, Director of Arts, Bristol City Council; Paul Elkin and Andy King, Curator and Assistant Curator of Technology, Bristol Industrial Museum; Nicholas Thomas, Director, City of Bristol Museum; Francis Greenacre, Curator of Fine Art, Bristol City Art Gallery; the staff of the City Records Office, College Green, and the Museum and Art Gallery Archives; Jerry Brooks, Librarian, Bristol United Press.*

# INTRODUCTION

**T**he City of Bristol Record Office and the City's Museum and Art Gallery are astonishing treasure houses, whose contents tell us so much about Bristol – how it began, what happened there, the ways of life of its citizens, its appearance at least during the last three hundred years: above all, this portrayal of the way it looked in the endless range of its moods. Probably no other place in the British Isles has been so comprehensively blessed with such a wealth of visual records that have survived. First came the series of maps, which chronicled its development in growing detail and accuracy from the sixteenth century; then the Braikenridge Collection, a unique assemblage of more than a thousand watercolours and drawings of our City as it appeared under the last of the Georges and the Sailor King; and so eventually, to the wonder of photography and the City Museum's exceptional holding of these often poignant images of the last hundred years and more.

James Belsey and David Harrison have selected some eighty photographs from Bristol's public collections and publish them here, some for the first time, with a dual purpose. First they use them to chart the technical development of photography and its gradual change from being an extension of the artist's hand and eye to a more purely commercial activity. And then they show the often supreme artistry and aesthetic brilliance with which our early photographers selected their subject and viewed it through the lens and with growing dark-room skill. For this reason, the authors have allowed their photographs to speak for themselves. Their notes and comments are concentrated at the end. In its preparation they have been well served by Jem Southam's and Christopher Binding's art work: the book's printing, too, is of a high quality.

Many of us have long believed that Bristol nurtured as talented a body of photographers as ever it did of painters. This collection upholds such a notion. Bristol has also been more than usually fortunate in those who have appreciated such a visual inheritance and have worked to preserve it and make it available. James Belsey and David Harrison are notable additions to that scholarly and sympathetic band, and we are indebted to them.

Nicholas Thomas,
*Director, City of Bristol Museum.*

3

# THE VICTORIAN CAMERA

## DAVID HARRISON

**T**he average family photographer today can pack into one pocket more photographic firepower than the great Victorian photographer could have dreamed possible. In a bag easily carried on one shoulder, he or she has the capacity to take photographs in semi-darkness, without focussing, setting exposure or speed, or even winding on a film. Compact telephoto lens make nonsense of distance: the speed of a bullet can be stopped by the magic of super-fast film and lenses and infra-red triggers. Special filters can create redder sunsets than Turner ever imagined, turn street lights into fairyland or create wild, surrealistic landscapes.

One photographic magazine recently carried a photograph of an owl pictured against the full moon. It was a picture that had everything – perfectly exposed, beautifully framed, delicately coloured and exquisitely composed. In fact the moon had been photographed in California: the owl in England six months later and the two slides sandwiched in a zoom copier which allowed the best of each slide to be used in the final composition.

None of the photographs in this book had the advantage of fast films (or even films at all, come to that) or cameras capable of the kind of rapid reaction that generates the most natural pictures. Take this passage from the first edition of *Amateur Photographer* magazine in October, 1884. "It is not generally known that Lady Brassey, the talented and successful author of *A Voyage in the Sunbeam,* is a first rate photographer. She seldom if ever goes on tour without a camera, lens, and a stock of dry plates. With rapid dry plates, quick lenses and a practiced hand the possibilities of photography are endless. To take a tiger in the very act of killing a buffalo excites surprise, perhaps incredulity. Yet it seems a lucky operator in India has accomplished the feat." What would that lucky operator have made of today's wildlife

One of the most famous photographs of all time. The Box Brownie girl who persuaded thousands that photography was simple . . . and fun.

An unsuccessful artist, William Fox Talbot achieved immortality with this and other photographic studies of Lacock Abbey in the 1830's.

photographers who can catch a kingfisher at the moment of hitting the water or a great whale throwing its enormous bulk out of the ocean?

Dry plates will need some explanation for those not familiar with the history of photography. They come into the story late in the latter half of the 19th century but the search for a cheap and efficient way of making permanent images starts much earlier. The rich always had portrait painters although no one will know how many minor blemishes, long noses, big ears and squints were tactfully overlooked by the painters. Portraits which have survived were generally those approved by the sitter and it seems safe to say that not every one was a totally accurate record. The middle classes could always plump for the cheaper option, a shadow picture named after French government minister M. Etienne de Silhouette because, like his policies, they were cheap and cheerful.

In 1786, an improved method allowed the profile to be cast upon a glass plate where it was engraved and features and details added. This had the advantage of creating a printing block so copies could be made. But the big problem was to find a device capable of producing a realistic image and then permanently recording it.

Image generation probably started with the camera obscura - that is, the principle of funnelling light through a tiny hole into a darkened room so that an upside-down image is projected on to an opposite wall or screen. It was an effect used at least as far back as the fourth century BC by both the Greeks and the Chinese, but it was Giovanni Battista della Porta, a scientist in Naples who in 1558 first proposed filling the hole with a lens or concave mirror to improve the image. From that discovery grew the camera obscura, two of which survive today in Bristol and Edinburgh.

The image could be created but how could it be preserved? It has also been known for centuries that light affected certain substances, fading some, darkening others. In 1727, a chemist called Schulze attached stencils to bottles of silver and chalk in nitric acid and, by exposure to the light, managed to print letters on the liquid. Twenty years later, another experimenter confirmed that silver was the key. Thomas Wedgwood, of the pottery family, and the chemist Humphry Davy experimented with paper and leather moistened with nitrate of silver, and managed to create good images, but were unable to fix them permanently. That discovery was left to a French army officer, Nicephore Niépce who in 1826 managed to record an image of the view from his home on a bitumenised pewter plate in a camera obscura. It took an eight hour exposure, and the image is faint, but it still survives today.

Louis Daguerre, a painter, heard of his experiment and the two men decided to co-operate on further research. Niépce died before any progress was made but Daguerre eventually found that a metal plate covered in silver iodide was light sensitive and that an image was formed which could be seen if the plate was treated with mercury. The process was published in 1839 and was an immediate success. Painter Paul Delaroche proclaimed pessimistically: "From today painting is dead." The prints were called Daguerrotypes and the process was much improved over the following years. An equally important advance however was the design by Josef Petzval of Vienna of a lens specifically for photography. It was added to a new camera designed by Peter Voigtlander in 1841 and, amazingly, the basic design is still in use today (as, of course, is the trade name Voigtlander).

The big drawbacks of the Daguerrotype were the ease with which it could be damaged and the incredible ritual of preparing and exposing the plates. These were covered in silvered copper, polished with jeweller's rouge, sensitised with iodine and bromine, exposed for at least 30 seconds, and developed in a special box containing mercury heated by spirit lamp. The image was finally fixed chemically, sealed with a solution of gold, heated and mounted. No wonder a Daguerrotype was expensive – and on top of all that, it couldn't be copied and the image was reversed unless a mirror or prism was put between the lens and the subject.

At the same time as Daguerre was perfecting his process, William Henry Fox Talbot was experimenting in a different direction. He was an unsuccessful amateur artist who longed for a method to fix natural images permanently. He used paper coated with salts of silver in a small wooden, home-made camera, taking pictures of his home, Lacock Abbey in Wiltshire. These images can still be seen today. More importantly, he also invented the negative process, the reversed image from which as many positives as needed can be printed. He called his process a Calotype, but the long exposure needed meant professionals preferred the Daguerrotype with all its own disadvantages. In fact both processes were soon displaced by wet plate photography, using glass plates coated with sensitive salts. Several experimenters, including astronomer Sir John Herschel, had experimented with the idea but it was the English sculptor Frederick Scott Archer who invented the collodion (gun cotton dissolved in ether) plate which was sensitive, easy to use and cheap. A variation, using enamelled tinplate, was the tintype.

Collodion plates were usually printed on albumen paper, invented in 1850 and capable of fine detail. A further invention in 1854 of a method of producing several portraits on a single plate, led to the Victorian craze for *cartes de visite*. There were *cartes* of artists, writers and actresses, even nudes and courtesans, but particularly the Royal family. One charming picture of Princess Alexandra giving a piggy-back to her daughter Louise sold at least 300,000 copies.

Daguerrotype or collodion, the new medium brought to public notice a new breed of photographer, both professional and gifted amateur. In America, Southworth and Hawes tried to capture something of the personality of the sitter (no mean task with exposure so long that many heads were either clamped or resting on hands to keep them still). There were the Rev. Charles Dodgson (Lewis Carroll) and his obsession for little girls; Julia Margaret Cameron and her portraits of Browning, Herschel, Tennyson, Darwin, Trollope, Carlyle and other intellectuals of Victorian society; the social documentaries of Hill and Adamson in Scotland; and the flamboyant bohemian Felix Tournachon (The Great Nadar) who took the first aerial photographs and portraits of the greats like Hugo, Wagner, Liszt, Verdi, Offenbach, Baudelaire and Balzac.

Photographers travelled far and wide – Francis Frith who brought back the wonders of Egypt; Auguste Busson who took three days to climb Mont Blanc with 25 porters to carry his equipment; Samuel Bourne who tackled the Himalayas; John Thomson bought back irreplaceable pictures of Imperial China. The achievements of these pioneers should not be under-estimated. Their equipment was large and bulky, and the collodion process, in which plates must be exposed while still wet, meant carrying a portable darkroom. This would have included a light tight tent, chemicals, cleaned glass plates, camera, plateholders, tripod and lens. Fresh water was also essential.

Then, in 1878, another major breakthrough – dry plates. Experiments had been going on for more than 20 years to overcome the problems of collodion and among the materials tried to keep the collodion plates moister longer were sugar, raspberry syrup, liquorice and beer.

The new plates used gelatine emulsion, were easily made and remained sensitive for a long time. Not only that, exposure could be cut to one tenth of the time that wet plates needed. All the photographer needed now was a camera, tripod and a load of dry plates which could be processed when he got home. And because the plates were of constant sensitivity, it was simple to work out exposure times. It also meant that for the first time, action photographs could be taken, and it was the gelatine dry plate which enabled Eadweard Muybridge to make his famous series of sequence photographs showing how animals and humans actually used their limbs and muscles in moving.

Cameras also improved greatly from this time onwards, with major advances in shutters and portability. But the real popularity of photography as a family hobby had to wait for George Eastman who in 1888 introduced the first successful roll of film camera . . . the Kodak. At last the mystical, long winded, often dangerous rigmarole of plates was not necessary. All the Kodak user had to do was point the camera and shoot (no focussing, no exposure measurements), send the camera and exposed film (100 pictures per film) back to the factory where the film was developed, the camera reloaded and returned to the customer. Eastman's slogan was "You press the button, we do the rest." By the end of the Victorian era, photography was within the reach of millions, thanks to Eastman's new five shilling camera, probably the most famous ever made; the box Brownie.

The first editon of *Amateur Photographer* gave hints on choosing a camera kit which gives a good idea of the dauntless nature of the early cameramen and women. First choose the format, from quarterplate (4¼" × 3¼") to large cabinet (12" × 10") remembering that the bigger the plate, the heavier the outfit. The larger sizes, said AP hastily, were not recommended to beginners. Then decide on the lens - single view; portable symmetrical; rapid symmetrical or rectilinear; or portrait. The rapid symmetrical was recommended as the best all-rounder and as free from distortion. The size of lens was decided by a simple formula – the focal length should be a little longer than the longest side of the photograph. Naturally each lens must have a set of diaphragms or stops, a cap and a metal flange to screw it to the camera. *Amateur Photographer* warned that so-called instantaneous dry plates were by no means instantaneous! Subjects in brilliant sunlight could be taken in a small fraction of a second, but the interior of a church might require half an hour.

The camera itself should be light and fold up for carrying. Foreign travellers to hot climes would need models made of well seasoned wood with brass corners. It should be rigid when open and the part to which the lens was attached should be capable of both horizontal and vertical movement. Add to these, plate carriers, a screw for fixing the camera to the stand or tripod, a focussing cloth (usually velvet lined with taminy); an instantaneous drop shutter and a carrying case. Then, of course, there was the developing and the basic kit should contain: portable, non actinic lantern, three developing dishes, three printing frames, sensitised paper, flat camel's hair brush, one bottle sulpho pyrogallol, 2 oz. of ammonia, 1 oz. potash ferrocyanide, ¼ oz. mercury bichloride, 4 oz. pulverised borax, 1 lb. pulverised alum, 7 lbs. soda thiosulphate, one tube chloride of gold. Imagine the effect on local wildlife if the photographer decided to dump half empty bottles in the river rather than haul them home.

A travelling ferrotype photographer.

But it is easy to mock, as with anything which has developed so far from the original as photography. In Victorian times, photography was new and exciting, still the preserve of the middle and upper classes but, for the first time in history, it was possible to see what someone several thousand miles away actually looked like: to picture the Sphinx or tribes of aborigines for people who would never leave their home villages; to have permanent records of families at a time of high mortality.

That first edition of *Amateur Photographer* summed it up rather well. "Less than half a century ago", wrote an unnamed enthusiast in 1884, "the art of photography was regarded by all but the very few initiated into the secret as being little short of magic; although by the improvements it has undergone from time to time it has, to a certain extent, become familiarised with many, it nevertheless continued to be regarded as an 'art and mystery' by a great majority of the public until within the last decade. During this period, however, a change has been experienced which may be pronounced as little less than a revolution – a change which has placed photography in the first rank as a study and amusement." He was referring to the invention of the dry plate and continued: "We believe that ere long photography will be generally regarded as a ready and pleasant dissipator of the *ennui* sometimes attending a prolonged residence in the country. Indeed we will go as far as to say that a set of photographic apparatus should be considered to be an almost necessary adjunct to every country house: to lady visitors especially would such afford the means of amusement, now that the process has been divested of its objectionable features. Personal pleasure may be found in photographing one's house, gardens, servants or domestic pets. All objects animate and inanimate are easy subjects for treatment by the new process and in a thousand ways would a knowledge of the art be a source of pleasure and profit, not only to country residents but dwellers in cities.

In the same magazine, two intrepid photographers describe taking pictures on a walking tour of Wales. One carried a 5" × 4" camera, rectilinear lens, cloth, camera legs and plates, weighing in all about eight pounds, and was extremely happy with the pictures he took, although not about dropping the camera in Swallow Falls at Bettwys-y-Coed and ruining it. The other took sciopticon camera, lens, slides, case and so on, weighing just five pounds. But his main object was geology, so he also had a heavy hammer and chisel and collected a hundredweight of rock specimens. He changed the plates under his bedclothes each night.

The advertisements, as always, give a good idea of what photography meant to the Victorians. They could buy a silver-steel rotary burnisher for burnishing portraits and making them equal to enamelled prints or have photographs mounted on canvas ("no gelatine used"). Mawson's Negative Varnisher was felt to be the best available, while Coventry Machinists' Company offered tricycles "especially adapted for amateur photographers on the road." All that was missing from the magazine were photographs.

By the end of the century, photography had come of age. Fox Talbot's vision of a medium in which the unskilled could record images permanently was reality. There were, of course, those who still asserted that photography was not art and that reality had no place in creativity. But already there were artists who saw the potential of the medium in much the same way that some modern artists have welcomed computer graphics as a new and exciting tool. In 1895, Gauguin could say: "Shall I tell you what will soon be the most faithful work of art? A photograph when it can render colours as it will soon be able to. And would you have an intelligent being sweat away for months to achieve this same illusion of reality as an ingenious little machine?" A few years later, Picasso commented: "Why should the artist persist in treating subjects that can be established so clearly with the lens of a camera. It would be absurd, wouldn't it? Photography has arrived at a point where it is capable of liberating painting from all literature, from the anecdote and even the subject."

# THE PHOTOGRAPHER
# AS ARTIST

### JAMES BELSEY

**A** photograph, the dictionary tells us, is a picture or likeness taken by means of the chemical action of light on a sensitive film made of a base of glass, paper, metal or some other suitable material. So far so good . . . but that dictionary definition takes us only so far along the road. It is just as important to understand that a photograph also happens to be an image – an image captured, created, sometimes even stage-managed, often composed and usually considered, consciously or unconsciously, by the person whose finger is on the shutter trigger. The image which results from the chemical process not only shows what the individual photographer wants us to see but it also tells us something about the person behind the lens.

There is a marvellous photographic portrait of those two outstanding image-makers of 19th century Bristol, the local artists Samuel Jackson and Francis Danby. Two men whose imaginations and whose art were charged by the Bristol landscape they knew so intimately: a landscape with its flower-studded, rolling Downs, its panoramic views to the hills of Wales, its ferociously romantic Avon Gorge, its busy quaysides and bustling streets and its almost arcadian Leigh Woods across the fearsome gorge with its massive cliff faces.

The celebrated photograph of the two artists was taken by S.P. Jackson, artist son of Samuel Jackson, in about 1855 and it hardly needs their typically Victorian costume to make it immediately evident that this is a photograph of its period. Jackson is portrayed in a sitting position. He sits awkwardly, self-consciously holding a walking stick in his right hand as if it were some sort of badge of office. In his left hand, even more clumsily, he is grasping an open book. The clear suggestion to the viewer is that this must be a book of paintings or sketchings. His fellow artist Francis Danby leans over, almost dutifully, his left hand helping to support the book they are examining. The background is meaningless, perhaps a sheet of cloth or paper suspended behind the two to prevent any distraction from the main tableau of characters. Both men are frozen into an unnatural immobility, not so much by the action of light on sensitive paper as by their own self-conscious rigidity and the uneasiness of the formal pose they are adopting. They are offering us an image of themselves and the photographer has arranged that image, and captured and presented it for us. It is a photograph no modern cameraman or woman would dream of taking.

Just as Danby and Samuel Jackson have left us their glorious images of landscapes and townscapes in their paintings, so S.P. Jackson has left us with his own little photographic legacy in this Victorian portrait of two interesting men. It is an image, an image you long to break down in a search for some sort of reality. For instance; what on earth happened after this photographic session was over and Jackson and Danby could breathe at last, put down that wretched prop of a book, stretch their limbs and clamber to a much more comfortable standing position? They would spring to life before our eyes and so create a scene which, if photographed, would offer an informal image we could understand and recognise more than a century later.

Conversely, there are a very few marvellously *modern*-looking images of another leading Victorian with strong Bristol connections, Isambard Kingdom Brunel, which were taken a couple of years later than the Jackson/Danby portrait, in about 1857. This famous series was explored brilliantly by the critic Rob Powell in his revealing, very satisfying touring exhibition *Brunel's Kingdom* which opened at the Watershed Gallery in Bristol in 1985. The accompanying book amplified his theme that our view of Brunel and his age is strongly influenced by the "official version" as seen in photographs and illustrations.

A contrast in styles: the awkwardness of Samuel Jackson and Francis Danby posing in a quiet Clifton square, and genuine tension captured on the faces of the Brunel entourage watching the launch of the *Great Eastern*.

The atmosphere in which the pictures of Brunel were taken was charged with drama. They show men who are tense, nervous and pre-occupied, mostly too busy to worry about the figures they are cutting in front of the man with the camera. This was the time when Brunel and his backers and engineers and workers were attempting to launch his huge ship the *Great Eastern* on the Thames. We see an anxious Brunel, top-hatted, cigar-chewing, fretful as he watches the scene and worries about the great launch. For one glorious moment a Victorian photographer forgets or ignores or somehow manages to break free from the conventions of his age to capture a moment of high drama. We immediately recognise it as a moment of "truth", as something that "actually happened". But it too is an image, an image we understand very well today through our constant exposure to newspaper and TV photographic images, many of moments of similar tensions. Are such pictures any less contrived for finding the "right" moment in an otherwise boring spectacle than S.P. Jackson's when he draped Danby over his father's shoulders and gave them a book to hold? It is a moot point.

Old photographs, therefore, should be seen to have much more than historic or nostalgia value. They are important documents of their age which tell us as much in their visual language as any books or letters of the time. The Brunel series of six taken at that *Great Eastern* launch attempt offer only two apparently unposed, unself-conscious studies which are glorious exceptions to the visual conventions of Victorian photography. The stiff, formal "construction piece" style of the double portrait of Danby and Jackson is the norm of 1850's photography. It does not take a great deal of knowledge of Victorian art to see and realise that mainstream, conventional Victorian photography owed as much to Victorian paintings in approach and style, aesthetics and subject matter as it did to the technical developments which had made photography possible. You can almost see the artistic aspirations at work as

the first Bristol photographers hurried off to familiar viewpoints which had been popular with professional and amateur artists for years.

The Avon Gorge drew them time and time again, almost always unsuccessfully. The Gorge is a heaven-sent subject for painters who can telescope, dramatise, heighten and concentrate a landscape. The Gorge seen in quiet greys and its drama limited by the frame size then available is a disappointing subject. It is aerial photography, particularly from balloons, and increasingly good colour film that makes the Gorge such a substantial subject for photography more than a century later. Leigh Woods, that great haunt of early 19th century sketching parties, was another magnet with its dappled light, its fantastically shaped, ancient trees, its sunlit clearings and its banks of grassy, natural lawns. It made a dreadful subject for anyone hoping with a camera to capture artistic images, producing instead flat, almost sullen pictures which had not a trace of that magical quality of paintings of the same place.

Just compare the prosaic photographs of the Gorge and Leigh Woods with, for example, the brilliantly evocative watercolour studies which Samuel Jackson made of the same scenes from the Clifton Observatory and in Nightingale Valley in the second quarter of the 19th century and you can see at once what the photographers were hoping to evoke . . . and what they failed to achieve. Gradually, photographers in Bristol and elsewhere began to discover subjects that were more suitable to the new visual form but which were still images of their time.

A great body of work by Victorian and Edwardian photographers who worked in Bristol survives in both private and public collections, showing that the city certainly played its part in the development of photography from the earliest days. For example, the very first recorded photograph of a ship was taken at the City Docks in Bristol. It is the famous study by William Fox Talbot, one of the pioneers of photography, of the *Great Britain*. Fox Talbot had travelled from his home in Lacock, near Chippenham, to capture the sight of the latest masterpiece created by Brunel – how impossible it is to escape from Brunel's shadow in almost any aspect of Victorian Bristol! The exciting new six-master, which had still to leave the docks on its maiden voyage, is pictured at an angle, moored alongside the Gasworks wharf on the north side of the Floating Harbour in about 1843. The picture is serene. Add paint, a little colour and a gilt frame and you might have a very satisfactory marine picture, the more interesting because it emphasises the highly decorated stern of the new ship.

In this, Fox Talbot was just the first of many. Shipping in the busy City Docks was an obvious subject for the early photographers, and it fulfilled many necessary requirements since painted studies of ships at sea or in harbour were a very well accepted branch of Victorian art. As techniques and camera equipment improved, ushering in a new breed of decidedly non-arty but very definitely commercial photographers, the studies of ships were increasingly less painting-like and more and more like the technical and commercial pictures they had become.

The townscape in Bristol, rather than the romantic landscapes of Danby and Jackson, offered substantial fare to the early cameraman. Narrow, old, tall-sided little streets had a special appeal to the Victorian imagination, whether in pictures or in scenes from books by writers like Charles Dickens. Bristol offered a wealth of such picturesque places, and it was not long after the start of photography that the City's back alleys were being recorded. One particular area was a magnet, that little run of hillside which slopes up from the City Centre to the base of the sharper Kingsdown shoulder. Here were some of Victorian Bristol's most horrible slums in a verminous, hideously overcrowded, disease-ridden network of stinking, high-level

Samuel Jackson. The Avon from Clifton Down, looking towards The Severn Estuary c. 1825.

The limitations of the early camera were starkly exposed when compared with the expansive treatment which a consummate artist like Samuel Jackson could give to the natural scene.

**15**

Fox Talbot's celebrated study of the *Great Britain* in 1843 awaiting its maiden voyage was the precursor of thousands of marine photographs taken in Bristol City Docks.

hovels where death and violence were everyday matters. But they were certainly picturesque if you managed to ignore the people, steel yourself to the stench and somehow take your photograph when no one was around. The Bristol record has captured several of them as still, silent, deserted, lifeless but aesthetically pleasing studies of romantic cobbled streets. They vanished in the latter part of the 19th century, cleared away in the dynamic slum clearance schemes of late Victorian Bristol.

As equipment improved and exposure time lessened, street scenes in the busy thoroughfares became technically possible. Coincidentally, equipment and printing became cheaper and more efficient, feeding a growing demand for photographic images. Commercial studios sprang up in the city to meet that demand and new markets were created in stiff, stilted portraiture – just how a painter would paint you, our ancestors were told – and in postcard townscapes that millions used annually as an easy, attractive form of letter-writing. The heightened Victorian image gave way to something more commonplace, workmanlike.

Old photographs are very much a part of the stock-in-trade of the local journalist. Delightful illustrations to brighten up any page and evoke a curious longing to be there, to skip back in time, to step into the frozen frame and meet the people. Readers send them in regularly to newspapers like the Bristol *Evening Post*. Photographs of the old street scenes, records of charabanc trips to the seaside, wildly busy studies of moments of great pageantry like Royal Jubilees or other important anniversaries. I have dealt with hundreds over the years, and they always amuse and fascinate me.

But my respect for the Victorian and Edwardian photographs of Bristol increased enormously when I first saw some of the City of Bristol's collections housed in the Bristol Museum and Art Gallery, the City's Records Office, the Industrial Museum and the Blaise Castle Folk

Museum. The collection has many marvellous individual pictures, images of such power that it is possible to get an idea of how creative, observant Bristolians saw their city and wished it to be depicted. The finest group of all is from the Fuller-Eberle album in the City Records Office, a collection of photographs from the estate of Ellison Fuller-Eberle, presented by his brother Victor Fuller-Eberle, Ref. No. 20849 (34). I was first shown the album in the late 1970's and was thrilled by its marvellous set of images captured at the very dawn of photography. David Harrison shared my enthusiasm the moment he saw the volume and we make no apologies for including so many pictures from this outstanding record of Bristol in the 1850's.

Of all the photographers who worked in Bristol around the turn of the century, only a few names are remembered today. Ivor Castle and Cyrus Voss Bark were news and general commercial photographers, some of whose prints still survive, but the best record of one Victorian professional at work must be the legacy left by John York who was based on Broad Quay. The exact dates are not known but Andy King of Bristol Industrial Museum places his important years in the period 1880 – 1914.

York photographed many subjects but mainly ships. Bristol City Museum and Art Gallery owns some 2,000 of his pictures and hundreds more are in the collection of the World Ship Society. He used glass negatives which even today give prints of startling clarity and depth. Industrial Museum curator Paul Elkin thinks he probably kept in touch with the harbour master and waited for incoming ships at Hotwells or by the Suspension Bridge. Within a day or so, he would have pictures of the ships which by then would be moored near his office and would offer them for sale. Most of the vessels in those days, of course, would be freight carriers rather than passenger, which explains why he took so many pictures of ships and so few of people. Little more is know about York but his photographs provide an admirable survey of the Port of Bristol a century ago.

The photographs Fuller-Eberle gathered in a bound volume are uncredited but some have been identified. The most beautiful are the work of Hugh Owen, an amateur photographer who was chief cashier of the Great Western Railway in Bristol, and who gave up photography after just eight years in 1855 because he objected to the stains on his fingers caused by the wet- plate process. He knew Fox Talbot and used his Calotype process of paper negatives. The second outstanding early photographer at work in Bristol was J.B. Hazard, whose pictures sometimes carry the initials JBH. The Owen and Hazard pictures and the Fuller-Eberle collection as a whole illustrate one of the themes of this book – the early photographer as artist – better than any other sections of the city's vast pictorial archives.

The most startling omission from the very wide range of subjects captured by the early photographers in Bristol is Georgian and Regency Clifton. You glimpse the famous terraces and crescents only occasionally and then only as an aside to some grand view of the Avon Gorge, the Clifton Suspension Bridge, Cumberland Basin or a dramatic vessel on the river or mud banks. The showier Victorian buildings of Clifton are lovingly recorded but the suburb's greatest architectural treasures seem to have held no attraction at all for contemporary photographers. This lack of any real body of photographs of old Clifton in the 19th century has been a source of irritation to historians ever since.

Why was it so? What was it that made photographers so clearly disregard attractions like Royal York Crescent, the Paragon, West Mall and Caledonia Place? In the late 20th century these are the streets and settings which get every photographer arriving in Bristol scurrying up Park Street to find the city at its most ostentatiously elegant. Fashion and taste must have played a great part in it. Regency architecture was only yesterday to Victorians, Georgian architecture only the day before that, and their own buildings were a conscious rejection of the asceticism, reason and simplicity of the earlier styles. Victorians loved gothic romanticism and heady Italian flamboyance. To them Clifton must have seemed a cold, dull display, its severity mercifully softened by their own, more colourful additions. And, too, there is Clifton's role in art at the time. Clifton and its terraces existed as a viewpoint, not a subject to be viewed, or so painters thought. You looked out from Clifton; you didn't look *at* Clifton. It is a shame. There must have been marvellous images to be filmed in Clifton's magnificent setting.

The subject which must have presented the Victorians with some of their most difficult, even agonising decisions was that most enduring of all in art . . . the nude. This brought photographers into the middle of the debate about the nude with all its super-subtle nuances which shroud that shadowy border between art and pornography, titillation and good taste. The new media threw up difficulties never encountered by creative people before. Contemporary paintings of the nude bore precious little resemblance to the physical reality of naked women and men. What could the photographer do to approach the nude in a creative way without crossing that dangerous borderline? As we now know a very great deal, and more than a century later photography has taken over the nude almost as its exclusive property. It wasn't always so. Among the early photographers very few – there were some noble exceptions – dared to come to terms with the subject. The standard answer to the dilemma was compromise, often using live models as if they were torn from the canvas of a painting and awkwardly posed against clumsy sets and backdrops, shading or obscuring intimacies like pubic hair to conform to Ruskin-esque ideals of the female body. These 'mock paintings' are laughably unreal.

In the collection of early photographs in the City of Bristol Records Office there can be found an even simpler compromise . . . to use the camera to depict an already idealised nude, in this case – E. H. Baily's delightful statue of Eve which now lies enticingly on the great staircase in the City of Bristol Art Gallery. She is a perfect example of Victorian 'good taste', respectably classical, undeniably sensual but never pornographic. Why try to capture such a spirit with real, live, flesh-and-blood woman when there was a statue which said it all? Why indeed, so the photographer never even made the attempt and instead photographed this lovely marble statue from every possible angle and always, naturally, in the best possible taste!

In this selection, we have taken care to show images which reflect the range of Victorian pre-occupations . . . with street life, with invention, with industry and, finally, with the magic of the dawn of the aviation industry in Bristol. All the strands of imagery and photography and all that they can mean come together in several of these photographs but I must confess a personal favourite, one that appeals to me on many levels. It is the epic picture of the ceremony which marked the opening of the Clifton Suspension Bridge on December 8th, 1864 – that man Brunel again.

As a journalist, I love its drama. As someone who has always admired Victorian art, I love its grandeur and the great sweep of its addition right to left, culminating in the vast piers of the bridge heightened by the darkness of Leigh Woods in the background. I love its sense of pomp, occasion and self-confidence. I love its lofty viewpoint and the way, typically, people merge into a crowd and the crowd is shown to be secondary to a great engineering achievement. It speaks volumes about the Victorian image of Bristol.

PLATE
ONE

PLATE
TWO

PLATE
THREE

PLATE

FOUR

PLATE
FIVE

PLATE
SIX

PLATE
SEVEN

PLATE
EIGHT

PLATE
NINE

PLATE
TEN

PLATE
ELEVEN

PLATE
THIRTEEN

PLATE
FOURTEEN

PLATE

FIFTEEN

PLATE
SIXTEEN

PLATE
SEVENTEEN

PLATE
EIGHTEEN

PLATE
NINETEEN

PLATE
TWENTY

PLATE

TWENTY ONE

PLATE
TWENTY TWO

PLATE
TWENTY THREE

PLATE
TWENTY FOUR

PLATE
TWENTY FIVE

PLATE
TWENTY SIX

PLATE
TWENTY SEVEN

PLATE
TWENTY EIGHT

PLATE

TWENTY NINE

PLATE

THIRTY

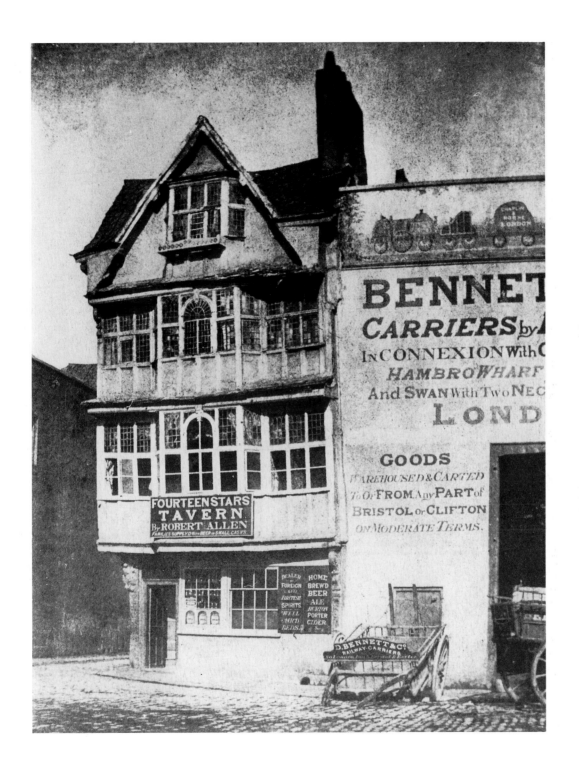

PLATE
THIRTY ONE

PLATE
THIRTY TWO

PLATE
THIRTY THREE

PLATE
THIRTY FOUR

PLATE
THIRTY FIVE

PLATE
THIRTY SIX

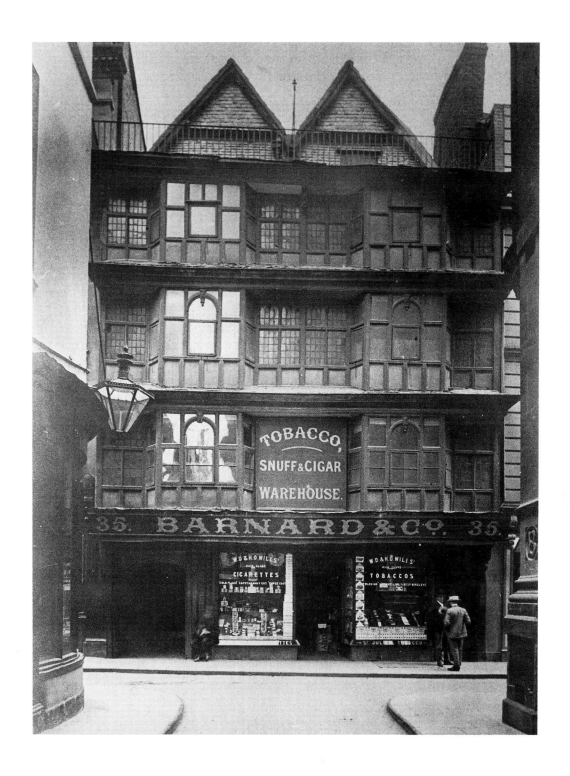

PLATE
THIRTY SEVEN

PLATE
THIRTY EIGHT

PLATE
THIRTY NINE

PLATE

FORTY

PLATE
FORTY ONE

PLATE

FORTY TWO

PLATE

FORTY THREE

PLATE

FORTY FOUR

PLATE
FORTY FIVE

PLATE
FORTY SIX

PLATE
FORTY SEVEN

PLATE
FORTY EIGHT

PLATE
FORTY NINE

PLATE

FIFTY

PLATE
FIFTY ONE

PLATE

FIFTY TWO

PLATE
FIFTY THREE

PLATE

FIFTY FIVE

PLATE

FIFTY SIX

PLATE
FIFTY SEVEN

PLATE
FIFTY EIGHT

PLATE
FIFTY NINE

PLATE

SIXTY ONE

PLATE
SIXTY TWO

PLATE
SIXTY THREE

PLATE
SIXTY FOUR

PLATE
SIXTY FIVE

PLATE

SIXTY SIX

PLATE
SIXTY SEVEN

PLATE
SIXTY EIGHT

PLATE
SIXTY NINE

PLATE
SEVENTY

PLATE
SEVENTY ONE

PLATE
SEVENTY TWO

PLATE
SEVENTY THREE

PLATE

SEVENTY FOUR

PLATE
SEVENTY FIVE

PLATE
SEVENTY SIX

PLATE
SEVENTY SEVEN

PLATE
SEVENTY EIGHT

PLATE
SEVENTY NINE

# NOTES ON THE PLATES

*The following abbreviations have been used to identify sources: City Art Gallery (CAG); City Museum (CM); City Records Office (CRO); Industrial Museum (IM).*

1  The photographer as painter. The image, the pose, the composition of this formal, 18th century-flavoured study of Redland Chapel in the 1850's are taken directly from the canons of British High Art. (CRO)

2  Stapleton Glen, 1850's. The Frome Valley was one of the most loved rural settings for Bristol artists like Francis Danby, but the camera could barely hint at its secluded atmosphere of water, woodland and dappled light, as this clumsy, lopsided photograph demonstrates. (CRO)

3  Stapleton Glen, 1850's and an altogether better attempt to portray the Frome Valley. Francis Danby executed some delightful paintings of the valley's characteristic mill buildings, and the photographer here wisely followed his example. (CRO)

4  The facade that launched a thousand chocolate boxes . . . the Victorian pastoral idyll of the rose-clad cottage, and with tea and coffee for sale too. Leigh Woods, 1850's. (CRO)

5  An exquisite summer scene in the heyday of the Empire. A middle class family in what passed for casual wear with a strangely rigged sailing boat at Hanham in 1894. The photographer has gone for the expected

reflective effect and the sails are too tangled with the tree for perfect composition but the whole picture suggests warmth and lazy, hazy summer afternoons nearly a century ago. (IM)

6  Harvest time, 1850's . . . the seasons dominated daily life during the mid-19th century in a way unimaginable in the age of central heating and universal electric light. The seasons' symbols, like this cornfield, were potent images. (CRO)

7  Trees in Leigh Woods. The woods inspired many local artists and the romantic setting and its much-loved images of dappled light and rich colours attracted early photographers too. They soon realised that photography could only capture these starkest sights of maimed oak trunks. (CRO)

8  Pond at Redland, 1850's and a typical study of the landscape where the growing city met the country. The path is today tarmaced and runs between Redland Green and Metford Road. The pond has long since been drained. (CRO)

9  Redland in the 1850's looking across the garden of Redland Villa to a pastoral setting now entirely covered by houses in Napier Road, Elgin Park and Woolcot Street. (CRO)

10  Lovers' Walk, Redland in the 1850's by J.B. Hazard. The imposing study of the beautiful avenue leading to Redland Court plays to all the new medium's strengths and Hazard's delight in the intricate tracery of boughs and branches is thrilling. (CRO)

11  Redland Court. A tree-dominated view of an important country house had long been one of British art's familiar subjects. Transposed to photography, the Cedar of Lebanon overwhelms all. The effect is marvellous, but almost certainly unintentional. (CRO)

12  Jacob's Wells Road in the 1860's. Bristol photographers soon learned the knack of capturing the sinuous patterns of street lines that twisted and curved in tune to the hilly contours. (CM)

13  The organ grinder, Bristol, 1850's. Street life fascinated the Victorians and its colourful characters and scenes provided a rich subject for art, literature and photography. (CRO)

14  Two roadmen in Redland, 1850's. The image is quintessentially Victorian with its clear message of the dignity of labour . . . a theme Ford Madox Brown was to express so clearly a decade later when he first exhibited his famous painting *Work*. (CRO)

15 A splendid family group, posed in a relaxed style which would have been impossible with the long exposures of a few years earlier. The older lady still looks nervous but the younger couple are obviously used to the camera. This is the Rowles family of Pill who built most of the Bristol Channel pilot cutters but the photograph is typical of many thousands of family groups who could never have afforded a painted portrait. (IM)

16 The wash tub, Bristol, 1850's. *Genre* painting, depicting often sentimental scenes of 'ordinary' life, was immensely popular with the Victorian middle-classes . . . the style was perfectly suited to the camera. (CRO)

17 Two boys playing, 1850's . . . the picture is posed and the study sentimental, but it has a period charm that remains attractive more than a century later. (CRO)

18 Garden tools, 1850's. Early photographers took the Still Life and made it almost their own, as this strong, carefully-arranged and observed study shows. (CRO)

19 The hand-written caption simply reads Hanham. The photograph is mid-19th century but its directness and simplicity clearly foreshadow the asceticism of some 20th century schools. (CRO)

20 The Avon Gorge, 1850's. Here a clearly self-confident J.B. Hazard successfully uses the bold device of photographing a winding machine set against the gorge's rocky scenery. The composition is faultless. (CRO)

21 A painter's photograph. The cobbles, the carefully ajar iron gate, the elegant pillars, the boy and the cart - all are carefully aligned to make one harmonious whole. The summer foliage adds the final touch: nature and man in partnership. (CM)

22 Steep Street (1), just above the City Centre, was a gift to photographers. Here, in the 1850's, Hugh Owen brilliantly conveys the cluttered, maze-like alley-plan and steep contours by skilful placing of the camera. (CRO)

23 Steep Street (2). A decade later and an altogether sharper, clearer but less atmospheric study. (CM)

24 The Blue Bowl Inn in The Pithay, 1860's. The familiar image of the narrow streets and irregular skyline, inn sign and cobbled street is sharply interrupted by the interested stares of the stilled citizens. (CM)

25 Mary-le-Port Street by Hugh Owen, taken in the early 1850's. The image, as in so much of Owen's work, is doubly poignant because the scene itself has vanished . . . in this case during the Bristol Blitz. (CRO).

26 Shadow and light in stark contrast in Hugh Owen's evocative study of Lewin's Mead in the early 1850's. As an architectural record alone, the picture is invaluable. (CRO)

27 Host Street by Hugh Owen, one of a brilliant series by this remarkable early photographer of the mid-19th century. Owen combined an artist's eye with a photographer's skill better than anyone in recording the architectural scene around him. (CRO)

28 The Good Old Days! One of the many slums which disfigured Bristol and every other large city at the height of wealth and power. The photographer has recorded the scene with the kind of horrified fascination that the Victorians had for the lower orders. The three adults and the group of children have been carefully placed to give a sense of scale. (CM)

29 Is there an unconscious sense of irony in this photograph with what appear to be brewery workers handling barrels outside a Baptist meeting room? The stiff poses, the anxiety to be in the picture are typical of the time but overhead the lantern is a nice touch, breaking up a rather boring roofline. (CM)

30 The Old Fox in Redcliffe with the famous brass and copper works on one side and Redcliffe Dining Rooms (seating 71 people) on the other. The framing is slightly off – the left side should end before the low building to bring in more of the Coffee Rooms sign – but that apart, it is a clear and concise record. (CM)

31 Hugh Owen's striking study of the Fourteen Stars Tavern in Countership in the 1850's, the architectural interest of the tavern set against the fascinating advertising adjoining it. (CRO)

32 Cottrells, the Bristol saddlers in 1899. The
33 grouping of the family is a little clumsy although the shyness of the woman contrasts well with the assertive stance of the man. The horse tackle hanging above makes an interesting pattern, balanced nicely by the checkerboard of the shopfront tiles. (IM)

34 Thomas Street, off Victoria Street, in the last quarter of the 19th century. The Three

Kings Inn, run by Malcolm Knee, was a famous hostelry of the time and obviously thought attractive enough to photograph. The street trader adds life but it is the building which dominates. A fine picture of record. (CM)

35 Hotwell Road at the end of the century. A peculiarly uninteresting shot but a good example of the early photographer's habit of snapping anything. There is no sense of photography imitating art here. (CM)

36 A splendid picture which is made rather special by the placing of the horse and trap in the foreground and the other spectators forming a perfect frame in the distance. This is Old King Street during heavy flooding in 1889. (CM)

37 Mary-le-Port Street, a picture taken from Wine Street in the 1890's which concentrates on architectural and historical detail where Hugh Owen would have looked for atmosphere. (CM)

38 This lovely study of St Peter's Hospital is by Hugh Owen. Taken in the early 1850's, it shows meticulous attention to architectural detail and the camera position focuses attention on the decorative facade. (CRO)

39 Leonard Lane, alongside the old city wall, between Small Street and Corn Street, photographed by J.B. Hazard in the 1850's. Slum clearances would remove such sights but artists, photographers and their clients were by no means unaware of the old world charm of Bristol's dilapidated inner city housing. (CRO)

40 A remarkable picture, 1880's or earlier. The camera has not been able to cope with the wide range of light and shade, making the foreground too dark and the background burned out. But the photographer has captured the converging lines in this narrow street and the almost silhouetted figures of the family in front. They have obviously stopped, and turned to look at something. The mystery adds to the brooding atmosphere of this scene in a masterly photograph. (CM)

41 St John's Gateway, early 1850's and Hugh Owen as artist/photographer supreme. The arch frames the view and the effect is both dramatic and timelessly beautiful. The picture is one of early photography's masterpieces. (CRO).

42 Broad Street (1), looking up towards Christ Church with the bright light and the

fascinated onlookers creating a stark, frozen moment. (CM)

43  Broad Street (2). The light is now behind the camera in this 1860's shot. Figures are lost, details softened. (CM)

44  The Saracen's Head at Temple Gate in the 1860's. The photographer skilfully stresses the contrasting rhythms of cobbles with the horizontal sweep of the building by deliberately highlighting so much of the road surface. (CM)

45  The Black Boy Inn at the top of Whiteladies Road. It was demolished in 1874 to clear the way for today's broad sweep up Blackboy Hill. (CM)

46  St Werburgh's Church on its original site in Corn Street. The eastern end blocked busy Small Street and in 1878, the church was demolished and rebuilt in Mina Road. This is an excellent photograph technically, avoiding converging verticals (the bane of architectural photography) yet still making the church the obvious subject. Not easy in a crowded street with limited viewpoints and a drawing reprinted in *Bristol: The Growing City* (Redcliffe Press, 1986,) is a much better record of both the church and the neighbouring buildings. (CM)

47  J.B. Hazard's uncompromising study of St Mary Redcliffe church in the early 1850's. (CRO)

48  Five-past one at St Stephen's Church in the 1850's. The carriages add a fascinating touch of scale to the church and tower soaring above them. (CM)

49  A fascinating picture from the 1890's of a highly unlikely subject. Horse-drawn trams may have caused less air-born pollution than the buses that eventually superseded them but they did have an obvious by-product which someone had to clear up. But why was the photograph taken? (CM)

50  The Victoria Rooms in 1866, looking a rather gloomy memorial to Victorian stability but with the interest of the carriages to break up the monotony. (CM)

51  A charming scene with horse cabs and carriages lined up outside the Royal West of England Academy, still boasting the original entrance up dramatic flights of steps. The composition is rather clumsy but the ornate lamp posts and the peaceful stretch of Whiteladies Road behind are delightful. (CM)

52  The new High Cross on College Green in the early 1850's, and J.B. Hazard places a formally posed figure in the foreground to give scale and interest. (CRO)

53  Victoriana triumphant! Bombastic, four-lantern gas lamp with suitably imposing ironwork railings in, aptly enough, Victoria Square in Clifton in the 1850's. (CRO)

54  A good record of two Bristol businesses: Simmons, who managed to combine tin plate and sheet iron working with ships' stores and G Wadge, who was both builder and carpenter and undertaker. St Mary-on-the-Quay and the ships' masts can be seen clearly in the background thanks to the remarkable depth of field. This was early enough for the spectators still to be fascinated by the camera. (CM)

55  A very early photograph of The Centre at the junction with Colston Street. Very atmospheric, with rows of houses climbing up the hill and the horse and men sharp and clear considering the lengthy exposure this would have needed. The row of shops to the left looks little different today, thanks to an imaginative rebuilding scheme. (CM)

56  An unidentified fire, probably in the area of The Grove judging from the General Hospital on the right of the picture. An opportunist shot and probably late in the century judging by the horse drawn vehicles in the foreground. (IM)

57  A view over the Cathay fertiliser works, taken from St Mary Redcliffe in 1890. The railway line no longer exists, except as a brief embankment and bridge, but the glass works cone to the right is now the Dragonara Glass Kiln restaurant. The picture is almost certainly a commercial photograph taken for the factory and is a useful record of the townscape, if little more. (IM)

58  Maurice Tetard takes off from the Downs in a Bristol Boxkite watched by two Edwardian ladies. The unknown photographer has generated a wonderful sense of occasion, with the women providing a dramatic counterpoint to the daring aviator in his extraordinarily flimsy contraption. At this time, his camera would have been firmly tripod mounted and aimed at the spot where the plane was expected to take off. There was no question of panning or a second try

and a perfect shot like this did have a large element of luck. Were the women posed or just happily placed spectators? If the latter, the photographer was a man with an unerring eye for where a good picture was most likely to happen, a vital quality in the days before motor drive. (IM)

59  A remarkable photograph of a coal miner underground in Easton Colliery in the early years of this century. This has everything which makes a good picture: atmosphere, drama, a sense of time frozen for a moment. It grabs the attention and holds it, a small piece of social history permanently recorded. It was this kind of realism which led the painter Gauguin to forecast that photography would soon be the most faithful work of art. Sadly no details could be found of how and why the picture was taken, but it stands on its own merit. (IM)

60  The Victorians loved machines with the fervour of a generation for whom they meant just one step from brutal manual labour. This is the rough cutting room in H. Croot and Sons. The photographer's delight in wheels and pulleys and the sense of quiescent power waiting to be unleashed is evident. A picture very much of its time. (IM)

61  A scene typical of hundreds of suburban and country stations during the great days of the railway network. This is Ashley Hill in Bristol in 1900 with a Duke class engine heading the train. A good composition with the bridge framing the train and delightful little station. (IM)

62  A cheerful little engine named Bristol with driver and fireman posing proudly at the controls. A workhorse pure and simple from the house of Fox, Walker although the photographer might have avoided the impression of a tree growing from the boiler. A picture of record. (IM)

63  A rather inelegant B & ER locomotive which has a strangely ramshackle look about it for a Victorian engine. It was converted to a 4-4-2 with tender and in 1893 was rebuilt in Bristol. It was scrapped in 1890. The railwaymen have been posed, with one man to show the scale of the huge driving wheel and the others as a framework at either end. (IM)

64  This shot just has to be posed. The two men dominate the exact peak of the hill at exactly the right angle while the horse drawn wagon and the new fangled steam lorry demonstrate

both a sense of tradition and willingness to move with the times. The influence of Ford Madox Ford and the Honest Toil school is very strong here. (CM)

65 An early photograph which demonstrates the immediacy of the new medium and also illustrates a newer craze – stereoscopic photography. This fire in 1859 at the Fuidge and Fripp sugar refinery was taken, probably by an amateur, as a stereoscopic pair for use in the viewers which countless households owned by the end of the century. Commercial photographers issued thousands of pictures in this form which gave a 3D effect when seen through a viewer. (IM)

66 The kind of photograph the Victorians loved – honest artisans carefully posed amid scenes of equally honest toil. This kind of shot derives directly from painters like Ford Madox Ford and the writing of William Morris and the utopian Socialist movement. The picture was taken around the turn of the century and is probably St Augustine's Reach. The photographer uses the beams and planks both to draw the eye into the picture and to frame it. (IM)

67 The ship Refuge stranded on Leigh Bank on March 13th, 1854 photographed by J.B. Hazard who lived in Dowry Square, just a few hundred yards away. (CRO)

68 The Avon Gorge in the 1850's with the Somerset pier of the abandoned Clifton Suspension Bridge gazing disconsolately at the Observatory on the opposite bank. (CRO)

69 The Avon Gorge by J.B. Hazard, 1850's. For all Hazard's gifts the view is as barren and desolate as contemporary paintings of this very popular subject were heroically romantic. (CRO)

70 A detail of the Avon Gorge . . . J.B. Hazard's photograph of the spa building Hotwells House which was demolished in 1867. The Colonnade to the right now adjoins the Portway. (CRO)

71 The iron screw tug Robert Forrest approaching Cumberland Basin in 1895. This picture was chosen not just for the content (although notice the attraction of peaceful Hotwells before the Portway) but for the astonishing clarity of the photograph. Sharpness and depth of field like this would be enviable even with today's superb lenses. It was taken by John York of Broad Quay, a superb craftsman judging from his many surviving pictures. (IM)

72 The Importer, one of many ships which ran aground at Hotwells. The photographer is unknown but is not thought to be J. B. Hazard. A good picture from a record point of view, but would a painter have allowed the masts to become visually entangled with Windsor Terrace and the riverside houses behind? (IM)

73 The s.s. Deseado moored at Mardyke in 1890. She was a steel screw steamer which carried oranges from Asuncion on the River Plate and was later lost at sea. The Industrial Museum has a detailed record to go with this picture. A painter would have enjoyed this scene with the houses climbing in serried ranks up the steep hillside, and the two figures in the foreground break up what would be a blank area. (IM)

74 The Waverley, one of a number of ships to bear the name. This was photographed in 1890 and is a good reminder of the great days of the Avon as a centre for boat trips. The splendid large paddle steamer in the background and the little girl with her inelegant dolls pram add life and interest to the view. (IM)

75 One of the earliest photographs of Bristol with ships moored outside the Sedan Chair Hotel and Tavern in the heart of the city. The atmosphere generated with primitive equipment and long exposure is impressive. (CM)

76 A stunning wide angle photograph of Cedarbank, the largest sailing ship ever to enter the city docks. It measured 326 ft long, 43 ft across and had a depth of 24 ft 5 ins. By comparison the s.s. Great Britain is 322 ft long, 50ft 6ins wide and draw 17ft. Cedarbank was a four masted barque built by Mackie and Thompson of Glasgow in 1892. It was pictured in Bristol two years later by John York, one of the best known Victorian photographers whose studio was on Broad Quay. (IM)

77 Wapping 1857 and a ghostly print that captures an evocative flavour of dockside Bristol with its warehousing and a skyline bristling with tall masts of shipping on the Floating Harbour. (CRO)

78 Pomp And Circumstance (1). The opening of the Clifton Suspension Bridge on December 8th, 1864 and an epic study of Victorian pageantry with an artist's overall view. The drama is seen from a distance, the composition draws the eye to the stark piers and great chains of the bridge. (CAG)

79 Pomp And Circumstance (2). Queen Victoria visiting Bristol in 1899, 35 years after the ceremony at Clifton. Photographic technique reigns supreme with sharp focus and countless details, and it's a pity that the Queen chose to hide beneath her umbrella. (CM)

# FOR FURTHER READING

*The Bristol Landscape* by Francis Greenacre and Sheena Stoddard
(City of Bristol Museum and Art Gallery, 1986).

*Victorian Painters* by Jeremy Maas (Barrie and Rockliff, 1969).

*Bristol In The 1850's* and *Bristol's Earliest Photographs* by Reece
Winstone (Reece Winstone, 1968 and 1974).

*Times Gone By – A Photographic Record of Great Britain 1856–1956*
(Marshall Cavendish, 1977).

*Camera – Victorian Eyewitness* by Gus Macdonald (Viking, 1980).

*The Birth of Photography* by Brian Coe (Ash and Grant, 1976).

*The World as It Was* ed. Margarett Loke (Hutchinson, 1980).

*Bristol – The Growing City* ed. David Harrison (Redcliffe Press, 1986).